Christ Circumcised

DIVINATIONS: REREADING LATE ANCIENT RELIGION

Series Editors: Daniel Boyarin, Virginia Burrus, Derek Krueger

A complete list of books in the series is available from the publisher.

Christ Circumcised

A Study in Early Christian History and Difference

Andrew S. Jacobs

PENN

UNIVERSITY OF PENNSYLVANIA PRESS

PHILADELPHIA

Published by
University of Pennsylvania Press
Philadelphia, Pennsylvania 19104–4112
www.upenn.edu/pennpress

Printed in the United States of America on acid-free paper
10 9 8 7 6 5 4 3 2 1

Library of Congress Cataloging-in-Publication Data

Jacobs, Andrew S.
   Christ circumcised : a study in early Christian history and
difference / Andrew S. Jacobs.
      p. cm. — (Divinations : rereading late ancient religion)
   Includes bibliographical references and index.
   ISBN 978-0-8122-4397-0 (hardcover : alk. paper)
   1. Jesus Christ—Circumcision. 2. Church history—Primitive and
early church, ca. 30–600. I. Title. II. Series: Divinations.
   BT318.5.J33 2012
   232.92—dc23
                                                    2011043922

For my family

Contents

Preface

> There were certain people, he said, who did not blush to write books
> even about the circumcision of the Lord.
>   —Guibert of Nogent (d. 1124)

Beginning in the twelfth century, after centuries of relative obscurity, Christ's foreskin was suddenly difficult to miss across Christian Europe. Monasteries in France claimed to possess fragments of what they called the *sanctus virtus* ("holy virtue"), and produced legends explaining how this fragment of divine flesh came to be in their possession: it had been brought back from the holy land by none other than Charlemagne.[1] Jacobus de Voragine, author of the widely read *Legenda aurea* (*Golden Legend*) in the thirteenth century, recounted what was by then a common tale: "Now concerning the flesh of the Lord's circumcision (*de carne autem circumcisionis domini*), it is said that an angel took it to Charlemagne, and that he enshrined it at Aix-la-Chapelle in the church of the Blessed Mary and later transferred it to Charroux, but we are told that it is now in Rome in the church called Sancta Sanctorum."[2] Of course, Jacobus expresses some doubts about this legend, and even provides a more circumspect proposal of what happened to the foreskin: "But if this is true, it certainly is miraculous! But since that very flesh is truly of human nature, we believe that when Christ rose it returned to its own glorified place."[3] The miracle of Christ's foreskin in European hands was already engendering skepticism in the twelfth century. Guibert of Nogent, a Benedictine monk with deeply held reverence for the resurrection body of Christ, complained about scurrilous and impious persons who claim to possess Jesus' tooth, his umbilical cord, and his foreskin.[4]

Despite monastic skepticism, the foreskin of Christ (or fragments of it) became ubiquitous. It was parceled into reliquaries, represented in art, and contemplated in devotional literature.[5] Catherine of Siena, a lay mystic in the fourteenth century, imagined the wedding ring made for a virgin bride of God (perhaps even herself) fashioned out of Jesus' foreskin.[6] Agnes Blannbekin, a Beguine nun also in the fourteenth century, reported that she had visions of swallowing the sacred relic "hundreds of times."[7] Birgitta, who founded the Bridgettine Order of nuns in fourteenth-century Sweden, left a devotional tract in which she and the Virgin Mary also discussed the whereabouts of Christ's foreskin (Mary assures her it is safe in Rome).[8] Very quickly, it seemed, the foreskin was on everybody's mind (and lips).

Post-Enlightenment readers may shudder (or titter) at benighted medieval Christians so taken with a relic that is, to say the least, a bit unseemly.[9] Yet to dismiss these monks, mystics, and pilgrims as merely superstitious is to overlook the theological creativity and innovation here at work. Christians in those centuries (like many people today) saw the body, and all its constituent parts, as a highly charged zone of signification, on which multiple boundaries were enacted.[10] In an extremely technical commentary on the Catholic mass, written in the late twelfth century, Cardinal Lotario dei Conti di Segni spent many chapters explaining the miracle of the appearance of Christ's real flesh on the altar. He paused, as he turned to discuss the transformation of wine into Christ's blood, to ponder what happened to all those parts Christ shed on earth (blood, hair, foreskin). Did Christ take all of these with him in the resurrection? Or was it true (as "some say") that Charlemagne received the foreskin from an angel, and that it resided now in the Santa Sanctorum of the Lateran Basilica? Lotario demurs: "Better to commit all things to God, than to dare to define something else."[11] The desire to take hold of Christ's flesh—on an altar or in a reliquary—articulated a central theological desire of Christianity to unite the human and divine materially. A few years later, Lotario, now Pope Innocent III, would preside over a council in that same Lateran basilica that made transubstantiation—the belief that Christ's true body and blood were present on the sacramental altar—the official doctrine of the Catholic church.

At the same time European Christians expressed their desire to breach the boundary of human and divine and grasp God's flesh, they also evinced fear of breached boundaries. As Miri Rubin has documented, the doctrine of transubstantiation brought with it a new and horrible slander against the marginalized Jews of Europe: accusations of host desecration, the torture of Christ's body anew by perfidious Jews seeking to reenact the Passion.[12] The fear that God's body, once reproduced on earth, could be hijacked and subjected to renewed tortures articulated a more generalized (and, as Rubin points out, gendered) fear of bodily, and religious, vulnerability. Yet as the visualizations of artists and mystics throughout this period show, that body stolen away into illicit Jewish space was *already* imaginable as a circumcised, and therefore Judaized, male body. The foreskin of Christ, that theologically innovative relic, might allow Christians to imagine, in complex fashions, their relationship to Jews and Judaism, and even imagine Christ in that Jewish matrix. Medieval western Christians struggled to negotiate a host of complicated boundaries: between Christians and non-Christians, religious and lay, men and women, flesh and spirit. The luminescent and strange relic of Christ's foreskin allowed Christians to peer beyond these boundaries, to internalize difference, to imagine an otherness within.

Ancient considerations of the foreskin of Christ are far less dramatic and ubiquitous.[13] Typically Christians before the sixth century focused their attention on the question of why the Christian savior would submit to the indubitably Jewish ritual of circumcision. That is, Christians before the rise of Islam focused more on the ritual of circumcision than on its remainder. Modern seekers of the "historical Jesus" have, since the 1970s, taken to casually affirming the Jewishness of Jesus, and so find his submission to circumcision unproblematic.[14] Bart D. Ehrman, in a popular book on the historical Jesus, remarks easily: "There's probably no reason to belabor the point that all of our sources portray Jesus as Jewish—he came from a Jewish home, he was circumcised as a Jew, he worshiped the Jewish God, he kept Jewish customs, followed the Jewish Law, interpreted the Jewish Scriptures, and so on. . . . The tradition of Jesus' Jewish origin and upbringing is firmly entrenched in all of our traditions at every level."[15] This assertion relies on modern notions of historical reconstruction, on a "historical Jesus" who did not exist in this way before the modern period. Ancient Christians more commonly agreed with the remarks of Cyril, the fifth-century bishop of Alexandria: "You might rightly be amazed at this: that he [Christ] of necessity came down from above into the land of Judea, among those by whom he was mocked impiously; there he was born according to the flesh. But, in truth, he wasn't a Jew, insofar as he was the Word, but rather from both heaven and his father."[16]

If Jesus was, to ancient Christians, not a Jew, why was he circumcised when he was "born according to the flesh"? What purposes—theological, cultural, social, and political—did Christ's circumcision serve? The ways in which Christians answered this question take us into the heart of early Christian ideas about flesh, spirit, and the haunting permeability of religious boundaries that stand at the heart of this book.

Splitting the Difference

Making Difference

This is a surprisingly long book about a small mark: the circumcision of Christ, as it was imagined and interpreted in the first several centuries of Christianity. I propose to use this curious sign to begin to rethink the historical problem of Christian difference. By the historical problem of Christian difference I mean this: how do we, as historians, devise a narrative that reconciles the persistent Christian discourses of unity and singularity with the undeniable existence of multiple, diverse Christianities in antiquity? As Rebecca Lyman has phrased the problem: "'Christianity' defined as 'orthodoxy' rests uncomfortably on a history of inner conflict and persistent multiplicity. This intractable problem of diversity together with the ideological claim of unity only reinforces the cultural uniqueness or ideological paradox of Christian exclusivity in late antiquity."[1] Like Lyman, I am suggesting our standard answers to this "intractable" historical problem need retooling.

Most narratives of Christian development have attempted to explain this historical problem of Christian difference using the language of boundaries, conflict, and exclusion. Two narrative models in particular have predominated, both of which rely on similar assumptions about boundaries and distinction. The first narrative may be labeled the "traditional model," deriving as it does from the self-representation of Christian development from within the tradition.[2] Given definitive shape in the fourth century by Eusebius of Caesarea (although important groundwork was already laid by the Acts of the Apostles),[3] this traditional model viewed the development of "the Church" as singular and organic, directed by providence and guided by the apostles and continuous ecclesiastical institutions.[4] Difference is understood as deviance ("heresy") away from a pure norm ("orthodoxy"). In confessional narratives of Christian history, such deviant difference is always subsequent, malicious, and identifiable as outside the bounds of authentic Christianity. Nonconfessional variations on this traditional model still posit an "original" Christianity, and explain variant forms of Christianity as later, derivative biformations or "syncretisms" (without overtly judging their theological correctness).[5] Traces of the notion of "difference as deviance" also survive in modern accounts that seek to elevate and celebrate the excluded "others" of this traditional model, the implicitly or explicitly preferred "road not taken" that would have avoided the undesirable (misogynistic or otherwise hierarchical) traits of "normative" Christianity.[6]

The second narrative, which has ostensibly displaced the traditional model in the academy, is credited to early twentieth-century philologian and scholar Walter Bauer and his work *Rechtglaübigkeit und Kezterei im ältesten Christentum* (*Orthodoxy and Heresy in Earliest Christianity*). Bauer's thesis, that Christianity was originally diverse and that centralization and enforcement of a unified, Rome-oriented theology was secondary, has become especially influential in scholarship since its translation into English in the 1970s.[7] The dissemination of the translated Nag Hammadi codices and other "nonorthodox" texts over this same period contributed to a growing counternarrative of early Christian difference that denied primacy to any single formulation of Christian identity. Instead, Bauer has conditioned historians to view the development of normative Christianity as the end result of a conflict with and triumph of a "proto-orthodox" party over equally "original" and authentic forms of early Christian thought.[8]

This counternarrative (embedded, by the end of the twentieth century, in incipient multicultural identity politics) seeks to undo the totalizing and triumphalist narrative of the traditional model, and yet retains one of its central assumptions: that normative early Christianity (whether we consider it the original message of Jesus or simply one among several equally authentic, competing Christian "trajectories") employed the construction of boundaries to exclude difference and otherness. Even more recent, self-consciously "post-Bauer" historiography, which "reject[s] [Bauer's] idea that we can narrate a monolithic story of heresy becoming orthodoxy,"[9] adheres to a model of exclusionary boundary drawing to explain Christian development and difference. Lewis Ayres, in a recent issue of the *Journal of Early Christian Studies* on "the problem of orthodoxy," remarks of these post-Bauer scholars: "They have shaped accounts of the emergence of defined orthodoxies from more pluralistic situations which preceded them and frequently from situations of exegetical uncertainty. Orthodoxy is constructed from a range of possibilities, some more prominent than others, some already seemingly marginal. Scholars working from a variety of perspectives and commitments now also tend to take for granted that the emergence of orthodoxy involves a concomitant definition of heresy as that which is excluded."[10] The perspective may shift, from Eusebius to Bauer to "post-Bauer," but the model of "definition" and "exclusion" remains standard.

Informing this historiographic model, at least since the 1960s, are socio-anthropological theories of the formation of self and community. In these theories of identity formation, the "self" can only emerge through the identification and exclusion of an "other."[11] The "other" may be real, imaginary, or some indeterminate combination of the two; what is important is the separation of "self" and "other" through the process of boundary formation and exclusion of an "other." Even when such boundary formation is incomplete or ineffective, historians of early Christianity still assume that it became "normal" for early Christians to desire theological and social unity and "normal" for them to strive for this unity through the identification, classification, and rejection of difference.[12] It is one goal of this book to move a step beyond both the "traditional model" and the Bauer-inspired counternarratives by interrogating their shared assumptions about sameness and difference, namely, the centrality of boundaries and exclusion in the shaping of early Christian identities.

When we take as normative the process of defining the self through the exclusion of difference, we gloss over some of the complex internal dynamics that shaped Christianity throughout the ancient period. It is of course self-evident that our early Christian sources quite frequently *speak* of "boundaries" and "others" and deviance and difference, and frequently profess a desire for exclusion, uniformity, and singularity. But what if such totalizing language serves not as a clue to a sincere desire for theological unity, but rather as a mask lightly covering over persistent—even necessary—fragmentation and dissolution? What if the singular language of orthodoxy does not seek to exclude, but rather to internalize and appropriate the so-called deviance of the other? What if the failure of this constant boundary formation to achieve such unity was not a bug but rather a feature of the discourses of early Christian difference? How would our perception of early Christian identity change, and what would this do to our assumptions about the very invention of the category of "religion" in the crucial period of late antiquity?

The Fantasy of Boundaries

The socioanthropological model of boundary formation and exclusion is not the only theoretical tool available to us in addressing the historical problem of Christian difference. A different theory of the interaction of difference and identity comes from the tradition of psychoanalysis, rearticulated recently in feminist and postcolonial appropriations of the work of Sigmund Freud, Jacques Lacan, and others.[13] Already, historians of the premodern period have made convincing (and appropriately contingent) cases for the use of a theory formed in the heart of modernity as a lens to reconfigure earlier subjects and topics.[14] Psychoanalytically informed theories of subjectivity and personhood, quite apart from any universalizing claims, provide (I suggest) a compelling and useful model for rethinking our historical narratives of early Christian difference.

In these models, "self" (and, by extension, participation in a coherent community of "selves," such as races, genders, or nations) is a partially realized fantasy from which the "other" is never completely separated. In this understanding of personhood, the "other" is for the "self" simultaneously an object of identification and distinction. There are no real boundaries; there is never exclusion.

Lacan famously drew on the idea of a child regarding herself in the mirror, realizing herself as a subject through the imperfect "other" reflected there: at once recognizable as the "self" ("she moves when I move, she looks like me") yet intuitively other, apart from the self ("she's over there, I'm here"), with a smooth integrity the child does not experience in her own porous and uncooperative body.[15] As Terry Eagleton puts it, "The object is at once somehow part of ourselves—we *identify* with it—and yet not ourselves, something alien. . . . For Lacan, the ego is just this narcissistic process whereby we bolster up a fictive sense of unitary selfhood by finding something in the world with which we can identify."[16] "Self" in its broadest sense then emerges out of an act of misrecognition, and this "fantasy of *ego*" perpetuates the mistaken notion that subjectivity is stable, bounded, and discrete. In reality, "I" exist by virtue of my fantasies of an "other" that is really just a reminder of that smoothed-out reflection of my own psyche. "The subject constructs itself in the imitation of as well as opposition to this image," asserts Ania Loomba.[17] Whatever sense of self I possess is an illusion that emerges out of fragmentary and imaginary negotiations of unreal and ideal selves and others. The "other" is not only an object of *distinction* and *difference* by which I know myself (the "not-I") but also an object of desire and identification for myself (the "ideal-I"). Identity is always already split against itself at the moment of its formation between "self" and "other." No boundary between self and other persists, except as a fantasy of identity. Because my subjectivity emerges out of a scene of imaginary boundaries between my "self" and "others," it is inherently unstable: it shifts and reconstitutes itself according to myriad psychic and material pressures and forces. It desires wholeness and a sense of permanence—thus the insistence on "myself," a coherent subjectivity that can speak in the first person—but that desire is constantly, and sometimes thrillingly, frustrated.[18] The sense of self is therefore always accompanied by anxiety and ambivalence.

Whether or not my internal psyche or yours actually operates this way is unfalsifiable, and to some extent irrelevant for my purposes. It is when we turn this model of subjectivity outward, into the realm of social relations, that I find it becomes illuminating and helpful. When we think of the boundaries of community along these same lines, as fantasies that both create and uncreate communal cohesion, we view the formation of such identities, and their disruption, quite differently. Take, for instance, the articulation of gender as a social category. On a socioanthropological model of gender construction, "male" comes to exist by distinction from and exclusion of "female." A boundary is formed between self ("male") and other ("female"); to cross that boundary is to transgress it knowingly in an act of deviance, whether we find such gender deviance laudable or not. Any attempt to critique the normativity of the male self—say, a feminist critique—must therefore operate from an a priori position of exteriority and marginalization: self and other, male and female, may be equalized but must remain bounded and distinct.

A feminist appropriation of psychoanalysis, however, presses that initial moment of differentiation and finds very different consequences. The articulation of "male" is not simply the recognition and rejection of "female." Rather "female" is simultaneously an object of distinction and identification: it is never fully externalized, but always part of the male "self." "Maleness" exists always in contradiction to itself, always reinternalizing and rejecting its other ("femaleness"). Sexism, from this perspective, is not the fear or oppression of an other, but rather the fear of the otherness *within*, the fear of the permeability of the self's own boundaries. Likewise the critique of the seemingly privileged edifice of "maleness" does not take place from the distant margins but from that newly recovered place within. To cross the boundary between "male" and "female," moreover, is not to transgress at all, but rather to acknowledge the illusory boundary between self ("male") and other ("female"). It is also simply to acknowledge the inherent instability and shiftiness of those gender categories. In this reading, "gender relations" become politically and socially more open to intervention.[19]

Similar conclusions hold with our reading of other groups' formations, such as race or nationhood. Instead of seeing the instability of racial categories or national identities as a sort of category failure—the desire to construct "whiteness" cannot outpace the messy realities of daily existence; the will-to-"Americanness" is constantly troubled by new and unexpected contingencies and border infiltrations—we instead read such instabilities as part of the very nature of categories: "whiteness" abhors but longs for its internalized racial otherness, "Americanness" shouts for borders that can never be securely established.[20] The politics of race and nationhood become much more pliable and open to critique when we begin to see that the very attempt to bound and define constitutes a hidden act of dissolution and blurring.

Other scholars precede me (and instruct me) in the appropriation of psychoanalytic theories of identity deployed in the social field of history. Anne McClintock's 1995 study *Imperial Leather: Race, Gender, and Sexuality in the Colonial Contest* employs psychoanalytic frameworks to untangle the politics of race, gender, and class from Victorian England to postindependence South Africa. McClintock follows in the footsteps of postcolonial theorists from Frantz Fanon to Homi Bhabha,[21] and feminist theorists such as Julia Kristeva and Luce Irigarary, all of whom have operated at the intersections of politically informed history and psychoanalytically informed theory: "Psychoanalysis and material history are mutually necessary for strategic engagement with unstable power," McClintock writes.[22] Practicing what she terms a "situated psychoanalysis,"[23] McClintock weaves together various strands of thought that have moved psychoanalysis from the realm of the therapeutic and individual to the study of the historical and social, demonstrating the analytic value in rethinking difference and identity. Moving away from a binary logic that automatically diminishes and partitions the "other" of identity, this new view of subject (and community) formation leaves the "self" and "other" of identity mutable and dynamic, embedded in the shifting realities of a material world open to ambivalence and anxiety.

History, Theory, and Hybridity

It will become evident in the course of this book how I think this new model of difference based on the fantasy of boundaries can help us interrogate identity and difference in early Christianity. I want to make it clear in this introduction, however, that this is not simply a case of theory swapping, that, weary of sociology and anthropology, I turn to the linguistically puzzling and intellectually challenging world of "situated psychoanalysis." Just as the psychoanalytic construction of identity can be theoretically useful in exploring issues of race, gender, and nation-state formation, it is specifically applicable, I argue, in the context of the late ancient Roman Empire. In the early Christian context, we have a social and cultural situation in which recent postcolonial interpretations of "empire" dovetail with the psychoanalytic framing of identity and provide new insight into the workings of the Roman Empire.

A contrast between the imperial logics of the Greeks and Romans is instructive to get our historical and theoretical bearings. We tend to think of "Greekness" (*hellenismos*) as it developed in the post-Persian period as hinging on a putative binary distinction between self and other, creating a coherent cultural and social self ("Hellene") through the articulation of an excluded other ("barbarian"). It is no surprise that the socioanthropological model of boundary formation and exclusion has proved particularly useful in illuminating this cultural ideal.[24] Roman imperial identity, however, coming fast on the heels of this "Greekification" of the East, understood itself to be operating very differently.[25] Throughout the imperial period (emerging already in the late republic) we can pinpoint no overarching ethnic or cultural totality of "Romanness" that defined participation in the empire, analogous to Alexander's *hellenismos*. Or rather, "Romanness" was not expressed through boundary and exclusion. *Romanitas* was not the imperialization of *Latinitas*,[26] and the political unity of Rome never mapped onto any consistent cultural homogeneity. To be sure, we see traces of a "Roman/barbarian" dichotomy in Latin literature,[27] as well as attempts to construct a coherent sense of self in contradistinction to "others." But whereas Greeks identified barbarians in order to draw distinction and boundaries, Romans identified the barbarians as a site for the exercise of Rome's civilizing power.[28] The other was not to be excluded; he was to be incorporated, otherness intact, into the Roman sphere of *imperium*. Jeremy Schott succinctly notes, "Rome sought to contain the threat of diversity by incorporating otherness within its borders, not through its elimination."[29]

As the Roman Empire grew, it imagined its origins not in the clearly bounded selfhood of ethnic autochthony—the mythical articulations, for instance, of ancient Greek identity[30]—but rather in domination and appropriation of difference.[31] From the rape of the Sabine women through the opening up of the Roman Senate to Gallic nobles, Rome's founding power was to seize, appropriate, and manage difference. Tacitus's version of Emperor Claudius's speech to the Senate, in which the emperor argues for the extension of senatorial status outside of Italy, captures how Rome's logic of empire differed from that of the Greeks: "What else was the downfall of the Spartans and Athenians except that—although they prevailed in arms—they bounded off (*arcebant*) those whom they conquered because they were foreign-born (*alienigenis*)? But our Founder Romulus was so wise that multiple peoples (*plerosque populos*) on the same day he held as enemies and then as citizens (*civis*)" (Tacitus, *Annales* 11.24).[32] Greek xenophobia and boundedness make way for Roman heterogeneity, a strategy, we are led to believe, that is ultimately more successful in the expansion and management of an empire.[33] Yet with that internalization of difference comes an anxiety about subjectivity: Juvenal, through his disaffected poetic character Umbricius, complains about the unctuous Syrian Orontes flowing into the Tiber, leaving its Greek dregs on once-pristine Roman banks (Juvenal, *Satura* 3),[34] even as his contemporary Martial marvels at the exotic cacophony (human and animal) in the imperial arena.[35] "The city of imperial splendour was full of reminders of the violence of conquest," Catharine Edwards and Greg Woolf have remarked.[36] As the city grew into an empire, Rome's power continued to be defined through an anxious ability to contain and absorb difference.

Conditioned as we are by Gibbon's eighteenth-century tristesse,[37] we imagine the boundaries of the empire from the third century onward slowly crumbling, barbarians first dribbling and then pouring over poorly guarded and ineffective borders.[38] Yet C. R. Whittaker's recent work on the Roman Empire's borders has asked us rethink the *limites* of Empire.[39] These were not, after all, boundaries but rather frontiers: sites for the negotiation and management of difference.[40] The physical limits of the Roman Empire, the maintenance of this frontier zone of difference, embodied the Roman ideology of power: not the (always failed and failing) imposition of homogeneity (Hellenism, for instance) but the majestic management of difference and otherness. The very ideal of Roman selfhood, constructed out of the power of imperium, depended therefore on the persistence of difference and otherness alongside and within the limits of empire. Difference can never be eliminated or covered over, but must remain visible in order to support the logic of Roman domination.

Identity in this Roman Empire is thus always split against itself, a self that must always confront, appropriate, and risk being destabilized by difference. Like the child of Lacan gazing into the mirror, the Roman comes to desire the other that defines his self, and yet fears its difference. One way to frame this cultural economy of the Roman Empire—always identifying, categorizing, and internalizing the difference of its subject peoples—is through the theoretical concept of hybridity, as elucidated by postcolonial theorists.[41] The critical force of the "hybrid" elaborates the psychoanalytic description of the self outlined above, in that it helps us to uncover the fiction of a closed, bounded identity. Language of purity and containment, focused on the fear of the (racial, ethnic, or religious) mixing of the hybrid, masks the very operations of appropriation of those feared "others," and covers over a reality that is always already mixed: "colonial specularity, doubly inscribed," writes Homi Bhabha, "does not produce a mirror where the self apprehends self; it is always the split screen of the self and its doubling, the hybrid."[42] Roman rule was always hybridized in this way, pulling the provincial "other" into the heart of the cultural, social, and imperial formations of self and community. Tacitus would have us believe that this internalization of the otherness of subject peoples lay at the heart of Roman imperial might; Gibbon would no doubt disagree. Postcolonial criticism would highlight the simultaneously successful yet deconstructive effects of Rome's imperial hybridity.

Rome's hybridized self becomes visible at the very site of its imperial articulation. The Roman appropriation of hellenism is an instructive case in point. The mastery of Greek literature, art, and philosophy by the Roman elites created visible and pervasive evidence of Roman imperial mastery. Greek language and literature became the cultural spoils of Rome, but were never fully internalized—that is, Greek culture had to remain legibly "Greek" in order to retain value within the logic of Rome's empire.[43] At the same time, Romanness—defined through cultural domination—exists only by virtue of the legible Greekness within. "Captive Greece captured the beastly victor, and introduced the arts to rustic Latium," Horace wrote (*Epistularum liber* 21.1.156–57). To be Roman, in this sense, is to possess Greece, maintaining its discrete otherness within. *Romanitas* is hybridized, even in its careful delineation of (and anxiety over) the otherness of the interiorized, defeated Greek.

We can recall Cicero's poignant depiction of the multitudes of Greek-speaking visitors to the city of Rome (*ex Asia atque Achaia plurimi Romae*) openly weeping upon seeing their native statues "carried away" to be displayed in the forum.[44] Cicero is attempting to evoke antipathy against Gaius Verres and sympathy for his Sicilian clients, but he is also framing the despoiled, and despairing, Greeks for the masterful Roman gaze alongside the *spolia* of their statuary.[45] The weeping Greek becomes for the Roman viewer an object of both desire (the vehicle of *paideia*, the value of which is confirmed only by the Greeks' keen sense of its material loss) and of fear and anxiety (as the weeping Greeks threaten to transform into the litigious Sicilians who were Cicero's clients). The presence of the Greek highlighted Rome's strength but also problematized the hybridity of Rome by pinpointing the otherness within.

Indeed, Rome's hybridized hellenism created the space for Greek resistance. As Rome literally and figuratively colonized the Greek past—erecting Greek statues in the Roman forum, purchasing Greek *paidagōgoi* to teach the *alphabeta* to Roman noble children—the ostentatious control over Greek difference served to value that difference. Rome viewed the Greek as *homo paedagogus*, "definitively characterized by paideutic activity,"[46] and thereby provided a means for the Greek to assert his own cultural subjectivity. With the power of hybridized imperialism comes the threat of the "mimic man," as Bhabha has argued.[47] As Rome's imperial appropriation of Hellenism spread across the face of the Mediterranean, so too did the phenomenon later dubbed by Philostratus the "second Sophistic," the renewal of Attic artistry that can be read as a response to Roman power: the exploitation of the ambivalent relationship between ruler and ruled, the mimicry of Rome's colonizing power.[48] As Romans appropriated Greekness—*because* they did so—Greeks found a means to resist Romanness.

The simultaneous appropriation and differentiation of "Greekness" in the early Roman Empire provides merely the most visible and closely studied example of political and cultural hybridity at work among ancient Romans, and a clear sense of how the hybridized Roman both created and (to an admittedly limited fashion) empowered the colonized "other." One of my assumptions throughout this book is that the overall Roman ideology of empire at work in late antiquity lends itself readily to an analysis of the hybrid self, the self that comes into existence not through rejection of "the other," but rather through a simultaneous distinction from and appropriation of that other. It is this strategy for identity and difference, I suggest, that is taken up in early Christianity. It is this desire for, and fear of, the other at the heart of the self that I argue becomes visible through the circumcision of Christ.

A Different Fetish

The circumcision of Christ is, as I said at the outset, a small mark, but a potent one. In the next chapter, I explore more closely the specific place of circumcision in the economy of signs that circulated to uphold (but also, potentially, to undermine) Roman power in the imperial period. This particular instance of the sign of circumcision, however—typical yet unique—can reveal a great deal about Christian appropriations of difference, identity, and power. It is, to borrow Anne McClintock's use of the term, a revealing fetish of late ancient Christianity. The term "fetish" arrives in McClintock's postcolonial study by the parallel routes of the history of religions, where it marks the materialist fixations of "primitive" religions, and theories of psychosexual development, where it figures as the displaced site of libidinous attachment.[49] McClintock sees in the fetish the possibility of a psychoanalytically informed social history, cognizant of ambiguity, ambivalence, resistance, and transgression.[50]

In its simplest sense, "fetishism" displaces desire, the fixation on an object that always represents something more. In McClintock's more complex reading, fetishism gives the social and intellectual historian a window into "the historical enactment of ambiguity itself." If a community's identity results from paradoxical gestures of distinction from and appropriation of an other (hybridity), then the fetish materially reenacts that paradox. McClintock writes: "The fetish thus stands at the cross-roads of psychoanalysis and social history, inhabiting the threshold of both personal and historical memory. The fetish marks a crisis in social meaning as the embodiment of an impossible resolution. The contradiction is displaced onto and embedded in the fetish object, which is thus destined to recur with compulsive repetition. Hence the apparent power of the fetish to enchant the fetishist. By displacing power onto the fetish, then manipulating the fetish, the individual gains symbolic control over what might otherwise be terrifying ambiguities."[51] The fetish embodies that moment in time when the self is formed, that moment of identification and differentiation and splitting; it embodies, and ameliorates, the anxiety of that moment (am I my-self or an-other?). McClintock takes examples of fetish objects that make sense of the triangulated discourses of race, class, and gender in Victorian England: the crisp, white linen blouse, the polished black boot, the leather "slave" band of a scullery maid. Social groups, she argues, also locate the paradox of communal identity in fetish objects: the map, the flag, and the statue that contain and embody the difference of "nation" or "empire."

The fetish object grants the historian a glimpse into the contradictory figurations of communal selfhood, what I am calling the historical problem of early Christian difference. Other scholars of early Christianity before me have attempted to describe analytically the dense, contradictory figural language often found in our ancient Christian texts. In two important essays,

Patricia Cox Miller has taken her cue from literary criticism: borrowing first the "hypericon" from W. J. T. Mitchell to imagine a "fundamentally ambivalent standpoint toward the desert and its role in the development of Christian anthropology";[52] and later the "grotesque" from Geoffrey Galt Harpham to articulate the "impossible split reference" that is neither "a mediation or fusion of opposites but the presentation or realization of a contradiction."[53] Like Mitchell's hypericon and Harpham's grotesquerie, the fetish provides an analytic tool that makes sense of—instead of explaining away—the contradictions and ambiguities of early Christian discourse: "Fetishes may take myriad guises and erupt from a variety of social contradictions. They do not resolve conflict in value but rather embody in one object the failure of resolution."[54] By historicizing the fetish, removing it (as McClintock does) from the "narrow scene of [Freudian and Lacanian] phallic universalism," we can open it up to "far more powerful and intricate genealogies that would include both psychoanalytic insights (disavowal, displacement, emotional investment, and so on), as well as nuanced historical narratives of cultural difference and diversity."[55] The fetish embodies the anxieties of identity, it replays them, it gives them shape that makes them at once manageable but never resolvable.

Christ's circumcision is such a fetish for early Christianity. A unique moment—by definition, it could occur only once—it is nonetheless repeated in multiple discourses of early Christianity: interpreted, manipulated, disputed (but never discounted), creating a site for the articulation of Christian paradox. When I first began this project, I assumed that the contradictions embodied and enacted by discussions of Christ's circumcision would center on the fraught Jewish origins of an increasingly non- and anti-Jewish movement. I found, however, that this was only one level on which the circumcision of Jesus embodies "the failure of resolution" in early Christianity. All manner of paradox and contradiction—of impossible, desirable otherness at the heart of the Christian self—are articulated in this sign, made visible and never fully resolved.

My contention throughout this book is that an exploration of the diverse and often unexpected ways that this curious mark on the body of Christ pops up in ancient Christian discourse reveals a great deal about the making of Christian culture and identity. Like late ancient Christianity itself (as I shall argue), Christ's circumcision is an ultimately unbounded and confounding object of speculation in late antiquity. I do not examine here discrete treatises or homilies "on the circumcision of Christ" (until the last chapter, which seeks out the first examples of such writings), but find my subject weaving in and out of a variety of other discourses: anti-Jewish apology, heresiology, theological essays, ascetic treatises, homilies, and biblical commentaries. Like Judaism itself—the "signified" to which circumcision metonymically pointed in the ancient world—Jesus' circumcision is found throughout these early Christian discourses, difficult to "pin down" precisely for its perfusion throughout the early Christian imaginary. The remarkable ubiquity of Christ's circumcision in so many diverse areas of Christian thought is our first hint that this small, diffuse mark might possess a larger significance for the study of early Christianity.

Our second hint comes in the paradoxical nature of this mark: circumcision, the mark of Judaism, commemorated and delineated on the body of the Christian savior. It confounds some of our basic assumptions about normative Christianity: the blemish of multiple particularities (Jewish, male) on a universal messiah. What's more, there is a curious insistence on this confounding mark in our early Christian sources: from the first century onward (when Christ's circumcision perhaps makes its first appearance), Christians find it useful in some way to embrace the paradox of the circumcised messiah.

In the following chapters I explore the specific instances of these paradoxical uses of the divine circumcision, from the Gospel of Luke to the Latin and Byzantine Feasts of the Cirumcision. In Chapter 1, I explore in more detail the concept of a Roman cultural economy of signs that made "otherness" both visible and manageable—and disruptive—as signs of Roman power. In this cultural economy, the stereotypical circumcision—despite its existence in a variety of Near Eastern groups—came to signify "Judaism" in the metaphorical and material Roman economy. Like all stereotypes, however, this signifying circumcision had two effects: it at once supported and undermined Rome's cultural economy. When the earliest followers of Jesus came to confront this economy of signs, "circumcision" likewise signaled the symbolic freight of Jewishness: rejected by the apostle Paul, it was curiously—and, perhaps, cannily—recouped by the Gospel of Luke, in possibly the earliest reference to Christ's circumcision.

Chapter 2 treats the attempts by Christians throughout the late antique period to create—and blur—the boundaries between Christianity and Judaism. Through an exploration of dialogue texts (both literary dialogues between Jews and Christians, as well as the internalized dialogue of question-and-answer texts) that feature the circumcision of Christ, we see how Christianity can simultaneous reject and reinscribe its own originary Jewishness. Chapter 3 turns from (anti-) Jewish texts to the welter of Christian heresiological writings: here, too, we see that the attempt to construct boundaries often covers gestures that reabsorb the strangeness of abject theological "others" (heresies) into the heart of orthodoxy.

In Chapter 4, I focus on a single text that incorporates much of the paradoxical productivity enabled by Christ's circumcision. Epiphanius's *Panarion*, or "Medicine Chest for Heresies," contains a long chapter in refutation of the "Jewish-Christian" sect of the Ebionites. It is Epiphanius, ventriloquizing these Ebionites, who first voices the desire and fear of Christ's circumcision for "orthodox" Christians: "If Christ was circumcised, so too should we be." Epiphanius's response masterfully rewrites Judaism, Christianity, orthodoxy, and heresy in a single stroke; this text, perhaps most forcefully of any in the entire book, shows us how boundary-creating discourse provided early Christians an apt and surprising vehicle for the retention and internalization of difference.

Chapter 5 takes the Bible as an object of centralizing unity among Christians and demonstrates how the very act of constructing a unified scriptural vision could reproduce and recreate fission and faction. Emerging in both literary and ritual circles, biblical commentaries and sermons—both on the Lucan description of Christ's circumcision and in other passages where Luke 2:21 serves as intertext—wrestle with the multifarious Christ through the encounter with God's multivalent Word, perhaps nowhere more divided than at Christ's most Jewish moment. In Chapter 6, we arrive at the formal institutionalization of Christ's circumcision in mainstream Christian discourse: the commemoration of the Feast of Christ's Circumcision, emerging in churches across the Mediterranean and the Near East in the pre-Islamic period. Here, the call to Christians "to become circumcised like Christ" places the paradox of difference and identity squarely in the heart of Christian ritual time and space. I conclude with some final thoughts on the question that haunts much of this book: could ancient Christians conceive of Jesus (male and circumcised) as a Jew, or did their conception of Jesus "passing" as Jewish allow them to rewrite notions of religion and identity altogether?

There is no single trajectory or ideological line that Christ's circumcision allows us to trace throughout the late antique period. Indeed, my argument is precisely that Christ's circumcision reveals the fiction of lines, the fantasy of boundaries, even as it permeates the diverse discourses of early Christian identity. The accumulated details contribute to a single argument throughout this book: that early Christian discourses of boundaries, differences, and distinctions consistently and paradoxically worked to erases boundaries, confound difference, and problematize distinction. That is, early Christian identity emerged out of the simultaneous making, and unmaking, of difference.

Chapter 1

Circumcision and the Cultural Economy of Difference

The point of new historical investigation is to disrupt the notion of fixity.

—Joan Wallach Scott

Circumcision and the Jews: A Sign to the Gentiles

Stereotype: The Jewish Body in the Roman Empire

In the early second century, the Roman historian Suetonius described an incident from decades earlier under the revenue-hungry emperor Domitian: "Besides the other [taxes], the Jewish tax (*Iudaïcus fiscus*) was pursued with especial vigor: for which those persons were turned over (*deferebantur*)[1] who either lived a Jewish life undeclared or who, lying about their origins, had not paid the levy imposed on their people. I recall being present, as a teenager, when an old man, of ninety years, was inspected by a procurator (and a crowded court!) to see whether he was circumcised" (Suet. *Dom.* 12.2).[2] This brief, brutal scene condenses for Suetonius's readers, and for us, the convoluted role of Jewish circumcision in the early Roman Empire: a sign of distinction, strangeness, even shame, that at once sets the Jew apart (here, for special taxation), but also incorporates him into the broader economy of Roman power. The circumcised genitals of the tax-dodging Jew are part of the juridical processes that make the empire function.

In this first, preliminary chapter I ask what kinds of meanings Jewish circumcision carried in the Roman context, and how those meanings were both appropriated and contested: first, by the Jews themselves; second, by the earliest texts of the Jesus movement (the writings of Paul and his followers, including the Gospel of Luke); and, third, by early gentile Christians seeking to grapple with the overdetermined Jewishness of their religious past. My basic argument, throughout this chapter, is that Jewish circumcision circulated as part of a cultural economy of signs in the early Roman Empire: the stereotypical function of circumcision supported, but also destabilized, Roman control and management of Jewish otherness. The cultural force of circumcision, and its ability to resignify in multiple contradictory ways among ancient Jews and Christians, must be understood in this Roman imperial context. Only by considering the cultural and political implications of Jewish circumcision can we begin to understand the implications of imagining this overcharged sign on the body of Jesus.

The increasing significance of Jewish circumcision among Roman authors as "the mark of Judaism" has been well documented in modern scholarship.[3] Indeed, by the early empire, Jewish circumcision was already something of an overdetermined symbol in Roman literature, as a mark of cultural difference and general ridicule among Roman literate elites.[4] For Horace and Persius, the superstition of the "clipped Jews" (*Iudaei curti*) is a social nuisance (Hor. *Sat.* 1.9.69–70; Pers. *Sat.* 5.185).[5] Martial jealously contemplates the sexual prowess of foreskinless Jewish men (*Epig.* 7.30.5), while Juvenal bemoans the weird Jews who "worship the sky" and "by and by, shed their foreskins" (*Sat.* 14.99).[6] The valences of circumcision in these writings varies considerably, from a sign of hypersexuality to cloistered superstition. The one commonality is that it signifies *Jewish*: "Jews did constitute an identifiable ethnic group in the varied social mosaic of the Roman Empire, and circumcision did serve as the chief mark of their distinctive way of life."[7] In fact, over the centuries spanning the rise of the Roman Empire—and the early spread of Christianity—Jewish circumcision became a part of a complex and labile cultural economy of signs: a system of symbols that made the otherness of provincial peoples at once distinct from yet legible to the controlling eyes of empire.[8]

I have already discussed, briefly in the Introduction, the particular mode of Roman imperial power: unlike that of "Hellenism," the founding power of Romanitas was the containment and appropriation—but never erasure—of "other" cultures.[9] A crucial component of this form of imperial control was a political culture based on knowledge of these others in Rome's midst. Clifford Ando, in his recent work on Roman religion, has brilliantly inspected one sphere of Roman life in which such epistemological discourse functioned:

when Romans courted the gods of their enemies (*evocatio*) or "translated" the religious beliefs and practices of other peoples (*interpretatio*), they were expanding the "empiricist" bases of their own imperial religion.[10] Ando's study, which stretches from Cicero to Augustine, suggests that the epistemological foundations of Roman society extended beyond what we might define as the narrowly religious: in war, politics, literature—"culture," writ large—Romans prided themselves on their ability to incorporate others into a distinctly Roman body of knowledge.[11]

In order to be effectively incorporated into Rome's epistemological structures, these other cultures could not be conglomerated into an amorphous "other," but must remain distinctive and distinguishable.[12] Roman imperial power, in part, operated through stereotype, "the primary form of objectification in colonial discourse."[13] The "effete Persian," the "educated Greek," the "painted Gaul," and, indeed, the "circumcised Jew" all functioned to render legible, and therefore knowable and containable, the variegated other populations that made up the Roman Empire.[14] Petronius, in the first century, casually and effectively deploys a host of such distinctive marks (as two of his characters argue about possible disguises to escape a sticky situation): "why not circumcise us," sneers one character, "so we look like Jews? And pierce our ears, so we can imitate Arabs; and whiten our faces with chalk, so Gaul thinks we're her citizens" (Petr. *Sat.* 102.14).[15] The comical list of specific traits (and others in the novel's scene) underscores the mastery implicit in Roman specular identification.

Stereotyping, like so many forms of epistemological colonial control, is simultaneously effective and unstable, the conveyer of ambivalent knowledge that makes empires work even as it undermines them.[16] On the one hand, stereotypes operate through repeated assertions of optical dominance. Yet at the same time these various signs may not be obviously "visible" to the Roman charged with decoding and categorizing the provincial others under his gaze, or may be misleading. Suetonius's tax-dodging Jew's circumcision was not visible; the magistrate, relying on the word of (it seems) a snitch (*delator*), removed the old man's clothes in order to prove what was otherwise not manifest to his juridical sight. Indeed, as Shaye Cohen has astutely observed, the stereotype of "the circumcised Jew" would routinely *fail* to mark out Jews in the ancient Roman city: first, because Jews were not unique in their circumcision; second, because clothing conventions dictated that male genitals were not routinely open to inspection.[17] Stereotypes are inherently unreliable, Jewish circumcision included.

Circumcision fails in another sense, of course, in that it (ostensibly) only marks out male Jews: what would Suetonius's judge open to inspection if the accused Jew before him were a woman? Later (as we shall see) Christians would seize upon this gender inequity to argue the essential incompleteness of the Jewish covenant.[18] But in the Roman system of signs the strangely gendered nature of Jewish recognizability reveals not only the gaps in Roman specular authority but also the ways in which Rome's cultural economy was itself deeply gendered, as are all colonial systems of stereotypes.[19] By this I do not simply mean that imperial powers dictate the visible markers for "male" and "female," although this is, to some extent, true in cultures that legislate codes of dress and comportment.[20] I mean that stereotyping regimes mark cultural actors as either viewers or viewed, and draw on common tropes of "male" and "female" to encode those roles.

We should recall Joan Wallach Scott's fundamental insight about gender systems: "gender is a primary way of signifying relations of power."[21] When the Roman Empire constructs a relationship of power based on specular prowess, it is creating a fundamentally gendered relationship with the provincials: the (male) Roman exerts his power over the (female) provincial through his masterful gaze, replicating the social norms of dominating male and dominated female as a basic unit of asymmetrical social interaction.[22] The indisputable maleness of the Jewish sign of circumcision is, therefore, ironic and even paradoxical: by submitting to a sign on his male sex, the Jew becomes the feminized subject of the Roman Empire.[23] The sign of maleness becomes a sign of feminine submission. In this gender reversal, circumcision signifies more, and less, than it is.

As a queered sign, therefore, circumcision (like all colonial stereotypes) is never accurate or straightforward. Stereotypes, however, do not need to be "right" to be culturally authoritative and do important political and social work. Suetonius's story suggests the confidence that imperial Rome had in its specular authority: the man who, presumably, was otherwise unclassifiable is certified as "Jewish" and levied the appropriate tax. Of course, as historians, we have no way of knowing whether this man was really Jewish, or simply appeared so (or even if he was "really" circumcised, or those viewing his naked body merely agreed that he was so). We can't even know if Suetonius really witnessed this scene, heard about it, invented it, or misremembered it. All we know is that this man's body, at least as reconstructed by Suetonius, represented to an audience (of onlookers, or readers) the economic circulation of signs in the Roman Empire. Stereotypes become true because they work.

Significant in the promulgation of the power of stereotypes is the moment *just before* the man's clothes are removed, his genitals exposed, his Jewishness confirmed. It is at this moment that the anxieties of imperial identity are made most evident: as Homi Bhabha writes, the stereotype "gives access to an 'identity' which is predicated as much on mastery and pleasure as it is on anxiety and defence, for it is a form of multiple and contradictory belief in its recognition of difference and disavowal of it."[24] This anxiety makes real the sensation of mastery and pleasure that follows immediately. That moment of uncertainty also creates the opening by which colonial power becomes dynamic, fluid, and contestable. Stereotypes demand a "fixity" that is, of course, impossible. I will return, in the final chapter of this book, to the problem of "passing" that is the flip side of imperial specular certainty. Here I simply note that the truth-making quality of colonial stereotyping relies on, and is undermined by, the very ambiguity of specular identification: Rome shows her power by forcefully removing an old man's clothes, but in that same gesture shows the limits of her optical acumen. Circumcision, in this optical cultural economy, therefore signifies doubly: as the sign of the Jew and as the sign of that economy's own potential failures.[25]

Claiming the Difference: Jews on Circumcision

At the same time that this Roman cultural economy of signs incorporated the circumcised bodies of Jews into the mosaic of imperial life, we see a shift in the way that Jews envisioned circumcision, as well. Certainly circumcision as a paradigmatic sign of Jewishness predates Roman attention to the sign. It is the mark of the Abrahamic covenant (Genesis 17) designed, according to tradition, to "mark out" God's chosen people from among "the nations."[26] In the encounter with Hellenism, the mark of circumcision became a sign of provincial barbarism and some enthusiasts of Greek culture, we read in a late second-century BCE text, "removed the marks of circumcision and abandoned the holy covenant" (1 Macc 1:15).[27] During Judea's brief imperial period under the Hasmoneans, forcible circumcision was used to bring conquered peoples into the religio-political fold,[28] but by the period of Roman rule its Judaizing force was contested: Herod, descended from one of those forcibly circumcised Idumeans and chosen as Rome's client king, was ridiculed by his Judean subjects as *hēmiioudaios*—a "half-Jew."[29] Even as Rome came to recognize and privilege the sign of the Jewish covenant, the Jews themselves were revisiting this doubled mark of covenant loyalty and imperial stereotype. As Shaye Cohen notes, "In the first century of our era, the practice of circumcision seems to have been widely debated by Greek-speaking Jews."[30]

Indeed in the first century, allegorically minded Jews in Alexandria—according to Philo—were spiritualizing the mark of Abraham, claiming that its symbolism trumped actual performance of the ritual.[31] Philo defended the literal practice of circumcision while trying to recoup its philosophical and symbolic value, although he himself displays little enthusiasm for the physical rite.[32] Often Philo and his nameless opponents are read on a sliding scale of traditionalism and assimilation. The so-called antinomians are eager to assimilate into Greco-Roman culture, while Philo—despite his own "disquietude" over circumcision[33]—is understood as holding the literal line of the Law regardless of his allegorical proclivities. Yet if we cast the terms of debate along political lines, the polarities might reverse. By turning away from physical circumcision, the antinomians are radically disengaging their Jewish identity from the Roman cultural economy of signs—refusing Rome's specular domination, camouflaged by philosophical generality; by contrast Philo, a member (after all) of a respectful legation of provincials to the imperial court,[34] preserves the physical sign of Jewish stereotype clearly distinguishable beneath the glossy sheen of hellenistic philosophical sophistication. At issue then is the external legibility of Jewish identity, condensed in the sign of circumcision.

For this reason, perhaps, we see increased attention to the particulars of circumcision among the burgeoning class of rabbinic sages. Cohen details a shift from the last centuries BCE, when "circumcision was deemed efficacious no matter how, under what circumstances, or by whom it was performed," and the "mid-second century [CE]," when some rabbis "distinguished non-covenantal circumcision, the removal of a piece of skin, from covenantal circumcision, or *berit*."[35] The mark became ritualized, part of a more elaborate process of entering into the covenant community. The surgical details of Jewish circumcision became more complex, as the rabbis insisted that Jewish circumcision, in distinction from other circumcisions, must not only remove the foreskin (*milah*) but the membrane attaching the foreskin to the glans (*peri'ah*).[36] Even the significance of circumcision for the rabbis seems more profound and cosmic: "the praise that circumcision received in rabbinic literature is entirely unprecedented and extraordinary."[37] Some scholars posit that this intensified attention to the particulars and glories of circumcision emerges from a tacit resistance to the rising tide of Christianity, which elevated Pauline discouragement of circumcision to an art form. Cohen, by contrast, wonders if this rabbinic mania for circumcision might bespeak an internal Jewish conflict, stretching back to the Maccabean conflict between "hellen-izers" and traditionalists.[38]

Without setting aside these important and overlapping contexts, I suggest we might also read the rabbinic elevation of circumcision as a means of ap-propriating, and resisting, the stereotyping functions of Roman culture. Much in the same way that Greeks under the Roman Empire continued to produce paideia, consumable but never digestible by their Roman rulers,[39] so too some classes of Jews produced an elaborated and utterly distinct form of circumci-sion that was visible to—but never totally comprehensible by—Roman au-thority. By assuming control over the mark of circumcision, and therefore their own Jewishness, the sages were also exerting paradoxical control over "the nations," now configured as "the uncircumcised."[40] Romans might think they were demanding a sign of provincial legibility, but the Jews were taking back control of that sign and the manner in which it might be apprehended.

If Cohen is right, and the surviving instructions for rabbinic conversion to Judaism in the Babylonian Talmud are of earlier, Palestinian origin,[41] then the framing of the ceremony—with circumcision at its heart—also tells us something about the configuration of circumcision at the heart of the Roman Empire of cultural signs.[42] The conversion begins with the approach of the proselyte, who must accept the role of Israel as "pained, oppressed, harassed, and torn." While some interpreters have tried to locate this fragmented sense of "oppression" in a particular moment of Jewish-Roman relations,[43] the ritualiza-tion of this sense of objectification surely speaks to a general sense of provincial marginality. The proselyte is then given both heavy and "light" instruction in the Law; specific mention is made of dietary restrictions and Sabbath obser-vance, two common stereotypes about Jews in the Roman world.[44] After being warned again about the marginality of Israel and its promise of a place in the world-to-come, the proselyte is circumcised. Sometimes he is even circumcised a second time if the first circumcision is deemed physically insufficient (i.e., the surgery has not removed enough of the foreskin): an assertion of control that borders on the excessive. Finally the healed proselyte is immersed in a ritual bath, given more (and less specific) instruction, and "*Voilà*, he is like Israel."[45] At every step the difference of Jews can be read in particularly Roman terms: from the acknowledgment of political subordination to accepting the sign (cir-cumcision) by which the Romans "read" Jewish difference. Yet in that very act of assuming the stereotypes of Judaism those terms are being reworked and recuperated, even resisted. The Jewish sign is Judaized.

Jews who insisted on the significance of circumcision, yet struggle to control and redirect that signification, are like Homi Bhabha's "mimic men," who take on with necessary imperfection the constructed image of the colonizers.[46] Bhabha attended to the Indian colonial scene, and the crucial slippage between *English* and *Anglicized*; in the Roman context, in which power derives from the (impossible) mastery of stereotypes, the difference between *Roman* and *Romanized* consists precisely in the cues and signs of difference and distinction. The *Romanized* Jew accepts the marks of colonial difference (circumcision) but in taking up this mark with fervor and a newfound attention to arcane, ritualized detail simultaneously slips beyond the Romanizing gasp. Jewish circumcision, like all stereotypical signs of imperial power, becomes "an ambivalent mode of knowledge and power."[47]

Old Covenant in the New: Resignifying Circumcision

New Testament Circumcision: A Sign of Trouble

The increased pressure on the Jewish signification of circumcision from within and without must frame our exploration of the earliest Christian texts on circumcision, and the circumcision of Jesus. That is, we must view attention to circumcision, and Jesus' circumcision, not just theologically but also politically and culturally. Circumcision appears throughout the Pauline texts that form the core of the New Testament, from the letters of Paul (both authentic and pseudonymous) to the Acts of the Apostles. Almost always circumcision is a sign of trouble and division:[48] "Then certain individuals came down from Judea and were teaching the brothers, 'Unless you are circumcised according to the custom of Moses (τῷ ἔθει τῷ Μωυσέως), you cannot be saved.' And after Paul and Barnabas had no small dissension and debate with them, Paul and Barnabas and some of the others were appointed to go up to Jerusalem to discuss this question with the apostles and the elders" (Acts 15:1–2). Paul himself frames this "dissension and debate" over circumcision in slightly more dramatic fashion: "You foolish Galatians! Who has bewitched you? . . . I wish those who unsettle you would castrate themselves!" (Gal 3:1, 5:12) Often this conflict over circumcision has been read as a theological struggle over the mechanics of salvation: what role should the "Law" (Torah) play in the new dispensation of Jesus the messiah?[49] We are to imagine conservative Jewish followers (the "party of James" [Gal 2:12]) resisting Paul's innovative preaching of a new, universal covenant outside the Law: salvation by faith, not works.[50]

To read circumcision only soteriologically—from the vantage point of competing theories of salvation—is to sidestep the very political tenor of the earliest decades of the Jesus movement. Likewise, to read Paul's resistance to circumcision in his letters merely as simply repudiation of Judaism (or Torah or Law or "works") is to divorce him too quickly from his very Jewish, Roman, first-century context.[51] As Paula Fredriksen has pointed out, it was those who insisted on circumcising gentiles who were the innovators, rewriting the standard apocalyptic script. In most of our early Jewish sources, those from "the nations" who were saved would not become Jews at the end of time, but would be included in the apocalyptic kingdom *as* gentiles: "Eschatological Gentiles . . . those who would gain admission to the Kingdom once it was established, would enter as Gentiles. They would worship and eat together with Israel, in Jerusalem, at the Temple. The God they worship, the God of Israel, will have redeemed them from the error of idolatry: he will have saved them—to phrase this in slightly different idiom—graciously, apart from the works of the Law."[52] Fredriksen points out that this eschatological adhesion mirrored the situation Paul likely faced on the ground in major cities of the Mediterranean: gentiles ("Godfearers") who attached themselves to the Jewish God and synagogue without entering into any process of conversion or entry into the Jewish covenant.[53] If we consider circumcision not only as a theological seal but also a social and political marker—a sign of participation in the Roman cultural economy—we can view the conflict between Paul and the "circumcisers" from quite a different angle.

Paul, the fairly conservative former Pharisee,[54] in resisting the wholesale application of the Jewish sign of circumcision, may be viewed as resisting Roman power in several ways.[55] On the one hand, we might imagine him along the lines of the later intellectual heirs of the Pharisees, the sages, who developed tight controls over ritualized circumcision and so partially recuperated their sacred symbol from the clutches of Roman imperialism. When Paul writes, "What is the use of circumcision? Much, in every way (πολὺ κατὰ πάντα τρόπον)" (Rom 3:1–2), we need not see this as a rhetorical concession. Rather we might sense the same admiration for and anxiety surrounding the cultural function of circumcision as we find later in the sages, who similarly proclaim, "Great is circumcision!" (b. Ned. 31a–32b). The value of circumcision lies in its appropriate application by Jews alone: in Roman hands, it is a tool of power and control over Jews.

Paul's aversion to gentile circumcision might also resist Roman power in more general fashion: by refusing to submit followers of Jesus to the scrutiny of Roman specular authority. Paul opts out of this cultural economy of signs, and so pronounces that "circumcision has no value, and uncircumcision [literally, 'foreskin'] has no value (ἡ περιτομὴ οὐδέν ἐστιν, καὶ ἡ ἀκροβυστία οὐδέν ἐστιν)" (1 Cor 7:19; cf. Gal 5:6, 6:15). Paul values circumcision at nothing, even though elsewhere it was "of use in every way." Paul is not simply denying the value of circumcision or the Jewish Law: he is denying value to circumcision *and* uncircumcision, that is, to the distinction between the two.[56] They cannot be used to segregate populations in the fashion that the Roman Empire insisted.[57] So too Paul tells the church in Rome: "circumcision is not in the visible flesh (οὐδὲ ἡ ἐν τῷ φανερῷ ἐν σαρκὶ περιτομή) . . . but rather a matter of the heart (καρδίας)" (Rom 2:28–29).[58] Located now in the heart, circumcision remains invisible to the powers of Rome that Paul, elsewhere, is careful not to oppose (Rom 13:1–7). The followers of Jesus who internalize the mark of Judaism are thereby made invisible to the powers of this world, stripped of the stereotypical signs that would allow them to circulate in the Roman imperial system. Circumcision remains the secret, hidden treasure of Israel.[59]

If Paul's reluctance to incorporate this visible sign of Jewish identity and Roman power into his gospel may be read (at least in part) as a form of cultural resistance,[60] then we may also reimagine "the circumcisers" as, in some ways, accommodating the cultural constraints of Roman rule. When "certain individuals from Judea" insisted to Paul's gentile adherents that they be circumcised to show they belong to the "Law of Moses," they were preaching gentile incorporation into that same Roman economy of cultural signs. Where Paul would have his followers float invisibly ("neither Jew nor Greek, neither slave nor free, no male and female" [Gal 3:28]), free radicals in the Roman body politic,[61] the circumcising apostles would fix them—like the old Jewish tax dodger of Suetonius's memory—firmly, and legibly, in that Roman system of stereotypes. If they shared Paul's apocalyptic worldview, the circumcisers may even have thought that God would himself require a similar system of symbolic legibility during his final judgment.

My intention is not to reduce the role of circumcision in the first generation of the Jesus movement to simply a cipher for politics: clearly, Paul (and his opponents) felt passionately about this particular sign and its role in the apocalyptic scenario they all believed would soon play out across the face of the *oikoumenē*. The distinct lack of emotion in the same debate, as narrated in Acts of the Apostles, must likewise be read both theologically and politically (Acts 15): the text is notable for its efforts to "make nice" with the power of Rome (a point I address more fully below), and also for its distance from Paul's fiery apocalyptic abolition of status, sign, stereotype, and hierarchy.[62] Once Paul and his circumcising opponents have died, his followers continued to imagine the role of circumcision in culture and salvation: now brought into contact, for the first time, with the person of Jesus.

Colossians: Circumcision Rewritten

Jesus himself seems not to have preached about circumcision (in favor or against), at least as far as we can tell from the gospels;[63] nor does Paul speak of Jesus providing any direct or indirect guidance on the question of circumcision.[64] Later interpreters of Paul, however, came to imagine the issues of Moses' Law and Jesus' messiahship in a more diachronic fashion: not only did old covenant expand into a new, universal relationship between God and humanity but there was also a chronological development *from* the old covenant to a new covenant. The person of Jesus was imagined to have transformed the covenant, and its sign: circumcision.

The Letter to the Colossians is considered by many scholars to be pseudonymous, possibly written soon after Paul's death in his name.[65] Even those who defend Pauline authorship admit that "Colossians does not manifest the urgency about the timing of the Parousia [Second Coming] that 1 Thessalonians, for example, has."[66] With this dampened eschatological heat comes a comparative warmth toward the hierarchical structures of the Roman Empire: the notorious "household code" (Col 3:18–4:1) that ties the domestic theology of Colossians much more clearly to the later, pseudonymous "Pastoral" Epistles 1 Timothy and Titus.[67]

It is also in the Letter to the Colossians that we find our earliest possible reference to Christ's own circumcision, a notably positive use of "circumcision."[68] The language is dense, and the Greek grammar multivalent.[69] In the midst of a warning against "philosophy and empty deceit," the author reminds the Colossians of the celestial and divine fullness of Christ in which they now participate: "For in him the whole fullness of deity dwells bodily (πᾶν τὸ πλήρωμα τῆς θεότητος σωματικῶς), and you have come to fullness in him, who is the head of every ruler and authority. In him also you were circumcised with a circumcision not made by hands (περιετμήθητε περιτομῇ ἀχειροποιήτῳ), by putting off the body of the flesh in the circumcision of Christ (ἐν τῇ περιτομῇ τοῦ Χριστοῦ), when you were buried with him in baptism, you were also raised with him through faith in the power of God, who raised him from the dead" (Col 2:9–13; NRSV modified). The letter continues to extol the life-giving virtues of the crucifixion, which abnegates the need to follow the Jewish Law (Col 2:14)—here specified not as circumcision, but rather "matters of food and drink . . . observing festivals, new moons, or sabbaths" (Col 2:16). Circumcision does appear once more in the letter, as a gloss on a Pauline slogan from Galatians 3:28: "there is no more Greek and Jew, circumcision and uncircumcision, barbarian, Scythian, slave, free-person, but Christ is all in all" (Col 3:11). As Harry Maier has pointed out, the particular resonances of the letter as a whole set this later reference to circumcised peoples firmly in the world of imperial triumph, not resistance to empire: the "circumcised and uncircumcised" march alongside the barbarian, Scythian, slaves, and free persons in organized unison.[70] A letter that contains both positively valued circumcision and Roman triumphal language (see Col 2:15) locates us in a rhetorical context far from Paul's earlier letters.

If circumcision is not a problem, as in Paul's earlier letters, what is it doing in this passage? The interpretation of Colossians 2:9–13 is made difficult by its abstruseness, particularly its use of terms in simultaneously literal and figurative fashion: Christ's "body" in the beginning of the passage is presumably real (a reference to the incarnation), but the body that is "put off" by followers later on would seem to be figurative (symbolizing their old lives). Likewise, Christ's burial is literal (he really died, and was really buried) but that of his followers is metaphorical: they "rise" from the baptismal font *as if* they have also been buried and resurrected. Then, finally, there is circumcision: it appears to be associated here, for the first time, with baptism (an analogy to which I return below), making it a circumcision "without hands" (sometimes translated as "spiritual" or "invisible").[71] But this analogy also confuses the literal and figurative: baptism itself is a material event—there is a body, and water, and space, and hands—yet its spiritual efficacy happens invisibly, apart from manual operation.

In this amalgamation of the material and spiritual, what are we to make of "the circumcision of Christ"? Is it figurative or literal, like his body and his burial? Greek, as English, allows for two grammatical ways to construe this possessive phrase. As a subjective genitive, it is the circumcision that Christ performs (presumably, on the letter's recipients). As an objective genitive, it is the circumcision performed on Christ. The phrase has been interpreted both ways, but never strictly literally: like the rest of the passage, "Christ's circumcision" enjoys dual signification, at once literal and figurative, subjective and objective. When the phrase is read as a subjective genitive, it is a figure for Christian ritual: Christ performs this "circumcision" on the recipients of the letter "without hands" (Col 2:11) in "baptism" (Col 2:12).[72] This typological "circumcision"/baptism allows a reconfiguration of language that, elsewhere in the Pauline corpus, we would read more literally: by partaking in "Christ's circumcision" (baptism), the recipients of the letter redeem their previous state of "uncircumcision" (Col 2:13: "you were dead in trespasses and the uncircumcision of your flesh" [τῇ ἀκροβυστίᾳ τῆς σαρκὸς ὑμῶν]). Here, "circumcision" and "uncircumcision" (or, as in Paul's other letters, literal "foreskin") are figurative states of membership in the Christian community, not literal signs of participation in the Jewish covenant or Law.[73] Circumcision is, in this sense, radically resignified through Christ: no longer a literal "stripping of flesh" (Col 2:11) that marks out God's people, but a figurative "circumcision." At the same time, however, we should note the relative conservatism of this resignification in political terms: where Paul might seek to liberate his gentile followers from the political signs of status and domination (among which Jewish circumcision numbered), here the value of status, sign, and identification is restored, albeit in a doubly symbolic manner.

What about the objective genitive reading of "the circumcision of Christ"—that is, how do we read this verse if it refers to the circumcision performed *on* Jesus? Here, too, the literal and figurative shade into each other. Notably, however, even when modern interpreters read this phrase objectively—the circumcision performed on Christ—they resist reading it as his literal, infant circumcision: "Some have taken the phrase to refer specifically to Christ's physical nature—*not to his literal circumcision* (Luke 2:21), but to his death (cf. Rom 7:4)" (emphasis added).[74] The path of this semantic redirection is not immediately obvious, since the crucifixion is not explicitly mentioned here. It is mentioned literally in Col 1:20 ("peace through the blood of the cross"); in this chapter, however, it is one more in a series of visceral metaphors: "He set this [the 'record against us'] aside, nailing it to the cross" (Col 2:14). Curiously, we have an instance here of an objective genitive ("the crucifixion performed on Jesus") being transformed into a subjective genitive ("the crucifixion performed *by* Jesus, on the Jewish Law").

Even assuming that enough connotations of baptism-as-death-as-crucifixion seep into the text to allow a reader to understand Col 2:12 in this way, we must still marvel a bit at the ingenuity of this reading. This interpretation is remarkable for the degree to which it maintains both the literality of Christ's circumcision ("flesh stripped away," here by crucifixion) and its figurality (it is still not circumcision, but "circumcision"). When James Dunn argues that the "circumcision of Christ" should be taken objectively (that is, a circumcision performed *on* Christ), he writes: "The final phrase, 'in the circumcision of Christ,' is best seen, then, simply as a summary expression of the larger imagery of the preceding phrases. This is, what is in view is not primarily a circumcision effected by Christ . . . but a concise description of the death of Christ under the metaphor of circumcision."[75] On Christ's body, the "circumcision of Christ" is simultaneously circumcision and "circumcision," crucifixion and "crucifixion," death and "death." Still, it is difficult to understand why modern interpreters insist that the "physical" circumcision is somehow *not* also his literal, infant circumcision.[76] The reference to "stripping of flesh" (Col 2:11) at the very least gestures toward literal, physical male circumcision; so too, beneath and within the chain of metaphors, of literal and figurative language intertwined, might we envision Christ's circumcision, as well. If this is the case, then Colossians 2:11 is the earliest surviving mention of Jesus' circumcision.

It is, of course, impossible to distinguish between the objective and subjective genitive here, and we must assume the writer of Colossians knew what he was doing when he structured the sentence with this ambiguity in place. Circumcision (which, elsewhere in the letter, rather neutrally equates to "Judaism") juxtaposed with Christ's body becomes a radical resignifier. It can emanate from Christ or remain on his skin's surface; in either case, it cannot help but be swept up in the cascade of literal and figurative corporeal moments of Christ's life that structure the entire passage. It may very well refer to Christ's crucifixion, because this section of the letter has so disembedded "circumcision" from its normal religious, political, and cultural significations. By bringing the circumcision into contact with Christ—wielded by him or against him—the author of Colossians has succeeded in prising it free not only of Roman control, as in Paul's letters, but of Jewish control as well. Whether Christ's circumcision is baptism or crucifixion or both, it is no longer a sign of the covenant of Abraham or the legible symbol of Roman imperial subjection. It is Christianized, and totally open to multiple new meanings.

Luke's Jewish Messiah for Gentiles

The author of the Gospel of Luke is slightly more willing to imagine the messianic circumcision. A set of parallel passages recounts the nativities of John the Baptist and (in Luke's account) his cousin Jesus. At the climax of both come their circumcision and naming: "And it was the eighth day, and they came to circumcise the child, and they called him by the name of his father, Zechariah" (Luke 1:59; NRSV modified); "And the eight days were fulfilled to circumcise him, and he was called by the name Jesus, which he was called by the angel before he was conceived in the womb" (Luke 2:21). Multiple parallelisms link these nativities:[77] both infants are announced by angelic visitors (Luke 1:11–20, 26–38); both infants have special names, divinely preordained (Luke 1:13, 60–63; Luke 1:31, 2:21); both births are bracketed by Temple worship (Zechariah does Temple service before John's birth [Luke 1:8–9], Mary and Joseph go to the Temple for purification after Jesus' [Luke 2:22–24]); and both children are the occasion for songs of praise from their parents (Zechariah [Luke 1:67–79] and Mary [Luke 1:46–55], respectively).

Both passages are also grammatically evasive on the moment of circumcision itself, as no finite verb ("he was circumcised") describes the act of circumcision. In John's case "they came to circumcise him" (ἦλθον περιτεμεῖν); in Jesus' case "the eight days of his circumcising were fulfilled" (ἐπλήρηθησαν ἡμέραι ὀκτὼ τοῦ περιτεμεῖν αὐτόν). The finite action in both instances is the "naming," not the circumcising. Despite this grammatical imprecision, these passages are almost always understood as narrating the circumcisions of John and Jesus.[78]

Nonetheless modern commentators have little to say specifically about Luke's circumcised messiah,[79] other than to note that this event combines with the rest of the "prologue" of the Gospel of Luke (Luke 1–2) to create a deeply Jewish point of departure for a messiah who will, ultimately, deliver salvation to gentiles.[80] Indeed, for most modern scholars Jesus' circumcision is absorbed into the larger question of Luke's (seemingly) incongruous emphasis on the particularities of Law and Temple in his universalizing gospel.[81] Of the four canonical gospels, Luke's is typically considered the most gentile in its orientation;[82] the author crafts a "gospel for the gentiles" both theologically (a "universal" salvation that supplants the old covenant [see Luke 16:16]) and stylistically (a more urbane, sophisticated literary presentation).[83]

Luke's incongruously Jewish opening chapters have vexed New Testament scholars for centuries. Early source critics explained these early, more Jewish passages as the calcified remains of an older gospel source preserved—like an extinct theological fly in more precious amber—in the layers of Luke's gospel.[84] This early stratum may retain early traditions about Jesus the Jew, but those early traditions are effectively neutralized by being preserved in a more evolved text. Later redaction criticism focused on Luke's authorial motives in combining stories of Jesus' Jewishness with theological messages of universal salvation.[85] François Bovon imagines the evangelist as a gentile who, once drawn to Judaism as a "god-fearer," now sees the value in leaving Judaism behind. So the narrative of Jesus' Jewish childhood becomes something like a fond memory that carries nostalgic value, but little theological significance.[86] Raymond Brown likewise understands "a Lucan view of the Jewish Temple and its ritual more in terms of nostalgia for things past, rather than of hostility for an active and seductive enemy."[87] Such commentary frames the first chapters of Luke, including the passage on Jesus' circumcision, as splashes of theological color: an acknowledgment of the resolutely past-tense significance of Israel, a kinder and gentler mode of theological supersessionism.[88]

A more creative redaction-critical explanation for the early emphasis on Law and Temple in Luke's work was raised by John Knox, and recently defended by his student Joseph Tyson.[89] For these scholars, the redacted fragments of Luke-Acts, replete with Jewish color, do not look back (in triumph or nostalgia) to a primitive moment of the Jesus Movement; rather, they bear witness to a later debate among gentile Christian groups in the mid-second century: the rise of Marcionite Christianity. In the early second century, Marcion preached a popular form of Christianity that sharply distinguished Christian salvation from the prior—material, legalistic, judgmental, and Jewish—covenant. Christianity, and Jesus, had nothing to do with the Creator God of the Old Testament and his Jewish worshipers, Marcion taught. His later detractors accused him of producing a corrupt and truncated New Testament, purged of Jewish elements, in order to spread his heresy.[90]

Knox and Tyson have argued that the reverse might be true: perhaps Marcion's shorter, less Jewish gospel preceded the canonical Gospel of Luke, indeed, prompted the fuller, Judaized nativity.[91] Speaking specifically of Luke 1–2, Knox writes: "Marcion would surely not have tolerated this highly 'Jewish' section; but how wonderfully adapted it is to show the nature of Christianity as the true Judaism and thus to answer one of the major contentions of the Marcionites! And one cannot overlook the difficulty involved in the common supposition that Marcion deliberately selected a Gospel which began in so false and obnoxious a way."[92] Although this last point may be somewhat unfair—no one has argued that Marcion had multiple narratives of Jesus' life at his disposal and quirkily chose the one least suited to his theological agenda[93]—the overall idea that proto-orthodox expansion can explain the textual and canonical history of Luke as well as Marcionite truncation has found some traction in recent years. Tyson concludes that "[the] work as a whole, Luke-Acts as we know it, surely served as a formidable anti-Marcionite text."[94] Central to Tyson's argument are the highly "Jewish" chapters of Luke 1–2,[95] particularly the account of the circumcision: "it is important to observe that the vital link with Judaism signified by Jesus' circumcision would have been highly offensive to Marcion and his followers."[96] Although creative in its canonical revision, the "Knox-Tyson theory" participates in a well-established scholarly attempt to explain—and explain away—the presence of such an anomalous feature as Jesus' circumcision in the gentile gospel. The time frame has simply been moved up several decades, and the target of Luke's anomalous narrative (Jews, gentiles, or Marcionites) shifted to suit. Redaction criticism, early and late, rhetorically isolates and, in a sense, evacuates the Jewishness of the circumcision of Jesus. It is not "really" a part of Luke's gospel, and therefore easy to read right past.

Two twentieth-century commentators have attempted to explain the Jewishness of Luke's first chapters, and the circumcision specifically, in a way that does not view these passages as anomalous to Luke's "real" theological perspective. Jacob Jervell sees no incongruity between the Law-fulfilling Jesus of Luke 1–2 and the messianic community envisioned generally by Luke-Acts.[97] For Jervell, the circumcised messiah fits neatly into what was, at its origins, a fundamentally Jewish-Christian messianic movement: "Luke must indicate that the Messiah Jesus is the genuine and true Messiah. Among other things, this is evidenced by the fact that he was circumcised according to the law."[98] Instead of the theological friction that most modern readers of Luke's nativity encounter, Jervell finds harmony, a gesture of inclusion rather than supersession.[99] Ultimately, Jervell does concede that the Jewish-Christian perspective of Luke, according to which a circumcised messiah makes sense, opens up to a more universal, gentile movement so that, in the end, the passage still derives from and speaks to a past-tense Jewish experience.

The most recent treatment of the circumcision of Jesus in the Gospel of Luke comes from theologian Graham Ward, who considers multiple reasons why the evangelist might have included an account of Jesus' circumcision.[100] Like Jervell, he resists redactional arguments that reduce the significance of the passage to a mere "remnant" embedded in a fundamentally gentile account of

salvation. Ward also wants to find something organic in Luke's unique inclusion of this scene. Ward suggests: "To speak of the circumcision was making
a cultural and political statement . . . . I suggest, whatever the implied reader-
ship of the text, a statement is being made here about embodiment (as early
Christian exegetes understood) and about Jewish masculinity (and by impli-
cation femininity). It is a statement not just about religious and ethnic self-
identity (as Jervell argued) but about the way certain figurations of the body
are invested with cultural status. It says something, then, about the politics of
embodiment."[101] Ward's insistence on the "politics of embodiment" is intriguing; unfortunately, he does not then specify what that "something" might
be that Luke is saying, other than that "Luke appears to be making a gesture
of resistance to a cultural hegemony."[102] I am nonetheless sympathetic to his
desire to move beyond the redaction-critical explanations of previous scholarship, away from interpretations that make the scene of the circumcision either
ironic or nostalgic, and ask the question from a different angle: why is the
gentiles' messiah circumcised?

Here we need to return to the political and cultural contexts of circumcision, and to the power of the stereotype in the Roman world. There is no
doubt that the Gospel of Luke is a document highly sensitive to empire: the
very chapter that mentions the circumcision is framed by "Caesar Augustus"
(Luke 2:1) and "Tiberius Caesar" (Luke 3:1).[103] Moreover, Roman power is
made to interact discursively with distinctive Jewish identity: the power of
the imperial city intersects with the bygone Jewish autonomy of the "city of
David" in Luke 2 just as the circumscribed power of the tetrarchs is subor-
dinated to "Pontius Pilate, governor of Judea" in Luke 3. Finally, the Temple
itself symbolizes acutely the domination of Rome over the province of Judea
in the late first century and early second century. Certainly the destruction of
that Temple in 70 CE would haunt those passages that portray Jesus and his
relatives moving through the sacred precincts.[104] Therefore I would heartily
agree with Ward that Luke is engaged with "cultural hegemony," more specifically, with the cultural economy of signs and stereotypes in which circumcision circulated.[105]

If Luke is not preserving a bygone sense of Jewish "self-identity" (his own
or another's), how might we interpret his intervention into the Roman cultural economy of stereotypes? Several alternatives are possible (and I think
any or all of them may be present to a certain degree: cultural discourse is
necessarily heterogeneous). Scholars have often read Luke-Acts as politically
conciliatory, portraying sympathy to the Roman Empire.[106] Paul Walaskay's

formulation is even stronger, claiming that Luke-Acts functions not only as an *apologia pro ecclesia* to the Empire, but as an *apologia pro imperio* to the church: "Luke . . . has high regard for the imperial government and for those who administer it."[107] If Luke is theologically structured, in part, as a positive response to the Roman Empire, we might read Jesus' circumcision as a concession to the cultural economy of symbols that permeated the empire. Where Paul resisted the legibility of circumcision as a sign of Judaism to the Romans, Luke embraces it: the circumcised messiah is "Jewish," therefore, only insofar as he is also *Romanized*, visible and comprehensible to the knowing eye of Rome. If the founder of the Way can be comprehended by the imperial gaze, so can his followers. The participation of the messianic and divine figure in the cultural economy of Rome paves the way for an entirely conciliatory discourse of Christian identity.

But the discourse of stereotype, "as anxious as it is assertive,"[108] is rarely so straightforward; even if Luke is seeking, on some level, to acknowledge and defer to the authority of Roman signs, he is also taking it upon himself to manipulate and reinterpret those signs. This paradox informs Homi Bhabha's understanding of the function of stereotype in the colonial encounter: the good colonial subject takes on the legible signs of identity expected by the colonizer, but in that gesture makes those signs her or his own. Roman stereotypes in the hands of an outsider—the provincial, the object of the gaze, not its master—are always potentially subversive.

Like the later sages, who would attempt to reclaim control over their sign from Rome through ritualization, Luke's circumcised messiah may be read through the lens of mimicry. By placing Jesus squarely within the cultural economy of Roman signs, by signifying him as *Jew* in the opening chapters, Luke can subvert both the sign *Jew* and the Roman system of signification that encodes it.[109] Gary Gilbert has pointed out the ways in which Luke's Pentecost narrative in Acts 2 adapts a "well-established method of political propaganda" and "presents an alternative to Roman ideology and challenges Rome's position as ruler of the inhabited world."[110] In a similar geographic vein, Laura Nasrallah explores how the journeys of Paul in Acts effectively "mimic the logic of empire without shading into mockery."[111] Both of these studies point out the ways that Luke mimes and appropriates Roman culture for theological (and political) purposes.

So too may we read the body of Jesus, appropriately—but a bit oddly—signified as that of a Jewish male. It is no stretch to read this sign, crafted in the shadow of an imperial census conducted at the city of David, as deliberately

engaging Roman cultural power in the provinces. Its value, however, is destabilized in Luke's hands, rendered opaque by the ambiguity of circumcision,
Law, and Temple throughout Luke-Acts. By only partially acknowledging the
power of Rome to assort and categorize its other subjects, Luke destabilizes
that power, makes it his own. At the same time, the desire of (some) Jews
to slip beyond the bounds of Roman specular authority is also thwarted and
undermined: Jesus is irrevocably (but still a bit ambiguously) marked by the
preeminent sign of Judaism at the same time he is inscribed (but also a bit
ambiguously) into the imperial Roman census. Just as the name given by God's
angel is also the name registered by Roman power, so too the covenantal sign
ordained by God is also the sign sought by Roman authority (as Suetonius's old
man attests). On the person of Jesus, both those systems of power and identity
are disrupted and reorganized. Jesus is Judaized, and thereby Romanized, but
in both senses he is not quite a Jew and not quite a Roman. It makes a kind of
sense that the sign unproblematically taken up by the messiah in the Gospel
of Luke should be cleanly demoted and minimized in the Acts of the Apostles.

In many ways Luke is Paul's intellectual and theological descendant, organizing what he perceived as Pauline principles (especially the mission to gentiles) in a nonapocalyptic register. But it is not quite accurate to say that Luke
and Paul agree on the role of "Law," or circumcision, in the new covenant.[112]
As I have suggested, for Paul circumcision was a dangerous sign at least partly
because it rendered the people of God legible and apprehensible to Roman,
worldly power. His successor in the letter to the Colossians first attempted to
resignify that sign, make it less dangerous, by bringing it into contact with the
body of Christ: there, circumcision was drawn into an opaque swirl of literal
and figurative signs of salvation. The author of the Gospel of Luke takes us
further, placing that sign directly on Jesus' infant body; there it acts not merely
as a sign of capitulation to Roman power, but as a mimicry of that power. Jesus
circumcised sets his followers on the path to the annulment of this doubly
Jewish-Roman system of signification.

Christian Circumcision

By the second century—around the time, possibly, that Luke's ambivalent
verses on Christ's circumcision began to circulate—gentile Christian authors
had begun contending with circumcision as a distinctly Christian sign. For
these Christians, circumcision condensed and refracted broader discourses

of stereotype, identity, and ambivalence. On the one hand, they intensified and amplified the Roman stereotype of circumcision as the paradigmatic, and ignominious, sign of "the Jew." That is, the sign that distinguished Jews from—and made Jews comprehensible to—Romans now performed the same functions in a new, gentile, Christian idiom. At the same time, however, non-Jewish Christians also arrogated positive Christian meaning to this sign, as they claimed for themselves the title of Israel.[113]

The doubled view of circumcision finds its way into anti-Jewish literature early on:[114] the *Epistle of Barnabas*, which probably dates from the mid-second century,[115] sounds the twin notes of repudiation and appropriation that will become standard in the stereotypical discourses of early Christianity. The letter as a whole interweaves a defense of Christian practices (such as baptism) and theologies (such as the passion and the new covenant) with rejections of Jewish customs and practices. The chapter on circumcision opens with a metaphor drawn from the Hebrew Bible that would become a favorite of early Christians, the "circumcised" hearts and ears (Deut 10:16, 30:6; Jer 4:4, 6:10).[116] The author goes further than this metaphorical, biblical language, however, and declares that God had *never* ordained fleshly circumcision for the Jews: "But even the circumcision in which they trusted has been nullified. For he has said that circumcision is not a matter of the flesh. But they transgressed because an evil angel instructed them."[117] This ascription of the rite of circumcision—alone among the Jewish covenant laws discussed in *Barnabas*—to an "evil angel" is an extraordinary step: "B. was not willing simply to argue for the truth of the purely symbolic interpretation of the rite (as he had for sacrifice, the temple, and the dietary laws), but to demonise it."[118] Even as this sign is plotted in a distinctly religious register (the domain of angels and demons), it is simultaneously removed from the *Roman* economy of signs: "But you will say: Surely the people were circumcised as a seal. So is every Syrian and Arab and all the priests of the idols: so are they also part of their covenant? Even the Egyptians have circumcision!"[119] Circumcision no longer retains its particular stereotypical signification in the Roman symbolic order, setting Jews apart from other provincial populations. A new system of stereotypes has taken its place; although circumcision still indicates the peculiar (demonic) quality of the Jews, Christians have seized that system of signs from Roman hands.

Yet as strong as *Barnabas*'s "demonization" of Jewish circumcision seems, his recuperation of the Christian meaning of this rite is equally remarkable. This chapter of the *Epistle of Barnabas* may contains the earliest example of

Christian *gematria*, the symbolic interpretation of letters through their numeric equivalents (possible since ancient languages used the same symbols for letters and numbers).[120] Here, the author draws on the circumcision of Abraham's household in the Hebrew Bible:[121]

> Abraham, who first made a circumcision, looked forward in the spirit
> to Jesus when he was circumcising, receiving the teaching of the three
> letters. For it says: "And Abraham circumcised from his household eigh-
> teen men and three hundred." What knowledge, then, was given to him?
> Learn that first there are the eighteen and then, after a pause, he says
> "three hundred." For "eighteen": *iota* is ten and *ēta* is eight: you have
> [the first two letters of] Jesus (Ιησοῦς). And because the cross was going
> to possess grace in the *tau* he also says "three hundred." So he shows
> "Jesus" in the first two letters and in the other one "the cross."[122]

Circumcision here is not just reinterpreted *through* Jesus, it is actually equated with Jesus, and the crucifixion, and the entire scheme of Christian messianic redemption. This remarkable act of resignification allows the author at once to repudiate Jewish circumcision (as it exists among actual Jews) and reappropriate it as a mark of distinction through (as) Jesus.

Other early Christians attempted to maintain this doubled view of Jewish circumcision, often through the prophetic metaphor of "circumcision of the heart." Justin Martyr's *Dialogue with Trypho the Jew* begins by locating his interlocutor, the Jew Trypho, squarely in the realm of the Roman political and cultural economy: "I am a Hebrew of the circumcision," Trypho supposedly tells Justin upon meeting him, "fleeing the war just now taking place, sojourning in Greece, mainly in Corinth."[123] "The war" refers to the so-called Bar Kokhba revolt—prompted, some scholars have posited, by a Hadrianic ban on circumcision[124]—which had left Jerusalem devastated and the very province of Judea absorbed and renamed. Trypho's situation, like that of Suetonius's old Jewish tax dodger, registers both the anomaly of the "other" in Roman society as well as his legibility to the imperial gaze.

Justin affirms the designating function of Trypho's circumcision: "For the circumcision from Abraham according to the flesh was given as a sign, so that you may be separated from other nations and from us; and so that you alone may suffer that which now you now justly suffer; and so that your lands may become deserted, and your cities burned up; and so that foreigners may eat your fruit in your presence, and not one of you may go up to Jerusalem. For not by anything else are you recognized among the other people than from the circumcision of your flesh."[125] The function of circumcision for Justin extends far beyond tax collection, however. The "just punishments" executed by the Roman army have a distinctly Christian logic: "Now these things have happened to you well and justly. For you have slain the Just One, and his prophets before him. And now you reject those who have hope in him and in him who sent him, the Almighty and the Creator of all things, God, and as much as you can you dishonor him, cursing in your synagogues those who believe in Christ.[126] For you do not have the authority to become murderous against us, on account of those who now are in charge."[127] "Those who are now in charge" are the Romans, but the real power at work is "the Almighty," who has devised a punishment for the blasphemous Jews as well as a sign to distinguish those who are to be punished. Circumcision is a Roman marker deployed by a Christian God. Once more the figure of Jesus—here crucified and daily avenged—intervenes to rewrite the script of Roman-provincial relations.

The figure of Jesus also reinscribes the sign of circumcision as a positive Christian marker, the "second circumcision" (δευτέρα περιτομή, drawing on the language of Joshua 5, wherein Joshua must circumcise the Israelites before they enter into the Land). In discussing the typological relationship of Joshua, son of Nun, with Jesus Christ (whose names are identical in Greek) Justin proclaims: "That one [Joshua] is said to have circumcised the people a second time with knives of stone, which was the pronouncement of that circumcision with which Jesus Christ himself has circumcised us from the stone and other idols."[128] This metaphorical "stripping away" of the religious life of pagan gentiles, prefigured in Joshua's circumcision of the Israelites entering the promised land, constitutes the positive, Christian distinction of Justin's "second circumcision": "our circumcision, which is the second (δευτέρα), having been instituted after yours, circumcises us from idolatry and from absolutely every kind of wickedness by sharp stones, that is, by the words of the apostles of the corner-stone cut out without hands [see Dan 2:34]."[129] Ultimately, this Christian circumcision marks out and distinguishes a new "people" as thoroughly as Jewish circumcision: "Jesus Christ circumcises all who wish—as was proclaimed above—with knives of stone; that they may be a righteous nation, a people keeping faith, holding to the truth, and guarding peace [see Isa 26:2–3]."[130]

As in the *Epistle of Barnabas*, the moral purification of Christian circumcision is identified with, and performed by, Jesus himself. Justin explains this through a numerical association between the law of circumcision and the resurrection of Jesus:[131] "Now the command of circumcision, ordering that these always take place on the eighth day, was an image (τύπος) of the true circumcision, in which we are circumcised from every error and wickedness through the one who rose from the dead on the first day following the Sabbath, Jesus Christ our Lord: for the first day following the Sabbath is also the first day of all the days, but according again to the count of the cycle of all the days is called the eighth, while it remains the first."[132] Resurrected on the eighth day of the week, Jesus both embodies and performs a "true circumcision," a moral purgation of the community formed in him. Christians are constituted (in Pauline language) as the body of Christ, and that body has been circumcised.

The association between resurrection and circumcision recalls the connection between circumcision and baptism that some scholars, as we have seen, find in Colossians 2:12. It is debatable whether Justin himself makes this connection, although twice in the *Dialogue* he seems to come close.[133] Early in the *Dialogue*, he exhorts Trypho and his companions to abandon Jewish "foolishness" and embrace true religion: "Wash therefore, and make yourselves clean, and remove the wickedness from your souls [Isa 1:16], as God orders you to be washed in this bath, and be circumcised in the true circumcision."[134] Later, speaking once more of "spiritual (πνευματική) circumcision," Justin remarks: "And we, who have approached God through him [Christ, the son of God], have received that circumcision not according to the flesh, but spiritually, which Enoch and those like him kept. And we have received it through baptism, although we were sinners, through the mercy of God, and it is allowed to all to receive it in the same manner."[135] Whether Justin has developed a specific theology of baptism as Christian circumcision is unclear; more clear, however, is the cluster of associations Justin has made between Christian morality, distinction, and superiority, all effected through circumcision and the resignifying person of Jesus.[136] By the third century, the Christian sign of circumcision was much more routinely identified with baptism.[137] Origen can speak of "the second circumcision of baptism" in interpreting the story of Joshua son of Nun,[138] even as he retains Justin's more general formulation of the "second circumcision of the vices."[139]

But just as Roman stereotypes simultaneously affirmed the totality of Rome while dangerously embedding the non-Roman other within, Christian circumcision likewise created and disrupted religious boundaries. In the mid-third century, Cyprian of Carthage was surprised to learn that at least one North African bishop was adapting the "law of ancient circumcision" to regulate infant baptisms in his church. Specifically, this bishop, Fidus, was taking up wholesale the "eight-day" standard of infant circumcision and using it to argue that no infant should be baptized before its eighth day.[140] This literal transference of circumcision law to baptismal regulation troubled Cyprian and his fellow bishops, precisely because it blurred the boundary between "old" and "new" Israel that circumcision normally articulated. They reiterated to the bishop that literal, Jewish, carnal circumcision had been but a "type" (*imago*) which had "ceased with the supervention of truth."[141] Cyprian and his episcopal colleagues find that they must insist on circumcision as an institution of distinction and boundary: "we think that no one should be kept from obtaining grace because of a law which was previously instituted, nor that spiritual circumcision should be impeded by fleshly circumcision, but that any person at any time should be admitted to the grace of Christ."[142] The problem is that the Christian signification of circumcision has become lost in a prior, Jewish signifying system. In order to correct this, Cyprian reintroduces the mediating sign of Jesus' body: "For the eighth day—that is, the first day after the Sabbath—would become the day on which the Lord rose up, and would make us live and would give us the spiritual circumcision: this eighth day, that is, the first day after the Sabbath, the Lord's Day, went before in an image. But this image has ceased now that the truth has supervened and spiritual circumcision has been given to us."[143] Through Jesus, Fidus must come to understand eight as "eight," and circumcision as "circumcision."[144] Otherwise, the distinction between Judaism and Christianity is lost.

Fidus's attempt to control the signifying power of circumcision may strike the bishops of third-century North Africa as overly "Judaizing" (although it seems Fidus was just as concerned with ancient concepts of hygiene), but in one sense it was entirely Christianizing. By seeking to institute and control a system of distinguishing signs—and by privileging circumcision in that system of signs—Fidus was following in the footsteps of Jesus followers from Paul onward. Christians, drawing on the stereotyping gaze of Roman imperialism (as did non-Christian Jews), were teaching themselves to view the world in a new way. The metaphorical, typological, and allegorical implications of circumcision as a sign of Christian distinction would continue to proliferate through late antiquity.[145] The person of Jesus—in direct and indirect ways—played a central role in this symbolic proliferation.

That the person of Christ, in his earthly incarnation, should function as a destabilizer and resignifier of cultural symbols reminds of us the great distance between early Christian concepts of divinity and history and our own. In the twenty-first century, it is commonplace to see Jesus as distinctly embedded in and defined by the world of signs, symbols, and values we imagine he inhabited. Christians and non-Christians alike assert, "Jesus was a Jew." Such a statement makes *sense* to modern readers: Jesus is explained by his symbolic world. Circumcision signifies Judaism, Jesus circumcised is Jewish. But early Christians, as we have seen in this chapter, did not engage so straightforwardly with their universe of cultural signs. The Roman economy of identity was charged with power, knowledge, and resistance, and to engage in that circulation of signs was to open up the possibility of resignification. Jesus Christ, incarnate *among* Jews, was precisely resistant to the signifying power of cultural signs. On his person, they could mean anew.

Circumcision, already an overburdened and contested sign before the spread of Christianity, acted as a kaleidoscope in which gentile Christians saw themselves reflected and refracted, and through which they also gazed upon their despised "other," the Jews. As we have seen, this simultaneous appropriation of and fear of the sign of circumcision amplifies and twists discourses of identity and stereotype already at work at the fractious contact zone of Jews and Romans. In the nascent literature of Christian difference—apologies, treatises, texts *adversus Iudaeos*—these contact zones are reconfigured and reimagined. In the texts that will become embedded in the New Testament, we see the first hints of this discourse of identity and difference through circumcision pushed onto the incongruous and unique body of Christ.

Chapter 2

(De-)Judaizing Christ's Circumcision
The Dialogue of Difference

> The *I* hides in the other and in others, it wants to be only an other
> for others, to enter completely into the world of others as an other,
> and to cast from itself the burden of being the only *I* (*I-for-myself*) in
> the world.
> —Mikhail Bakhtin

Circumcision and the Dialogic Imagination

Over a quarter century ago, the historian of early Christianity Robert Markus elegantly noted: "The history of Christian self-definition cannot be written in terms of a steady progression from simple to complex. In one sense the whole of the church's history is a growth in self-awareness; every important encounter with a new society, a new culture, with shifts in men's assumptions about their world, themselves or God, with upheavals in the values by which they try to live, brings with it new self-discovery. Psychologists have long been telling us that we discover our selves only in encounter: what is self and what is not self are disclosed to us in the same experience."[1] Markus envisions the early Christian "encounter" as the site of both estrangement and self-discovery, in the same moment recognizing "the other" and (thereby) creating an awareness of "the self." More recently, in an essay likewise surveying the theoretical developments of the study of early Jewish and Christianity identities, Judith Lieu notes with approval the historian's focus on the continuous construction of communal "boundaries," rhetorical and yet effective means of distinguishing "self" from "other": "While not the only model for understanding the construction of identity, an emphasis on the function of boundaries has proved particularly fruitful in recent analysis of identity."[2]

Yet as Lieu goes on to suggest, the repetitious effort to draw boundaries between "Jew" and "Christian" in the ancient world hints at the instability of these same boundaries: "selectivity, fluidity, dynamism, permeability are all intrinsic to the construction of boundaries. . . . Where rhetoric constructs the boundary as immutable and impenetrable, we may suspect actual invasion and penetration."[3] Like Markus, Lieu focuses on texts in which Christianity and Judaism rhetorically enact their difference with the "other" in order to produce something like a coherent self, an "imagined homogeneity."[4] For both scholars, it is the moment of putative boundary making, as the "self" gazes at and engages with the "other," that fascinates. Our ancient Christian sources abound with such moments of encounter, of back-and-forth between Christian and non-Christian. Indeed, much of our textual resources constitute a cacophonous series of dialogues, a library of discourses fixated on that moment of differentiation: heresiologies, apologies, and texts *adversus Iudaeos* that place the Christian self in "conversation" with a heretical, pagan, or Jewish other.

Literary theorist Terry Eagleton articulates how identities emerge out of chains of overlapping dialogues: "Like the rough ground of language itself, cultures 'work' exactly because they are porous, fuzzy-edged, indeterminate, intrinsically inconsistent, never quite identical with themselves, their boundaries modulating into horizons."[5] For Eagleton, as for Lieu, communal identity ("culture") claims a wholeness and finitude that masks fragmentation and incompleteness: the "boundary" between persons and groups, on closer examination, turns out to be an ever-receding horizon. Eagleton's comparison with the "rough ground of language"—which also aims for a precision that is lacking in the execution—further echoes the dialectic ground of early Christian culture. As Mikhail Bakhtin long ago asserted, and his cultural studies descendants have elaborated, "language—like the living concrete environment in which the consciousness of the verbal artist lives—is never unitary."[6] Our encounters with the world, framed by language, are (in Bakhtin's now familiar terms) dialogical—"an encounter within the arena of an utterance, between two different linguistic consciousnesses"[7]—and therefore can never be reduced to a singular, "unitary" selfhood. Dialogue provides the appearance of discrete identities, a formal separation between self and other (speaker and addressee); yet at the same time it confounds those identities, grounding them necessarily in a temporary space of identification (communication).[8] Dialogue creates difference and yet elides that same difference; as Eagleton suggests, "culture"

operates in much the same fashion. "Self" can only ever emerge from the dialogic imagination as the strange and contingent interaction with the "other."[9]

The notion that identity emerges within a cacophony of strange, overlapping voices—that the singularity of identity is, in actuality, a product of
multiple voices or, to use Bakhtin's felicitous term, "heteroglossia"[10]—would
surely come as little surprise to the architects of the ancient Roman Empire,
as we have already seen. To a world teeming with unfamiliar signs and sounds,
the Romans (as they told themselves) brought order, meaning, and stability.
The vast frontiers of this empire did not coalesce around the homogeneity of a
nouvel Hellenism, but through a carefully managed spectacle of heterogeneity.
To be Roman was to exert an ostentatiously precarious control over an omnipresent parade of "others"; to engage with, and even internalize, their strange
voices. To consider Roman power, therefore, is to contemplate the triumph
of the dialogic imagination of Rome—the back-and-forth between domestic
metropolis and alien provinces—on a grand cultural and political stage.[11]

To reimagine in a similar fashion the formation of early Christian culture
as the product of a shifting and unstable dialogic imagination is, in some
ways, to continue and expand the work on "others" and boundaries that presently permeates the study of ancient religious identities, particularly our many
"dialogue" texts.[12] To read such texts dialogically, in a Bakhtinian sense, is to
refuse the absolute separation of self and other that ancient Christians anxiously demand. Dialogues do not merely construct a boundary, isolating and
segregating a Christian from a non-Christian. Dialogues internalize the other,
creating fissures and contradictions within.[13] If Christians persist in defining themselves in contradistinction to some other—pagan, heretic, or Jew—
they make that other an indispensable part of "Christianness" (in the same
way that "Rome" comes to be understandable through its relationship to "the
provinces").[14]

In this chapter I turn to examine the circumcision of Christ in a variety
of "dialogue" texts in order to interrogate more deeply this Christian dialogic
imagination, which both projects outward and internalizes a necessary other.[15]
My goal is to highlight the ambivalent and incomplete separation of "self" and
"other" that lies beneath the totalizing veneer of early Christian discourses,
with particular attention to Judaism. On Jesus' body, the otherness of Judaism
both articulates and disrupts the Christian self. Christ's body becomes the site
of a "de-Judaization" that is always incomplete, that continues to echo with
the sound of Jewish origins.

I examine here two types of dialogue texts. I begin with the formal, "external" dialogues: texts that depict the explicit interaction between Christianity and Judaism. First, I look at Justin Martyr's *Dialogue with Trypho the Jew* and Origen's *Against Celsus* (with particular focus on the passages in which the pagan writer Celsus introduces a fictitious Jewish interlocutor to debate Jesus and the Christians). We have already met Justin and Origen in Chapter 1, where they contributed to the general transformation of Jewish circumcision into a distinctly (yet ambivalently) Christian sign. In this chapter, we see both Justin and Origen authoritatively appropriating the voice of Jewish otherness in the production of Christian truth and laying the groundwork for establishing Christ's circumcision as thoroughly Jewish even as it articulates a logic of Christian supersession of Judaism. In stark contrast to these texts of seeming dialogic realism stands the later *Altercation of Simon the Jew and Theophilus the Christian*, a possibly early fifth-century dialogue that survives in a Latin recension. Here the voice of the other is but a tinny echo of an earlier Jewish intransigence, drowned out by the Christian voice in a manner that makes all too clear the ease with which a Christian could master and swallow up Jewish otherness.

In the final section of this chapter I turn to an internalized mode of Christian dialogic: the emerging literary genre of "question-and-answer" texts (*erotapokriseis*), in which the Christian subject is formally split—"never quite identical" with itself, in Eagleton's words—in the fractured production of an ideal Christian identity. Here anonymous Christian ignorance replaces earlier Jewish opposition, creating a more subtle interiorization of Jewish challenge. Both sets of dialogic texts, the external dialogue and internalized erotapokriseis, inscribe the unrealized desire to establish that "horizon" where Judaism ends and Christianity begins. That horizon of religious difference remains intractably hazy: in the dialogic imagination of Christ's circumcision, Christians repeatedly internalized the stark otherness of Judaism. Their differentiating rhetorics disclose a sense of permeability and indeterminacy that re-Judaizes even as it de-Judaizes.

Talking Back: Christian Dialogues

When analyzing the numerous dialogues of early Christian literature, scholars are often caught up in trying to tease out the social reality of the dialogue setting.[16] Some historians prefer to read these texts addressed to "outsiders"— such as the second- and third-century apologies, or the various adversus

Iudaeos texts framed as responses to intractable Jews—as evidence of real, antagonistic interaction.[17] The apologists are responding to real pagan criticisms (and perhaps even expect that the imperial authorities to whom they address their "defenses" will be sympathetically responsive); the treatises adversus Iudaeos are likewise reacting to the criticisms of real Jews encountered in the public square, in formal or spontaneous debate. Others prefer to interpret these texts as internal documents, produced to delineate the boundaries of Christianity for insiders using the fiction of external animosity.[18] The intended audience is not a Roman governor or recalcitrant synagogue, but the occasionally wavering convert, or the dedicated neophyte eager to bolster his or her newly adopted religious persona. A common assumption on all sides of such debates is that these Christian texts of dialogue give us insight into an evolving and hardening array of Christian boundaries: whether the "pagan" or "Jew" addressed in the Christian text is "real" or not, he or she is believed to create for the Christian a clear sense of the otherness that must lie beyond the Christian pale.

I propose instead to hear these texts as part of the religious and cultural polyphony that produced Christianity, the anxious heteroglossia of Christian culture: the multiple and contradictory discourses that are jarringly juxtaposed in the service of crafting a social identity. Such a reading does not deny that Christians might have intended their texts for pagan or Jewish audiences, with missionary or polemical goals; nor does it rule out the possibility that these texts served internal purposes of reassurance and self-definition (or even, as scholars often end up claiming, that such texts could serve multiple purposes).[19] My goal is to shift our understanding of these "self-differentiating" texts altogether, away from assumptions about boundaries and the establishment of difference.

The textualization of religious difference may bring not logical resolution but dialogical irresolution: the problems of difference (and similarity) are not resolved, but rather enacted, creating the *sense* of a boundary (between speaker and interlocutor) without finite closure. The heteroglossic nature of Christian religious culture is thus produced and reproduced: projected ostensibly "outward" into the person of a Jewish "other," but safely constrained within the lines of a Christian text. The circumcision of Christ, likewise the strange container of difference on the paradigmatic body of the savior, emerges as the particularly apt signal of such a project.

Justin Martyr and Trypho the Jew

One of the earliest appearances of Christ's circumcision in early Christian literature is in the only surviving second-century "Jewish-Christian dialogue" text, Justin Martyr's *Dialogue with Trypho the Jew*.[20] Justin is notable among the earliest Christian writers for demonstrating his mastery of "orthodox" Christianity through literary refutations of deviant heresy, recalcitrant Judaism, and impious paganism.[21] It is tempting to read Justin as an orthodox triumphalist, whose multivocality gave his readers of a sense of security and the ability to "answer back" authoritatively to any and all outside criticism. Yet Justin's texts, particularly the very long *Dialogue*,[22] also disrupt that sense of security by preserving, even hypostatizing, such criticism. The *Dialogue* is a notoriously difficult text to parse—both in historical and literary terms—as a straightforward text of Jewish-Christian differentiation. Despite Justin's frequently rancorous tone throughout the long *Dialogue*,[23] the very dialogic nature of the text hints at ongoing communication and rapprochement: the shared desire to determine what divides Jew from Christian cannot help but gesture at what holds them together. I am not suggesting that, beneath a veneer of discourtesy and acrimony, Justin is trying to get in touch with his "inner Jew"; to the contrary, I think the text lays out for us the ways in which gentile Christians of the second century felt haunted by that "inner Jew," and sought to confront, domesticate, and humble him. Yet at the same time, this early text illustrates the ways in which such efforts at confrontation and domestication lack clear resolution.[24]

The discussion of Christ's circumcision in the *Dialogue* exemplifies the frustrated attempts of Christianity to confront its originary Jewishness. The appearance of this stereotypical mark of Jewish identity and symbol of "the Law" on Jesus' body should be especially noteworthy in a text whose "core . . . is the vindication of what today we would call supersession" (to quote Tessa Rajak),[25] focused particularly on the failure of that Jewish Law. For much of the *Dialogue*, Justin and Trypho debate Jesus' status as the true messiah, with particular focus on his fulfillment of prophecy.[26] In earlier chapters, Justin manages to convince Trypho that many scriptural elements of the messiah could be seen in the life of Jesus. Trypho, however, balks at the virgin birth. He dismisses Justin's Greek version of Isaiah 7:14, and instead asks whether it wouldn't make more sense to believe that Jesus was appointed to the messiahship because of his perfect conformity to the Law of Moses. Could this not be the basis on which Jew and Christian come to agree on Jesus as the Christ?

At this moment of potential dialogic convergence, Justin pulls away dramatically. The bulk of the Law, he insists, was *not* given to the Jews as a source of redemption, but rather as a punishment and mark of their continual disobedience.[27] If the Law is not a sign of salvation, it cannot be a mark of the Savior. Trypho tries again. He points out that even Justin's own description of Jesus suggests otherwise, that Jesus *did* bear the mark of the Law and could therefore satisfy Jewish expectations: "But *you* have confessed to us (σὺ γὰρ ὡμολόγησας ἡμῖν) both that he was circumcised and that he kept all of the legal precepts (τὰ νόμιμα) ordained through Moses!"[28] (It is worth noting that there is, in fact, no point in the *Dialogue* prior to this assertion where Justin makes such a "confession" to Trypho.) Trypho insists that Jesus' exemplary and voluntary Jewishness can provide a key to the messianic rapprochement of Jew and Christian.

Justin, however, continues to demur. Justin does not deny that his "confession" accurately portrays what Justin believes about Jesus' life (i.e., he was circumcised); but neither does he accede to Trypho's reading of Christ's circumcision. Instead, Justin chooses to recontextualize Jesus' circumcision and, along with it, Jesus' seeming submission to Jewish Law. According to Justin, circumcision in this one, special case is no longer a sign of Jewish obeisance, but rather a unique symbol of divine redemption: "And I replied: 'I have confessed it, and I do confess. But I confessed that he underwent all of these things not as if he were made righteous (δικαιούμενον) through them, but bringing to fulfillment (ἀπαρτίζοντα) the dispensation that his father—creator of all things, Lord, and God—wished. For likewise I confess that he underwent fatal crucifixion and that he became a human being and that he suffered as many things as those members of your people arranged for him!' "[29] Christ's circumcision did not demonstrate Jesus' admirable Jewishness: on the contrary, it was of a piece with the redemptive suffering "arranged" by Trypho's Jewish *confrères*, a mark not of fraternization but of alienation. Despite appearances, Christ's submission to the Law connotes the eradication of legal righteousness, and the establishment of the boundary between Jew and Christian. Circumcision was just one more indignity that Christ suffered in order to redeem humanity, to end the "old dispensation" of the Lord and bring the righteous to a "new dispensation" (a non-Jewish dispensation) ordained by God.[30]

This biographical redirection mirrors Justin's cosmic reinterpretation of the Law, and the division between Christianity and Judaism. In a move that is theologically unsurprising, but still notable in a "dialogue," Justin claims to understand the Jewish Law more accurately than his Jewish interlocutor. The fact that the Christian savior took the Law upon himself (through such acts as circumcision) appears, in part, to authorize this rhetorical move: now Christians who understand the full scope of salvation through their redeemer can likewise understand in fullness the older dispensation of the Law which that savior took on himself. Yet upon closer examination, Justin's argument remains tantalizingly vague.[31] On the one hand, the very Jewishness of Christ's circumcision provides Justin his warrant for a superior understanding of the Law: he can correct Trypho's misapprehension of Jesus' acts and therefore the true relationship of Law and messiah. On the other hand, the uniqueness of Jesus' circumcision also allows Justin to argue for the dissolution of that Law. Jesus' circumcision is Jewish (in that it opens up the Jewish Law to the clear perception of Christians), yet non- (or even anti-) Jewish (in that it reveals that Jews do not understand the true meaning of their own Law).

The mechanics of this doubled understanding of Christ, circumcision, and Law are not fleshed out. Justin merely asserts that—somehow—Jesus' participation in the rite of circumcision provides the rationale for its discontinuation. The fact that Justin follows up his point on the Mosaic Law with a typical litany of patriarchs "righteous before the Law" only muddies his point further.[32] For Christ was precisely not "righteous before the Law," but rather (Justin argues) he was righteous despite, and within, the Law. Only the Jews, Justin remarks (and Trypho curiously concedes) actually needed the harsh yoke of the Mosaic Law, "because of the hardness of their hearts and their tendency to idolatry."[33] Neither the righteous patriarchs before the Law nor their spiritual descendants (the Christians) had need of such a burden. Where, then, does that leave Christ? Would he not have demonstrated the impermanence of the Law much better by not submitting to its yoke?

As we shall see, later interpreters of the divine circumcision handled the logic of Christ's circumcision with more finesse and creativity. Yet, I suggest, the incompleteness of Justin's own argument is exactly the point in the *Dialogue*: in it, we hear the articulation of anxiety about Justin's Christian identity, an anxiety that is neither dismissed nor glossed over. An earlier moment in the *Dialogue* clarifies this resistance to an absolute resolution of the difference between Jew and Christian. When Justin delivers his dictum on the negative, pedagogical nature of the Jewish Law (imposed because of the "hardness" of the Jews' hearts),[34] Trypho challenges him. Trypho queries Justin: "But if someone, who knows that this is so [i.e., the Law does not contribute to righteousness], after he knows that this one is the Christ, and clearly he has believed in him and he wishes to obey him and *also* to observe these [laws], will he be saved?"[35] Justin makes his own curious concession: "I said: 'As it seems to me, Trypho, I say that such a one will be saved, as long as he doesn't struggle in any way to convince others (I mean those from among the Gentiles who have been circumcised from error through Christ) to keep these things with him, saying that they won't be saved unless they keep them. Just as you yourself did at the beginning of these speeches, proclaiming that I wouldn't be saved until I kept them!' "[36] Justin draws the barest line between Christians who keep the Law, but don't bother their gentile coreligionists, and Jews like Trypho, who will not realize the "truth" about their own Law and will insist on imposing it on others.

But Trypho astutely notices how Justin hedges here ("as it seems to me," ὡς μὲν ἐμοὶ δοκεῖ); when pressed, Justin admits that not all Christians remain in communion with Christians who follow the Law. As for himself, however, as long as the Law-abiding Christians do not "compel" others to follow their example, "so I proclaim it is necessary to admit as our own and keep fellowship with all of them, as kindred spirits (ὁμοσπλάγχνοις) and brothers."[37] Already by the early second century, the fraught question of "Jewish Christians" articulated a keen anxiety among the self-proclaimed, gentile "orthodox":[38] what constitutes the lines of division (the horizon) between Judaism and Christianity, and when and how can that boundary be breached? (I return to this question, in its robust fourth-century flower, in Chapter 4.) Justin's own answer is contingent and uncertain, foreshadowing his equally uncertain discussion of the Law inscribed on Christ's own person in the circumcision.

As this earlier discussion in the *Dialogue* suggests, the brief moment of unease surrounding Christ's circumcision and Justin's halfhearted attempts to suggest that this sign was, at once, a disapprobation of Jewish Law and a key to special Christian insight into that Law bespeak a profound blurring of distinction and problematization of difference. By the end of the *Dialogue*, difference seems to win the day over reconciliation: both Trypho and his attempts to secure a scriptural and theological middle ground with Justin are rejected. Yet this is far from a triumphalist Christian text; Trypho also remains unconvinced of Justin's arguments, and there is no conversion of the Jewish interlocutor to constitute the *Dialogue*'s "happy ending."[39] This ambiguous conclusion suggests, again, that we should direct our attention away from any unequivocally triumphant message of Christianity facing and defeating its Jewish "other" (whether real or imaginary), and focus instead on the ambivalent, dialogic process in which this confrontation is framed. The point seems to be not so much erasure or capitulation of "the other," but rather the preservation of that still, disturbing voice within Christianity. Justin leaves various questions of Christian truth relatively unresolved in this text; even the central Christian argument against Judaism—true "Law" versus Torah, true "Israel" versus the Jews—is ultimately disrupted by the dialogic back-and-forth, the heteroglossic lack of clear differentiation.

In a text whose fundamental purpose would seem to be the articulation of the difference between Judaism and Christianity, absolute difference from the Jew is deferred. The brief discussion of Christ's circumcision neatly encapsulates both the desire for certainty and the deferral of that certainty. Since Christ's circumcision cannot, for Justin, affirm the sort of valorization of Jewish Law desired by Trypho, it must (somehow, even paradoxically) affirm the contingency and impermanence of that Law. Yet this assertion of the Jewish Law's impermanence is only possible because the Jewishness of Christ's circumcision establishes a dialogic space in which Trypho and Justin can communicate, in which Justin can assert that his knowledge of Jewish Law is superior to that of the Jews. Christ's circumcision, a small feature in this very long text, becomes a resonant echo of Trypho himself: the reminder, and remainder, of the Jewish voice required to establish Christian truth that can therefore never be fully silenced.[40]

Origen and Celsus

An even more complex interweaving of the "other" voices of Christian difference appears in the next century in Origen's *Against Celsus*, written at the behest of Origen's patron Ambrose.[41] Although ostensibly an "apology" addressed to a (dead) pagan critic, this text is also an illuminating counterpart and double to Justin's "anti-Jewish" dialogue with Trypho. First, scholars have suggested that the interlocutor of Origen's apologetic text, Celsus, a younger contemporary of Justin, may have composed his *True Doctrine* as an answer to Justin's several "philosophical" Christian texts.[42] We are therefore picking up the threads of a century-long dialogue between parties seeking to "out-know" and thus outargue their opponents, an empire-wide antiphony of religious differences.[43] Second, Origen's response to Celsus also takes the form of a literary dialogue after the fact: Origen composes his defense of Christianity against its long-dead pagan despiser as an interlinear response, preserving large chunks of Celsus's own words and responding to them piece by piece. Because of this purposefully dialogic format, Origen's apology *Against Celsus* sounds like a chorus of juxtaposed, competing religious voices.

Scholars usually read this text with an eye to "Christian-pagan" relations in late antiquity. But the insistent interplay of pagan, Christian, and Jewish voices also creates a deliberately tangled interpenetration of Christian self and Jewish other. The Jewish voice plays a significant role in this "anti-pagan" apology. In addition to the posthumous voice of Celsus and the determined responses of Origen, we also hear the careful interpellation of a dissonant Jewish voice claimed by both Celsus and Origen. Celsus's Jewish voice comes in his introduction of a prosopopoeial first-century Jew as a mouthpiece for criticisms of Jesus and of Jewish converts to Christianity.[44] Origen's responding Jewish voice comes through his display here (as throughout his oeuvre) of "firsthand" knowledge of Jews and Judaism acquired in the course of Origen's scriptural and exegetical studies.[45] We could read this Jewish interpellation as Origen's reappropriation of the Jewish origins of Christianity, made necessary by the caustic and deprecating Celsus, as Origen claims early on: "Celsus . . . thinks it will be easier to falsify Christianity, if, by making accusations against its source, which lies in Jewish doctrines, he would establish that the latter is false."[46] But when we turn to the appearance of Christ's circumcision in this text, we gain a clearer sense of the way Judaism blurs Origen's Christian apology.

Origen turns to Jesus' circumcision during a long defense of Jewish customs and "wisdom."[47] Part of Celsus's argument against gentile Christianity relied on the appropriateness of ancestral customs. According to Origen, Celsus conceded that, for the Jews at least, there might be some value in preserving Jewish custom, but there was no reason for non-Jews to adopt it: "Now if, accordingly, the Jews should cloak themselves in their own law, this is not to their discredit, but rather to those who abandon their own [ways] and make themselves over into Jews."[48] Celsus insisted that there was nothing particularly special about Judaism, and it was therefore unsuitable and even culturally treasonous for good Hellenes to abandon their traditional practices to follow some dead Jewish criminal.

Origen, in order to prove the superiority of Christianity, chooses first to prove the superiority of Judaism, "which has a certain greater wisdom not only than that of *hoi polloi*, but also of those who bear the semblance of philosophers."[49] Origen argues that the intellectual and historical priority of Judaism over Hellenism makes it precisely the sort of universally admirable system of belief that should be adopted by all, even gentile Greeks.[50] Celsus (at least in Origen's citation) had listed several aspects of Judaism that acted as the Jews' false basis for superiority: their concept of heaven; their worship of a single, "highest god"; circumcision; and abstention from swine. Older, and better, nations could likewise boast of these practices and, Celsus concluded, were more impressive in their religious and cultural accomplishments.[51] After a brief defense of the Jewish concepts of heaven and monotheism,[52] Origen turns to circumcision.

Origen's opening discussion of circumcision already betrays a certain ambivalence with respect to the comparative value of Judaism and Christianity. Origen first asserts, against Celsus, that Jewish circumcision is distinct from (and, consequently, superior to) the rite as practiced by various Near Eastern pagans: "the reason for the circumcision of the Jews is not the same as the reason for the circumcision of the Egyptians or Colchians; therefore it should not be considered the same circumcision."[53] The praise of the singularity of Jewish circumcision is, however, undermined in the very next chapter, when Origen discusses the origins and function of circumcision in more detail: "So even if the Jews boast of circumcision (σεμνύνωνται τοίνυν Ἰουδαῖοι τῇ περιτομῇ), they will distinguish it not only from the circumcision of the Colchians and Egyptians, but even from that of the Ishmaelite Arabs, even though Ishmael was born of their own forefather Abraham, and was circumcised along with him."[54] A historical and scriptural gloss typical of the hyperlearned Origen, this evocation of the Ishmaelite double of Jewish circumcision also subtly chastises the "boasting" Jews, reinscribing Jewish inferiority alongside the scriptural and exegetical prowess of the Christian.[55]

This double-sided interpretation of Jewish circumcision is the context in which Origen introduces the circumcision of Jesus, in a manner that likewise preserves the Jews' superiority while introducing a note of disrepute. In describing the unique circumstances of Jewish circumcision, Origen speculates that it was "on account of some angel hostile (πολέμιον … ἄγγελον) to the Jewish people that this [rite] is even performed, who was able to injure those of them who were not circumcised, but was weakened against the circumcised."[56] He arrives at this theory through an ingenious interpretation of the enigmatic passage in Exodus 4, where Zipporah's emergency roadside circumcision of her son somehow fends off Yahweh's murderous attack on Moses.[57] Like most late ancient readers of this strange incident who discounted the possibility of a direct theophany of a transcendent God into his creation, Origen understood the agent of death as an "angel" of the Lord, and he posits:

Now I think this angel had power against those who were not circum-cised from the people and generally against all those who worshipped the Creator alone (πάντων τῶν σεβόντων μόνον τὸν δημιουργόν), and he was powerful as long as Jesus had not taken on a body. But when he did take it on, and his body was circumcised, all [the angel's] power against those who were [not] circumcised in this piety (θεοσέβεια) was toppled: by his ineffable divinity Jesus toppled him [i.e., the angel]. Therefore it is forbidden to his disciples to be circumcised and it is said to them: "For if you are circumcised, Christ is of no benefit to you." (Gal 5:2)[58]

The rite of circumcision, according to Origen, affirms the superiority of the Jews: after all, the "hostile angel" has singled out the Jews because of their proper worship of the "Creator alone," in affirmation of the uniquely cor-rect nature of their monotheistic worship. Presumably, such angelic avengers already held sufficient sway over the idolatrous pagans.[59] Yet the mark of the Jewish covenant is also revealed to be, at root, little more than a prophylac-tic talisman nullified by Jesus' incarnation. Christ's circumcision, therefore, reveals the hidden truth of Jewish covenant practice: even as it is superior to the polytheistic idolatry of the gentiles, it is but a stopgap measure long since eradicated by the new covenant of salvation.

This introduction of Jesus' circumcision into Origen's discussion of Jew-ish superiority over hellenistic "wisdom" in his defense of Christianity weaves together several disparate threads of early Christian apology. On the one hand, Judaism is plotted as superior to paganism because it constitutes the true rev-elation of divine philosophy, of which Plato's later contribution is but a pale imitation.[60] On the other hand, Judaism is portrayed as defunct, no longer the bearer of this divinely inspired wisdom: the narrative of Christian supersession (over Jews *and* pagans) is inscribed on Christ's own body.[61] By taking circum-cision upon himself, Christ both affirms the significance of the Jewish ritual and yet renders it moot and past tense. This overlay of supersession directly onto Christ's person is so complete that Origen can introduce here (without attribution) Paul's later voice, from the Letter to the Galatians, the point of departure for most Christian argumentation against circumcision. The obso-lescence of the Law is portrayed as synchronous with Christ's observance of that Law.

Yet this polyphonous synchronicity renders supersession ultimately ambivalent, as well. As in Justin's *Dialogue*, transcendence of the Law is

accomplished at the moment of Christ's submission to the Law. In the treatise
Against Celsus, we are at least given a glimpse into the mechanics of such a potentially counterintuitive argument: a cosmic drama and angelic avenger are
conjured "behind the scenes" in order to explain first the institution and then
the eradication of this Jewish ritual. Yet the Jewishness of the ritual on Christ's
body, at the beginning of the incarnation, remains incontestable, indeed, absolutely requisite for the logic of Origen's argument to make sense.[62] Christianity must, therefore, be constantly reminded of the remainder of Jewishness
at its origins even as it persists in pushing an increasingly supersessionist line.
The artful heteroglossia of Origen's apology affirms this doubled position of
recuperation and repudiation of Christianity's Jewish origins. The Jewish voice
functions at once as critic and defender of the truth of Christianity: Celsus's
prosopopoeial Jew provides Origen with as many occasions for defending
Christian novelty against Jewish critique as it does for defending Jewish custom against pagan disrespect.[63] The invocation of Christ's own circumcision
at this nexus of identification and differentiation embodies the multivalence at
work in the production of insistently porous Christian boundaries.

Simon and Theophilus

The *Altercatio Simonis Iudaei et Theophili Christiani* (the manuscript title of
which already betrays something of a change in tone from Justin's "dialogue"
and Origen's "reply") reads much differently from older dialogues (although
some of the content may be drawn from earlier texts).[64] The *Altercation* in the
form we possess it probably dates from the late fourth or early fifth century,[65]
and is ascribed by the late Latin bibliographer Gennadius to an otherwise
unidentified Evagrius.[66] The Jewish interlocutor, Simon, is flat and listless,
providing little more than prompting for the much more fulsome and lively
(and aggressive) replies of the Christian, Theophilus. "Proba mihi," Simon
repeats throughout the *Altercation*, "Prove it to me," and Theophilus proceeds
to prove most convincing.[67] Simon's compliant requests for more "proof" and
"evidence" might read like the plaintive inquiries of a thick-headed catechumen, were it not for Simon's occasional, and faltering, resistance and Theophilus's sneering responses: "You speak like a Jew."[68] It comes as little surprise,
then, that at the end of the *Altercation*, all of his questions answered, Simon
the Jew converts: "Bearer of salvation, Theophilus, good doctor of the sick,
I can say nothing more: command me to be catechized and consecrated by

the sign of faith in Jesus Christ. Indeed I think that, through the imposition of hands, I shall receive cleansing from my transgressions."[69] That Simon's conversion should be the "happy ending" of this later dialogue demonstrates already its distance from the dialogic imagination of Justin or Origen.

In a somewhat different register, then, this late Latin dialogue appropriates and integrates the Jewish voice into Christian truth. This Christian mastery of the Jewish voice—both repudiating and revaluing the Jewish origins of Christianity—is once more signaled by the intervention of Christ's circumcision. The circumcision of Jesus is introduced in this instance by Theophilus the Christian, in the midst of his "proof" that Christ is the prophesied subject of Isaiah 7–8. Simon had suggested, through an intertextual reading of Isaiah 37:22 ("The virgin daughter of Zion has despised you and mocked you") that the "virgin" of Isaiah 7:14 allegorically represented Zion. Theophilus counters that Simon's allegory is nonsensical. Isaiah's earlier prophecy had spoken of a *literal* child, "who ate butter and honey" (Isa 7:15), was born of "David's lineage" (Isa 7:13), and who in his infancy received the "strength of Damascus and the spoils of Samaria" (Isa 8:4).

Theophilus proceeds to lay out the correct interpretation of the Isaiah passage, which subordinates any allegory to the literal interpretation: "First, it is explained that Christ ate butter and honey, in accordance with the birth of all infants. We believe this and so we maintain our faith; and certainly he was circumcised on the eighth day."[70] The author of the *Altercation* introduces here an argument that was used earlier against docetists and Marcionites: a literal reading of Isaiah 7 proves Christ's fleshly infancy and consequently the reality of his human form.[71] Like all children (according to this reading), Christ ate the food of infants: butter and honey. Furthermore, in proof of his real childhood, he was really circumcised. The logic seems to be that, since Christ was demonstrably a child (as his infant circumcision proves), he would certainly have eaten the foods of a child (butter and honey) and, therefore, so far fits the literal description of the child in Isaiah's prophecy. The ritual of circumcision in this interpretation has little or no resonance with Judaism:[72] its purpose is to reinforce Christ's literal fulfillment of Isaiah's prophecy. Only when the literal significance of the passage has been understood should allegory be introduced: the "butter and honey" of Christ's infancy are additionally understood to be the "anointing of the spirit" and the "sweetness of his teaching, which we follow and so we attain faith." The "spoils of Samaria" are likewise first read literally—as the gifts of the Magi—before being allegorized as the pagan abandonment of idolatry in the face of Christ's truth.

This christological interpretation of Isaiah 7–8 might not seem particularly noteworthy but for the strange insertion of Christ's circumcision. Of all the signs of Christ's infancy that might be drawn from the gospels—swaddling, being carried, and so on—why single out such a Jewish proof in the service of refuting Jewish biblical exegesis? Partly (as we shall see) the author is laying some textual groundwork for the more robust reinterpretation of circumcision to come later in the dialogue. But I suggest he is also inverting commonly held values of Christian Old Testament interpretation. In other exegetical duels over this Isaiah passage, we tend to see the Jewish side coded as literal (the "Virgin Birth" is no more than the prediction of the birth of King Hezekiah to his "maiden" mother) while the Christian side is figural: Justin's own interpretation of Isaiah 7 in the *Dialogue with Trypho* stands as an early and classic example.[73] Here, however, the Jewish position is represented as too freewheeling and allegorical—the "virgin" as Zion—while the Christian insists that the literally carnal interpretation must take priority. In essence, Theophilus reverses the exegetical stream: claiming both the "carnal," or Jewish, interpretation alongside the allegorical, spiritual reading. Jesus' circumcision, then, represents this Christian absorption of Jewish carnality. Just as Christ took on circumcision, but seemingly only as proof of his universal humanity, so too Theophilus appropriates the fleshly, Jewish mode of reading as part and parcel of universal Christian truth.

Simon is, predictably, convinced by Theophilus's Christianizing interpretation.[74] The discussion moves on to other aspects of Jesus' messiahship, and soon to the new covenant ushered in by Christ's advent. Simon returns to the question of circumcision: "We indeed read many things, but we do not understand them in that way. So I want to understand, one by one, each of the things I ask you to be proven by the evidence of truth. Now, because God instructed that circumcision be performed, which he first entrusted to the patriarch Abraham, and which you professed earlier that Christ underwent (*quam circumcisionem Christum habuisse superius professus es*), how then are you going to persuade me to believe, you who forbid circumcision?"[75] Simon picks up Theophilus's earlier thread of the circumcision of Christ in such a way as to allow Theophilus to introduce the familiar Pauline trope of Abraham's righteousness "before he was circumcised" (*priusquam circumcideretur*; see Rom 4:10). For Theophilus, Abraham's dual status—uncircumcised believer and circumcised believer—presages the dual nature of the universal church, "showing that two peoples would come into the faith of Christ: one would come having been circumcised and one would come still having the foreskin." Following Simon's lead, Theophilus moves directly from Abraham's circumcision to Christ's: "For if Christ had not been circumcised, how would you believe me today or the prophets, who say that Christ came from the seed of David? Circumcision is in fact a sign of race, not of salvation (*circumcisio enim signum est generis, non salutis*)."[76] Theophilus's response is, as before, a mixture of literal and figurative interpretation, of de-Judaizing and re-Judaizing exegesis. For, on the one hand, the general thrust of Theophilus's interpretation is spiritualizing and universalizing: the "old covenant," and its sign of circumcision, point inevitably to the extension of salvation to all peoples, Jewish and gentile. It is, as Justin had insisted to Trypho, not a sign of salvation but one of "race" (*genus*). Theophilus adds to Justin's earlier reading of Christ's circumcision the notion of messianic condescension: Christ had no need of circumcision, but took it upon himself so that Jews would willingly receive his message of salvation. He condescended to the Jews by taking on their "racial" sign; although, tellingly, Theophilus does not explicitly state whether this condescension actually makes Christ Jewish, or functions merely as a strategic disguise (I return to this question in my concluding chapter). Indeed, we are led to believe that Christ is an antitype of Abraham, who is both "uncircumcised" and "circumcised," the father of Jews and gentiles alike.

For Theophilus, circumcision—even (and especially) the circumcision of Christ—is the Jewish sign of the former covenant that, ultimately and paradoxically, leads Jews away from that former covenant. The "Law" both makes and unmakes the Jew. As if to drive home the doubled nature of circumcision, as the mark of Jewish "race" and the sign of that race's absorption into a universal salvation, the *Altercation* then introduces the example of the Lawgiver himself: Moses. Simon asks about the salvific circumcision of Exodus 4:25, prompted perhaps by Theophilus's claim that circumcision does not bring "salvation" (*salus*).[77] Although no avenging angels appear in the *Altercation*, we should recall Origen's similar association of Exodus 4:25 with the circumcision of Christ. Theophilus's interpretation is even more straightforwardly christological: "All things, whatever [Moses] did, he was anticipating them in Christ's image. Surely his wife Zipporah, who circumcised the boy, is understood as the synagogue. Moreover, what she says, 'Let the blood of the boy's circumcision cease,' means that at the time of Christ's advent the circumcision of boys stopped. And so God says the following to Moses: 'Build for me an altar of uncut stones (*lapidis non circumcisis*), as also you will not bring an iron tool on them' [Deut 27:5], because certainly in his coming Christ was to build a church of uncircumcised people (*de populo incircumciso*)."[78] In the case of

Abraham, the sign of circumcision had signaled the coming church comprising both Jews and gentiles. Christ's circumcision is "racially" more ambivalent (does assuming the Jewish "sign of race" make Christ himself a Jew, or is he just passing?), but also is effected in order to bring Jews out of their former covenant into his saving church. Finally, in this strange story from the life of Moses—who does everything as an "image of Christ"—the advent of Christ (and, we should understand, his own circumcision) answers the prayers of "the synagogue" that infant male circumcision "should cease" and to construct a church built of "uncut" (*non circumcisi*) gentiles. All circumcising roads, including Jesus' own, lead Jews out of their own circumcising covenant. In the subsequent sections of the *Altercation*, Theophilus explains to Simon the true circumcision "of the heart," and continues leading him down the path to conversion and baptism.

On first blush, the *Altercation* presents a typical, de-Judaizing Christian interpretation of circumcision: the faithfulness of Abraham before circumcision, the temporary nature of the Law of Moses, the transformation of incomplete and prefigurative "signs" into full salvation at the coming of Christ. But the dialogic format of the *Altercation*, the back-and-forth between suggestible Jew and authoritarian Christian, injects a subtle nuance of re-Judaizing into the discussion, only heightened by the prominence of Christ's own circumcision. For while the truth of circumcision remains ineluctably Christian, it is also persistently Jewish: this "sign" creates the *genus Iudaïcum*, the "Jewish race," even as it instructs them on how to give up their "genus" for Christian salvation. Circumcision, the ambivalent circumcision of Christ in particular, functions as a shorthand not for the eradication of Judaism in favor of Christianity, but for the transformation of Judaism into Christianity. Furthermore, it is a transformation that remains conspicuously visible, on the surface, apparent to the triumphant, spiritual church of the gentiles. Even at the climax of the *Altercation*, when Simon pleads to progress (like a catechumen) from instruction to the baptismal font, Theophilus's response invokes not the new covenant, but the old: "A blessing indeed! So Isaac blessed Jacob, and through his hand received blessing, so that the greater might proceed from the lesser, so also Ephraim and Manasseh were exchanged by the imposition of hands."[79] Again, Christian triumph echoes in the voice of the "old covenant" (the blessings of the patriarchs, here read as an allegory for the choosing of the "younger son" over the elder). The appropriation of the Jewish voice, almost comically subservient in the *Altercation*, remains audible and essential to the spiritual victory of Christianity.

Justin's *Dialogue* and Origen's apology *Against Celsus* ventriloquize the voice of Jewish others, and are two of our earliest Christian writings to hint at the complex, and unresolved, boundaries with Jews and Judaism through Christ's circumcision. Scholars of Christian difference in antiquity have often been tempted to seize upon this presentation of "the other's voice" in such texts to reconstruct some historical account of Jewish and pagan opposition to Christianity (the Quest for the Historical Trypho or Celsus, perhaps). Yet the circumcision of Christ, whose unavoidable difference destabilizes Jewish-Christian boundaries, suggests that something more intricate is taking place within early Christian dialogues with Jewish others. The entirely schematic format of the *Altercation of Simon and Theophilus*, in which a two-dimensional Jewish character is led like a marionette to the baptismal font, makes this point even more clearly: in tracing the interaction of Jewish and Christian voices in late antiquity, we may do better to attend to the dialogic genre rather than to the historicity of characters and events.

It is important to recognize that the format of these texts conveys as much ideological meaning as the content. By producing dialogues, these three authors conveyed the Christian desire to speak, at times, in the voice of the other: to sound like "the Jew" or "the pagan" (or, in Origen's case, both). We need not read the attempt to erect a firm boundary against Judaism as merely reactive ("they're just responding to criticism from Jews"), nor explain the tenuous and often contradictory nature of those boundaries as a result of the primitive level of religious development ("they're still figuring out what they believe").[80] These externalized dialogues of difference that draw on the irresoluble multivalence of the divine circumcision, in my reading, are deliberately and productively heteroglossic in their articulation of Christian identity vis-à-vis Judaism.

Especially the *Altercation*, from a later period than Justin's or Origen's texts, on the other side of the Constantinian divide, illuminates the hybrid character of the early Christian dialogic imagination. That is, beyond the debates about the historicity of Trypho, Celsus, or even Celsus's prosopopoeial Jew,[81] the *Altercation* underscores the degree to which Christians conjured a Jewish voice to serve their own needs. Simon, the weakest member of the chorus of Jewish voices surveyed here, makes all too clear the Christian desire to exert control over "the Jew" on the written page. Even if we can convince ourselves that we hear traces of a "real Jew" somewhere in Simon's obsequious interlocution,[82] we must confront him as a creature of Christian literary projection. In fact, Simon's character rang so false for Adolf von Harnack that he served as a centerpiece for the German church historian's argument about the fictitiousness of all such "Jewish-Christian dialogues."[83] For Harnack, unable to believe that Simon was anything more than a cipher, the actual target of such texts, from Justin's *Dialogue* onward, were heretics and pagans, not the moribund Jews who had slinked off after their rejection of Christ and their failed rebellions.[84]

But if Simon's flatness makes us recognize the artifice involved in the Christian production of these ancient Jewish voices, the robustness of Justin's Trypho and even Origen's own ambivalence in the face of a rhetorical Jewish opponent lead us to acknowledge the flip side: that, for all of this literary invention and artifice, Christians were drawn to elaborate the image of the Jew as their troubling interlocutor. The dialogic imagination of early Christians did not erase and silence those Jewish voices, but preserved them. The fact that Simon turned so easily to the baptismal font may lead us to question the "historical Simon," or even his authentic Jewish credentials; it should not, however, lead us to ignore his necessary *Jewishness*, the framing of Christian mastery as an encounter with a Jew, the transformation of a Jew, and a desire to confront and domesticate Jewishness within Christianity.

The circumcision of Christ encapsulates this hybridizing impulse: the Jewish remainder that completes Christian identity (and yet, at heart, potentially disrupts it—for what is to stop suggestible Simon from turning into troublesome Trypho?). Just as Christ's circumcision for these authors leaves the indelible trace of the Jew on the savior's body, the trace that somehow speaks against the totality of Judaism, so too the careful retention of a Jewish voice in the service of a refutation of Judaism instructs us on the ways in which Christians blurred their own literatures of difference. This blurring is neither a sign of confusion or hesitation on the part of the dialogue writers nor a sign of religious immaturity, but—like the divine circumcision itself—a discourse of dialogic multivocality that makes Christian culture "work."

Posing the Question: "If the Savior Was Circumcised . . ."

As I suggested above, the Jewish interlocutor in the *Altercation of Simon and Theophilus* often sounds more like an unformed catechumen, eager to be brought into the Christian mysteries, than a resistant and recalcitrant religious outsider. In the dialogic space of the *Altercation*, this confusion of self and other strikes me as intentional: a way of more fully assimilating that otherness into the orbit of Christian control, of taming and yet retaining the hetero-glossia of religious identities. The suggestive overlap of Jewish resistance and neophyte ignorance leads me to introduce a second set of texts into my ex-ploration of the dialogic imagination of Christ's circumcision. These are texts from the fourth through seventh centuries that more fully internalize that "other voice" of Christian identity, texts that scholars have dubbed *erotapokri-seis* (following a middle Byzantine neologism) or "question-and-answer texts."

As a genre, the erotapokriseis emerge out of the literary flotsam and jet-sam of classical paideia, perhaps like the novel or the gospel.[85] Various pre- and para-Christian authors made use of the "question-and-answer" format (known classically as ζητήματα or *quaestiones*) within treatises, letters, or other for-mal genres.[86] Philo of Alexandria subjected biblical texts to a "question-and-answer" treatment in the larger context of his scriptural commentaries,[87] and late ancient Aristotelian and Platonic instructors also found the process a use-ful instructional tool. The isolation of the question-and-answer format as an independent, self-conscious genre, however, seems to be the innovation of Christian authors in the fourth century.[88] Some Christian writers, such as Augustine, located their erotapokriseis in specific social contexts: an identified questioner has approached them (often in writing) and requested guidance, which is then provided in a responsive, question-and-answer framework.[89] Other Christians chose to leave their questions and answers floating in a kind of anonymity, identifying neither the questioner nor (except to the extent that we can identify an author at all) the answerer.

My exploration of the dialogic imagination of Christ's circumcision pro-vides, perhaps, a further context for the rise of this variegated genre in Chris-tian literary circles in the early period of the Christian Roman Empire: the cultural hybridity and heteroglossia that characterizes Roman political power and Christian religious culture. Just as the production of external dialogic texts—Justin's anti-Jewish *Dialogue* or Origen's anti-pagan treatise *Against Celsus*—might allow for uncomfortable otherness to be confronted, controlled, domesticated (and yet, importantly, never eradicated), so the erotapokriseis could take this effort at internalizing otherness one step further by substitut-ing Christian naïveté for external criticism.[90] Questions that in other contexts seem shocking or challenging coming from a non-Christian (on scriptural in-consistencies, or the impossibility of Christ's incarnation or resurrection)[91] are softened by being reframed as innocent Christian queries. Whereas a pagan or Jew might aggressively challenge Christian theology or exegesis, a Christian neophyte transforms incisive critique into simple curiosity.[92]

For this reason, perhaps, the challenge of Christ's circumcision to Christian identity emerges in its most direct form in the erotapokriseis. In the external dialogues—Justin, Origen, the *Altercation*—an unspoken anxiety of otherness lurked beneath the de-Judaizing, and re-Judaizing, efforts of our authors. These dialogues framed Jewish challenges to Christianity in a variety of ways: Christians selectively appropriated scriptural Law, they were inconsistent in their veneration of God's covenant, and so forth. While Christ's circumcision partially, and variably, might answer these charges, it was never allowed to raise the explicit question: "But doesn't Christ's circumcision somehow make Christians Jewish?" Yet it is, in some respect, this unarticulated anxiety that necessitates meeting and domesticating the otherness of Judaism through Christ's circumcision: the fear (or, perhaps, desire?) that the original Jewishness of Christ, the apostles, the Scriptures, might unwittingly infect Christians. We find the direct formulation of this potential effect of Christ's circumcision in one of the earliest fulsome question-and-answer texts, that of Ambrosiaster.

Ambrosiaster

The shadowy figure dubbed "Ambrosiaster"[93] organized his late fourth-century *Liber quaestionum* as a series of scripturally ordered queries.[94] Yet this scriptural arrangement, upon closer examination, contains and reframes larger, and perhaps more troubling, questions of Christian faith and knowledge. Using this organizing rubric, Ambrosiaster can subsume monotheism under the "Old Testament" (*Quid est deus?*) and Trinitarianism under the "New Testament" (*Si unus est deus, cur in tribus spes salutatis est?*). The "questioner" throughout is invisible and, in fact, exists only as a series of tabular questions appended to the beginning of the text:[95] he is the disembodied voice of Christian inquiry, whose interrogational bona fides is evident in the instructional (if, occasionally, confrontational) tone Ambrosiaster takes in his answers. There is likewise no preface, leaving us to imagine a context for the *Liber quaestionum*. Given the context of other contemporary Latin erotapokriseis—found in letters and treatises of Jerome and Augustine, for instance[96]—we can most easily envision Ambrosiaster acting as the ecclesiastical authority setting out to correct the average Christian reader and direct her or him away from possible error. That is, much like the external dialogues examined above, Ambrosiaster's *Liber quaestionum* is concerned with boundaries. The desire to keep the putative questioner on the right theological track lends a distinctly polemical and, at times, apologetic edge to Ambrosiaster's "answers." His particular attention to Jews and Judaism has even led some scholars to posit that Ambrosiaster was a former Jew, on the theory that no zeal matches that of the convert.[97] But as we have already seen in the externalized dialogues of Justin, Origen, and the *Altercation*, more compelling concerns about identity and otherness might lead a Christian to appropriate and repudiate the voice of the Jewish other.

While Ambrosiaster's chapter traditionally titled "Adversus Iudaeos" might seem a logical place to investigate his attitude toward the Jewish heritage of Christianity,[98] more telling are those briefer quaestiones that approach Christianity's latent Jewishness obliquely. In the obscure chapter "De lingua Hebraea" (*Liber quaestionum* 108), Ambrosiaster uses philology to engage the ongoing polemical debate between Jews and Christians over the legacy of Abraham, a debate ostensibly stretching all the way back to the time of Jesus and Paul.[99] Ambrosiaster begins by addressing the assumption (shared by his contemporaries and, it should be noted, by modern biblical scholars) that "Hebrew" derives from "Heber" (Gen 10:24–25, 11:14–17), a patronymic that would have associated the Hebrews (and their Jewish descendants) more specifically with the "family of Shem, by family, language, land, and nation" (see Gen 10:31).[100] Nothing could be further from the truth, Ambrosiaster asserts: *Hebraeus* actually comes from (*H*)*Abraham*.[101] The Hebrew language, Ambrosiaster goes on to explain, is the divine tongue of creation, spoken by Adam in Eden and extinct after the confusion of languages at the Tower of Babel.[102] Later this language—which, Ambrosiaster points out, no longer has "any land or any people" (*neque terram . . . neque gentem*)[103]—was restored by God's chosen ones, Abraham (from whom the language now took its name, *Hebraeus*) and Moses.[104]

That Ambrosiaster intended this somewhat esoteric discussion of languages and names to reverberate in Jewish-Christian debates over Abraham's spiritual patrimony seems clear from one trenchant New Testament example of a "Hebrew" invoked in the course of his answer: the apostle Paul. Paul famously referred to himself as a "Hebrew born of Hebrews" (*Hebraeus ex Hebraeis*; Phil. 3.5). For Ambrosiaster, however, Paul's boasting of his "Hebrewness" was due to his likeness in piety to Abraham, not his ethnic or linguistic origins among the Jews.[105] In a few dense paragraphs on a seemingly esoteric topic, Ambrosiaster takes the ethnic and linguistic core of "Jewishness" as it was understood in his day, and thoroughly de-Judaizes it: Hebrew means Abrahamic, Abrahamic refers to piety, and even the apostle Paul, whose ambiguous Jewishness might trouble early Christians, is rendered safely, and unequivocally, non-Jewish.

The question of Christ's circumcision—another moment at which Christianity might seem perilously Jewish—receives a similarly fine treatment. The question arises early in the section reserved for quaestiones novi testamenti, immediately following a question on the baptism of Jesus: "Why was the Savior—even though he was born holy (*sanctus*) and was called Christ the Lord at his very birth—baptized, even though baptism takes place on account of purification and sin?"[106] Assuring the questioner that Christ was, indeed, born without sin and therefore had no need of baptism (indeed, this is why John hesitated: Matt 3:14–15), Ambrosiaster explains: "It was fitting that he should be as an example to those who would later become 'sons of God' [John 1:12], whom he taught would be made sons of God through baptism."[107] The very next question pursues this idea of Christ's exemplary activity on earth: "But if the Savior was baptized so that he would be as an example, why did he, having been circumcised, forbid others from being circumcised?"[108] Ambrosiaster begins his response in a manner befitting a treatise structured according to New and Old Testaments: "The circumcision of the foreskin (*circumcisio praeteriti*) was a dated commandment (*temporis mandatum*), which rightfully possessed authority until Christ; so that it remained in force until such time as Christ was born, who was promised to Abraham, so that, as for the rest, circumcision has ceased since the promise has been fulfilled."[109] Ambrosiaster invokes a familiar patristic strategy for explaining the difference between Old and New Testament obligations, used also in the *Altercation*: a "difference in times" by which Christ's advent created a cosmic rupture between then and now, a Jewish past and a Christian present.[110] Of course, this has the effect of relegating Ambrosiaster's Jewish contemporaries to a state of hopeless anachronism, but at least provides an opportunity for understanding their willful blindness to New Testament truth. Ambrosiaster also creates a space within his own orthodox religion for an account of the Jewish past: it is the prehistory of salvation, a time of commandments once honored but now "fulfilled."[111]

As Ambrosiaster continues, however, we see that his Christian appropriation of the Old Testament promise is not quite so gracious. After affirming Abraham's covenant in Genesis 17, Ambrosiaster proceeds to transform it entirely. I cite the rest of his "answer" in full, continuing directly from the quotation above:

Now, Isaac was promised as a type of Christ (*figura Christi*). For God said to him: "in your seed all nations will be blessed (*in semine tuo benedicentur omnes gentes*)" (Gen 22:18); this is Christ. Indeed that faith which Abraham received was restored by Christ, with the result that "in the seed of Abraham" (which is Christ) "all nations will be blessed." Such was Abraham's promise.

Therefore circumcision was the sign of the promised son—that is, Christ. At his birth it was fitting for the sign of the promise (*signum promissionis*) to cease; nevertheless also that the one who was promised should himself receive the sign of his father (*signum patris*) when he came, so that he would be known as the one who was promised to justify all the nations (*gentes*) through faith in the circumcision of the heart. Now since bodily circumcision (*circumcisionis corporale*) was a seal (*signaculum*) of the son born according to the flesh to the father, Abraham, so too for those born according to the spirit the circumcision of the heart is a spiritual sign; therefore it is more correct, after Christ, no longer to require circumcision according to the flesh.[112]

Ambrosiaster's exegetical logic is typically dense, and begins by reframing the "promise" invoked earlier in his answer. We learn, immediately, that Christ was the promised "child according to the flesh" of Genesis 17, while Isaac was merely a "type" (*figura*). Therefore, as the fruit of the promise, it was fitting for Christ to receive the "sign of the promise," that is, circumcision. Already the voice of Christian identity is shaded by Jewish undertones. Christ's circumcision—as the child of Abraham's flesh, as part of the "promise" made in Genesis 17—might appear no different in kind from the circumcision of any Jew, past or present: also performed on children of Abraham's flesh, also in memory of the "promise" made in Genesis 17. This interplay of *carnalis* and *spiritualis* then becomes a lynchpin in the rest of Ambrosiaster's answer.

For if the "promised son" explains why Christ was circumcised, it does not yet answer the question as it was posed: why should not every Christian take this physical circumcision as a literal example and follow suit? (Especially considering the immediately preceding quaestio, in which Christ's baptism served exactly this exemplary purpose.) Ambrosiaster explains that precisely because *Christ*, and not Isaac, fulfilled the ancient promise to his "father" Abraham, it was fitting and necessary that the seal of that promise should no longer be necessary. Instead, a "spiritual circumcision of the heart" must take its place for those children born according to the "spirit."[113] In fact, we learn, this was the entire purpose of the promise, its sign, and its fulfillment, for the key passage in the Genesis covenant for Ambrosiaster is Genesis 22:18, "in your seed shall be blessed all the *nations*," that is, all of the gentile Christians, the spiritual "children of Abraham." Despite its carnality, embedded in the logic of the Abrahamic covenant, Christ's circumcision reveals the truth about circumcision in general: that this Jewish sign was, in truth, a sign to the gentiles, and always had been. Ambrosiaster's answer doubly inscribes the (seeming) Jewishness of Jesus and the absolute non-Jewishness of Christianity in the same stroke.

In this one condensed dialogic moment, we glimpse both the desired "horizon" between Christianity and Judaism and its determined lack of definition. Christ, in his circumcision, embodies this moment of heteroglossia, particularly through his representation of both "carnal" and "spiritual" truths. On the one hand in this passage, as elsewhere in the *Liber quaestionum* (and throughout early Christian writings) the categories of carnalis and spiritualis function as a shorthand for the qualitative difference between Jews, mired in the blindness of the fleshly Law, and Christians, liberated by spiritual grace.[114] So the Christian questioner can rest assured that he need not fear finding himself on the wrong side of that divide: he is a spiritual "son," like all faithful believers, part of the blessed "nations." Christ's revelation of the truth of circumcision thus affirms the Christian's spiritual superiority.

Yet we note that this spiritual surety is guaranteed by the son "according to the flesh," whose literal, physical descent from Abraham—as well as his submission to the literal, physical seal of circumcision—will always, of necessity, create a kind of kinship with "real" Jews. Christ's circumcision is effective in its revelation and fulfillment because it is carnalis, in exactly the fashion that the Jews persist in their circumcisio carnalis. We have already seen how the Jewishness of Christ's circumcision remains visible in the external dialogues, affirmed by the literal voice of Jewish interlocutors. Although here the Jewish interlocutor has been replaced with a faceless Christian, the visibility of the Jewish other remains, on the surface of Christ's body and in the theological logic of his actions. It is not enough for the Christian to claim spiritual truth, he must also acknowledge its fleshly basis. In Ambrosiaster's terse reply we hear the doubled voice of Christian dialogic: the utter rejection, and appropriation, of Jewish otherness.

Ps.-Athanasius and "Duke Antiochus"

By nature, the erotapokriseis is a flexible form—much like biblical commentary, which I discuss further in Chapter 5—ever expanding to include more questions, different answers, and varying voices of Christian inquiry. The relatively well-known *Liber quaestionum* of Ambrosiaster itself comes down to us in multiple textual traditions, with contents ranging from 115 to 151 questions and answers.[115] Pseudonymous sets of questions in the later Latin West and Greek East provided a similarly flexible format, not only for containing the anxiety of theological uncertainties but for safely expanding the subtextual chorus of voices in this Christian heteroglossia.[116] The internalized anxiety over the circumcision of Christ, we should not be surprised to learn, receives ongoing attention in this format.

The question-and-answer text known as the *Quaestiones ad ducem Antiochum* was, by the seventh century or so, ascribed to Athanasius of Alexandria. While Athanasius's writings provide one of the many sources for the compilation of this erotapokriseis text, its authorship and provenance are otherwise unknown.[117] The most common surviving Greek version probably dates from the seventh or eighth century,[118] and possibly betrays the influence of the rise of Islam;[119] these *Questions to Duke Antiochus* may even have been edited and adapted until the time of the Crusades.[120] While most erotapokriseis can be considered something of a hodgepodge, bringing together heresiology, scriptural commentary, philosophy, cosmology, and a myriad other Christian discourses, the *Questions* is a notably disjointed conglomeration of a wide variety of sources held together by little more than an enduring title and textual transmission.[121] Various "sources" can be identified—especially prominent Christian writers of the fourth, fifth, and sixth centuries—but my interest here is not source criticism. Rather I seek to gain insight into the ways ancient and early medieval Christians created a space for the dialogic cacophony of different voices even as they were ostensibly refining and narrowing the bounds of "orthodox" identity. Certainly a loud voice in that babel, for the author(s) of the *Questions*, was the insistent voice of Jewish criticism and the equally pressing call for sharp, diverse responses.[122]

The question concerning Christ's circumcision comes among other discussions of ritual correctness, stated here even more baldly than in Ambrosiaster's *Book of Questions*: "Why, since Christ was circumcised, are we not also circumcised like him?"[123] Here is Athanasius's answer in full:

Christ, being the Son of God, came to fulfill the Law, so that he would not be considered hostile to God (ἀντίθεος) nor opposed to the God who has given the Law (ἀντίδικος τοῦ θεοῦ τοῦ δεδωκότος τὸν νόμον). For early and late have the Jews accused him of this. But since he fulfilled the requirements of the law on our behalf, we are no longer under the law, but under grace. Therefore Christ tells us through Paul: "but if you are circumcised, Christ will be of no benefit to you" [Gal 5:2].

The result therefore is that we recognize clearly that all those who have been circumcised are strangers to Christ (ἀλλότριοι τοῦ Χρισ-τοῦ), whether they are believers or unbelievers, Jews or Greeks, since they boast in the Law of Moses and do not follow Christ.[124]

For just like all those who, supposing they can offer sacrifice to God through blood and senseless creatures, nullify and make abominable the bloodless sacrifice of Christ: so all those who have been circumcised in the flesh revile and reject the spiritual circumcision, that is, holy bap-tism; for the one is like the other.

For not in the Law did Christ render the devil and the demons powerless, nor did he effect salvation through it: but in the cross. So the demons do not look upon the Law with fear and trembling, but rather when they see the cross they tremble and flee, and they are rendered powerless and chased away.[125]

Several arguments from earlier dialogues and other Christian explications of the circumcision of Christ are expressed here in a variety of "voices." On the one hand, Christ seems to ameliorate his own baffling circumcision with the Pauline exhortation on the uselessness of the act (recall that Origen simi-larly juxtaposed Paul's words with Christ's actions). For Ps.-Athanasius, these words remind good Christians that circumcision becomes the ultimate mark of non-Christianness, by which both "Jews and gentiles" can be recognized and excluded. Like all other marks of the "Law of Moses," such as sacrifice, cir-cumcision is rendered ineffective by the world-transforming act of Christ's sal-vation in which all Christians should hope to participate. Do demons quake at the sight of sacrifice or (we are led to imagine) circumcision? No, it is the sign of the cross that drives away evil.

Such an answer is, of course, a perfectly reasonable explanation for Chris-tian noncircumcision, ultimately reaching back to interpretations of Paul him-self: to trust in the Law is to doubt in the cross, and lose salvation. This answer does little, however, to explain *Christ's* own circumcision. Surely it was not to mark him as outside the community of the faithful? Surely good Christians posing the query are not to understand by this response that Christ himself misplaced his trust in the Law? No, the beginning of the response clarifies this for us—in some ways. For, as we can see, Christ's circumcision was at once a scrupulous adherence to the Law and a total obliteration of that Law.

First there is the idea of Christ's ministerial condescension, which we saw Theophilus invoke in the *Altercation*. For Jews—both in the period of the New Testament and, we learn, even unto the (nebulous) time of the questioner—"have accused" Christ of being "hostile to God" (ἀντίθεος) the Lawgiver. Circumcision removes this argument and proves Christ's connection to God's (earlier) Law. More than that, however, Christ "fulfilled" the Law. This notion of "fulfillment," which also appears in some biblical commentaries on Jesus' circumcision, draws partially on the claim in Matthew 5:17 that Jesus came "not to abolish the Law, but to fulfill it." While modern biblical scholars may argue that the evangelist's intent here was to intensify and internalize the precepts of the Torah,[126] ancient and medieval Christians understood "fulfillment" rather differently, as the response makes clear. Here "fulfillment" means something like "filling to the brim" or "paying in full."[127] Jesus has not simply observed the Law (perhaps a more straightforward sense of "fulfillment"); he has entirely satisfied it for all future generations, to the point that any further observance of the Law is not only moot but counterindicated. Thus, Jesus can go on to proclaim (through Paul) that circumcision is "of no benefit," for Christ's observance of the Law has completely filled it out.

Although the responder goes on to trace out the implications of this fulfillment (specifically, the fact that circumcision now serves only and entirely as a negative marker of "outsider" status for Christians), it is worth lingering over this creatively reimagined moment of Jesus' circumcision. At this moment, gesturing ritually to his Jewish contemporaries and future Jewish critics, Jesus is at once embodying and emptying out the content of the Law. He is, at this one charged instant, completely filling and completely full of the Jewish Law, so completely full of Jewishness that he uses up all of the positive Jewishness in the cosmos. This Christian internalization of Jewish otherness, otherwise feared and derided in this short chapter and throughout the rest of the *Questions*, is compelling, to say the least. The reader must imagine Jesus at one and the same moment as intensely, overwhelmingly Jewish in his fulfillment of the Law (otherwise, some trace of obligation might remain) even as he *de*-Judaizes salvation for all time. The potentially threatening identification with a Jewish Jesus with which the question began has been only partly allayed: Jesus' Jewishness lingers, potently, at this originary moment of Christian salvation. Any boundary making effected later in the response can therefore only be partial and incomplete. The other voice of the Jewish Law, "senseless" and "bloody," echoes still.

Other Voices

Historians of early Jewish-Christian relations have, understandably, attended with some eagerness to the echoes of other voices embedded in ancient Christian dialogue texts. The temptation to recover the elusive voice of Jewish resistance as a counterpoint to the sheer volume of Christian polemic and apology is a worthy project. My goal in this chapter has not been to undermine such a task, but rather to nuance it. For the Christian act of appropriating and speaking in a Jewish voice conveys more than inadvertent historical data; it provides insight into the convoluted and contradictory processes by which ancient Christians formed their collective religious identities. The literary staging of a dialogue might preserve some authentic Jewish point of critique or belief; it also subsumes and internalizes that critique into the lines of a Christian text and transforms that Jewish voice into one carefully managed strain in the chorus of Christian culture.[128]

The circumcision of Christ, appearing occasionally in these dialogue texts, provides one tool for untangling this staged antiphony of Christian and Jewish voices. The freighted symbol of Jewish identity in the ancient Roman world could not but disrupt any sense of secure religious boundaries when imagined on the body of the Christian savior. Like the remainder of Jewishness on Christ's body, Judaism in these texts is not elided or eliminated: it is preserved and hypostatized, reincarnated time and again, contained (perhaps) but always present. In some of the texts I have examined, such as Justin's *Dialogue*, the problem of Judaism remains conspicuously unresolved. In Origen's *Contra Celsum* and the later Latin *Altercation of Simon and Theophilus*, the circumcision of Christ signals how Christians could rewrite Judaism as a legible symbol of Christianity itself, transmuting the negatively coded Jewish traits of "Law" or "flesh" into positive Christian values. I introduce the erotapokriseis texts as an internalized form of Christian dialogue to demonstrate how profitably Christians might imagine their own identity as a chorus of (not always harmonious) voices even as they insisted on the monophonous singularity of orthodoxy. For Ambrosiaster or the serial authors of the *Questions to Duke Antiochus*, Christ's circumcision at the same time celebrated and amplified anxieties about boundaries, making Jesus into a paradigmatic symbol of Jewish-Christian paradox and contradiction.

While these dialogic "encounters" with the other serve the particular goal of creating a sense of Christian community, the strategies by which other voices are conjured to construct Christian culture were neither unique nor entirely invented by Christians. That "culture" should be hybrid, polyphonous, and embedded in an asymmetrical confrontation with "others" lay, as we have seen many times so far, at the heart of Roman imperial identity. We must also keep in mind, however, that, by staging in so spectacular a fashion that confrontation with the "other" inside the empire, the Roman self was also rendered unstable, liable to the threatening otherness within.

Likewise circumcision, this symbol of Jewishness par excellence, came to be incorporated into the fractured singularity of Christian identity on Christ's body. This assumption of Jewish otherness becomes visible to us through texts that most clearly and deliberately stage the multiple voices of self and other composing Christianity: the dialogue texts. Here, in texts traditionally read as the vanguard of religious boundary formation, we glimpse the partial and even contradictory ways in which Christianity configured itself vis-à-vis the Jewish other. Much like the cultural economy of Roman imperialism, moreover, this Christian staging of the simultaneous repudiation and internalization of difference could generate a fragile sense of self, always vulnerable to the other it maintains within.

Yet even as we can sketch a plausible historical context for such a maneuver in the analogous operations of Roman imperial culture, we can also attend to the lasting effects of this sly internalization of Jewish otherness that always supports yet threatens the coherence of cultural identity. Perhaps the Christian absorption of its originary Jewishness, evident in these dialogue texts through the paradoxical circumcision of Christ, has left its lasting marks on the formation of cultural identities even into our postmodern period.[129] At the very least we can appreciate the resonances between the premodern and the postmodern that are made visible. Although speaking of twentieth-century articulations of race and hybridity, Robert Young's description of "culture" works well for the strategies of an early Christian dialogic imagination as well: "Culture never stands alone but always participates in a conflictual economy acting out the tension between sameness and difference, comparison and differentiation, unity and diversity, cohesion and dispersion, containment and subversion."[130] As we turn now to consider a different category of Christian other, the heretic, we should nonetheless keep this sense of culture—unified and divided, contained and subverted—close at hand.

Chapter 3

Heresy, Theology, and the Divine Circumcision

> The various means of *purifying* the abject—the various catharses—
> make up the history of religions.
> —Julia Kristeva

Abject Heresy

In the fifth century, Vincentius of Lerins famously described Christian orthodoxy as "that which everywhere, always, and by everyone was believed."[1] Traditionally, we have understood Vincentius to be asserting the continuity of orthodoxy through time and space.[2] Yet we might hear this claim to singular discourse differently within the political framework of the late Roman Empire. As I explained in Chapter 1, no overarching "Romanness" defined participation in the Roman Empire. Rather, the empire existed by virtue of its ability to contain and manage difference. Reading historically between Vincentius's lines, then, we might hear him trumpeting not continuous assent stretching back to the time of the apostles, but rather a more fluid economy of doctrinal control patterned on the cultural economy of Roman authority.[3] Orthodoxy literally comprises all manner of Christian belief, even that which it seems to reject.

In this chapter, I explore how the articulation of orthodoxy and heresy simultaneously asserted and negated Christian boundaries, visible through the variegated uses of Christ's circumcision in theological debate. I argue that the logic of ancient Christian orthodoxy, despite its own rhetoric, was not a logic of the exclusion of the theological "other," but a logic of the partial absorption and internalization of that "other." As I lay out in the introduction, scholars treat Christian theological assertions of orthodox unanimity with a healthy skepticism: no longer do we believe that heresy constitutes deviation from a continuous line of orthodox truth stretching back to Jesus. Yet we remain drawn to models of binary self-definition, imagining that orthodoxy constitutes a "self" coming into being in direct relation to a heretical "other," a figure of opposition identified (or constructed) to sharpen the boundaries of individual and communal identity.[4] There are, however, other ways of tracing the curious and complex methods by which individuals and groups define "self" and "other," models that may, in fact, fit better the fluid cultural economies of late Roman identity, and illumine the strategies by which orthodox Christianity likewise strove for dominance.

Whereas anthropologists and sociologists might view the formation of the "self" as a scene of definitive rejection of the "other," psychoanalytic theorists like Julia Kristeva (drawing, ultimately, on Freud and Lacan) speak of *abjection*:[5] a violent expulsion of "otherness" that is, by virtue of its very processes, always incomplete and recursive.[6] Elizabeth Grosz comments on abjection: "The subject must disavow part of itself in order to gain a stable self, and this form of refusal marks whatever identity it acquires as provisional, and open to breakdown and instability."[7] For Kristeva, the abject can be any reminder of that incomplete disavowal, which gives the lie to bodily and subjective coherence: food, excrement, a cadaver.[8] The abject is neither object (Other) nor subject (Self); it occupies an uncomfortable "in-between" space that challenges the boundaries of identity. To confront the abject—in Kristeva's psychoanalytic terms—is to confront the impossibility of my-self, to return to a moment (horrifying or purifying) before "I" existed.

Kristeva writes of this more subtle and unstable process of distinction between "self" and "other": "We may call it a border; abjection is above all ambiguity. Because, while releasing a hold, it does not radically cut off the subject from what threatens it—on the contrary, abjection acknowledges it to be in perpetual danger. But also because abjection itself is a composite of judgment and affect, of condemnation and yearning, of signs and drives."[9] The abject is "a frontier" that engenders "a sublime alienation" from our own sense of self.[10] By identifying and actively expelling from within ourselves the object of horror, of fear, of "otherness," we acknowledge that it is already a part of us, and so it creeps back in. The abject, according to Kristeva, initiates both horror and pleasure; our sense of self is threatened, but we delight in that momentary loss of subjectivity ("joy" or *jouissance*). The abject, the part of us we expel and yet acknowledge, creates simultaneously fear and desire at the edges of personhood.

In her classic essay on abjection, Kristeva explores the role the abject can play in individual psychic development—from childhood phobias to literary expression—and also how abjection (in her view) has been manifest in various rituals of defilement, purification, and atonement in the history of religions.[11] In this setting, the function of abjection, she suggests, moves from the individual to the social: "Abjection is coextensive with social and symbolic order, on the individual as well as on the collective level."[12] Anne McClintock extends these social implications yet further still: "Abjection traces the silhouette of society on the unsteady edges of the self; it simultaneously imperils social order with the force of delirium and disintegration. This is Kristeva's brilliant insight: the expelled abject haunts the subject as its inner constitutive boundary."[13] In this reading, identity—individual and communal—is always already split at the moment of its formation between "self" and "other." The "self" is, in fact, a fragile fantasy; the "other" an omnipresent, and internalized, reality. The abject reminds us of this fragmented reality, and so traumatizes and energizes the self and society.

The fear and desire for the abject resonate in interesting ways with the postclassical Roman context.[14] As I have suggested in earlier chapters, Rome remained imperial not because it rejected the "otherness" of the provinces, but precisely because it never needed to: it created an economy of cultural difference that produced an internally heterogeneous and hybridized "Romanitas."[15] The provincial other existed as distinct from, yet as part of, Rome. As the analyses of Kristeva and McClintock suggest, the cultural economy crystallizing in the Roman Empire was productively unstable: unity emerged through the display of and triumph over an abject other that could, in turn, never be eliminated but always interiorized. The Greek slave, the painted Gaul, the circumcised Jew—all marked as not "really" Roman, yet nonetheless made part of the Roman Empire—could all engender this sense of repulsion and attraction, the "inner constitutive boundary" of Roman identity and power.

To locate early Christian orthodoxy in such a sociopolitical framework, then, is to imagine the assertion of singular unbroken truth also as a kind of fiction of self and other, a scene of "expulsion" that masks much more complex strategies of appropriation and internalization. Just as Roman imperialism relied on (and was repulsed by) the triumph over and absorption of the otherness of the provinces, so Christian orthodoxy comes into being through a triumph over and absorption of the "otherness" of heresies. The heretic is the abject whom the orthodox Christian faces with both horror and pleasure: without him, the orthodox cannot exist, and yet (and so) the heretic remains thoroughly within the logic of Christian orthodoxy. Defeated, he is absorbed; absorbed, he is never fully defeated. Over time, these twin processes of Roman imperialism and Christian orthodoxy will become intertwined and mutually reinforcing.[16]

The circumcision of Christ signals this early Christian scene of orthodox abjection. As in the Christian differentiation from—and reinternalization of—Judaism I explore in Chapter 2, in intra-Christian theological debates this troublesome sign represents broad issues writ small. In a variety of theological controversies the circumcision of Christ appears as an incidental and often surprising aside, unveiling the tenuous, even illusory, boundaries between orthodoxy and heresy. Jesus' circumcision, in its unquestionable otherness and necessary Christianness, provides the orthodox an opening through which to master and internalize the theological difference of their opponents: how the heretical is not rejected—made utterly other—but rather abjected, distinguished in a manner that recognizes its necessary persistence within the orbit of orthodoxy. The divine circumcision ultimately also points to the unending work of orthodoxy, which must constantly patrol a border that is, in fact, "above all ambiguity."[17]

I focus here on two broad themes of Christian orthodoxy that span the second through sixth centuries: first, the relation of "old" and "new" covenants as embodied in Scriptures; second, the metaphysical and ascetic articulations of the person of Christ. Both cases disclose the abject quality of developing discourses of heresy and theology. The divine circumcision is that anomalous oddity that unfolds the deeper contradictions of Christian orthodoxy, revealing, within a discourse of theological purity, traces of "otherness" that can never be fully expelled.

The (Dis-)Unity of Scriptures

One early, and persistent, subject of Christian theological debate was the continuity of divine revelation, especially as it was embodied in Scriptures. While acknowledging a need to distinguish the "new" revelation of Christ in some fashion from the "old" covenant of the Jews as found in the (now) Old Testament, gentile Christians of the second through fifth centuries ultimately rejected what they depicted as a theology of absolute discontinuity.

Our standard histories of Christianity suggest—with implicit or explicit approval—that these orthodox groups were seeking a kind of *via media* with respect to Judaism: a theological porridge that was neither "too Jewish" nor "not Jewish enough," but somehow "just right."[18] Such a historical narrative, ultimately, relies on the terms of the heresiologists themselves, who were determined to distinguish their own supersessionary logic from that of "heresiarchs" such as Marcion or Valentinus.

The case of the second-century "gnostic" Valentinus is instructive in this regard. Valentinus was deeply interested in the links between "old" and "new" revelations, illumined through creative interpretive strategies, especially *allegorēsis*, that articulated both continuity across and distinction between the two testaments.[19] Yet Valentinus's attempts to link the narratives of creation with the teachings of Jesus and the apostles were decried by the orthodox as a "dismemberment of truth," "changing" and "refashioning," and even "abusing" the natural order of scriptural revelation.[20] Even so, by these same sorts of creative reading practices—allegory, typology, "spiritual" exegesis—the orthodox likewise attempted to create meaningful links between the revelation to the Jews and a distinctive Christian theological view of salvation.[21] The orthodox walked a fine heresiological line: the same spiritual scriptural strategies employed by Valentinus to relativize the "old" revelation were used by the orthodox to recuperate that revelation. At times, the line blurs: when does a "spiritual" reading of Old Testament history cross that boundary, from preservation of a sacred past to its rejection? What—apart from orthodoxy's strained insistence—fundamentally divides Irenaeus's theology of "recapitulation" from the *Apocryphon of John*'s equally creative reimagination of Eve's redemption?[22]

As we might expect, the divine circumcision could profitably intervene on the side of Christians who wished to assert the continuity of old and new revelations. The circumcision of Christ resisted any "spiritualizing" interpretation for its utter literalness: even when it signified something "more profound" or spiritual, its materiality and reality were never in doubt. Christ's circumcision was real, not allegorical, and must therefore, somehow, speak to the literal Law and the unity of scriptural revelations. Yet at the same time the mark of the old covenant on the new savior created a rupture: Christ's circumcision was constantly and inventively reinterpreted in the heat of theological debate, never allowed to indicate the continued force of the Old Testament Law. A double-sided moment of biblical juncture and disjuncture, this jarring scene from the infancy of Christ provided an opportunity for the orthodox camp to absorb and internalize both the value of Jewish "Law" (otherwise rejected) and the creative interpretive practices of the "heretics" (also mistrusted), all the while asserting boundaries against these theological "others." The Christian Old Testament becomes the site of orthodox abjection.

Tertullian and Marcion

In the mid-second century, Marcion, a wealthy bishop's son, arrived in Rome preaching a form of Christianity that explicitly divided the Jewish God, salvation, and Scriptures from Christian community: the God represented by Christ was a "stranger God," totally distinct from the plodding, material God of the Jews.[23] To this end, Marcion preached from a brief version of the Christian Scriptures, including a version of the gospel based on the Gospel of Luke. Needless to say, the passages regarding Jesus' circumcision and presentation at the Temple were not included: as Irenaeus aptly put it, Marcion "circumcised the Gospel according to Luke."[24] Tertullian tells us that Marcion mocked the infancy accounts found in other versions of the gospel: "Away with Caesar's taxing censuses, with filthy lodgings, and filthy swaddling clothes, and hard stables! Let the shepherds take better care of their flocks. And let's not have the *magi* tire themselves out from their long trip; I give their own gold back to them! . . . Let the infant be not circumcised, lest he should suffer! Nor should he be brought to the Temple, lest his parents be burdened by expensive offerings; don't put him in Symeon's hands, lest he sadden the old man to the point of dying! Let that old woman shut up, lest she bewitch the boy!"[25] Marcion's sneering summary of the gospel nativities conveys what he finds to be an inappropriate and even ludicrous emphasis on the materialistic demands of the Law at the dawn of a new, spiritual age: *magi* with their gold, expensive offerings in the Temple, spiritually exhausted Jewish prophets, and, of course, the fruitless suffering of an infant's circumcision. Marcion's critique emerges from within one of the critical discourses of early Christian self-definition, one also embraced by the orthodox on occasion: that the Jewish "Law" was outwardly and inwardly distinct from Christian salvation. For Marcion, that other Law was in part emblematized by a needless act on the infant Christ's flesh.

In his long refutation of Marcion composed several decades after Marcion's time, Tertullian responded by recuperating the value of Jewish Law, and not merely as a typological prologue to Christian faith. Tertullian praises the humane practice of routine slave manumission; he admires the restraint of violence promoted by the *lex talionis*; and he commends the frugal temperament encouraged by the laws of *kashrut*.[26] Tertullian's goal is to demonstrate the continuity between Jewish Law and Christian grace, and thereby disprove the radical disjuncture between "old" and "new" covenants preached by Marcion. Tertullian's warrant for this rhetorical move—apart from sheer assertion—is, however, unclear. How, for example, can Tertullian praise the moderation of the Mosaic law of measured punishment when, elsewhere (much more in concert with Marcion), he avidly decries the "old law" which "used to take vengeance by the sword's retribution, and pluck out an eye for an eye"?[27] How does Tertullian so openly reject Judaism in one context (for instance, his treatise *Against the Jews*), and so admiringly internalize its value in another?[28] One answer, I think, lies in Tertullian's unspoken reliance on the cultural economy of signs that defined the Roman Empire in which he lived: while Marcion seeks to triumph through the erasure of the "other," Tertullian prefers to recoup the "other's" symbolic value for his own dominant theology. To speak in a more theoretical vein: the Law, for Tertullian, is not rejected but abjected, maintained as the "inner constitutive boundary" of difference. Marcion, the heretic whose preaching dovetails, at times, too closely with Tertullian's own, becomes lodged within, as well.

Christ's circumcision discloses Tertullian's double-sided discourse of rejection and appropriation. Like Marcion, Tertullian scores points by mocking his opponent's account of Christ's origins. According to Marcion, Tertullian writes, Jesus simply "appeared" one day and began preaching in the villages of Galilee: he "plopped down," "all of the sudden," "without any warning," "going straightaway from heaven to the synagogue" in Capernaum.[29] Why, Tertullian asks, should Jesus have first appeared in Galilee—and not, say, Marcion's province of Pontus—if he were not coming to fulfill the prophecies of the Old Testament? Why, moreover, would he go straight to a synagogue, if his intention were not likewise to fulfill and honor the Old Testament Law? How could Jesus have been heard by the assembled Jews, Tertullian presses, if they did not already know him as one of their own? Tertullian cleverly dissects Jesus' actions as reported in Marcion's own shorter gospel in order to make his point: "Watch him come into the synagogue: certainly to the lost sheep of the house of Israel. Watch him offer the bread of his teaching to the Israelites, the first-born favorites (*prioribus . . . Israëlitis*). . . . How could he have been admitted into the synagogue—unexpected and unknown—no one knowing for certain his tribe, his people, his house. . . . Surely they were mindful of the fact that, unless they knew that he was circumcised, he was not to be let into the most sacred places (*sancta sanctorum*)."[30] According to Tertullian, even Marcion's abbreviated gospel attests to the Jewish origins of Christianity, literally embodied by Christ: in his movements, in his activities, on his person through circumcision.

Of course, Tertullian will not then proceed to defend the full participation of Christians in Jewish Law. He will, in fact, along with Marcion, understand by Jesus' proclamation, "The Law and the prophets were in effect until John" (Luke 16:16), that "a certain boundary (*quendam limitem*) has been established between old things and new, where Judaism should stop and Christianity begin."[31] Tertullian's "certain boundary (*limes*)" is an evocative image; on the one hand, it reminds us, as I have suggested, of the political economy of the Roman Empire, likewise reliant in porous *limites*.[32] At the same time we recall the "inner constitutive boundary" of the abject ("above all, a boundary"), which lies both within and outside the orthodox subject. Once more we see that, for Tertullian, the Law does not prompt rejection, but abjection: the keen, uncomfortable, yet pleasurable awareness of a difference that dissolves upon contact. The divine circumcision—an emphatic metonym for Jesus' Galilean birth, his synagogue preaching, and his respect for Jewish Law—creates that keen awareness, dissolves the "certain boundary" between self and other. Not only the otherness of Jewish Law but that of Marcionite heresy is absorbed in the halo of this circumcision. The orthodox, like the Jews (and unlike the Marcionites), affirm the utility and sanctity of Jewish Law; the orthodox, like the Marcionites (and unlike the Jews), reject the Law as an imperfect vehicle of salvation.

I think we miss some of the subtlety of heresiology in general if we attempt to explain away Tertullian's double-edged discourse here through recourse to theological necessity or convenience: it is not merely "reactive" theology, concocted in the face of a Marcionite challenge. Likewise, I am leery of "explaining away" Tertullian's paradoxes and conundrums solely through recourse to his noted rhetorical prowess.[33] The power of Tertullian's rhetoric of orthodoxy is not simply stylistic, but lies in its ability simultaneously to reject and absorb the "other," to assert difference and yet internalize that difference into the heart of Christian truth.

Augustine and Faustus

Some two hundred years later, Augustine (who, like Tertullian, composed a treatise *Against the Jews*) engaged in a similar debate over the continuity of scriptural revelation with his erstwhile Manichean coreligionists.[34] Mani in the third century, like Marcion in the second, had preached a radically discontinuous form of Christianity:[35] the old God of the Jews made way for the new God represented by Christ; the old allegiance to materiality made way for a new appreciation and striving for the spiritual; and the old forms of the Jewish Scriptures were now forever disproven by the revelations of the New Testament.[36] By the fourth century, Manichean Christianity had penetrated well into Mediterranean society, dovetailing with the growing elite interests in biblical interpretation and ascetic practice.[37] Augustine had, as a young, urban professional, spent a great deal of time among the Manicheans of North Africa and Italy, and upon his transfer of allegiance to "Catholic" Christianity was eager to establish his orthodox bona fides by decrying his former brethren.[38]

Faustus, a popular Manichean intellectual (mentioned by Augustine in his *Confessions*),[39] is the mouthpiece of a dangerously attractive brand of Latin Manicheism conjured as Augustine's opponent in a treatise of about 400 CE. The *Contra Faustum* is written as a sort of interlinear response to a book by Faustus "published against correct faith and Catholic truth," alternating between Faustus's text and Augustine's (usually much longer) responses.[40] The result is a pastiche dialogue, as Augustine decides it is "fitting to place his words under his name, and my response under mine."[41] Already the format of the treatise—a kind of heresiological drama—highlights the degree to which orthodox and "heretical" voices of biblical interpretation shade into each other.[42] Between the "proximate otherness" of Manicheans and Catholics stands the Jewish Law:[43] a sign of Faustian rejection and Augustinian abjection.

At issue, for much of the constructed back-and-forth of the *Contra Faustum*, is the status of the narratives, laws, and themes of the Old Testament and the reliability of the New Testament. Like Marcion's brand of Christianity— which also persisted well into the fourth century—Manicheans sought an absolute distinction between the old, Jewish covenant and the new Christian mode of salvation.[44] Also like Marcion, Manicheans saw this distinction mapped in the respective testaments of the two religions.[45] In the *Contra Faustum* particularly, the relation of—or distinction between—these two written testaments stands at the heart of the debate. For Faustus, the Old Testament is a "poor, carnal thing" when compared with the promises of the New Testament,[46] a mere repository of the "errors of Judaism and a semi-Christianity."[47] Because of the error-prone nature of the Jewish Old Testament, Faustus (like Marcion) argues not only the necessity of rejecting the Old Testament but also the need to prune the New Testament of obvious corruptions from the earlier, bankrupt revelation. A firm scriptural boundary is in order to secure theological accuracy.

What's more, Faustus finds in this doubled operation of scriptural emendation a common desire between Manichean and Catholic Christians. Faustus suggests that Manichean Christians operate no differently with regard to the New Testament than do the Catholic with respect to the Old: do not Augustine and his colleagues strip away the precepts and laws from the Old Testament, under the thin pretense that, although ordained by God the Father, "these things were only required of the Jews until the coming of Jesus"?[48] Faustus insists upon the exegetical proximity of the two groups, as both Manicheans and Catholics strive to forge tight, clear religious boundaries:

> Therefore, just as you allow in only the prophecies from the Old Testament, and the civil and common commands pertaining to the discipline of life, but you set aside (*supersedistis*) circumcision (*peritomen*), and sacrifices, and the sabbath and its observance . . . for what reason should not we also allow in from the New Testament only what was said in honor and praise of the majesty of the Son . . . and ignore the rest (*dissimulavimus caetera*)? . . . I'm thinking of his being born shamefully from woman, his being circumcised like a Jew (*circumcisum Iudaice*), his having sacrificed like a gentile, his being baptized in humiliation, being led around by the devil in the wilderness, and tempted by him as pathetically as possible.[49]

How, Faustus presses, is Manichean treatment of the New Testament any different than orthodox treatment of the Old? Do not both ensure that the "new" salvation is not tainted by the prior revelation to the Jews through a clear process of scriptural rejection? The example of Christ's circumcision is particularly significant here: if Augustine's friends are so comfortable dispensing with Old Testament circumcision, how can they countenance it in the New Testament, on God's very body?

Augustine frames his response as one of biblical fidelity, insisting that the Scriptures cannot "lie" or distort, and it is therefore inappropriate to "correct" them through shifty editing or dissembling.[50] Such a frame allows Augustine to respond by comparing the veracity of Jesus' apostles with the mendacity of Faustus's beloved Mani. The former are patently trustworthy, the latter is (Augustine asserts) frighteningly absurd. In this passage, he compares Christ's infancy (including the circumcision) with Mani's cosmology: "The former [the apostles] preach that Christ was circumcised (*circumcisum*) in the flesh which he received from the seed of Abraham; Mani preaches that God in his two natures was cut up (*concisum*) by the race of shadows.[51] The former that a sacrifice was offered for the infant flesh of Christ, because at that time it was done piously; the latter that an element, not of flesh, but of the divine substance, to be offered up to all the demons, was introduced into the nature of an enemy race."[52] Augustine continues in this vein, moving through all of Faustus's purported neotestamentary improprieties. Where Faustus rejected the emptiness of Old Testament Law in the New Testament, Augustine asserts the primacy of New Testament apostolic witness over the sheer craziness of Mani's mythologies. To trust the apostles means to trust the New Testament as the church has received it, with its insistence on the continuity of Old and New Testaments.

This response, in some measure, dodges Faustus's central scriptural claim, perhaps because it cannot so easily be answered. Despite Augustine's insistence on apostolic and scriptural fidelity, he will find ways to argue against the authority of key passages in the Old Testament, and even explain away the more Judaizing aspects of the New Testament. The two parties would seem to agree on central points concerning the Law, Jews, and the new revelation. As Faustus says earlier in the treatise: "I myself say that the Law is not circumcision (*circumcisionem*), or the sabbath, or sacrifices, and all other such things of the Jews; but that which is truly the Law, that is, 'Do not kill, do not commit adultery, do not bear false witness" [Exod 20:13, 14, 16], and so on. To this Law, which was long ago spread among the gentiles . . . the Hebrew writers insinuated themselves, like leprosy or boils, mixing in these most vile precepts of their own, which focus on circumcision (*peritomen*) and sacrifice. But come now: if you are truly a friend of the Law, condemn with me the ones who dared to violate her!"[53] Augustine, with all sincerity and disdain, refuses Faustus's invitation, insisting that he has repeatedly acknowledged that many Old Testament precepts were "brought to fulfillment through the grace of the New Testament, and others . . . are shown to have been set aside through the truth that has been revealed."[54] In this crucial respect, Augustine agrees with Faustus: the new revelation, through Christ, shows the need to dispense with the earlier, Jewish covenant (embodied for both, in part, by circumcision).

Yet Augustine insists that there is a clear difference between the Manichean brand of supersession, which is fantastic and mendacious, and the orthodox brand, which is faithful and reliable. Their difference also lies in the degree to which Augustine refuses Faustus's absolutism, his sheer and utter rejection of the Jewish Law in all its guises. Both sides insist on a "difference in times" that renders the Old Testament laws (and their Jewish practitioners) moot;[55] yet Augustine, like Tertullian before him, insists on retaining and internalizing that Law in all its troubling Jewishness. The Law cannot be rejected: it remains abject. Again, like Tertullian, Augustine's warrant for this doubled gesture is the action of Christ (as "faithfully" reported by the evangelists), who embodied for Christians the simultaneous rejection and appropriation of Jewish Law.

That such a method of reinternalizing the value of Jewish Law against heretics might be problematic is evident in Augustine's turbulent correspondence with Jerome where, again, the issues of Jewish Law, scriptural continuity, and heresy are at stake. At one point, Jerome insinuates that Augustine's defense of the straightforward truth and value of *all* Scriptures makes him little better than a Judaizing "Ebionite."[56] Augustine, in turn, holds his line on the accuracy and message of Jesus' veterotestamentary observances: "Nor do I think that the Lord was falsely (*fallaciter*) circumcised by his parents!" he insists.[57] Of course, Augustine agrees with Jerome (and, we might add, Faustus) that although "then [the Law] was approved, now it is detested";[58] again, the line between heresy and orthodoxy, with respect to scriptural continuity, is a fine one.

Augustine's desire to straddle that line—to internalize the literal value of the Jewish Law while insisting that a "difference in times" creates a sufficient boundary with contemporary Jews—speaks again, I think, to the particular logic of orthodoxy at work here. For Augustine and Tertullian, the mastery of Christian orthodoxy becomes evident through simultaneous gestures of rejection and recuperation of "others": through abjection. To cede ground to devious, fallacious, and absurd theological opponents (whether they be Jews or de-Judaizers) is to compromise the fullness of Christian orthodoxy. Better to paint those theological "others" as deficient and incomplete: the circumcision of Christ, a sign overspilling so many theological boundaries, provides the necessary authority to make this rhetorical move.

To recognize Jesus' circumcision as the abject sign of the Law is to nuance our understanding of a discourse of orthodoxy that embraced supersessionism but rejected the "extremism" of Marcion or Mani. The totalizing orthodoxy that emerged as triumphant in the fourth and fifth centuries did not merely triangulate between scriptural poles, like a cunning politician wooing diverse constituencies. Rather, this brand of orthodoxy positioned itself on the very edges of a blurred boundary between truth and falsity. The divine circumcision endorses the truth of the Law, yet allows Christians to negate that Law's force. Marcion's new gospel and Faustus's revised Scriptures are only partially refuted by the logic of Jesus' circumcision; their impulse toward revision and rescription are pulled back within the stream of orthodox Christian truth.

The Personae of Christ

In other heresiological contexts, the divine circumcision emerges in arguments centered more specifically on the person of Christ himself. The multiple nature of Christ's person is not unrelated to the connection (or disjunction) between Old and New Testaments. Marcionites and Manicheans both (according to their detractors) believed that a rejection of Judaism and its Scriptures entailed a rejection of the Creator God and his material works. These brands of Christianity therefore decried the physicality and materiality of the divine in all forms, including Christ on earth. Indeed, one of Tertullian's smaller treatises in refutation of Marcion and other "docetic" heretics was entitled *On the Flesh of Christ*, a defense of the reality of Christ's fleshly existence.[59] Marcion's rejection of the nativity accounts, according to Tertullian, was expressly "so that [Christ's] flesh will not be proved."[60] The pollution of flesh and materiality, for Marcion, was connected to the limitations of the prior, superseded covenant.

For Tertullian, the continuity of sacred histories and revelations necessitated the doubled reality of Christ's person as fully flesh and fully divine. In *On the Flesh of Christ*, Tertullian practically luxuriated in the stark contrast between exalted God and his demeaned flesh.[61] The distasteful reality of Christ's fully fleshly existence is necessary to understand the scope of his divine exaltation: "What's more unworthy of God? What is more blushworthy (*erubescendum*): to be born, or to die? To bear flesh, or the cross? To be circumcised, or crucified (*suffigi*)? To be in a cradle, or a coffin? To be laid down in a manger, or laid to rest in a tomb?"[62] The incongruous conjunction itself speaks to Christ's divinity: who else but God, Tertullian asks, could contain within himself such impossible contradictions?[63] "It must be believed," he famously proclaimed in this chapter, "because it is ridiculous (*ineptum*)."[64]

The impossibility of Christ's person is asserted again and again in theological debates, and in this section I focus on two related discussions: the convoluted debate over Christ's divine-human "nature(s)" and the controversial imitation of Christ by ascetic elites. Again, we see the divine circumcision intruding—at unexpected moments—in order to assert and rehearse and appropriate the contradictions and incongruities of Christ's person. In these debates, the question is not so much whether to reject or accept Christ's circumcision but rather what to do with that theological fact. The confounding multiplicity of Christ—contemplated and imitated—creates, once more, a boundlessness at the inner limits of Christianity: it is the humanity, and inhumanity, of Christ, we find, that engenders the abject impossibilities of orthodoxy.[65]

Christological Anxieties: Nature and Corruption

Toward the end of the fourth century, Athanasius of Alexandria commented on a recent christological controversy in the city of Corinth, the details of which are preserved in a letter written by Athanasius to the Corinthian bishop, Epictetus.[66] The debate has been characterized by scholars (following the lead of Epiphanius of Salamis, who preserves Athanasius's letter)[67] as an "Apollinarian" controversy over the manner in which Christ's humanity and divinity were joined together. One side, apparently, posited that God's Word was only loosely united to the person of Christ by "attribution, and not by nature" (θέ–σει καὶ οὐ φύσει).[68] The other side pushed a diametrically opposite line: that the union between human and divine natures was so total that Christ's physical body was, in some sense, divinized, that "the Word has been transformed into flesh, bones, hair, sinews, and the whole body."[69] By the time Athanasius has caught wind of the debate, it has been (it seems) successfully resolved; nonetheless, the pro-Nicene bishop of Alexandria feels compelled to provide his own opinion on the matter.

Athanasius declares both of these groups heretical, describing their arguments as "absurd," "insane," and "stupid."[70] Yet Athanasius's rebuttals are carefully crafted to allow him to recuperate core elements of both sides of this debate: the consubstantiality of the Son and the Father (pushed to a physicalized extreme by one side) and the distinction between human and divine natures (relegated to mere "attribution" by the other side). Again, I think we do a disservice to Athanasius's theological creativity if we characterize his position simply as the moderate "middle way" between the "too-human" and the "too-divine" savior. Athanasius was not merely perfecting the recipe of humanity and divinity that would produce a theologically palatable person of Christ but was rather crafting a sophisticated method for both rejecting and reappropriating the theological positions of heretical opponents.

Once more, the circumcision of Christ helps us track Athanasius's orthodox logic. In this case, however, it is difficult to ascertain who first broached the significance of the circumcision: the Corinthians or Athanasius himself.[71] At the beginning of his letter to Epictetus, Athanasius cites with stupefaction the various, contradictory arguments put forward in the "minutes" of the debate, which he has received:[72] "Who has heard in a church, or from anyone among the Christians, that the Lord carried around a body by attribution, and not by nature? Or who was so impious as to say and also to assert that that divinity, which was consubstantial with the father, περιετμήθη and that imperfection came to be out of perfection?"[73] The word untranslated here, περιετμήθη, can have several meanings, including "was circumcised." In context, it may simply mean that the divinity "was curtailed" (modern English translators have gone both ways).[74] Whether speaking of circumcision or curtailment, this line seems to be associated with the party arguing for a divine Christ-body. Yet it is difficult to determine whether these words come from the "consubstantialists" themselves (perhaps attempting to praise the degree to which God humbled himself in the economy of salvation) or by their "attributionist" opponents (perhaps in order to point out the absurdity of the consubstantialist position). As we shall see, though, Athanasius clearly hears in this a reference to Christ's circumcision.

Athanasius proceeds against both "heretical" parties in Corinth. Against the "consubstantialists," he argues for the absolute humanity of Christ, and the absolute distinction between God's divine nature and our human nature; against the "attributionists," he argues for the full divinity of the Word that was completely united to the human Jesus. It is clear here, as in Athanasius's voluminous writings on the incarnation, that the union itself constitutes a primal scene of abjection: the joining of the divine Logos to humanity can only serve to highlight, for Athanasius, the abject horror of human corruptibility, even as it corrects it. Virginia Burrus aptly notes that Athanasius's "incarnational Christology remains haunted by the shame it attempts to refuse."[75] Athanasius's after-the-fact intervention into a christological debate succinctly conveys this haunted theology.

Athanasius begins by claiming that, if God's nature and the human body could somehow be absolutely united in divinized flesh, why go through the bother of having the Son of God become incarnate in a specific time and place, born of Mary? It was, Athanasius points out, to assure us of Christ's total humanity: so we are told by Scriptures that Mary "brought forth" a son, that she "wrapped him in swaddling clothes," and, later, that "blessed are the breasts at which he sucked" (Luke 1:27, 1:31, and 11:27).[76] Likewise (also in Luke) Gabriel refers to the child born *of her*, not simply *in her*, to emphasize the truly human nature of his body: "This is the body circumcised on the eighth day, this body Symeon received in the crook of his arms, that became a child, and grew into his twelfth year, and became thirty years old. For it was not the very nature of the Word which, being altered, was circumcised; for it is unalterable and unchangeable, as the Savior himself says."[77] Athanasius here follows the narrative of Luke 2, making clear that he is not speaking merely of curtailment but literal circumcision performed on Jesus in his infancy. The circumcision of Christ—a radical alteration to Jesus' human form—shows that his body could not have been divine, for God cannot be changed or altered. Here Athanasius drifts toward the theological position of the "attributionists," who would surely agree that a clear and bright distinction must be made between transcendent Godhead and limited humanity. The circumcision would effectively cut off the man from the God.

Yet for those who might see in this statement an affirmation of the "attributionist" perspective, Athanasius continues directly: "But indeed *in* the body being circumcised, and being carried around, and eating, and tiring, and affixed to the tree, and suffering, was the impassible and bodiless Word of God."[78] Here, the nub of the "consubstantialist" position is neatly recouped, and the abject horror of humanity diverted. All of the "changes" ascribed to the fully human Christ—the first of which is, again, circumcision—have theological meaning only if the Word is fully united to that mutable human. "On this account, then," Athanasius adds, "did the sun, upon seeing its Creator raised up in a humiliated body, withdraw its rays and cast a shadow on the earth."[79] The Word truly became flesh, Athanasius asserts with the consubstantialists, and the Creator was united with his creation.

Athanasius even admits that he is upholding at the same time the contradictory positions of the two Corinthian camps: "And it *was* a paradox, that he who suffered also did not suffer: he suffered, because his own body suffered and he was in that suffering body; he did not suffer, because the Word, which is God by nature, is unsuffering ($\dot{\alpha}\pi\alpha\theta\dot{\eta}\varsigma$). And the bodiless one was in the suffering body, but the body had within it the unsuffering Word."[80] At this point, we can suspect that Athanasius is not simply "working out" the complex metaphysics of his incarnational theology, prompted by the controversies in Corinth.[81] Rather the Alexandrian bishop is exploiting an opportunity to demonstrate the triumph of Nicaea,[82] the full and total confession of faith so powerful that it can defeat—and yet absorb—the theological assumptions of multiple opponents. And, once again, we see how the subtle mention of Christ's circumcision (perhaps here even manufactured out of the felicitous multiple meanings of *peritemnō*) can enable this polyphonous, even "paradoxical," logic of orthodoxy. It is the double-speaking sign that allows Athanasius to affirm Christ's total humanity and his divinity, to emphasize union and distinction. That this sign also signals an unspoken "otherness"—a Jewish particularity placed at the head of a series of universal "human" activities (eating, growing, tiring)—works also to the advantage of Athanasius's subsuming theological logic.

Yet the price of triumphantly subsuming "the other" is, as in many hybrid political and religious discourses, an attendant anxiety and uncertainty of self. Just as Augustine's fierce defense of scriptural unity against Faustus could be construed by Jerome (his putative theological ally) as heretical Judaizing, so too orthodox reliance on the "paradox" of Christ's person, read through Christ's circumcision, could also disclose the anxiety of internalized otherness. In the next century, as christological controversies came to a head, Patriarch Nestorius of Constantinople chided Athanasius's successor Cyril for overly emphasizing the union of God and man in Christ. Nestorius writes: "To attribute also to the godhead the properties of the flesh . . . is, my brother, the act of a mind truly led astray. . . . I won't even mention how circumcision, sacrifice, sweat, hunger, and thirst, which happened to his body on account of us, are worshipfully united to the divinity. If these are taken with reference to the divinity, and falsely, there is cause for just condemnation against us as slanderers."[83] Like Athanasius, Nestorius betrays anxiety when confronted with the abject scene of christological union: too much emphasis on this "union" of divine and human natures misconstrues the fundamentally unchangeable essence of the Godhead. To ascribe circumcision to Christ is one thing; to ascribe it to God is quite another. But whereas Christ's circumcision for Bishop Athanasius had signaled orthodox ability to both reject and subsume the errors of heretics—the totalizing power of the abject—here abjection produces a profound theological disquiet. When the success of orthodoxy rests on "paradox," on rejection and appropriation in the same discourse of heresy, the risk of slipping into error remains always present, the fiction of a coherent, pure selfhood always precariously threatened from within.

The ecumenical councils of the fourth and fifth centuries did little to ease christological anxieties, particularly in the Christian East. The Council of Chalcedon (451) asserted the "two natures and one person" of Christ, but led to increasing debate over how, precisely, this dual unity played out in Christ's physical, moral, and incarnate person. At heart was the necessity of Christ's similarity to humanity—an essential component of the divine economy of salvation—and the preservation of his divinity. If Christ were too divine, he could not be said to have fully taken up—and, thus, saved—humanity. Were he too human, his efficacy as the divine Son of God on earth might be hampered. Athanasius had confronted diametrically opposed positions regarding the degree to which Christ's human person was imbued with divinity, and the circumcision—a sign of human frailty on Christ's flesh—allowed him to articulate a paradoxical theological position. More than a century later, the debate over Christ's humanness once again dwindled down to a minute consideration of Christ's body.

In the early sixth century, a party of Christians who insisted on the abundance of divinity in Christ's earthly incarnation began to consider whether Christ's flesh—like ours—could be subject to corruption. This embrace of so-called *aphtharsia* (to its opponents: aphthartodocetism, all too reminiscent of the docetic heresy of the Marcionites, Gnostics, and Manicheans) split apart the already scrambling opponents of the Council of Chalcedon throughout the sixth century. As political and theological fissures broke apart the churches of the eastern Roman Empire, two bishops in and out of exile, former allies who rejected the two-nature Christology of Chalcedon, broke over their understanding of Christ's human nature. Julian of Halicarnassus and Severus of Antioch had met in Constantinople and again in exile in Egypt in the early sixth century. Later, inspired (as he claimed) by Severus's own careful articulation of the hypostatic union of God and man, Julian proposed that Christ's body was *aphthartos*, "incorruptible," because of the power of the divine nature.[84]

Severus found this doctrine both blasphemous and distracting in the larger quest to resist the christological errors of Chalcedon. His irritation against these "phantasiasts" (φαντασιασταί) is evident in a letter written to a certain Caesaria sometime during his long, post-518 exile from his patriarchate. The "phantasiasts," it seems, had invoked Christ's circumcision in defense of their doctrine of Christ's bodily incorruptibility: "They think they are propounding and saying something against which it is impossible to argue: 'If our Lord underwent the circumcision required by the Law, "when," as the gospel says, "eight days were accomplished for circumcising him, and his name was called Jesus," what happened to his foreskin?' "[85] It's difficult to know how the circumcision entered into this argument. The awkward citation of Luke 2:21 against their own theological interests suggests the "phantasiasts" are responding to a rebuttal of their position. A detractor asks, "If Christ's body was incorruptible, how could he be circumcised, as we read in the gospel?" They respond: "If he was circumcised, where is his foreskin?" Such a response sacrifices scriptural integrity for the integrity of Christ's impermeable skin. It is even possible that—unique among readers of Luke 2:21 in antiquity— Severus's opponents understood this gospel passage to mean that, although the time had come for Jesus' circumcision, no circumcision actually took place.[86]

No surprise, then, that Severus—who associates the "phantasiasts" with the docetic and Bible-defacing Manicheans—should begin by falling back on Scripture: not only the gospel account but also Paul's reference to Christ as "minister of circumcision" (Rom 15:8), affirming the "promise to the patriarchs" in Genesis, and asserting his primacy as the "seed of Abraham" (Gal 3:16).[87] Based on these passages, the fact of the circumcision for Severus remains incontrovertible. On the question of the foreskin, however, Severus hedges a bit. The one shouldn't have anything to do with the other, he argues: "Just because nothing is written about the portion of himself that was cut off (I mean the foreskin), we will not therefore refrain from confessing that he was circumcised in reality."[88] What Scripture leaves unspoken, Severus primly scolds, it is best not to guess about.

Whatever happened to that foreskin on earth during Jesus' life, Severus remains confident in its ultimate fate: "When he rose from the dead, he took that also, inasmuch as it is a portion of the whole body, and he preserved it with this without corruption according to ineffable methods which he understands."[89] Severus is certain of this because of his faith in the resurrection: "For we also shall receive our own body complete at the resurrection, not carrying the diminution caused by sores or other injuries, but whole and perfect." The "whole and perfect body" of the resurrection relies, of course, on Christ's salvific assumption of that body: as Athanasius and Cyril of Alexandria both insisted, the corruptibility of the human body was forever transformed by the incarnation.[90] In his assurance of Christ's "whole and perfect body," even retrieving from its mysterious hiding place its temporarily forfeited foreskin, Severus inclines toward precisely the same desire for bodily wholeness and perfection that—we presume—led the followers of Julian of Halicarnassus to insist upon Christ's earthly incorruptibility as well.

To be sure, Severus insists as Julian never would on Christ's earthly sufferings, among which he pairs the crucifixion and the circumcision. Even these moments of paradigmatic disintegration of the flesh, however, are infused with the aphthartodocetic desire for wholeness, perfection, and bodily integrity. Severus draws an analogy between the purificatory operations of Christ's crucified body, citing John Chrysostom, and his circumcised body:

> "But why is he slaughtered at the height of the tree, and not under a roof? In order to purify the nature of the air, therefore, it is done high up, without a roof above him, but heaven. For the air was purified by the sheep being sacrificed high up. But the earth also was purified; for the blood dropped from the rib upon it."[91] Accordingly therefore, if on this analogy the foreskin that was cut off touched the earth, it assuredly also sanctified it, and by methods which he himself understands who was voluntarily circumcised, he assuredly, as I said before, preserved it; and at the time of the Resurrection he rose with the whole body complete and without corruption, having this portion also undiminished.

The parallel between the crucifixion and circumcision is not unique to Severus,[92] but the logic here is particular to his argument against—and appropriation of—the carnal theology of the aphthartodocetists: both circumcision and crucifixion are marked, for Severus, by the paradoxical linkage of human suffering and divine redemption. The foreskin, like Christ's crucified flesh, must drip with a blood that impossibly purifies the ground of corruption.[93] The very human (and corrupt) bloodiness of Christ's suffering upon contact with the atmosphere is immediately transformed—and transforms—into something else altogether: incorruptible sanctification.

Both Severus and Julian were seeking ways to reduce the distance between Christ's (and humanity's) suffering and the incorruptible nature of the divine. Chalcedonian Christology did not insist sufficiently upon the divinity of Christ incarnate. Julian's theological instincts led him to a firm boundary marked out by Christ's body, to an ultimate rejection of the human and the affirmation of the sanctifying incorruptibility of the divine. Severus's comparable desires led him not to rejection, but abjection: the bloody human flesh of circumcision (and crucifixion) expelled yet held close. Christ's most vulnerable—and discarded—piece of flesh rises with him in incorruptibility. The heretical impulses of Julianist Christology are never outside Severus's own contemplation of Christ's body: they form the inner boundary of an impossible orthodoxy.

Christ the Ascetic

Closely related to these ancient christological concerns were rising anxieties over asceticism modeled on the physical person of Christ; in these ascetic debates, too, we find the circumcision limning the abject space of divinized humanity (or humanized divinity). From early on in the emergence of a distinctly Christian form of *askēsis*, the particular practices of renunciation were viewed (in part) as an attempt at *imitatio Christi*, and Christ's own earthly actions were scrutinized for guidelines. Christ's human life modeled a path to human divination. Yet while some Christians promoted ascetic virtue as the physical path to spiritual excellence, others feared that extreme asceticism suggested a fundamental mistrust of the goodness of God's creation, and, ironically, a rejection of the physical reality of Christ's incarnation. At issue, once again, is the degree to which Christ's humanity can be acknowledged and appropriated in Christian theory and practice. And, once again, the circumcision signals a series of partial disavowals.

Amphilochius of Iconium, Gregory of Nazianzus's cousin and a strong proponent of Nicene orthodoxy in the later fourth century,[94] more than once found himself targeting Christians who (he claimed) negated all fleshly existence in an attempt to live "as angels." His treatise conventionally titled *Against the Heretics* is directed against an overly zealous ascetic group (perhaps the Messalians)[95] that preached, among other points, vegetarianism and the abandonment of family ties. Based on Amphilochius's own rebuttal, it is likely that this group claimed—as part of their ascetic philosophy—the example of Christ's simple life on earth, in rejection of family and glory.[96] Amphilochius also saw distinctly christological implications in their ascetic rejection of human life. According to Amphilochius, all of Jesus' human activity, from birth and circumcision to death, occurred "so he might fully convince everyone that he had really assumed humanity, and that he was not a mere appearance (δοκήσει), and did not come as a phantom (φαντασίᾳ) on this earth."[97] By claiming the banner of imitatio Christi, and by rejecting their own humanity, Amphilochius's opponents (he suggests) are no better than docetic heretics.

Amphilochius's argument is not only christological but scriptural, as well.[98] For much of this treatise, Amphilochius focuses on the negative repercussions of his opponents' ascetic abstention from food, which is part of God's created order. To prove his point he lifts citations from the Old Testament, and the "holy patriarchs," and then turns to the New Testament: "Now these things come from the Old Testament: but let us show them also from the

Gospels themselves, that Christ and the apostles also partook of food and did not prevent eating. First Christ was born from the ever-virgin Mary, and he was circumcised on the eighth day according to the law of Moses, and reared by Joseph and the Blessed Virgin Mary; and he was present at the Temple of God as often as the Law proclaimed, until he reached thirty years old: for it was not possible for him not to go up there each year for the festival of the eating of the Pascha."[99] We might ask why Amphilochius not only refers to Christ's eating of meat at the annual Passover feast in Jerusalem but also throws in references to his birth from "ever-virgin Mary," his rearing by Joseph and Mary, and his circumcision on the eighth day. On the one hand, we could infer that, by itself, a reference to Christ eating paschal lambs might be dismissed by Amphilochius's opponents as mere condescension to the times, a contingent activity not binding on those seeking to imitate his sanctity. By incorporating Christ's birth from Mary ("ever-virgin": Amphilochius is no enemy of asceticism properly framed), Amphilochius expands Christ's carnivorousness into a broader approbation of human existence within the created order. The image of the loving "holy family" models the affective bond between parents and children against asceticizing heretics seeking to disrupt the social order of this world. The introduction of Christ's circumcision expands Christ's example even more broadly, emphasizing not only Christ's truly human birth, and his attention to his fleshly family, but also the continuity of the "Law of Moses" and ascetic imitatio Christi that structures the entire treatise. Christianity cannot, Amphilochius argues, operate through rejection of the Law or the body or humanity. Like Christ, Christianity must somehow ingest the meat of the Law, and thereby affirm the human body.[100]

To call humanity an abject sign in Amphilochius's treatise may seem unwarranted: surely, if anything, Amphilochius celebrates the humanity of Christ in his rebuke of overzealous asceticism. Yet I suggest Amphilochius's very fulsome praise of humanity signals its otherwise abject quality in Christian ascetic discourse. Witness the extremes to which Amphilochius goes in his argument. It is not enough for Christ to eat meat, he must eat the meat of sacrifices—every year, for thirty years—at the Jewish Temple. It is not enough for Christ to demonstrate his approval of family and worldly life by partaking in "family time," he must even be circumcised as an infant to prove the value of the human body and human social relations. In order to shame ascetic "extremists" who reject their own humanity, Amphilochius not only humanizes Christ but places this paradigmatic object of ascetic imitation firmly within the heart of Jewish ritual and religious otherness.

It goes without saying, perhaps, that Amphilochius was *not* trying to convince Christians—ascetic or otherwise—to start circumcising their sons, or make annual pilgrimage to the ruins of the Jerusalem Temple. Rather, Amphilochius renders Christ's humanity in all of its particularity and full-bloodedness: his is not just generic "flesh" but embedded humanity. To imitate Christ, then, should be to imitate his full humanity—meat-eating, family-loving, Law-abiding—as well. Humanity is not only recuperated from ascetical rejection, its particularity is elevated to impossible heights. Ultimately, paradoxically, Christ's own humanity—glutted with sacrificial meat, pared down by the alien rite of circumcision—is potentially estranged from the Christians who seek to imitate him, those Christians who are the target of Amphilochius's treatise. The incongruous sign of Jesus' circumcision, among the other signs of human particularity, make vivid—abject—the shock of Christ's humanity. In so ostentatiously countering the antisocial claims of the heretics, then, Amphilochius perhaps ends up conceding value to them.

Even as Amphilochius in the East could exuberantly proffer Christ's human existence to curb what he viewed as ascetic overenthusiasm, western debates on the ascetic life could call Christ's body to testify for the opposite position. One late fourth-century debate over ascetic zeal in the city of Rome shows how anxiety over the intersection of divine spirit and human flesh might spill over into various heresiological concerns—scriptural, ascetic, and christological—and how the divine circumcision could play an unexpected role in the process. Jovinian, an Italian monk, had written a treatise defending the equal merits of married and ascetic Christians.[101] Jovinian's attempt to rein in what he saw as overly fervent (and, possibly, Manichean)[102] ascetic theologies drew down the wrath of various Latin fathers, including Jerome, who inserted himself into the controversy all the way from his monastic perch in Bethlehem.[103] Jerome's response is particularly interesting for my purposes, as his defense of ascetic merit against the "heretic" Jovinian makes Christ himself into the masterful heresiologist, appropriating the theological alterity of his opponents as a model for his Christian imitators.[104]

Jovinian, like his eastern contemporary Amphilochius, feared that the ascetic excesses of his fellow Christians drifted too close to the errors of heretics: Marcionite rejection of the heroes of the Old Testament (who married, ate meat, and reproduced rather frequently and freely); Gnostic abhorrence of the material cosmos (created by God the Father through his Son); and Manichean preaching of an ascetic elitism of "elect" set apart from the less favored masses. Jovinian was not against asceticism, but sought to modulate the overzealous fashions of Egyptian and Syrian asceticism making a splash in Rome. For Jovinian, asceticism should draw equally from the continuity of Scriptures and the duality of Christ: Law and the flesh must be acknowledged, incorporated, and drawn into the proper Christian life, not set aside or rejected.

Among his several arguments, Jovinian invoked Scripture and nature in his defense of a moderate ascetic theology. Jovinian cited Christ's presence at the wedding at Cana (John 2) to argue that the savior, like the Old Testament patriarchs, must have approved of the institution of marriage since he blessed it with his presence. Elsewhere, Jovinian gestured to the human body itself as evidence, saying (according to Jerome), "And why were genitals created, and why were we made in this way by our most wise creator, such that we suffer such burning desire for each other, and we delight in this natural coupling?" In his blistering response to Jovinian, Jerome rejected these tepid attempts to embrace the goodness of creation and the exemplarity of the patriarchs. Jerome does not desire the rough rejection of the Manicheans, nor the pallid compromise of Jovinian, but rather delights in the open-ended friction of abjection: where Law and flesh appear on Christ's body, they must paradoxically and abjectly resignify. In response to Jovinian's scriptural and anatomical points, Jerome sees fit to reimagine the paradigmatic example of Christ, modulated through the uncanny sign of Christ's circumcision.

On the point of our physical nature, Jerome holds up the naked, anatomically correct body of Christ as his ascetic exemplar, perhaps in an effort to rhetorically shame Jovinian:[105]

> Our Lord and Savior, who, although he was in the form of God, lowered himself to assume the form of a slave, having been made obedient to his Father even unto death, a death on the cross, why was it necessary that he should be born into these body parts which he did not use? Indeed, he who was circumcised so that he could demonstrate his sex (*qui certe ut sexum ostenderet etiam circumcisus est*). Why did he castrate[106] John the apostle and the baptist with desire, whom he caused to be born as men? We therefore who believe in Christ, we follow his example! And if we knew him in the flesh (*iuxta carnem*), let us now not know him according to the flesh (*secundum carnem*).[107]

The invocation of Christ's body in response to Jovinian's argument "from nature" is, it must be said, ingenious. Jovinian had evoked generic flesh, the generic male body (that of himself or his reader). Christ was of course also "fully human" in form and substance, therefore his male body could answer Jovinian's "immodest" query even better than Jerome's own imperfect ascetic flesh.

Yet even as it is fully and paradigmatically human, Christ's body contains opposition and contradiction: living *iuxta carnem* but not *secundum carnem*, never rejecting the human body (Jerome is no Manichean or docetic), but also not accepting the corruptibility of everyday flesh. Christ embodies abjection, the liminal and paradoxical state within which the ascetic must find his exemplar. Why was Christ circumcised? To demonstrate the reality of his sex, and to model for his followers the willing "castration" of that sex: to model, for ascetics like Jerome, the renunciation of sex through an unambiguous sign of male sexuality (an operation on the genitals). Christ's appropriation of this sign serves for its inversion: sex and sexuality, through the hyperreal body of Jesus, connote their opposites.[108]

Jerome clearly found Christ's circumcision a congenial bodily sign through which to imagine the mimetic abjection of ascetic flesh. Later in the treatise, Jerome again raises Christ's circumcision in response to Jovinian's scriptural argument from the wedding at Cana. After invoking his own silent, scriptural witnesses in favor of virginity—the virgins of Matthew 25 and Revelation 14—Jerome turns to Jovinian's exegesis of John 2: "I shall respond to this most briefly: just as he who was circumcised on the eighth day, and for whom a pair of turtledoves and two young doves were offered as a purification sacrifice . . . sanctioned Jewish custom (*iudaicam consuetudinem*) so that he would not seem to ascribe to them just cause to have him killed as one who destroyed the Law and condemned nature; just so this too was for us. He who came once to a wedding taught that you should be married only once. For at that time it was possible to hinder virginity, if we did not place marriage after virginity, and chaste widowhood in the third rank."[109] Christ's presence at the wedding is revealed as a cunning stratagem, the only possible way to introduce the preferability of the virginal state to a population not yet ready for this higher calling. Indeed, Christ was modeling restraint by his selective matrimonial attendance: inasmuch as one marriage is preferred by Christ's attendance at only one wedding, how much more should *no* marriages be praised, Jerome suggests.

The introduction of the divine circumcision as an analogous stratagem is revealing: for Jesus allowed himself to be circumcised (and sacrifices offered on his behalf) not in order to show approval of Judaism but rather to forestall the inevitable criticism of the Jews. To defeat the Jews, he appropriates the sign of their religious particularity, rendering them inert.[110] To forestall the antiascetic heretics of the first century (and the fourth), he attends a wedding, shrewdly seeming to bless the matrimonial state, but working toward a higher sanctity.

Amphilochius and Jovinian (it seemed) tried to temper the shock of Christ's full-blooded humanity by embracing and accepting it: heretics, they argued, did not appreciate the miracle of Christ's incarnation, and so foolishly—even diabolically—rejected it. As defenders of moderate ascetic bodies against heretical assault, however, Amphilochius and Jovinian were not particularly successful. Amphilochius's treatise was lost in a sea of Greek writings from Cappadocia, briefly revived in heretical debates of the sixth century, and otherwise lost to semiobscurity. Jovinian—an educated, mainstream Roman Christian, from all we can tell—found himself at the center of attacks from multiple sides. Jerome's attack came from the furthest distance, and carried the most punch.

The human body, it seemed, could be neither simply accepted (as Amphilochius and Jovinian proposed) nor rejected (as the Manicheans and aphthartodocetists taught). It is a problem that cannot be resolved, but must hover at the borders of ascetic selfhood: it is, in other words, abject. Jerome in his later life was notable for his dogged insistence on the perdurance of sexual identity in the resurrection,[111] as Caroline Walker Bynum and others have noted.[112] Often Jerome's intransigence on this subject is viewed as a problem (resolved by more agile minds, such as Augustine's): the proponent of transformative asceticism so fears "change" that he lugs gender hierarchy with him even into the afterlife.[113] Yet Christ's abject body suggests a more subtle model for understanding the body's inevitable gender. Its masculinity was true and intact, yet signified otherwise; so too the ascetic Christian could aspire to a Christlike body that could signify in multiple, even contradictory ways.

That these concerns over flesh and humanity and Scripture and law should become so clearly illumined in debates over asceticism, the aspirational imitation of Christ's impossible humanity, points us to a broader conception of the logic of Christian orthodoxy. Christ models for Jerome not just the triumph over the body but the triumph over heresy: Christ repeatedly absorbs the "otherness" of his opponents, disarming their criticisms, even as he absolutely inverts the signs of their identities. He models this triumphant absorption of theological otherness even in infancy, ordaining his own circumcision; faithful Christians like Jerome thus learn to imitate Christ not in the circumcision of their genitals, but in the strategic manner of confronting, defeating, and appropriating the alterity of heretical opponents. Orthodoxy for Christians such as Athanasius, Jerome, and Tertullian is not about rejection, but abjection. In this sense, the heretic himself is the abject figure of Christian identity: the inner constitutive border of religious self that enables that self's very existence.

Abject Theology

One of the few modern Christian theologians to engage actively, and repeatedly, with Christ's circumcision is Graham Ward, one of the fathers of the Radical Orthodoxy movement.[114] In a series of essays, some of which are excerpted in his 2005 collection *Christ and Culture*, Ward figures Christ's circumcision as part of an all-encompassing theology of displacement. Christ's body assumes a mark of undeniable particularity—both male and Jewish—but also reconfigures that mark through his everpresent divinity:[115] "the explicit displacements of his own physical body"[116] render obscure—perhaps even moot—Christ's otherwise overdetermined physicality (male, Jewish, and so forth). The ultimate disappearance of that body in the ascension, leaving the communion of believers as Christ's "body," completes the circuit of displacement: "The body of the gendered Jew expands to embrace the whole of creation."[117] Ward argues that feminist theologians who express concern at the intersection of male divinity and patriarchy "fail to discern the nature of corporeality in Christ."[118] By taking on gender, Jesus transcends gender (and, we presume, the specificity of Judaism as well),[119] and so does Christian theology: "The body of Jesus Christ, the body of God, is permeable, transcorporeal, transpositional. Within it all other bodies are situated and given their significance. We are all permeable, transcorporeal and transpositional."[120]

I find Ward's arguments interesting precisely for the points at which they extend our ancient theologies of the divine circumcision into a postmodern register. For Ward, Christ's human body (which is also a scriptural body) is a paradox: divine through mortality, "multigendered" through masculinity, universal through Jewish birth, circumcision, and naming. It is also "all-compassing," both rejecting and absorbing the "failure" of feminist theological criticism (which, as Virginia Burrus astutely points out, takes for Ward the role of ancient christological heresy).[121] Ward answers but internalizes the problems of Christ's gender; his (Jesus') masculinity is neither an object of rejection—as it is for Ward's feminists—nor a subject of identification—as it might be for those feminists' theological opponents: it is abject, "hover[ing] at the border of the subject's identity, threatening dissolution."[122] Orthodox

Christology does not resolve these threats, it incorporates them: this, for Ward as for Athanasius, is the power of orthodoxy.

It is also, as we have seen in our ancient authors, the danger of orthodoxy: its "threat of dissolution." In her trenchant engagement with Graham Ward, Virginia Burrus notes that "Ward seems to fear, as the ancient fathers also feared, that without the threat of heresy theologians have nothing to say."[123] Abjection energizes, and enervates, the fragile subject with the internalized threat of otherness: orthodoxy is animated by the heretic, which it must constantly repudiate, replicate, and finally absorb as the difference that hovers within. Triumph and failure, pleasure and horror, attend to the scene of abjection: so, too, they haunt the orthodox confrontation with, and existence through, heresy.

Whether the psychosocial specter of abjection must continue to haunt Christian theology at the site of Christ's scriptural and material configuration takes us beyond the concerns of this book. It may be, as Burrus has suggested elsewhere, that an embrace of strains of humiliation and shame also intertwined with ancient Christian thought may create a sufficient antidote to the oppositional discourse of orthodoxy that exists on the abject border of heresy.[124] What is clear from the ancient Christian thinkers examined here is that, even as the circumcision of Christ created an opportunity for certain Christians to promote a dominant orthodoxy that identified, decried, and ultimately internalized the "otherness" of its opponents, it also made clear the limits of such a discourse of orthodoxy. Christ's own bodily inscription of otherness modeled both the triumphant absorption of the other—as Jerome would have it—but also the threatening and ineradicable presence of that other, as the christological fears of Nestorius articulate. These intertwined discourses of heresy and orthodoxy, it would seem, will always signal their own discontinuity and rupture. The divine circumcision marks out this site of theological abjection.

Chapter 4

Dubious Difference
Epiphanius on the Jewish Christians

> Fixity of identity is only sought in situations of instability and dis-
> ruption, of conflict and change.
> —Robert J. C. Young

What Does Jewish Christianity Do?

At the nexus of Judaism and heresy lies "Jewish Christianity," a concept that
signals the myriad ways that orthodoxy imagines religious truth might mean-
der into a dangerous intermediary terrain: a space of otherness that is Judaized,
but not quite Jewish. The term "Jewish Christian" itself does not exist among
ancient Christians,[1] functioning rather (in Daniel Boyarin's formulation) as a
"term of art in a modernist heresiology."[2] This modernist term covers a vast
and impossible terrain, like the endless stretches of dragon-infested ocean on
the edges of a medieval map. After listing roughly eight ways in which modern
scholars deploy "Jewish Christianity," Karen King remarks: "These items refer
variously to ethnicity, religious beliefs or practices, historical events, sectarian
groups, and literary or hermeneutical practices, making 'Jewish-Christianity'
a particularly exasperating case of classificatory imprecision."[3] For all of its
imprecision, however, "Jewish Christianity" and related "terms of art" litter
the historiographic tracks of recent early Christian (and, to a lesser extent,
ancient Jewish) studies.[4]

The term has primarily been used by modern scholarship to interrogate
the so-called Parting of the Ways, the moment (or moments) at which the
sibling religions of Judaism and Christianity became mutually exclusive.[5]

Jewish Christians in this reading are those persons who refused to take either path but continued to claim a predifferentiated religious identity. Sometimes they are "ethnic Jews" seeking to fold a messianic Jesus into their "traditional" religious lives; at other times they are gentile Christians wishing to imbue their new faith with a requisite antiquity, or even exoticism.[6] These Jewish Christians lurk, like obstinate religious anachronisms, on the margins of a burgeoning orthodox Christianity that has rejected the performance of the Law and comprises mostly gentile converts. As in the case of many ancient heresies treated in modern scholarship,[7] the Jewish Christians are sometimes colored with a nostalgic, even romantic hue because they suggest forgotten apostolic and messianic origins. Peter Tomson writes: "What we need is a paradigm that fully integrates the Jewish and Jewish-Christian practice and beliefs of Jesus and his disciples. On that view, the subsequent anti-Jewish affirmation of Gentile Christianity would imply an inner conflict with the Jewish foundations of its own tradition. Conversely, Judaeo-Christianity, though being anathematised, would have been carrying on an authentic element of Christianity."[8] The figure of Jesus (and, to a lesser extent, his original disciples) endows subsequent "Judaeo Christians" with an "element" of "authenticity" that is clearly privileged over the "conflicted" and unfairly anathematizing gentile Christians.

For scholars less nostalgically inclined, Jewish Christians are more like fossils in the early Christian record, whose presence, once properly excavated, can help us more finely appreciate the development of all branches of Christianity.[9] Taking seriously the taxonomy of ancient Christian heresiographers, modern intellectual excavators piece together the literary remains of such exotic "missing links" as Nazarenes, Nazoreans, Elchesaites, Ebionites, and the like to reproduce a system of thoughts, beliefs, and practices that can stand alongside other "lost Christianities."[10] In lieu of skeletons we reconstruct literatures, "Jewish-Christian gospels," only occasionally supported with speculative archaeological remains;[11] these texts provide a foil to better understand the gentile, de-Judaized Christianity that became normative. To choose a more colorful metaphor: the multifaceted and antique stratum of Jewish Christianity becomes a primeval prism, out of which flow the myriad colors of ancient Christian orthodoxy and heresy.

More recently, however, students of ancient religion of a more skeptical stripe have attended to the role of Jewish Christianity in the construction of religious boundaries and identities, eschewing recovery for rhetoric.[12] Studies of early modern science and empire have shown the crucial role that classificatory systems play in the production of political knowledge and power. Central to such systemic projects are those interstitial figures between the straight taxonomic lines: the mixtures, the mongrels, the hybrids.[13] In *Border Lines*, Daniel Boyarin argued that ancient Christians constructed a hybrid Jewish Christianity in order to distill by contrast pure religious categories and, further, to form part of the epistemic production of the very category of "religion";[14] these hybrid heresies embody "the difference that enables unity itself."[15] In this way, Boyarin reverses the heresiological stream: purity and unity do not precede, but rather flow out of, the construction of a *Mischlinge*, a purposeful "mixture" the function of which is to create religious boundaries. Jewish Christians play a key role in this border patrol: "The Ebionites and Nazoreans, in my reading, function much as the mythical 'trickster' figures of many religions, in that precisely by transgressing borders that the culture establishes, they reify those boundaries."[16] Taking my cue from Boyarin, in this chapter I also focus on the traces of religious hybridity embedded in the newly bounded "religion" of Christianity. As we have already seen, the particular modes by which the Roman Empire managed and controlled difference resulted in a productive, yet disruptive, hybridity within the imperial self. In contrast to the prismatic reading of Jewish Christianity that characterizes earlier studies, teasing out "original" trajectories that have blurred together, I pursue a more specular model: heresiology as a strange mirror, in which the hybridity that makes Jewish Christianity heretical is reflected back and internalized in the production of Christian truth.

Students of Jewish Christianity can gain much insight from theoretical discussions of hybridity.[17] Theorist Robert Young has pointed out that "the need for organic metaphors of identity or society implies a counter-sense of fragmentation and dispersion."[18] The very process of confronting and defeating the "hybrid" necessarily acknowledges the danger of fragmentation and reveals the illusion of purity and containment. I do not mean, by this, that "real" hybrids threaten "really" pure societies or identities: rather, the *construction* of a theoretical "hybrid" who stalks the boundaries of a theoretically pure society or identity reveals the inherently destabilizing processes of any totalizing discourse of self. "Whiteness" is constructed in fear of the "mixed race" in such a manner that "whiteness" itself is revealed to be a teetering illusion. Hybrids are not discovered but rather invented; they do not prove the truth of pure, prehybridized selves, but rather concoct them (and reveal their fictiveness). As I noted in Chapter 2, Young sees culture (or orthodoxy in this case) as participating in a "conflictual economy" that embodies "tension between sameness and difference, unity and diversity, cohesion and dispersion, containment and subversion."[19] For early Christians, the "tensions between sameness and difference," between "Jew" and "Christian," are lodged in this hybrid Jewish Christianity, projected outward but never quite dislodged from the heart of the Christian self.

The Ebionites and Epiphanius

Of the various Jewish-Christian sects scholars purport to extract from the heresiological record, the Ebionites hold a particular pride of place:[20] they are mentioned in multiple ancient sources, from Irenaeus in the second century well into the more stable heresiological lists of the fifth century, and figure prominently in the project of defining orthodoxy throughout late antiquity.[21] For their heresiological utility, they are matched only by the Manicheans and gnostics. They articulate multiple Christian boundaries: scriptural (Irenaeus chastises them for reading only one gospel);[22] theological (according to Tertullian, they deny the divinity of the Son);[23] and ritual (they insist on observing the Jewish Passover, the Saturday Sabbath, dietary laws, and, naturally, circumcision). Origen complains in the second book of his response to Celsus, the pagan detractor who chastised Christians for abandoning the traditional Law of the Jews: "[Celsus] has not noticed this, that those from among them [i.e., the Jews] who believe in Jesus have not abandoned their paternal Law. For they live according to it, being named (ἐπώνυμοι) after the poverty of the Law which they have accepted. For 'the poor' is called 'Ebion' among the Jews, and those from the Jews who have received Jesus as Christ are styled as Ebionites.' "[24] For Origen, as for so many ancient and modern students of the Ebionites, the continued observance of the Law signals the bright line between the orthodox Christian and the heretical Jewish Christian.[25]

Among such observances, of course, we find circumcision. Irenaeus, the first extant author to refer to the Ebionites by name, conflates their scriptural and ritual oddity. Not only do they restrict themselves to Matthew's gospel, but they interpret the "prophets in a somewhat singular manner: they practice circumcision, preserve the observance of those customs which are enjoined by the Law, and are so Jewish in their manner of life that they even adore Jerusalem as if it were the house of God."[26] When Tertullian surveys a cloud of second-century heresies in his *Prescription Against Heretics*, he remarks that, when Paul "inveighed against those keeping and observing circumcision and the Law, this was Ebion's heresy."[27] It is often the unpalatable Jewishness of the Law that makes Ebionite heresy so grotesque to the orthodox. In a homily on Abraham's circumcision, Origen easily conflates Jewish and Ebionite error on this score: "For not only are fleshly Jews concerning the circumcision of the flesh (*carnales Iudaei de circumcisione carnis*) to be refuted by us, but also some of those who seem to have taken up Christ's name but nevertheless think that fleshly circumcision (*carnalem circumcisionem*) should be received, as the Ebionites and anyone else who strays with them by a similar poverty of understanding."[28] Here the Ebionites become something like "intellectual Jews," complementing the "fleshly Jews" who must be refuted. Yet their intellectual communion with "fleshly Jews" is signaled by the Ebionites' assumption of a bodily, fleshly mark: circumcision. Ebionite heresy, for all of its various theological permutations, is visible primarily in flesh, in a practice that inappropriately puts Christians in a Jewish skin.

One of the Ebionites' most fulsome detractors is Epiphanius of Cyprus, who is also the only writer to link Ebionite circumcision explicitly with the circumcision of Jesus.[29] In the late 370s, drawing on his earlier theological treatise, the *Ancoratus*,[30] Epiphanius produced an elaborate and compendious *Panarion* (*Medicine-Chest*) against heresies.[31] "Heresy" in early Christianity, as we have seen in Chapter 3, produces a fractured orthodoxy, in which difference is continuously expelled and reappropriated. Epiphanius's long heresiography totalizes this process of abjection: history, geography, and religion are all distorted yet comprehended underneath Epiphanius's knowing gaze.[32] Indeed, for Epiphanius error is coterminous with truth, and so heresy must stretch to the beginning of human history and the ends of the earth: twenty heresies (including the four "mother heresies" of barbarism, Scythianism, Hellenism, and Judaism [see Col 3:11]) predate Christ's incarnation, and sixty have emerged since then. All of them are knowable, containable, and refutable within the scheme of Christian truth: Epiphanius's treatise, in fact, offers "remedies" for each denominated erroneous poison.

Epiphanius inveighs with typical venom against three sects that "nullify the New Testament" truth with the "old religion" of Judaism.[33] Epiphanius finds the Ebionites especially odious.[34] In fact, the chapter against the Ebionites is one of the longest in the *Panarion*; it is twice the length of the two chapters against Cerinthians and Nazoreans (the other two Jewish-Christian heresies) combined.[35] Epiphanius draws on earlier writings against the Ebionites, especially Irenaeus, but also claims firsthand knowledge of Ebionite texts and customs, and incorporates a great deal of "original" material.[36]

Throughout the chapter Epiphanius harps on the abhorrent mingling and mixing of the Ebionites. Their founder, Ebion, was a "many-shaped monstrosity" (πολύμορφον τεράστιον):[37] "If someone should assemble for himself an adornment out of different precious stones and an ensemble of muticolored garments and doll himself up conspicuously, just so even this one perversely, taking every doctrine whatsoever—fearsome, destructive, repulsive, misshapen and unlikely, full of contention, from each and every heresy—patterned himself after all of them. For he has the Samaritans' repulsiveness but the Jews' name, the viewpoint of the Ossaeans, Nazoraeans, and Nasaraeans, the image of the Cerinthians, and the evil manner of the Carpocratians. And he has the Christians' name alone."[38] A melting pot of heretical nonsense, lacking coherence or even good taste, the Ebionites offend by their senseless refusal to be either correctly Jewish or piously Christian, while claiming to embody both Judaism and Christianity. Their handling of Christ's circumcision, as we shall see, typifies their monstrous and diabolical error.

For Epiphanius, the Ebionite attempt to stand "midway" between Judaism and Christianity renders them "null."[39] Their pretensions at fulfilling both religions are a mockery, a monstrosity; every attempt to draw on Jewish or Christian religious identity just demonstrates their founder's "poverty of understanding."[40] Epiphanius makes a pun on the name of the sect's founder, Ebion. Indeed, Epiphanius is one of the few Greek Christian sources to insist that the group took its name from an individual, and not from a custom of communal poverty or (in more heresiological vein) "impoverished" faith and intellect.[41] Epiphanius scolds the Ebionites: "Their boastful claim, if you please, is that they are poor because they sold their possessions in the apostles' time and laid them at the apostles' feet [cf. Acts 4:34–35]; and thus, they say, they are called 'poor' by everyone. But there is no truth to this claim of theirs either; he really was named Ebion."[42] Epiphanius's insistence on the eponymous nature of the Ebionites fits his naming pattern throughout the *Panarion*: more often than not, heretics bear the names of their founders, and in this they separate themselves from true Christians, who bear the name of Christ alone. Additionally, Epiphanius here divorces the Ebionites from their claims to authentic Christianity. They claim their "poor" name links them directly to the apostles, suggesting an original purity to their brand of Christianity. Epiphanius knows better.

Epiphanius details the ways that the Ebionites are neither Jewish nor Christian, despite their claims to both traditions.[43] The litany of the Ebionites' defective Christianity is familiar, drawn to a great extent from earlier heresiologists, but in Epiphanius's telling designed to highlight their nonsensical theological eclecticism. For instance, while Ebion preached a predictably "Jewish" Christology—he "determined that Christ was from the seed of a man (ἐκ σπέρματος ἀνδρός), that is, Joseph"—later Ebionites diverged: "his partisans, as though turning their own mind to something incoherent and impossible, recount different things from each other about Christ."[44] Absorbing the influence (as Epiphanius guesses) of the Elchesaites, some say he was the "first man," others "a spirit" who has come many times, or perhaps only once, when Jesus was baptized. Epiphanius sneers, "Great is the dizziness among them from the different suppositions made about him in different times and places."[45] Sometimes Christ is a "mere man" (ἄνθρωπον ψιλόν),[46] sometimes he is a "manlike pattern (ἀνδροείκελον ἐκτύπωμα) invisible to human eyes, ninety-six miles tall."[47] Modern students of Jewish Christianity carefully parse Epiphanius's multiple sources—were Ebionites primitive Christian Jews, or sophisticated Jewish gnostics?[48]—but for Epiphanius the insolubility of their confusion and contradiction is the point.

The Ebionites' New Testament is similarly mutilated and misunderstood: they read only a "Hebrew Gospel," which is probably nothing but a bad translation of the Gospel of Matthew,[49] "adulerated and mutilated,"[50] "falsified,"[51] and "counterfeit."[52] In all his twisted translation and interpretation, "Ebion makes himself manifest in many forms, as a kind of monstrosity as I have shown."[53] Naturally Ebionites also mangle central Christian rituals, often pointing to their butchered or fantastic Scriptures for support: multiple baptisms, rejection of celibacy,[54] vegetarianism,[55] annual Eucharists celebrated with "unleavened bread" and "water only."[56] In all ways that they claim Christian truth, in belief and text and practice, they show themselves to be false and twisted: "how many other dreadful and falsified things, things filled with depravity, are observed among them!"[57]

Yet perhaps more noteworthy than Epiphanius's refutation of the Ebionites' Christian error is his insistence on their faulty Judaism. Epiphanius's response to the Jewish claims of the Ebionites, I suggest, is more crucial to his own hybridized orthodox Christianity. Perhaps it is important to note that, throughout this treatise, we have no way of verifying Epiphanius's claims about the Ebionites (or any other heresy, for that matter);[58] as Joseph Verheyden notes, "Several elements [in Epiphanius's chapter] are most probably inaccurate or simply historically incorrect," although he graciously concedes, "this does not make his presentation completely worthless."[59] We do know, however, that Epiphanius focuses on those issues he finds to be the most insidious and in need of "antidote": the particular ways in which Ebionites misapprehend Judaism, therefore, must be those ways that could most easily "infect" and poison Epiphanius's fellow orthodox travelers. That is, in the Jewish heresy of the Ebionites, as portrayed by Epiphanius, we catch a glimpse of Epiphanius's own hybridized, Judaized orthodox desires.

Before coming to the issue of Christ's circumcision, Epiphanius addresses the Ebionites' corrupt appropriation of Jewish Law and Scriptures. He notes that they reject all the prophets who came after Moses and Joshua: "They confess Abraham and Isaac and Jacob, Moses and Aaron, and Joshua son of Nun (but only because he was Moses' successor, but he was not anything). After these they confess none of the prophets, but even anathematize and jeer at David and Solomon, and similarly they set aside Isaiah and Jeremiah, Daniel and Ezekiel, Elijah and Elijah: for they do not heed them, blaspheming their prophecies, but they accept only the Gospel."[60] Epiphanius's criticism seems to be that, in their Christian zeal ("accepting only the Gospel") the Ebionites have deformed their Jewish Scriptures. Perhaps this is why Epiphanius's books of "the prophets" seem to echo the Jewish canonical ordering (the historical and prophetic books together), rather than that of the Christian Septuagint.[61] In addition to mutilating the prophetic books, Epiphanius adds, they do not even "accept Moses' Pentateuch in its entirety," replying (to Christians, or Jews?), "What need is there for me to read what is in the Law, when the Gospel has come?"[62] A strange response from Judaizing Christians, to be sure, and perhaps an even stranger criticism from a heresiologist appalled by the inappropriate admixture of Jewish Law into Christian practice.

But the Ebionites are, it seems, perennially confused in ways that Epiphanius is not. For, despite their strangely de-Judaized Jewish Scriptures, the Ebionites try to pass formally as Jewish, while calling themselves "Christians": "Ebionites have elders and heads of synagogues, and they call their church a synagogue, not a church; they take pride only in Christ's name."[63] They think they are true descendants of the patriarchs and the Law, when in fact they follow a "lame-brained" heretic:[64] "The misguided Ebionites are very unfortunate to have abandoned the testimonies of the prophets and angels and content themselves with the misguided Ebion—who wants to do what he likes, and practice Judaism, even though he is estranged from Jews (ἀπο᾿ Ιουδαίων ἠλλοτριωμένου)."[65] Ebion may try to look like the Jews, but he is, in essence, a "stranger" to them. Epiphanius, however, seems to know Jews and Judaism not like a stranger, but like the most informed insider. In this, we shall see, he is the true follower of Christ.

Ebion's Circumcision, and Christ's

Like so many of the other lamebrained customs and assertions of the Ebionites, their practice of circumcision proves their lack of religious coherence.
Similar to their "adulterated" Scriptures or their "limping" teachings,[66] their
insistence on circumcision becomes emblematic of the mishmash that is Jewish Christianity: "They are proud to possess circumcision and even boast that
this is the seal and the imprint of the patriarchs and the righteous ones who
have conformed to the Law, for which they suppose they are equal to them. Yet
what's more, they wish to derive proof for this from Christ himself, just like
the Cerinthians.[67] According to their silly reasoning they also say, 'It is enough
for the disciple to be as his master [Matt 10:25]. Christ was circumcised; you
be circumcised too!' "[68] The rationale for Ebionite circumcision rests both on
the precedent of Jewish authority—the patriarchs and "the Law"—and the
aspiration of imitatio Christi, the embodiment of Christian faith through the
paradigmatic example of Jesus. They claim Judaism and Christianity at once,
sealed and imprinted in their insistence on the validity of circumcision.

Epiphanius denies the Ebionites their reliance on Jesus as a guarantor of
the Law: not because Christ and the Law are distinct, but precisely because
they are so intimately connected. Epiphanius will not deny the significance of
Christ's circumcision; in fact, he will reclaim it from the heretical interpretation of the Ebionites. Epiphanius had described Ebion as "estranged from
the Jews"; to Christ by contrast, "the Law is not a stranger" (οὐ τὸν νόμον
ἀλλότριον).[69] Indeed, Epiphanius highlights Christ's circumcision against
the Ebionites because it demonstrates the real nature of this "seal and imprint"
among the Jews. Like Ebion, Epiphanius assumes an essential continuity between the circumcision of the righteous patriarchs and that of Christ: the
truth of Judaism is revealed in Christ's circumcision. So we learn that Christ
ordained his own circumcision "to affirm that the circumcision he had given
long ago had served legitimately,"[70] and specifically to confirm his own command that Abraham and his descendants be circumcised.[71] What was Christ
affirming about the patriarchs and their Jewish progeny by taking this sign
upon himself? The Jews' essential ignominy: "The visible circumcision was
instituted because of Abraham's doubt. . . . Because of the doubt that had led
Abraham to say, 'Shall a son be born to him that is a hundred years old?' [Gen
17:17], [God] laid physical circumcision on him and his [kin] to keep them
from forgetting the God of their fathers when enslaved by the idolatrous,

unbelieving Egyptians. They would see their circumcision, be reminded and feel ashamed, and not deny him. And until Christ this remained the case, and because of it he too consented to be circumcised."[72] On the one hand, Epiphanius argues that the Ebionites' ignorance of the true meaning of circumcision makes them like contemporary Jews, who have also been displaying a marked lack of faith and "poverty of understanding" before and after Christ's advent.[73] But this similarity to errant Jews merely makes the Ebionites (like the Jews themselves) bad participants in the old covenant. The fact that so many Jews, along with the circumcising Ebionites, continue to deny the true God is not lost on Epiphanius, or his readers. We begin to sense the utility of crafting "real" Judaism through the lens of Christ's Jewish circumcision: under Christ's peculiar aegis, Epiphanius can construct "real" Judaism entirely along Christian theological lines.

If the Ebionites fatally misunderstand the Jewish Law (just like the Jews!), they also misapprehend the true fulfillment of Jewish prophecy signaled by Christ's circumcision. Here Epiphanius turns not to Abraham, but to Moses, as he explains how Christ's circumcision fulfills a "prophecy" uttered by Moses' wife Zipporah on the road to Egypt.[74] Epiphanius explains, "For in this the saying of the Law was fulfilled, one that had stood until his time, and was abolished and yet brought to fulfillment in him—the words of Zipporah, 'The blood of the circumcision of my child has ceased.' "[75] Zipporah's words (in the Greek version of Exodus) to the "angel who was sent" to attack Moses and was fended off by the prophylactic roadside circumcision are taken here as a prophecy about Christ.[76] When Christ (the promised "child") was circumcised, the "blood of circumcision" ceased forever to flow: the "type" of circumcision was fulfilled and the ritual rendered moot. This "prophecy" places both the "fulfillment" and "abolition" of circumcision in the time of the patriarchs of the Jews. Were the Ebionites truly to follow the "Law and the prophets," the real foundations of Judaism, they would know to abandon ritual practice rather than persist in it.

Later, when Epiphanius discusses the ridiculousness of Ebionite observance of the Sabbath and other Jewish legal niceties, circumcision—and the particular circumcision of Christ—rears its head once more. Epiphanius points out rather smugly that the Sabbath and circumcision have the potential to cancel each other out for a boy born on the Sabbath (here he follows Jesus' example, again, in John 7:19–24): if circumcision is delayed in honor of the Sabbath, then the commandment to circumcise on the eighth day is abrogated; conversely, if circumcision is performed on the correct day, the Sabbath has been violated.[77] Like Zipporah's prophecy, this built-in abrogation of the Law is, according to Epiphanius, deliberate and affirmed by Christ's own circumcision, "prescribed by him in the Law and dissolved and fulfilled by him in the gospel."[78]

We must attend with care to Epiphanius's exegetical logic here: Christ in no way undermines the Jewish foundations of Law and prophecy through his circumcision, but rather affirms their deeper truth. The Law instituted by Christ is inherently self-abrogating, and this is proven by Christ's own observance of that Law: both observance and elimination of the Law must be inherent to the truth of Judaism. Ebion is therefore doubly ludicrous to combine Law and Christ to justify his own circumcision, fundamentally misunderstanding their relationship: Epiphanius quips that the Law of circumcision was "snipped off (περιτμηθείσης) altogether in [Christ] and abolished through him."[79] Epiphanius, unlike that "stranger to the Jews" Ebion, sees the truth of Judaism reflected clearly in the circumcision of Christ.

Like waves that dash in vain against God's natural boundaries, or serpents that devour their own tails, the circumcising Ebionites have "prematurely cut themselves off (ἑαυτούς κατατέμνοντες), and annulled from the beginning the very things of which they boasted."[80] By contrast, Christ's circumcision provides Epiphanius with a sure touchstone of authentic Judaism. The orthodox Christian, who reviles the Jewish religion, can demonstrate superior knowledge of it against the "heretic" who tries to validate its practices. As Daniel Boyarin notes, in discussing the anti-Judaizing rhetoric of Epiphanius's colleague Jerome, "the assertion of the existence of a fully separate-from-Christianity 'orthodox' Judaism functioned for Christian orthodoxy as a guarantee of the Christian's own bounded and coherent identity and thus furthered the project of imperial control."[81] Epiphanius's display of "real" Judaism in refutation of the pseudo-Jewish Ebionites is, in some respects, an ideological tour de force: a demonstration that imperial Christianity can, with ease and agility, control knowledge of that deeply ingrained "other," the Jew.

That Epiphanius must rely on the Jewish truth of Christ's circumcision, however, makes this an ambivalent show of strength, and a contaminated project of categorization and separation. Epiphanius cannot merely "know" the Jewish truth from the vantage point of the well-informed outsider. It is a truth he must internalize, since it is inscribed on the body of his savior. The truth of Christ's circumcision—which, as we have seen, is the "truth" of Judaism—necessarily draws Judaism intimately into Christian discourse, with the result that the orthodoxy produced in response to the blasphemy of the

Ebionites must be an equally hybridized truth. The appropriation of Judaism that led the Ebionites astray, transforming them into nightmarish, polymorphic "monsters," is therefore ironically and craftily reproduced in Epiphanius's own interpretation of the circumcision of Christ.

At one point, Epiphanius gives multiple reasons for Jesus' circumcision: "First, to prove that he had actually taken flesh, because of the Manicheans, and those who say he has [only] appeared in a semblance. Then, to show that the body was not of the same nature as the Godhead, as Apollinarius says, and that he had not brought it down from above, as Valentinus says. Also to confirm the fact that the circumcision he had given long ago served legitimately until his advent, and to deprive the Jews of an excuse: for, if he had not been circumcised, they could have said, 'we could not accept an uncircumcised messiah.' "[82] The first set of reasons looks inward, in anticipation of heretical christological error: varieties of docetism, or disbelief in the "real" body of Christ, and their heretical "opposite," a Christology that proposes a superpresent, even divine Christ-body.[83] The second set of reasons for Christ's circumcision looks outward, in concession to Jewish adherence to the Law: the Jewish Law (as we have seen) is affirmed in its antiquity and legitimacy, and Jews are furthermore provided with a helpful sign to correct their disbelief in the messiah's arrival. Epiphanius reiterates these two categories of explanation for Christ's circumcision later in the chapter, arguing that Jesus was circumcised "to deprive the Jews of their excuse [and] for the refutation of Manicheans and others."[84] That is, Christ in his circumcision initiated an internal discourse of exclusion of heresy at the same time as he opened himself (and his followers) up to the otherness of Judaism. Such intimate interlacing of heresiology and attention to Judaism is neither unique nor surprising.[85] Yet this rejection of heresy and internalization of Judaism are, at least, ironic in a tract written against a Judaizing heresy. The circumcision of Christ, representative first of a bad, inappropriate, and blasphemous (Ebionite) hybrid religious identity, is also being corralled, through an analogous (if not homologous) process into a good, appropriate, and fully orthodox, hybridized religious identity.

These hybrid religious identities are only affirmed and redoubled in one of the most famous sections of *Panarion* 30, Epiphanius's long "digression" on the tale of Count Joseph of Tiberias, a former Jewish functionary in Palestine who, after a series of varied encounters with Christianity, ultimately converts, befriends Constantine the Great, and literally builds up orthodox Christian presence in the holy land.[86] Joseph's own conversion narrative is remarkable enough—as much for his resistance to Christian truth as his eventual championing of it—but perhaps more significant to Epiphanius's larger project of the appropriation and Christianization of true Judaism are the series of other converts and crypto-Christians in Joseph's narrative: Joseph's former employer, the Jewish patriarch Hillel, secretly converts on his deathbed; later an "elder, and scholar of the Law" comes to an ailing Joseph, and "whispers" encouragement that he accept Jesus as Lord (Epiphanius affirms he has heard similar stories himself); and an anonymous ex-Jew mentioned at the beginning of Joseph's story, like Joseph, lives an orthodox life among Arian heretics in Scythopolis.[87] Each of these figures is Christian, but not quite: embodying the truth of Judaism, which is the acceptance of Christianity.

The hybrid nature of Epiphanius's orthodox "antidote" to the Ebionites' confused Jewish Christianity already appears in the care with which he articulates the "real" Judaism that the Ebionites have misapprehended. That this "real" Judaism emerges through Christ—indeed, on his very body—gives Epiphanius the opportunity to comprehend the paradigmatic mark of Jewishness as a sign of Christian truth. We have already seen him argue, for instance, that the true nature of Jewish Law is revealed through the circumcision of Christ and transformed into a symbol of Christian orthodoxy. In other instances Epiphanius similarly identifies a fundamental "truth" of Judaism, misapprehended by the Ebionites, and uses Christ's circumcision to elucidate and internalize this "truth" into Christian orthodoxy.

To take one example, Epiphanius both condemns and then curiously appropriates the gendered nature of Jewish salvation. Epiphanius chastises Ebion for clinging to a sign of salvation (circumcision) that "deprived" women "of the kingdom of heaven."[88] Yet it is precisely through participation in this same masculine ritual that Christ opens the doors of that kingdom to women: "For he came and fulfilled it, and gave us the perfect circumcision of his mysteries—not of one member only, but by sealing the entire body and cutting it off from sin. And not by saving one portion of the people, males alone, but by truly sealing the entire Christian people, men and women both."[89] Christ "fulfills" by participation in the Law, so that the Jewish cutting of his male body enacts the "cutting off" and "sealing" of the entire communal body of Christ, "men and women both." There is, of course, a careful slipperiness here, as Epiphanius elides Christ's *literal* circumcision, performed on his human body, with a broader conception of typological "circumcision," understood already by some in the fourth century as the "seal" of baptism.[90] But this slippage is neither accidental nor merely rhetorical, but rather central to Epiphanius's construction of orthodoxy. The "coming" and the "fulfilling" of this type are located squarely in the physical rite of Christ's own circumcision with the result that only by inscribing an indubitably male, Jewish circumcision on himself can Christ affirm the two-sex seal of Christian baptism. The gender singularity of Jewish circumcision is not abrogated or denied by Jesus; he affirms it, embodies it, and so bestows it on all Christians.

In the same way that the maleness of Judaism is absorbed into a two-sex Christianity, a "Jewish" focus on Jesus' humanity is also internalized into an "orthodox" Christology giving equal weight to Christ's human and divine natures.[91] As we have seen above, some Ebionites understood Christ to be a "mere man," and therefore subject to the Law as they were. Such a misappropriation of the nature of Jewish Law leads the Ebionites astray, producing a defective, heretical Christology. Epiphanius points out the flaw in their logic: if Jesus was a "mere man," how can his acts be taken as divine, and therefore worthy of imitation? After all, Eıpiphanius points out, a "mere man" in his infancy cannot choose to be circumcised: it is something done to him without conscious consent. Epiphanius remarks: "If [Ebion] had said that Christ had come down from heaven as God and been circumcised on the eighth day by Mary, then—since he was God and would be allowing for this by his own consent—this would provide the scum with the argument for circumcision."[92] Ebion cannot use the argument provided by Epiphanius, however, because his faulty reliance on Judaism denies Christ's divinity.

Epiphanius, however, can affirm both Jesus' humanity (as the Jews do) as well as his divinity through Christ's circumcision:

> We say that he has both come from heaven as God and stayed in the Virgin Mary's womb as long as any baby, to take his incarnate humanity in its fullness from the virgin womb, and provide a dispensation in which he was also circumcised—truly, and not in appearance, on the eighth day. "For he came to perfect the Law and prophets, not to destroy them" [cf. Matt 5:17]—not to proclaim the Law as foreign (οὐ τὸν νόμον ἀλλότριον), but given out of himself and remaining in types until him. Thus, the lacks in the Law would be fulfilled in their turn, in him and by him, so that the types, come to spiritual fulfillment, might be preached in truth.[93]

On the one hand, Christ's true humanity emerges through "true" Judaism, that is, it is proven—as even the Ebionites might have argued!—by Christ's submission to Jewish law. Yet by decreeing this Jewish ritual even as an unborn infant in the womb, Christ also shows the glory of his ever-present divinity. Epiphanius, combining the same seemingly incompatible elements as Ebion (Law and Christ, humanity and divinity, Judaism and Christianity), produces a fully orthodox Christology. Where Ebion's hybridized Jewish Christianity fails—indeed, on the same grounds on which it failed—Epiphanius's hybridized orthodoxy succeeds.

Hybrid Orthodoxies

What is noteworthy here is the discursive reversal, the disavowal of the heretic who blurs religious boundaries coupled with a meaningful transgression of those same boundaries in the name of orthodoxy. The uncanny signifier of Christ's circumcision, I suggest, erodes the "partitions" of Judaism and Christianity at the very site of their formation. A reader might argue that Epiphanius was forced to attend so diligently to Christ's circumcision by its inclusion in the gospel account and the attempts of Jewish Christians to exploit it for their own heretical ends. Epiphanius's own hybridizing reversal, then, would be unwitting and provoked. Certainly the scholarly preoccupation with Epiphanius's "sources" suggests that he was, to a great extent, an antiquarian and reactive heresiologist: compiling texts and stories and rumors to be mocked and refuted, but with no creative theological program of his own.[94]

Yet notably the Ebionites never cite the gospel story of Jesus' circumcision, at least according to Epiphanius. Indeed, he spends a great deal of time discussing their "gospel," and notes that it lacks any nativity (which, after all, in the canonical Gospel of Luke also serves to affirm Jesus' divinity): "The beginning of their Gospel is: 'It came to pass in the days of Herod, King of Judaea, that a man, John, came baptizing with the baptism of repentance. . . .'"[95] While we obviously have no reason to trust Epiphanius's description and citations of the "Gospel of the Ebionites" (although scholars, traditionally, have placed great weight on them), we also have no particular reason to believe his description of Ebionite theology. My point here is not to call Epiphanius's trustworthiness into question (an argument that seems patently unnecessary and unhelpful) but rather to point out that the imitation of Christ's circumcision, located so squarely in the *Panarion* among the heretics, may have been a much more free-floating idea in the fourth century than Epiphanius is willing to let on. That is, something more compelling in the circumcision of Christ afforded Epiphanius the opportunity to transform Ebionite blasphemy into Christian orthodoxy.

That orthodox Christians found their Jewish, heretical, and pagan "others" compelling is no surprise: the allure of the other undergirds much of Epiphanius's literary output, and made him a prominent figure of fourth-century Christianity. That the compulsion of the other should lead to such an utter absorption of otherness brings Epiphanius's technology of orthodoxy into alignment with the broader technologies of Empire by which Rome isolated, marginalized, and appropriated the non-Roman within.[96] I do not suggest that Epiphanius set out deliberately to mirror or mimic the Roman logic of empire; rather that, for a figure such as Epiphanius, it seems, strategies of Roman power made sense in the context of Christian orthodox triumphalism. Such a double logic of ancient religious identity—singular and totalizing, yet hybridized and contradictory—emerges in the context of a Roman Empire that produced dominant identity through a "conflictual economy," simultaneously subordinating and absorbing the otherness of the provinces. To cite Young's discussion of hybridity once more: "authority becomes hybridized when placed in a colonial context and finds itself layered against other cultures, very often through the exploitation by the colonized themselves of its evident equivocations and contradictions that are all too apparent in the more hostile and challenging criteria of alien surroundings."[97] Jewish Christianity, in this reading, serves as the strange counterpart of a purely orthodox, imperial operation: the careful articulation, and appropriation, of Jewish "otherness." Indeed, to the extent that Jewish Christians "really" existed in the fourth century (or could be so labeled by their "orthodox" accusers), their attraction to the customs or beliefs of the Jews may be no different in kind from that of the heresiologists themselves, compulsively drawn to articulate a more authentic Judaism and to seize it back from the "heretics." The compelling allure of Judaism at once threatens and enables the articulation of imperial Christianity, producing hybridized religious identities—orthodox and heretical—in the same gesture.

We see this allure and fear in the Christian community of Epiphanius's younger contemporary (and future enemy), John Chrysostom. In many ways Epiphanius and John are parallel figures: monastically inclined bishops whose strong rhetoric influenced and inflamed theological and social debates across the eastern Mediterranean.[98] The church historian Socrates recounted their eventual, fatal antipathy, casting curses that, supposedly, resulted in Epiphanius's death and John's deposition from the See of Constantinople.[99] In the

380s, in the decade after Epiphanius composed the *Panarion,* John was still a popular preacher in Antioch. It was there, in the years 386–87, that he preached eight infamous sermons "Against the Judaizers," which later manuscripts would, more simply, label *Against the Jews.* Given the hybridized orthodoxies and heresies we have already seen in Epiphanius, it should not surprise us that later audiences did not so carefully distinguish between John's Judaizers and his Jews: both became complementary occasions for the expression of totalizing visions of Christian truth.

Breaking off from a proposed series of anti-Arian homilies, John announces that he feels pressed to address "an illness which has taken root within in the body of the church. We must first uproot it and then consider those outside (τῶν ἔξωθεν); first treat our own (τοὺς οἰκείους), and then take care of strangers (τῶν ἀλλοτριῶν)."[100] From John's point of view, a rhetorical shift occurs: from addressing heretics outside the church to those within his congregation who have been "infected" by a dangerous bug. Yet this infection itself comes from without: from the synagogue, a locus of pure otherness.[101] Indeed, the admixture of Judaism into John's heresiological anxieties creates a kind of identity confusion. When John recounts an infuriating moment, stopping a man from dragging a woman into an Antiochene synagogue (apparently to make her swear a business oath there), John refers to the offender as "an ugly and insensitive man, who seemed to be a Christian (δοκοῦντος εἶναι Χριστιανοῦ)—for I would not call the person daring to do such things an unalloyed (εἰλικρινῆ) Christian."[102] Obviously the "insensitive" man did consider himself a Christian, as did the rest of the Judaizing objects of John's vituperative and caustic preaching. Like Epiphanius, John finds the inappropriate mingling of Judaism and Christianity disgusting. He is fed up with "those saying they consider our things, but are eager for theirs,"[103] and charges them: "if you think Judaism is true, why do you annoy the church? But if Christianity is true (as of course it is!), then stay, and return with it."[104] While traditionally the Judaizing Christians are understood as outliers, drifting away from the secure ramparts of a clearly self-differentiated, non-Jewish Christian church,[105] more recent readings have understood John's violent rhetoric precisely to be imposing distinction where no such clear boundary seems to exist.[106] Antioch, a culturally promiscuous city, has engendered forms of religious life that John finds intolerably intermingled.

One of the ways these Judaized Christians adulterate their orthodoxy (from John's perspective) is by celebrating Jewish festivals.[107] His third homily "against Judaizers" is "against the celebration of the first," that is, the Jewish,

"Passover." John is, by turns, cajoling, threatening, and frightening; he holds up the authority of the "Fathers" of Nicaea against the wisdom of "the Jews." Chrysostom then introduces a slightly conflicting authority, Jesus: "Then also Christ, on account of this, made the Passover with them: not in order that *we* might do it with those people, but in order that he might elicit truth from the shadow. For he also submitted to circumcision, and observed the Sabbath, and completed the festivals, and ate unleavened bread, and did all of these things in Jerusalem."[108] It's unclear who has introduced the example of Jesus, although typically John is understood as responding to an argument from the Judaizers.[109] Even if his rhetoric is reactive, however, it is also theologically creative: like Epiphanius, John understands the allure of Jesus' Jewish activity, and invites his congregation to imagine Christ circumcised (and Sabbath-observant, and kosher, and so forth). So he frames Jesus' contingently Jewish body, and then suggests a new way of understanding it, as a kind of typological pantomime: "So why did Christ do it at that time? Indeed the old Passover was a type of the one that was going to come, and it was necessary for the true one to replace the type; having displayed the shadow earlier, then he brought the truth to the table: when the truth has been brought forth, the shadow has finally disappeared and it has no occasion. Don't propose this now, but show me that Christ commands that we do this! For I show the opposite: that not only doesn't he command us to observe this, but even he released us from this obligation."[110] Christ moved in a world of Jewish prehistory, of alien fantasy, of shadows. His followers move in a world of Christian truth, of light, of reality. The allure of Christ's activity is not removed, but recontextualized; he is allowed to remain Jew*ish*, although not really a Jew (and certainly not an exemplar of Jewish Law), and his participation frees Christians from all Jewish necessity.

We witness in Epiphanius's and John's hybridized religious truths the impossibility of orthodoxy itself, the ultimate instability of a religious discourse grounded in totalized truth and uncrossable borders. Even—or especially—at the moment in which unitary truth is forged, the edifice of orthodoxy cracks, the discourse of singular truth slips, and the shadow of the "other" creeps in. The circumcision of Christ represents that shadowy moment, the crack and the slippage, fittingly. "This is the moment of aesthetic distance that provides the narrative with a double edge," Homi Bhabha writes, unintentionally evoking the confounding knife poised over Christ's foreskin; a moment which "represents a hybridity, a difference 'within,' a subject that inhabits the rim of an 'in-between' reality."[111] The edgy truth of late ancient Christian orthodoxy—which so carefully modeled singularity, uniqueness, and totality for the faithful—is that it exists always "in between," internalizing the difference that it has disavowed. Working through the double-edged sign of Christ's circumcision, orthodox Christianity subversively mirrors the hybridity of Jewish Christianity, successfully constructing, appropriating, and internalizing the (now corrected) religious truths of the Jewish "other."

Chapter 5

Scriptural Distinctions
Reading Between the Lines

The infinite rippling of commentary is agitated from within by the
dream of masked repetition.
—Michel Foucault

Commentary and Difference

In Jerome's notorious quarrel with Rufinus at the beginning of the fifth century, spanning theological and social networks from Rome to Bethlehem, the
churlish monk had occasion to define the nature of commentary:[1]

> For what qualities do commentaries possess? They explicate another's
> words (*alterius dicto*); they lay out in plain speech what was obscurely
> written; they disclose the opinions of many people, and they say: "Some
> explicate this passage in this way, others interpret it in that way"; they
> strive to establish their own meaning and understanding by these wit-
> nesses for this reason: so that the sensible reader, when he reads diverse
> explanations (*diversas explanationes*), he learns which of the many are
> acceptable or unacceptable, so he may judge which is trustworthy. And
> so, like a good money-changer (*trapezita*), he may reject the money of
> counterfeit coinage. Should the one who has placed the interpretations
> (*expositiones*) of so many persons into a single work which he is explicat-
> ing be held liable (*reus*) for the diverse interpretations (*diversae interpre-
> tationes*) and the meanings which contradict themselves?[2]

In defending himself against accusations of heresy and hypocrisy, Jerome articulates the contradictory and incongruous structures of early Christian commentary.[3] By "clarifying" the plain speech of the Bible, commentaries highlight the Bible's obscurity; they collate meanings "which contradict themselves" in order to arrive at singular truths.[4] They are, at base, peculiar texts of paradox.

Early Christians believed that Scripture conveyed a single, unified *skopos* ("point of view"), but that it did so through disjointed and abstruse means.[5] Augustine, who marveled at the means by which a transcendent God reached out to a broken human race, saw the infinite variety of Scriptures. "How much in so few words (*quam multa de paucis verbis*)!" he remarked in his *Confessions*,[6] and later in his treatise *On Christian Doctrine*, "For how much more generously and generatively (*largius et uberius*) in the Divine Words could the Divinity have been provided, than that the same words may be understood in multiple ways, which are approved by other no less divine examples?"[7] The narrow, unchangeable words of the Christian Bible practically vibrated with possibility, but by the same token generated a great deal of "semiotic anxiety."[8] How were Christians to elicit singular truth from God's "generative" scriptural bounty?

Commentaries both ameliorated and highlighted this anxiety.[9] In commentary writing, the critical distance between "text" and "meaning" is glossed over but cannot be completely effaced. Ostensibly, meaning is anchored by the text: God's scriptural truth acts as surety against the wobbly and tendentious opinions of a fallible humanity.[10] But the very operations of commentary undermine this surety: "claiming merely to repeat the original text, commentary presents itself as a repetition of 'sameness,' when in fact it operates differently," as Elizabeth Clark reminds us.[11] In this different repetition of sameness we see not the failure but the power of commentary writing to craft Christian identity. Commentary writing confronted and channeled the multiplicity of scriptural meanings, so that even the "contradictory meanings" of Jews and heretics might be made to speak in an orthodox Christian voice.

That Christian culture should produce polyphonous commentaries in order to arrive at singular interpretations of Scripture will not surprise students of the late Roman world, which was itself a site of surprising and confounding juxtapositions.[12] The physical space of the empire was, as we have seen, a never-quite-coherent collection of provincial "others," whose difference was both distinguished from and incorporated into Romanitas.[13] "Roman religion" in the imperial period likewise constituted a bewildering overlap of "foreign" and "native" cults, imported into and exported out of the city of Rome.[14] Even Roman culture—in its aesthetic and poetic and literary forms—routinely and creatively juxtaposed diverse and variegated fragments: a "jeweled style," as Michael Roberts dubbed it; "a subjective disassembly and reconstitution," in the words of Catherine Chin: a cultural style that dis- and rearticulated fragments to create the present from the past, the "native" from the "alien."[15]

As a genre, commentary is particularly suited to the recombinatory aesthetics of late Roman culture.[16] In commentary writing all manner of elements are brought together and reconstituted in order to form a new literary object; yet the recombined ingredients—*lemmata* (disarticulated passages, sometimes in multiple versions), individual opinions, grammatical and syntactical interventions—remain clearly discrete. In biblical commentaries, Christians could play with and build on this particular aesthetics. Like the Roman Empire itself, Christian Scripture—through commentary—could enact a kind of unity by incorporating fragmentary difference. Corralling multiple (even contradictory) voices, Christians forced them to sing in a single chorus.

Not surprisingly, interpretations of Christ's circumcision illustrate particularly well the dissonant harmony of Christian scriptural voices. Christ's body, like the Scriptures themselves, was a multivocal, multivalent site for the contemplation of Christian identity: both were God's Word made visible, and both problematically escaped the limits of their mundane revelation. The body of Jesus participated in humanity, but was by definition utterly unique. So, too, the Christian Bible existed in human language but transcended the limits of human discourse. The circumcision of Jesus, as an object of scriptural commentary, allowed Christians to ponder the contradictions at their foundations. As I discussed in Chapter 1, a single scriptural verse narrates Jesus' circumcision, Luke 2:21: "and then the eight days were fulfilled to circumcise him, and he was called by his name, Jesus, which he was called by the angel before he was conceived in the womb." A relatively straightforward narrative verse,[17] Luke 2:21 provided occasion for early Christian commenters to contemplate their own internal contradictions in the safely transcendent spaces of the divine: the Bible and Christ's body.

Like the grammatical and philosophical commentaries with which educated Christians would have been familiar, biblical commentary was an expansive genre.[18] Commentaries might emerge out of the lecture notes of a prominent teacher,[19] or the collected sermons of a preacher on a fixed set of public readings.[20] Commentaries might be designed for public consumption or private circulation or even personal study. The only constraint on commentary as a genre—particularly early Christian scriptural commentary[21]—is that it creates interpretive meaning (or meanings) through explicit reference to a base text.[22] Several of the commentaries I consider in this chapter originated in oral performances, but were ultimately incorporated (by their authors or others) into various written formats, further flattening their diverse elements by constraining them within the Christian page. Some commentaries were further disarticulated and recombined in the commentaries of later writers, or in anonymously (or pseudonymously) compiled commentary collections. In all cases, however, commentary crystallizes and captures the other within Christianity, creating a confounding space within which to contemplate and interiorize the difference that haunts the pages of the Christian Bible.

Origen: "Circumcised with Him"

The earliest known commentary on Luke 2:21 comes in the third century, from the tireless Origen.[23] Origen's highly intellectualized view of the cosmos and Christian redemption was, as modern scholars note, centered on God's Word in Scriptures.[24] He produced countless pages of commentaries and preached daily (according to some sources) from every book of the Christian canon. Both his sermons and his commentaries were collected, edited, and published, circulating as foundational texts of Christian biblical interpretation throughout late antiquity.[25] His collected *Homilies on Luke* survive principally in the fourth-century Latin translation of Jerome, illustrating the elasticity of the performative and textualized genre of "commentary" in the late ancient world.[26] (And providing another layer of recombination, as well, in the transformation of Greek orations into Latin texts.)

In Origen's typically thorough fashion, he does not get to the middle of Luke 2 until his fourteenth homily, which treats Luke 2:21–24. Throughout this homily, Origen is careful to weave together the potentially clashing threads of Jewish Law (and flesh) and Christian salvation (and spirit). At times, Origen understands the passages allegorically: of the avian offerings at Luke 2:24 he proclaims: "these aren't the kind of birds that fly through the air, but a certain divine quality appeared, more majestic than human contemplation, under the guise of the dove and turtle-dove."[27] The "time to purification" in Luke 2:22 can similarly refer to "the true purification that will come upon us after some time . . . even after the resurrection from the dead."[28] As in so many of his homilies and commentaries, Origen presses his audience to think through and beyond the surface of the text, to extend the logos into a meditation on the ultimate truths of God's cosmos through figurative interpretation.

But Christian spirit never completely overcomes Jewish flesh in Origen's commentary, as both remain firmly locked in the divine body in which Christians participate.[29] John David Dawson, defending Origen against modern misreadings, notes, "In Origen's view, salvation requires a radical transformation of the body, but it cannot entail its replacement, even as allegorical reading requires deepening and extending, but not replacing, the text's literal sense."[30] Dawson's defense of Origen may go a bit too far; Origen does, after all, suggest in other writings there are points in the biblical text where literalism must be eschewed entirely: the text (logos) even demands it.[31] Rather, as Virginia Burrus recently argued, the materiality of language (like our material bodies) is a space within which our fallenness is at once evident and joyously transcended.[32] To push continually into spiritual interpretation is to feel exquisitely the instructively dissolving bounds of the physical letter.

Origen's doubled vision of language and materiality informs his comments on the circumcision in Luke, when he seems to be in tension with his own spiritualizing tendencies. Origen introduces the extreme opinions of "those who deny that our Lord had a human body, but [claim] he was concocted out of celestial and spiritual stuff."[33] These unnamed misreaders also "deny the God of the Law, and they say it was not him, but another by whom Christ was sent to preach the gospel."[34] Against these docetists and (we assume) Marcionites or gnostics, Origen upholds the reality of Christ's flesh—"soiled" like every "soul clothed in a human body," although without sin[35]—and he upholds the reality of Christ's submission to the Law.

But Origen has not come simply to praise Jewish flesh and Law, nor simply repudiate heretics. Origen's audience is both implicated in and shielded from the carnal realities of Christ's acts. Origen twice repeats that Jesus was circumcised "for us."[36] Yet he was circumcised and subsequently purified so that his followers would not need to be: without sin, he died to sin "so that we, who have died, in his death to sin, may live henceforth without sin and vice. . . . Just as 'we died with him' when he died and rose with him at his resurrection, so we were circumcised with him and after the circumcision cleansed by a solemn purgation. And so now we have absolutely no need of fleshly circumcision."[37] According to Origen, all Christians participated in Christ's fleshly circumcision and so have no more need to be circumcised. The purification of Christ's flesh in circumcision was effective for all people for all time: the circumcision of *his* flesh obviated the circumcision of all other flesh. Here Origen cites Colossians 2:11, which refers in cryptic fashion to "the circumcision of Christ" (περιτομή τοῦ Χριστοῦ): "In him also you were circumcised with a circumcision made without hands, by putting off the body of flesh in the circumcision of Christ." As I briefly discussed in Chapter 1, this clause that may be subjective or objective—the circumcision performed on Christ or by Christ—is by Origen's time frequently understood to refer to baptism ("a circumcision made without hands"). Paired as it is, however, with Jesus' literal circumcision in Luke 2:21, it cannot help but lose some of its metaphorical gloss: even if it points ultimately to Christian baptism, the passage also indicates, with carnal certainty, Jewish circumcision on Jesus' body. We see a similar spiritual-physical "bait-and-switch" in a surviving fragment of Origen's homilies preserved in Greek, in which he asks: "For what reason was this sign (σημεῖον) not elsewhere, but in the circumcision of [Christ's] private parts (αἰδοίου)? Since it was necessary that a good progeny (εὐπαιδία) come into being through him as an instrument, it was necessary for the indication of good progeny (τὴν τῆς εὐπαιδίας σημείωσιν) to appear through him."[38] Here the "good progeny" is at once spiritual and physical: Christians are Christ's spiritual descendants just as Jesus was Abraham's physical descendant, and so the mark of the former (spiritual baptism) is indicated by the mark of the latter (physical circumcision). The two descents, spiritual and physical, blur in a haze of cross-signification.

Christian readers are left to wonder: what exactly are they participating in? How are Christians "circumcised with Christ"? They might think, at the beginning of the homily, that (in defiance of docetists and Marcionites) they are participating in the routine acts of Jewish childhood: circumcision, naming, purification at the Temple, affirming their historical affiliation with the Creator God of Moses. Yet at the end of Origen's comments, these acts on Jesus' body are transformed into something utterly unique: "And so his death and resurrection and his circumcision were all done for us."[39] Just as Jesus' death was not like our death, and his resurrection certainly set him apart from humanity, so his circumcision cannot speak solely to the fleshly covenant of the Jews. At the same time, in its indubitable—indeed, requisite—materiality, it cannot simply speak to the spiritual ritual of Christians. It must lie somewhere in between, or above, Jewish flesh and Christian spirit.

As a sign of doubled signification, Christ's circumcised body also bridges the poles of orthodoxy and heresy. In this brief commentary on Jesus' circumcision, Origen is able simultaneously to repudiate Marcion's docetic extremism—look, real flesh!—and yet recuperate precisely what was attractive about Marcion's Christology: the transcendence from carnal to spiritual, from pollution to purity, from one Law to "another Law" (*aliae legi*).[40] Origen is often painted, following his late ancient detractors, as an inveterate allegorist, floating inappropriately free of the physical or historical grounding of the biblical text. Yet in his interpretation of Christ's circumcision, we witness a Christian mind drawn to both flesh and spirit, attempting to align both, and able to do so only on the incongruous (textual and physical) body of Christ. "For Origen," Virginia Burrus notes, "Word is always becoming flesh and flesh is always the becoming of Word."[41] On Christ's body, these dual acts of becoming are frozen, juxtaposed as if on a split screen, condensing the mysterious capacity of biblical revelation to signify multiply, and contain difference.

Ephrem: "The Circumciser of All"

Origen's reading of participation in Christ's circumcision confronts, but never resolves, the scriptural contradictions between flesh and spirit. Other early Christian interpretations of Luke 2:21 similarly engage Christian Scripture's challenging dichotomies. I propose we read one of Ephrem's *Hymns on the Nativity* as a ritualized commentary that confronts the multiple, incongruous layers of scriptural textuality. Ephrem performed sixteen festival hymns celebrating the paradoxes of the incarnation and advent of Christ, probably on Epiphany.[42] Some time after Ephrem's death, these songs were combined with other metric hymns on similar topics, and circulated as Ephrem's *Hymns on the Nativity*.[43] *Hymn 26* was not one of these original festal hymns, but was collected with them because of its focus on the infancy of Jesus and the mysteries of birth, creation, and divinity. If the hymn was not originally festal, it was certainly commentarial: the hymn's structure is highly scripturalized, which is why I believe we can read it as a commentary along the lines of the other texts treated in this chapter.[44] Brief comments on the events of Matthew 2 and Luke 2 surround a christological interpretation of the seven days of creation. Stanzas 1–2 consider the "first year" and "second year" of the redeemer's childhood;[45] stanza 3 analogizes the illumination of Christ's birth to the initial moment of creation; stanzas 4–10 compare Christ's advent to the graduated creation of Genesis 1–2; and stanzas 11–13 explicate Luke 2:21–24.

Hymn 26, like many Christian commentaries, is particularly concerned with the problem of biblical harmony: the two nativity accounts (which are not explicitly harmonized by Ephrem) enfold a creation account that attempts to integrate the Fall of Genesis 3 into the seven-day creation account of Genesis 1. The Old and New Testament accounts are themselves then harmonized: the old creation of Genesis is mapped onto the new creation of the gospel accounts, crystallized in Christ's birth and advent. This palimpsest commentary reaches a pinnacle with the stanza on Jesus' circumcision:

> Let the eighth day that circumcised the Hebrews
> confess Him Who commanded His namesake Joshua
> to circumcise with the flint the People whose body [was] circumcised
> but whose heart was unbelieving from within.
> Behold on the eighth day as a babe
> The Circumciser of all came to circumcision.
> Although the sign of Abraham was on his flesh,
> the blind daughter of Zion has disfigured it.[46]

Here we find not only Jesus being circumcised (Luke 2) but also Joshua (Jesus' namesake, in Syriac as in Greek) recircumcising the Israelites about to enter the promised land (Joshua 5) and Abraham, who first received the covenant of circumcision (Genesis 17). Christ is both object and subject of circumcision— "the circumciser of all came to circumcision"—an example to Joshua and the follower of Abraham's example. Throughout this hymn, the infant Jesus straddles the entire biblical narrative, from the first illuminating moment of creation to his own redemption of humanity.

This one stanza, this one act of circumcision, functions as a microcosm of Christ's exegetical elasticity: in contemplation of the circumcised circumciser, Ephrem can collapse the multiple layers of the biblical text into a single, compact point. Christian biblical meaning, emblematized in Christ, can likewise straddle past and present, Old and New Testament, in a similar tour de force. Ephrem's Syrian context may provide some explanation for this desire to harmonize: certainly by the fourth century a popular gospel harmony circulated in Syriac alongside the four "divided gospels."[47] This gospel harmony was probably known to and used by Ephrem, and may even have encouraged certain harmonizing tendencies.[48] Nevertheless the desire to press together the various layers of scriptural history, from creation to redemption, is far from unique to the Syrian context, and commentary writing—which was simultaneously selective and supplementary—serves this task admirably.

Ephrem's act of commentarial condensation, however, leaves an important remainder, which is also partially symbolized by and visible in the act of circumcision: the "blind daughter of Zion," the intransigent "People" who fit so awkwardly into the narrative of biblical salvation that not even two flinty circumcisions on their bodies are sufficient to penetrate their hard hearts. In other hymns, Ephrem invokes Jesus' seeming Jewishness to shame the Jews that crucified him: "Woe to the circumcised who were not ashamed to mock the Lord of the circumcised. If he had been uncircumcised, then there would have been cause for his death!"[49] Christine Shepardson attempts to untangle Ephrem's complex use of sacred (Jewish? Christian?) history in such engagements with Scripture: "Jesus' very Jewishness, as evidenced in scriptural history, supports, Ephrem argues, Christians' interpretation of the history of Israel as the Jews' voluntary forfeiting of their divine covenant."[50] That Jews should be both signaled by yet alienated from circumcision when it is on Christ's body also reflects the challenge to and promise of Ephrem's totalizing biblical *skopos*. He cannot recombine these multiple biblical moments without acknowledging the Jewish people who also see themselves therein; but by his very act of exegetical prowess he has demonstrated Jewish deficiency, and wrested the Law from their hands. He can only do so, however, by leaving Christ's body deeply embedded in that Law. It is, at best, an ambivalent act of partial expulsion and abjection.

Ambrose: "Fashioned Under the Law"

Ambrose of Milan's sole New Testament commentary was on the Gospel of Luke, and shares Ephrem's and Origen's ambivalence about Jewish law and flesh.[51] Ambrose drew freely on the multiple, sometimes incongruous opinions of previous exegetes, especially those of Origen.[52] (Indeed, Jerome's disdain for Ambrose's use of Origen's exegesis of Luke apparently led the monk to produce his own translation of Origen's homilies, from which I cite above.)[53] Like Origen's commentary, Ambrose's originated in sermons that he then expanded and edited for publication.[54] In his prologue, Ambrose frames Luke's gospel as a particular challenge to the spiritually minded exegete: "indeed it is historical (*est enim historicus*)," Ambrose says of the gospel, with what might be a little distaste,[55] more given to "describing things than explaining commandments."[56] Ambrose reflects here the predominant opinion of early Christian commentators, who paid relatively scant attention to Luke. For morally inspiring narrative, Matthew was the gospel of choice; for spiritual edification, the Gospel of John drew the lion's share of attention. Luke, the "ox" of the gospels, was rarely given the same amount of exegetical attention. (Mark was generally ignored.)[57] Nonetheless, Ambrose insists, all of the evangelists partake of the three gifts of wisdom: moral, rational, and natural. With Luke, a reader must be prepared to struggle a bit against the text's earthy style "upon entering into this struggle of consecrated arguments."[58] Few passages provide the opportunity to show how Luke can convey the spiritual within the carnal more than the scene of Jesus' circumcision.

After interpreting Mary's silent consideration of the shepherds in Luke 2:19 (an example for other ascetics to learn silently from their own episcopal "shepherds"),[59] Ambrose turns abruptly to Christ's circumcision, although without directly citing Luke 2:21: "And then the child is circumcised," he writes, the child about whom we are told "a child is born unto us, a son is given unto us" (Isa 9:6).[60] Ambrose, like other commenters on Luke 2, finds particularly compelling Christ's double submission to "the Law": first in circumcision, next in the presentation at the Temple.[61] Origen had made these acts, like the crucifixion and resurrection, at once an admonition to docetic heretics and one more part of Jesus' uniquely redemptive biography. Ambrose follows suit, taking a page—literally—from the letters of Paul. First he explains Christ's circumcision using Galatians 4:4: "Indeed he was fashioned (*factus est*) under the Law so that he might win those who were under the Law."[62] But Ambrose is not satisfied to understand the Law as a literal, and repeatable, series of covenantal and ritual obligations, and those "who were under the Law" to be won over quickly disappear from his view in a figural haze. The circumcision and the presence at the Temple become a metaphor— "the purging of trespasses"—and then an allegory—"through the circumcision on the eighth day the future purgation of all fault in the age of the resurrection was prefigured."[63] Between Law and type, Jesus' real and physical (and Jewish) circumcision is partially blurred.

Later in the same commentary, when Ambrose discusses the baptism of Jesus, the reality, physicality, and Jewishness of Christ's circumcision are once more introduced and refracted. Again, Ambrose puts Pauline language to use, in an even more innovative fashion:

> The Lord came to the font; now all these things were done for your sake. For those who are under the Law, as if he himself were under the Law (although he is not under the Law), he was circumcised, so that he might acquire those who are under the Law. But for those who were apart from the Law, he dined in fellowship with them, so that he might

acquire those who lived apart from the Law. He was made weak for the weak through bodily suffering, so that he might acquire them. Afterwards he was made all things for all people: poor for the poor, rich for the rich, weeping for the weeping, hungry for the hungry, thirsty for the thirsty, flowing forth with abundance (*profluus abundantibus*).[64]

Whereas for Origen Christ's circumcision was elevated among the acts of divine redemption, here it is reduced to a form of spiritual condescension. Jesus now, like Paul (1 Cor 9:20–22), came "as if under the Law, although not under the Law," and the circumcision was—apparently—part of this Jewish disguise by which he could win those "under the Law" (the requirements for winning gentiles involved the less physically challenging "dining in fellowship"). Of course Ambrose knows, and his readers know, that despite his perfect semblance of Jewishness, those "under the Law" will not be won over. If this is not the failure of Jesus (how can it be?), Ambrose's readers know where to place the blame. Judaism is acknowledged—even appropriated (contingently) on Christ's body—but ultimately it fails.

Jesus was (again, like Paul) "all things for all people." Jew, gentile, poor, weak, rich, hungry, and weeping: so many faces and yet, of course (as Ambrose teaches in this commentary), Christ came to initiate a particular and specific economy of salvation.[65] That is, he may have come as many things for many people but really conveyed one, specific message to one circumscribed group of believers. This saving economy can be decoded—through the rough terrain of overly worldly concern with historical narration—even from the Gospel of Luke. For, like Jesus and Paul, Ambrose's Bible can also be "all things to all people." Or, at least, it can seem to be all things to all people: the Bible (like Christ circumcised) can even seem Jewish, yet its true voice (as Ambrose teaches) is the voice of Christian orthodoxy.[66]

Cyril of Alexandria: "Proof of His Kinship"

The fullest elaboration of Jesus' circumcision in the Gospel of Luke comes from the fifth-century patriarch of Alexandria, Cyril.[67] Cyril composed a raft of scriptural commentaries (not all extant), on Old and New Testament books during his long episcopal career.[68] In them he often postures aggressively against heretical, pagan, and Jewish opponents of Christian truth.[69] Cyril's confrontations with Jews (both social and literary) often focused on a kind of tug-of-war over the Scriptures,[70] a struggle interiorized into his biblical commentaries and evident in his interpretation of Jesus' circumcision.

Ancient Christian commentary was a genre that collected and produced fragments, and was often in turn refragmented in distribution. Cyril's commentary on Luke survives in scattered bits and pieces: some preserved as homilies (in which form they may have originally been delivered) in the original Greek and a Syriac translation, some preserved under his name in various Greek *catenae* ("chains" of exegetical comments) compiled by later Byzantine Christians.[71] The scattered nature of Cyril's comments on Luke's gospel affirms the fragmentary and recombinatory nature of late antique Christian scriptural commentary: a multivocal conversation (often fractious and inconsistent) within the "orthodox" construction of the Bible.[72] Beneath the authoritative "voice" of the Alexandrian patriarch, we sense in the scriptural locus of Christ's circumcision not a secure anchor of religious identity, but rather a moving and unstable target.[73]

Cyril, like Ambrose, reads the circumcision of Christ through the lens of the transformative and paradoxical "dispensation" of Christ's condescension to human form: "Therefore he bent down his neck under the Law with us, doing this as part of his plan (τοῦτο πράττων οἰκονομικῶς)."[74] Cyril cannot help but hear, and convey, his reader's surprise and anxiety over this moment of unpalatable Jewishness at the dawn of the Christian era: "But when you see him observing the Law, do not be taken aback (μὴ σκανδαλισθῇς), nor place the free one down among the slaves: rather consider the depth of his plan (τῆς οἰκονομίας τὸ βάθος)."[75] As in Ambrose's commentary, we learn, all is not what it seems. Cyril's exposition will both elucidate why God's "plan" (*oikonomia*) should entail this mark of Jewish submission and alleviate the anxiety he assumes Christians must feel at contemplating the Jewish mark on their Christian God.[76]

Cyril accomplishes this rhetorical feat by highlighting the absolute Jewishness of this act and the ways in which it obviates that Jewishness. First, Cyril explains Jesus' total submission to the Law of circumcision: "Therefore Christ has bought off from the curses of the law those who are under the law, even though they were not keeping it. How has he bought them off? He fulfilled it: and in another way, so that he might absolve the charges of the transgression in Adam, he obeyed and made himself tractable to every bit of it on our behalf to God the Father."[77] Christ kept the Law perfectly, so perfectly that even those gentiles who weren't keeping the Law (but were nonetheless somehow bound to it), were "bought off" from its curses. (Or else Cyril means here to indicate that those Jews of the time "who were under the Law" were not even keeping it themselves.) Cyril's "fulfillment of the Law" (cf. Matt 5:17), however, signals more than scrupulous observance: it means that he has "paid in full" the burden of the Law. Jesus' circumcision was so perfect that it has fulfilled the obligation for all time.

The fact that the Christian savior submitted so perfectly to the Law now enables his Christian followers to exert exegetical authority over that Law, even over the imperfectly observing Jews. Christians now see the "bigger picture" that the Jews lack, including Paul's dire warnings on circumcision: "But come now again and let us see through examination what is this puzzle (αἴνιγμα), and of what sort of mysteries is the event to be disclosed to us. Blessed Paul said: 'Circumcision is nothing and uncircumcision is nothing' [1 Cor 7:19]. But it is possible to say something to this: Did the God of all then ordain through the all-wise Moses that a 'nothing' should be observed (τὸ μηδὲν τηρεῖσθαι), even dangling a punishment over those who transgressed it? I should say so!"[78] According to Cyril, Christ's physical circumcision actually affirms Paul's assertion of the "nothingness" of the Jewish covenant rite.[79] He goes on to explain exactly *how* it means nothing through a complex intertextual play (I cite at length, continuing immediately from the previous citation):

> For whatever there was in the nature of the thing itself, that is, the carnal fulfillment, is absolutely nothing; but it engenders the figure of a mystery, quite agreeably; or, rather, it possesses the concealed manifestation of the truth. For it was on the eighth day that Christ rose from the dead, and he gave us the circumcision in the Spirit. For God ordered the holy apostles: "Go forth and make disciples of all the nations, baptizing them in the name of the Father, and the Son, and the Holy Spirit" [Matt 28:19]. For we say that the circumcision in the Spirit has been fulfilled especially in the time of holy baptism, when Christ also shows that we share in the Holy Spirit. For again as a figure of this was that other, ancient Jesus [i.e., Joshua], who was general after Moses.[80] For he made the children of Israel cross the Jordan, and then, stopping, right away he circumcised them with stone knives [Josh 5:1–3]. Therefore whenever we cross the Jordan [i.e., in baptism] then Christ circumcises us in the power of the Holy Spirit, not purifying flesh, but rather clipping off the defilement in our souls.[81]

The swirl of biblical citations—beginning with Paul, working through Matthew and Joshua—effectively dislodges the reader from the moment at the beginning of the Gospel of Luke under examination. What begins as "nothing"—the physical rite of circumcision—ends up replete with the power of the Holy Spirit. Jesus' circumcision ripples outward to the resurrection, the "great commission," the seal of baptism, and the baptismal waters of the Jordan River, the site of another "circumcision" of another "Jesus."[82] This revelation that the Law is grace, that circumcision is baptism, and that purity is spiritual is thus made possible (in Cyril's reading) through the unique confluence of Scriptures on Christ's own body.

Yet a twinge of anxiety remains: Christ did not demonstrate the "spiritual" circumcision of baptism through baptism alone, but rather through literal circumcision. He was circumcised like a Jew, and the taint of offense (*skandalon*) remains, even ventriloquized by Cyril in his homily. In a fragment preserved in the catenae (and which Cyril may have adapted from earlier commentators on Luke), Cyril confronts Christ's possible Jewishness head-on:

> Again, when the Son was with us, although he was God by nature and Lord of all, by this he does not dishonor our own measure, but comes under that Law with us, even though as God he is the Lawgiver: he is circumcised on the eighth day along with Jews (μετὰ Ἰουδαίων), so that he may confirm his kinship (τὴν συγγένειαν). For the messiah [Christ] was expected from the seed of David, and he offered the proof of his kinship. For if even though he was circumcised they said, "We do not know where he comes from" [John 9:29], had he not been circumcised according to the flesh, and kept the Law, their denial would have had just cause (πρόφασιν εὔλογον). But after he was circumcised, circumcision stopped, since that which was signified by it was delivered to us, that is, baptism.[83]

Here the crux of Christians' anxiety about their own Jewish origins is articulated: do we not imagine, Cyril says, that Christ was circumcised precisely because he was "kin" with the Jews? Yes, Cyril admits; but it is a "kinship" that is subverted and truncated on both sides. Christ's submission to the Law was a strategy, a means of defusing future Jewish critique (Ephrem had made the same point). Although Cyril can briefly gesture to Jesus' desire to save the "remnant of Israel" later in his commentary,[84] both commentator and audience know that, in fact, the Jews—Christ's own "kin"—*did* irrationally reject him, despite his unnecessary submission to their Law: they *did* proclaim (unjustly, we now learn) that they did not know "where he comes from" (cf. Matt 13:55 and parallels).

At this point, not only the Law (Judaism) is overwritten by Christ's circumcision, so too are the Jews themselves. Just as Christ's submission to the Law reveals that it is "nothing," his kinship with the Jews reveals that the Jews themselves are "nothing." By submitting to the Law, Christ shows its emptiness; by becoming a Jew—or, perhaps, almost a Jew? a human "among Jews"?—Christ demonstrates their faithlessness. By intertextualizing Paul's comment that "circumcision is nothing," Cyril argues that the full meaning of this weighty comment, the full exegetical triumph over Judaism and the Jews, only emerges on Christ's circumcised body. Cyril's commentary suggests that the definitive Christian answer to the *skandalon* of Judaism can only be found by internalizing that Jewish "otherness" as completely as Christ did.

Proclus of Constantinople: "Deep Mysteries in Common Language"

Perhaps around the same time that Cyril was delivering his homilies on the Gospel of Luke,[85] Bishop Proclus of Constantinople (the second to hold that see after Cyril's archrival, Nestorius) delivered a sermon on Luke 2:21–24.[86] Later manuscript collections would assume that Proclus was preaching on the "feast of the circumcision," but, as I discuss in Chapter 6, such an early dating for the festival seems unlikely. Rather, as we see through Cyril and other preachers of the fourth and fifth centuries, the scriptural exposition of Christ's circumcision and presentation in the Temple were becoming increasing significant biblical moments, deemed worthy of public exposition. Proclus's preaching, like Ephrem's a century earlier, is not engaged in a broader investigation into Luke's Gospel (so far as we can tell from his extant sermons).[87] Although brief, however, it provides an opportunity for Proclus and his audience to meditate upon the paradoxes of God's presence on earth: bodily and scriptural.

Proclus begins by contemplating the inherently incongruous nature of Scripture: "The language (λόγος) of divinely-inspired Scripture is common (κοινός), but it teaches a great and deep mystery (μέγα καί βαθὺ μυστή–ριον)."[88] Christ on earth embodied this same incongruity of the "common" and the "deep": "What a great and amazing matter! He was an infant on earth, according to the flesh, and at the same time he filled the heaven. He received circumcision: while enthroned with the Father he was under the Law. Moses' own Master observed Moses' commandment."[89] Just as the poor verbiage of the Bible masks God's mysteries, so the inferior and circumcised body of the infant Jesus conceals a truth of mastery and transcendence.

Like Origen, Proclus sees Jesus' submission to Jewish Law as part of his tremendous condescension to human flesh. Citing Paul, Proclus remarks: "Before the incarnation he was not under the Law, but when he 'was born of woman' [Gal 4:4] he became someone who observes the Law."[90] Several times Proclus draws this parallel between Christ as incarnate and as Law-observant: "That it was lowly and absolutely unworthy of his inherent magnificence to submit to the Law, I agree with you! But was it not also likewise lowly to share our flesh and blood?"[91] Later, again, Proclus equates Jesus' becoming part of the "seed of Abraham" with "sharing with us (ἡμῖν) flesh and blood."[92] Explaining his equation between Jesus' Jewishness and his humanity, Proclus introduces a key passage from Philippians: "Did he take the 'form of a slave' [Phil 2:7] if he was not in submission to the Law? For it is the nature of a slave to be under Law. So the one who was a free person according to his own nature took the form of a slave: he was circumcised according to the Law."[93] The rough texture of overlapping scriptural citations, much like Cyril's rapid intertextual fire, effectively blurs the frame around Christ's "unworthy" Jewish moment.[94] His circumcision is transformed into the mark of a slave, like the tattoos by which slaves were recognized in the Roman world.[95] This slave mark is, in turn, analogized into "our flesh and blood," the mark of shame that all humans carry. We are all slaves, we are all under some "law," we are all redeemed in this "great mystery."

Certainly part of Proclus's exegetical work here is to alleviate any anxieties about Jewishness: not only was Jesus' submission to the Law overwritten by his true nature ("enthroned with the Father," "Moses' Master"), it was also merely part of his condescension to human form ("the form of a slave").[96] Yet at the same time Proclus cannot completely disguise the particularity of Jesus' act. It was not any mark, but the mark of circumcision; he did not submit to any law, but the Law of Moses; he was not of any "human seed," but the "seed of Abraham." Proclus's brief engagement with Luke 2:21 reveals, perhaps, the underlying conundrum of any christological biblical interpretation: to what extent must the faithful interpreter effectively reconcile the "commonness" (of language, of Law, of circumcision) with the "deep mystery" (of incarnation, divinity, and transcendence)? To engage with the Bible is already to enter into this "common discourse" (κοινὸς λόγος); can that commonness—indeed, that Jewishness—ever be completely effaced? The anxieties attendant upon deep mysteries in human—Jewish—flesh will continue to mark commentaries on Luke 2:21.

Philoxenus: "We Do Not Dare to Ask"

Throughout the fourth and fifth centuries, the prismatic lens of Scripture refracted not only the tangled relations between Jews and Christians (and between Old and New Testaments) but also those between Christian movements divided over doctrine. Already in the third century, Origen had seen in Christ's circumcised body a refutation of (and the appeal of) docetists and Marcionites. By the fifth century, the particularities of Christ's person had come to overwhelm the interpretation of the divine Word. In Chapter 3, I discussed the ways that Christ's circumcision could be made to speak to multiple sides of proliferating ancient christological debates; we should not be surprised to see the multifarious lines of Scripture reflective of these debates, as well.

Philoxenus, bishop of Mabbug (Hierapolis), on the eastern fringe of the Roman Empire, was a staunch defender of "orthodoxy" against the "Nestorians";[97] that is, he embraced a form of "miaphysitism" that opposed the definition of Christ promulgated at the Council of Chalcedon.[98] Philoxenus's Christianity was formed at several fractious borders: between "Nestorian" and "monophysite," "Persian" and "Byzantine," "Greek" and "Syriac."[99] For Philoxenus, correct doctrine was intimately woven into the fabric of scriptural interpretation, down to the least stroke and letter. Interpretation was necessary, therefore, to gain knowledge of God in an appropriate manner. For this reason interpretation was also highly fraught: incorrect reading led to incorrect doctrine, to false and misleading knowledge of God. The scriptural text must, therefore, be absolutely reliable (as Origen would insist),[100] and totally harmonious in all of its parts (as Ephrem believed).[101] Among Philoxenus's many theological treatises and letters that survive from his episcopacy, we possess fragments of commentaries on three gospels: Matthew, Luke, and John. According to a scribal colophon in one early manuscript of Philoxenus, the bishop of Mabbug produced a joint "commentary on the gospels of Matthew and Luke."[102]

In the 1970s, two dissertations translated and commented on Philoxenus's *Commentary on Matthew and Luke*. J. W. Watt followed the collocation of fragments suggested by André de Halleux's masterful biography of Philoxenus; his version of the text, from several manuscripts, was published in this reconstructed order of scriptural passages.[103] Douglas Fox transcribed and printed the majority of the oldest surviving manuscript of the commentary, but disputed de Halleux's contention that these fragments (and others, purportedly from a *Commentary on John*) really derived from a commentary, per se: "Only ten out of twenty-nine fragments speak of a Philoxenian 'commentary' in an unqualified way, and when the contents of those ten fragments are examined it becomes clear that what has been called Philoxenian commentary is something other than the systematic exegesis of a biblical book."[104] Similar comments dot his own commentary on Philoxenus's supposed commentary: "it is difficult to believe that this came from an exegetical work in any formal or technical sense."[105] Several scholars of Philoxenus—including de Halleux himself—have criticized Fox's argument that we should not consider Philoxenus's use of scriptural texts as "commentary."[106] Indeed, his formalistic approach to "commentary" seems overly strict, even in the limited scope of early Christian texts. It is more helpful to think of "commentary" as a kind of epistemology: a way of knowing that is fundamentally scriptural and expansive.[107]

Yet perhaps Fox is eliciting a discomfort out of Philoxenus's own commentarial texts. David Michelson has pointed out, in a recent dissertation on Philoxenus, that the Syriac-speaking bishop's own commentaries call the project of "commentary" (and scriptural interpretation in general) into question. On the one hand, Michelson (following earlier scholars) highlights the earlier theological and textual influences on Philoxenus. Philoxenus stands in a particular Origenist tradition of textual Christology, mediated by the ascetic writings of Evagrius of Pontus.[108] In this line of thought, an awareness of the relation between Christ as the incarnate Word and Scripture as God's revealed word must always be present, such that Christ, commentary, and the individual Christian are mutually intertwined.[109] For speculative mystics such as Origen and Evagrius, this opened up to the attentive reader of Scripture exciting opportunities to contemplate the nature of the Trinity itself.[110] But the intense monastic theology of Evagrius in particular also highlighted the limits of language, as another form of bodiliness that could point to, but never fully encompass, the divine. Interpretation of Scripture was desirable, but always potentially limiting and misleading.[111]

As one of the first generation of serious, post- (and anti-) Chalcedon theologians, Philoxenus seems much more sensitive to the perils of christological exegesis than either Origen or Evagrius (both of whom were repeatedly condemned during theological debates of the fourth through sixth centuries).[112] As Michelson points out, Philoxenus is leery of the potential for biblical commentaries (such as those of the "Nestorians") to produce faulty doctrine. Philoxenus's own commentaries, therefore, routinely call the utility of commentary writing into question: "To coin a phrase, Philoxenos' 'commentaries' on the gospels perhaps should be seen as 'anticommentaries.'"[113] Scripture must be apprehended, of course, but the interpreter must be chastened and humble, on guard against the vainglorious and proud exegesis that will plunge him into heretical doctrine.[114]

Philoxenus's comments on the circumcision and Luke 2, then, have the twofold purpose of expressing correct doctrine and warding off the overly curious and intellectualized interpretations of his theological opponents. At two points, in the surviving fragments of the *Commentary*, Philoxenus brings up the circumcision. In the first set of comments, he seems to be addressing those proponents of aphtharsia, or "incorruptibility" of Christ's human body, who denied the circumcision altogether:[115] "But the blasphemers say, 'If something had been cut off from his body in circumcision, they would have shown to us what became of that part of the flesh which had been torn out, by which, if it had been thrown into the earth and corrupted, would be made false that [word] of the prophet [in] which he said, "You will not give your Holy One to see corruption" [Ps 16:10].' But if this is not fit to be imagined, what they say [that Jesus was not circumcised] stands and they speak things which suit the Manicheans, according to the church."[116] We recall the curious Caesaria, who inquired after the foreskin of Christ in a similar fashion in correspondence with Severus of Antioch (which I discuss in Chapter 3). Like Severus, Philoxenus finds the entire discussion inappropriate, "not fit to be imagined" (*lâ payâ detetranâ*), the sight of the rotting foreskin of Christ cast onto the ground in his infancy. Philoxenus's imputation to the heretics of the designation "Manicheans" may refer not only to their impossible view of Christ's body but also their willingness to edit Scripture (here, apparently, removing Luke 2:21 altogether) to suit their theological aims.

Philoxenus gives us more of a taste than Severus, however, of the intertextual gambits employed by his theological opponents, who replace the impossible image of Christ's corruptible flesh with the praise of incorruptibility found in the Psalms. The next fragment of Philoxenus's commentary may continue directly, insofar as it refuses "Manichean" scriptural antitheses: "So we do not say that 'his body saw corruption' [cf. Acts 2:31]; and we do not dare to ask, 'What came from the cutting of his circumcision?'"[117] Philoxenus refuses to be painted into an exegetical corner: he will deny neither Acts 2:31 (by removing "not" from the verse) nor Luke 2:21 (by asking an impossible "follow-up" question). Nor, as we learn in the next passage, will he work to make the two passages understood together: "For if they continue in audacity, as though supported without sense on the surface of the word (*berayothâ de-malthâ*) of Scripture which says, 'But his body did not see corruption' [Acts 2:31], they should learn from where it is written that it does not say this about the circumcision but about the resurrection."[118] On the one hand, according to Philoxenus, his heretical opponents are dancing "on the surface of the word," refusing to see the verse on incorruption in context: a plain reading for "sense" will show that the passage in Acts was speaking of the resurrected body, not the entirety of Christ's incarnation. Yet Philoxenus is not calling for a more complex reading, asking the heretics to dig beneath "the surface." In fact, he is resisting their attempts to link verses together across the life of Christ, to knit a more richly intertextual christological interpretation of Jesus from the texts of the gospels. In this section, Philoxenus is producing an antimidrashic commentary.

Daniel Boyarin has usefully defined midrash as "the radical intertextual reading of the canon, in which potentially every other part refers to and is interpretable by every other part."[119] We have seen such midrash at work in most of the other early Christian interpreters of Luke 2, from Origen to Proclus. Yet Philoxenus finds such intertextual inflation unsatisfying, even dangerous. He insists that the Acts passage must be locked in place and speak *only* of Christ after the resurrection. What Michelson has interpreted as "anticommentarial" tendencies in Philoxenus may be read as more precisely antimidrashic: a fear that, once the individual *lemmata* and verses of the Bible are jostled loose, unanchored, they may float too easily into the dangerous waters of heresy. Philoxenus makes it clear how tempting those waters seem: "And so if this is a mystery (*razâ*) of the dispensation, have faith that even the cutting of Christ's circumcision was united to his person[120] in resurrection, and corruption did not have dominion over it, as the living and life-giving body of God. And do not seek impiously where that part is until the time of the resurrection."[121] Philoxenus will admit—after much demurral—that Christ's flesh did not decay or become corrupt like normal flesh (presumably he does not think that the foreskins of every Jewish infant have been united postmortem with their original owners). The "life-giving body of God" reclaimed its lost fragment in the resurrection (as Severus also claimed), unable to cede that one piece. Yet to seek any further—to understand through, perhaps, other intertextual readings—would be "impious." Like that "life-giving body," the text of Scripture must remain mysterious and ultimately impenetrable to human understanding. Commentary for Philoxenus is about the restriction of meaning and investigation, not its expansion.

It is, of course, a difficult stance for an expositor of Scripture to maintain and, later in his commentary, Philoxenus softens his position a bit. Philoxenus broaches the circumcision at least once more, again in refutation of heretics who willfully misunderstand the nature of Christ's body and "reject his corporeality." If Christ's advent was merely a "likeness," Philoxenus chides, then all the benefits of the incarnation were merely a "likeness" as well! "For on this account he became man, to make us sons to his Father," he asserts. "He was manifested as corporeal to change us to his spirituality. He was born of a woman to give birth to us of the Holy Spirit. He received circumcision and kept the Law to free us from its subjection and redeem us from its curse.[122] He grew in stature to bring us to completeness and perfection."[123] If Christ's appearance cannot be dismissed as a mere docetic "appearance," neither was it quite what it seemed: spiritual flesh, giving birth when born, circumcised to refute circumcision, immaturity engendering perfection. Such willingness to peer beneath the surface of God's word is more suggestive than the previous fragments, more open to the paradoxes of Christ's material manifestation. Yet, even here, Philoxenus's interpretation of Scripture is ultimately reactive and restrictive, refusing to extend beyond the language of Luke's nativity, unwilling to expand his vision of Jesus beyond very narrow textual boundaries.

Philoxenus's resistance to a midrashic approach to christological interpretation of the Bible may be a reaction to contemporary Christian parabiblical elaborations of the sacred history, akin to the aggadic midrash of the rabbis. A sixth-century text known as the *Cave of Treasures* recounts human history from Adam through Christ's resurrection, linking events geographically and typologically throughout. In the text, the binding of Isaac is related thematically to Christ's circumcision. An earlier version simply says, "And at eight days, Joseph circumcised him [Jesus] according to the Law."[124] A later emendation makes it clear that this obeisance to the Law did not entail suffering: "it didn't happen the way the wicked Cyril and accursed Severus said, who ascribed suffering to the eternal essence."[125] The author of the *Cave* is willing to concede Christ's circumcision, but only on the understanding that the act entailed no bodily suffering.

Christian midrash on Christ's circumcision develops this tension throughout the sixth century in later infancy gospels. Earlier infancy gospels, such as the *Infancy Gospel of Thomas* or the *Protevangelium of James*, did not dwell on (or even mention) the circumcision of Jesus.[126] Likewise the so-called *Gospel of Pseudo-Matthew*, which may date anywhere from the sixth through eighth centuries in its Latin form,[127] mentions the circumcision but simply includes a verse adopted from Luke 2:21: "On the eighth day they circumcised the child, and called his name Jesus, which he was called by the angel before he was conceived in the womb."[128]

Two later infancy gospels, probably originally composed in Syriac, do elaborate on the circumcision. The so-called *Arabic Infancy Gospel* not only mentions the circumcision but contemplates the fate of that much-discussed foreskin:[129]

> When the time of the circumcision was at hand (that is, on the eighth day), the little child was to be circumcised according to the Law. So they circumcised him in the cave. That old Hebrew woman took that piece of skin; but others say that she took the umbilical cord, and stored in an old jar of oil of nard. She had a son, an unguent dealer, and, giving it to him, she said, "Beware lest you sell this jar of unguent of nard, even if you're offered 300 *denarii* for it!" And this is the jar that Mary, the sinful, bought, and she poured it over the head and feet of our Lord Jesus Christ, which then she wiped with the hair of her own head.[130]

Here is an answer to the question posed mischievously by the proponents of aphtharsia and rejected out of hand by Severus and Philoxenus: If Jesus was truly circumcised, what happened to his foreskin? The answer is ingeniously intertextual: it remained hidden, in a jar, waiting to be reunited in anointing with Jesus before his crucifixion. The *Armenian Infancy Gospel*, which may date from the period of Philoxenus's and Severus's conflicts with the Julianists, approaches the circumcision quite differently:

> When the child was eight days old, Joseph said to Mary: "What shall we do with this child, since the Law requires to have circumcision on the eighth day?" Mary said, "Let it be according to your wish; do as you please." And Joseph rose up quietly and went to the city of Jerusalem and brought with him a wise man, good, compassionate, and God-fearing. And he was well-versed in the Law; and his name was Joel. And they came to the cave where the child was. But when he drew the knife, it would not cut into him. And when they saw this, they were very much amazed and said: "Behold, no blood dripped from the child." And he was given the name Jesus, as he was named by the angel.[131]

The final line makes it clear that this passage is a midrash on Luke, echoing as it does the final words of Luke 2:21. The viewpoint is thoroughly aphthartodocetic, proposing a nonintuitive reading of the verse—if not, in-deed, simply overwriting it—in a manner that suits the author's christologi-cal doctrine. That such narrative commentary might circulate alongside the canonical gospels, even as it potentially contradicts them, should lead us to reconsider the complex and even contradictory relationship between text and commentary in late ancient Christianity.

These later infancy gospels are midrashic in the sense that they "fill in" narrative gaps of the biblical text with legendary material and theological spec-ulation. In the same way, Philoxenus's heretical opponents filled in the christo-logical gaps of the gospel accounts with pertinent biblical verses on messianic incorruptibility. Of course, midrashic "gaps" do not exist until they are created in the minds of readers: "gaps" reveal interpretive desires, not authorial lapses. Philoxenus's resistance to midrashic intertextuality directly mirrors, then, the legendary fulsomeness of the (possibly) contemporaneous infancy gospels, in that the bishop seeks to close the gaps, tighten up the text, and foreclose the possibilities of intertextual, imaginative interpretation. No "otherness" can penetrate the tightly circumscribed text of Philoxenus's gospel commentary. Yet Philoxenus cannot utterly exclude the heretical other from the pages of his commentary: even when he refutes them, and forcefully excludes their opin-ions from his commentary, they remain hovering, like maleficent marginalia, around Philoxenus's anxiously guarded gospel.[132]

Others Within

As the source of Christian identity, the Bible marked out and contained dif-ference. Scripture provided Christians with the means to contemplate, even appropriate, the "other" and also the means to bound off—contingently, momentarily—that other. Scriptural commentary provided the textual ex-pression of this doubled desire to expel and contain. The other is invoked in myriad guises: as Jew, as heretic, in the past or in the present; even the words of Scripture themselves can seem alien, in need of taming into recognizable shape. "Herein lies the beauty of commentary," Elizabeth Clark remarks, cit-ing Michel Foucault: "[commentary] allows us to say something other than the text itself but on condition that it is the text itself which is said, and in a sense completed."[133] The act of commentary tames the other, but masks its own tracks in so doing. The other, by contrast, is conquered but preserved in the pages of the commentary. Christ's body—a manifestation of the Word of

God, like the Scripture—mirrors and models this internalization of the other. It is a double mark on God's Word—on the page, and on the body—that creates diverse spaces for the appropriation of the other. Even Philoxenus, who of all the commentators surveyed here most resists the play of otherness in God's Word, cannot fully resist the lure of a body equally desirable to the orthodox and the heretic.

The ability of commentary to contain otherness within its pages both energizes and undermines its ability to produce singular biblical meaning. It is, on the one hand, a demonstration of the power of Christian meaning making to draw even the most paradoxical ideas into the totalizing orbit of orthodox truth, an act Catherine Chin has called "scriptural spoliation."[134] Origen can manipulate heretical opinion and Cyril can speak in the voice of Jewish doubt and disbelief. Yet it is, on the other hand, a slippery power: to display control over others is to imply the loss of control. To defeat error is to leave the traces of that error, indelibly.

In his polemical definition of commentary, Jerome had compared the careful interpreter of Scripture to the expert "money-changer," separating authentic meanings from counterfeit. Even this gesture of masterful discernment, however, invokes its own failure: the success of the counterfeit, the incorporation of error, the misapprehension of self and other. Christ's circumcised body comes to represent not only the multiplicity and promise of scriptural commentary but its peril as well. The "otherness" within—even when carefully managed and maintained—is never eradicated, but remains always lodged uncomfortably in the babel of Christian biblical meaning.

Excursus: Interpreting Colossians 2:11–12

One other New Testament passage—Colossians 2:11–12—may also speak to Christ's circumcision: "In him also you were circumcised with a spiritual circumcision, by putting off the body of the [*Greek variant*: sins of the] flesh in the circumcision of Christ; when you were buried with him in baptism, you were also raised with him through faith in the power of God, who raised him from the dead"[135] (NRSV). As I discuss in Chapter 1, modern scholarship goes through some contortions in order to *not* see Jesus' literal, infant circumcision in this passage: crucifixion, baptism, resurrection are all envisioned here instead. (Quite possibly the author—not Paul, but a close follower—envisions the beginning and ends of Christ's life converging with the new Christian in the baptismal font.) This passage's grammar is much more ambiguous than Luke's—is Christ circumcising or being circumcised?—and so provides less of an opportunity for early Christians to inhabit the contradictions of Scripture. We have already seen that Origen draws Colossians 2:11–12 into his commentary on Luke, where it creates a more clearly metaphorical and spiritual space around Jesus' physical circumcision.[136]

In general, Christians came late to the systematic interpretation of Paul's letters (except, of course, for Origen; his commentary on Colossians has not, however, survived).[137] Perhaps inhibited by gnostic and Marcionite adoration of Paul,[138] "orthodox" Christians shied away from direct, sustained engagement with Paul's texts. In the fourth century, however, interest exploded: homilies and commentaries proliferated across the Greek- and Latin-speaking Christian worlds.[139] Even so, Colossians rarely attracted significant attention; most commentary on Colossians that survives comes from Christian writers who made a point to comment on all of Paul's letters (which, for the post-Nicene church, comprised fourteen letters, including Hebrews). I include a few examples of such commentary here, primarily as a contrast with the Luke commentaries examined above. Two differences between readings of Luke and Colossians will be immediately evident. First, early Christians generally did not read "the circumcision of Christ" in Colossians 2:11 as referring to the circumcision performed *on* Christ, but rather a circumcision performed *by* Christ on his followers (that is, they read it as a subjective genitive instead of an objective genitive). Second, whereas commentaries on Luke elicited the productive ambiguities of God's physical and textual bodies, Colossians allowed interpreters to envision yet a third body of Christ: the communal body of the church as constituted through ritual.

John Chrysostom delivered dozens of homilies on all of Paul's letters, Colossians included: as Margaret Mitchell has detailed, John had a special affinity for and love of Paul.[140] In his sixth homily on Colossians, he provides a clear ritual exegesis of the transformative nature of the circumcision performed by Christ:

> No longer, [Paul] says, the circumcision in a knife, but in Christ himself: for the hand doesn't perform this circumcision (as in that case), but the spirit; and not a part, but he circumcises the whole person. For in both cases it is a body: but whereas that one is circumcised in the flesh, this one is circumcised spiritually. And not as Jews: for it's not flesh but sin that you're shedding. When, and where? In baptism! And what he

calls "circumcision" he also calls a grave (ταφόν). . . . But he speaks of something greater than circumcision: for they did not just cast away the circumcised part (τὸ περιτμηθὲν), but they destroyed it, they demolished it.[141]

John envisions Christ as the instrument of circumcision, analogous to the knife, stripping away the "body of sins" (a common textual variant in the Greek in the fourth century, perhaps drawn in from Romans 6:6) like a foreskin and utterly annihilating it in the baptismal font. The logic of circumcision remains physically palpable: there is cutting, stripping, and bodily transformation ("in both cases it is a body"). But instead of something Jewish, John places this bodily reshaping in the context of rebirth in the baptismal font.

Other Greek-speaking contemporaries of John commented on Colossians, as well. Theodore of Mopsuestia, like John, learned his exegesis from Diodore of Tarsus and, like John, produced a series of commentaries on Paul's letters. Unfortunately, these commentaries survive only in fragments in the Greek exegetical chains and in some Latin translations. From what remains, however, it is clear that Theodore's take on "the circumcision of Christ" is not substantially different from John's, but differs in scope. Instead of the "shedding of sin," Theodore sees this circumcision more cosmically: "by 'circumcision' he means the removal of mortality (*mortalitatem ablatio*)."[142] A brief comparison between the circumcision of Christ and regular circumcision illuminates the greater magnitude of the former: "removing a little piece of the body in that case has no usefulness, but in this case such a great thing as mortality is taken away in the superior transformation of our body (*in melius corpore nostro transformato*)."[143] That the circumcision is "of Christ" is added, Theodore remarks, so that Christians may recall the future promise fulfilled in Christ, who rose from the dead as the "first fruits" of the resurrection. Finally, Theodore makes clear where this total transformation of the body occurs: "in baptism," where Christians begin to anticipate a future existence free of mortality and sin altogether.[144]

In all of these commentaries, Christ is simultaneously a model—the perfect, sinless, immortal body—as well as the agent of circumcision. Severian of Gabala, John Chrysostom's enemy and rival in Constantinople, explains succinctly when he interprets Colossians 2:11: "That is, the one circumcising us (περιτεμὼν ἡμᾶς) from the sin of the flesh through baptism has given life in himself, such that baptism in Christ is spiritual circumcision: for he excises (περικόπει) the sins of the faithful."[145] Christ circumcises the pious in the baptismal font, stripping away sin and death, and creating a new communal body of Christ that reflects his own bodily (spiritual) perfection. Ambrosiaster, writing in the Latin West slightly before the Greek commentators, envisions this communal body of Christ stripped of the errors of paganism, the "worship of the elements" (*elementorum cultura*), by Christ's circumcising baptism: "from earthly to heavenly, from human to divine, converted from error to truth, mingled with his head and his authority through love."[146]

Interpretations of Colossians serve a different function in early Christian thought from interpretations of the circumcision in the Gospel of Luke. In Luke, Christian interpretation comes face to face with the paradox of otherness within, projected onto the twin bodies of God (incarnate and scriptural). In Colossians, however, the focus on Christ creating a purified communal body through baptism leaves no room for the other, except as that remainder which is left behind and (in John's phrase) "destroyed" and "demolished." Yet as we shall see in the next chapters, the rhythms of ritual invoked in interpretations of Colossians 2:11–12 will rarely allow for such tidy boundaries.

Chapter 6

"Let Us Be Circumcised!"
Ritual Differences

> Is circumcision, for example, an exterior mark? Is it an archive?
> —Jacques Derrida

Festive Difference

Ritual and Difference

Jonathan Z. Smith has explained ritual as "above all, an assertion of difference," and explained that ritual is "concerned with the elaboration of relative
difference that is never overcome."[1] We see ritualized the "difference that is
never overcome" clearly in early Christian commemoration of Christ's circumcision, on January 1. We have seen, in the previous chapters, how early
Christians transformed the stereotypical signifier of Jewish identity into a malleable, even contradictory sign of Christianity: in texts, homilies, treatises, and
letters, in discussions of theology, Scripture, and practice. The Feast of the Circumcision ritualizes and inscribes these paradoxical discourses into the heart
of the communal body of Christ: a thoroughly gentile body that had, by the
end of late antiquity, duly imbibed Paul's warning that "if you let yourselves
be circumcised, Christ will be of no benefit to you" (Gal 5:2).[2] Five hundred
years after Paul wrote to the Galatians, a local council of bishops in Tours,
most likely adapting existing liturgical practice, pronounced: "So during the
interval from the Birth of the Lord to Epiphany, every day is a festival, with
the exception of that three-day period on which, in order to stamp out the
custom of the pagans [i.e., New Year's festivals], our fathers established that

special services should be held on January 1, so there may be chanting in the churches, and on the eighth hour on that same day a Mass of the Circumcision may be celebrated as is fitting to God."[3] Liturgical historians usually take this brief notice as our earliest evidence for the ritualized memorial of Christ's circumcision.[4]

By the sixth century, the Feast of the Circumcision was one of several festivals that had been introduced to commemorate, and allow participation in, events from the lives of Jesus and Mary.[5] Late ancient churches made these crucial moments from the life of Jesus part of their public, liturgical life. As Christians gathered together for these festivals, their communal identities were discursively shaped and scripted. Ritual, as Smith reminds us, simultaneously addresses and problematizes difference. What differences were brought to the fore as Christians came to celebrate a rejected sign on the body of their savior, publicly and communally marking this Jewish ritual on Jesus' body through their own Christian ritual?

I begin this final chapter in the story of Jesus' circumcision in late antiquity by engaging the question of time, difference, and community: calendars and festivals (in antiquity as today) created distinctive communal identities, but also acknowledged "other" times and temporalities. Early Christians were sensitive to the ways that public celebration could enact distinction from "others" (pagans and Jews), but could also open up the occasion to blur those distinctions. I consider the evidence for the beginning of the Feast of the Circumcision among other feasts of the life of Jesus (such as Epiphany, Christmas, and the Feast of the Presentation) before considering two main pieces of evidence for how Christians understood their commemoration of and participation in Christ's circumcision: two sermons, one in Latin, the other in Greek, both probably from the fifth century or early sixth century.

Throughout this study I have engaged primarily with written remains; now, as I consider the ritual lives of Christians, we might feel the historical distance between text and reality yawn a bit more gapingly. We should, perhaps, be leery of inferring too much from textual remains: how can we glean the feeling of ritual—by which I mean both its embodiment and sentiment—from literature? Michael Penn, in his study of the early Christian kiss, helpfully notes that, no matter what manner of evidence we possess, we are always examining a world of discourse: "An individual's perception of reality does not stem from a reflection of the real, but is mediated and manipulated by cultural discourse."[6] Ritual does not precede language, nor does language always fail to represent an elusive bodily truth. Rather, in the liturgical language ritual difference is made and unmade. In both of the homilies I examine in this chapter we see Christians yearning for difference even as they so ostentatiously reject it: the strangeness of the heretic, the hard-hearted anachronism of the Jew, the ignorance of the pagan all find a place on Christ's infant body in the circumcision, and within his communal body in the Feast of the Circumcision.

Christian Festivals and Ambivalent Difference

"Festivals offer a convenient vantage point from which to analyze collective identities," writes Daniel Stökl Ben Ezra.[7] Punctuated marks in a communal stream of time, festivals are notable both for their regularity and irregularity: they come at predictable times (weekly, monthly, annually, and so forth) and yet interrupt the routine passage of time. Festivals shape time and society through the structured disruption of both.[8] Festivals are also sites for the assertion of and resistance to power. In the Roman world, festivals and the calendar operated as instruments of empire and accommodation.[9] Just as Roman space became a container for other spaces, the provinces, so Roman time could also enlarge and contain other times. Time in the provinces, or even in the capital city itself, could march to multiple rhythms.[10]

Michel Foucault linked the containment of otherness within space (what he terms *heterotopia*) with an analogous containment of otherness within time: *heterochrony*.[11] He gives two examples—the museum and the cemetery—both of which show the complexity of space-time, its ability to structure life and community through difference and incongruity.[12] The Roman Empire, from its very foundations, was masterfully heterochronic. One of Julius Caesar's acts as dictator in 45 BCE was to reorganize and regularize the Roman calendar, asserting control over the punctuated rhythms of Roman time. As Denis Feeney has noted, one of Caesar's motives was to realign the social sense of time with the actual solar year: "it was for the first time feasible in the Mediterranean world to have the civil and natural years in harmony under the same standard of representation."[13] The power to align the "civil and the natural" has been, at different periods in history, one of the essential gestures of empire: the calendar becomes a totalizing tool, in Caesar's hands, akin to the map or the globe.[14]

Yet as Feeney also points out, Caesar's calendar was an ambivalent tool of empire, since its "reach was not really universal: it was not a universal grid for all the peoples of the Empire, but it retained its specific power for Roman citizens as a context for apprehending and exploring Roman identity."[15] Provincials could use the Roman calendar to synchronize, or hybridize, "local" and "imperial" time without fully ceding the former to the latter.[16] Likewise, Roman time itself was hybridized in the imperial center: Caesar intentionally used "Greek and Egyptian science" in his calendrical reckoning, employing an Alexandrian astronomer named Sosigenes to direct the reform. Augustus, in the next generation, monumentalized this hybrid Roman-provincial time when he reorganized the Julian calendar in 8 CE and constructed a massive *horologium* (a "timepiece," tracking the days of the solar year) in the Campus Martius: the temporal indicator was an Egyptian obelisk, which cast shadows on "zodiacal demarcations . . . annotated in Greek."[17] The incorporation of provincial science and monuments into the architecture of Roman time is certainly an imperial act (time is literally marked by spolia) but also one that retains difference within, a theme that should by now be familiar to us as a hallmark of Roman imperialism.

We can see this same Roman sensibility of containing and refracting difference at work when early Christians contemplate time's shaping of communal identity, flowing in a calendar, punctuated by festivals. Our earliest evidence about how Christians viewed communal time puts the emphasis on difference, distinction, and superiority. The *Didache*, a possibly first-century manual of Christian ritual and morality, instructs on weekly fasting: "Your fasts should not stand with those of the hypocrites; for they fast on the second and fifth days of the week [lit., 'of Sabbaths'], but your fasts should be on the fifth day and the Preparation [day]."[18] Here Christian weekly time is inscribed with, and against, Jewish time. The days are calculated according to the Jewish Sabbath (usually the days are translated into English, for clarity, as "Monday" and "Thursday," and "Wednesday" and "Friday," respectively); even "Friday" is here labeled the day of Sabbath "preparation" (παρασκευή).[19] At the same time, of course, Jews are called the "hypocrites" (we are not told why), and the days of Christian fasting are distinguished from theirs.[20] Calendrical and festival distinction from Jews recurs in similar "church order" texts throughout late antiquity.[21] Christian time marches alongside, but conspicuously apart from, Jewish time. The difference is pointed, all the more so because it is made visible.

Much debate exists among historians of Christian festivals and liturgy as to how and when Christians developed a distinctive sense of religious time.[22] The study of ancient Christian festival time is therefore itself marked by ambivalence and resistance. Students of ancient Christianity held, earlier in the twentieth century, that before Constantine—that is, before "the world" so unpredictably irrupted into the church—the sole time that mattered was the cosmic time of salvation, and only gradually did the mundane calculation of days overtake the celestial: no longer did festivals look forward to the *eschaton*, but now they peered backward to commemorate biblical events.[23] Directly opposite those scholars positing an original, unique timelessness within ancient Christianity stand those scholars who posit the absolute interpenetration of worldly time into Christianity, arguing that every Christian festival borrows from or overwrites other religions' sacred days.[24] Both methods of studying Christian time and festivals invoke ideas of syncretism, "borrowing," and "holdovers," explaining how early Christian festivals mimic and incorporate religious others (either as a form of "corruption" or as the very genesis of Christian festival time).[25]

This language of temporal entanglement in some ways merely reflects our sources, which likewise struggle with time and the other. We recall John Chrysostom railing against members of his church who attend the New Year's or Passover festivities at the synagogue (as I discuss in Chapter 4). Two understandings of Christian time are present in the same literary source. Some Christians insist on temporal distinction (John); others seek a more relaxed kind of temporal affiliation (the "Judaizers"). How do we make sense historically of what's going on in fourth-century Antioch? Do we privilege the viewpoint of John, and write off the Christian synagogue attendants as innovators, Judaizers, or syncretists? Do we side with the synagogue attendants, and accuse John of innovating in his desire to separate Christian and Jewish festival life? Do we speak ecumenically (but historically, perhaps, unhelpfully) of "Christianities," overlapping in space but disjointed in time?

Or do we step back from the tangle of calendrical rhetoric and think instead about how time functioned in the construction of community in the Roman world? Both John and his targets frame their festival observance, their sense of Christian time, around the religious difference of the "other" (in this case, the Jews). Jewish time stands in contrast, whether positively or negatively. After all, we have no sense that the Christians against whom John rails are substituting Jewish for Christian observance: rather, they are supplementing their Christian time with the time of the other.[26] John, likewise, creates a contrast, a dual stream of time playing out between "us" and "them." The practical outcome for both John and his opponents is different but, I suggest, the desire remains the same: to experience Christian time in close and clear contrast with the time of the "other."

Even in the case of the debates over Easter, which threatened to collapse the difference between Christian and Jewish time, we sense the same desire to distinguish yet contain difference. The so-called Quartodecimans (or, in Greek, *tessareskaidekatitai*) calculated Easter based on the soli-lunar Jewish calendar, so that it fell at the same time as the Jewish Passover. The "orthodox" accused these Christians of deviant calendrical behavior, Judaizing by adhering too closely to a Jewish, fleshly, literal interpretation of the Old Testament commandments concerning Passover.[27] Presumably, such festival calibration would also require consultation with the Jewish leaders who set the festival dates for their synagogues.[28] Not just ancient bishops but modern historians as well sense a kind of Judaizing in this festival conformity, as Stephen Wilson writes: "Both in terms of chronology and content the Quartodeciman celebration made the Christians almost indistinguishable from the Jews, at least to an outsider."[29] The assumption is that religious difference fades in the face of temporal unity: Christians aligning their festivals with the Jewish calendar must be seeking, even hazily, a kind of religious rapprochement.

Yet calendars do not necessarily work this way: indeed, incorporating the "other" into a punctuated calendar of festivals may be precisely a gesture of superiority and distinction.[30] To celebrate the Christian Pasch alongside the Jewish Pesach may be no more a gesture of reconciliation and rapprochement than two counterdemonstrations in front of the White House deliberately scheduled on the same afternoon.[31] One of our earliest sources for the Quartodeciman commemoration of Easter may be the rabidly anti-Jewish homily of Melito of Sardis, *Peri Pascha*: indeed, Alistair Stewart-Sykes has gone so far (following previous scholars) as to see in Melito's anti-Jewish homily a "Christian haggadah," not only drawing on the festival timing of the Jewish Passover but even miming its form.[32] Yet no one would argue that the *Peri Pascha* represents an attempt at forging Jewish-Christian unity.[33] The appropriation of Jewish time—if, indeed, it was part of Melito's Easter commemoration—both mimics and overwrites that time.[34]

Throughout early Christian festival life, this tense awareness of other times ticking alongside the sacred life of the church remains palpable. Our evidence for Christian calendar and festivals is sparse before Constantine's promotion of Christianity as a public, monumental religion.[35] By the fourth and fifth centuries our evidence grows more plentiful,[36] and we find Christians theorizing their own sense of communal, even imperial, time.[37] Even before January 1 became the Feast of the Circumcision, it was a day to inscribe Christian difference in the shadow of the Roman Empire. Augustine preached a sermon in Carthage, on January 1, 404,[38] in which he (like Caesar some centuries before) tried to reorient his community's sense of time with respect to the natural world.[39] In this case, he preached an enormously long sermon against the depredations of the "pagan" festival of the New Year, imploring his congregants not only to resist the lures of idolatry but to rethink their sense of the sweep of time.[40] The sermon manipulates time on multiple levels, not only reimagining the first day of the year as a time of fasting instead of revelry but also the history of human culture and God's cosmic calendar.[41] Even the length of the sermon, possibly approaching three hours, itself manipulates time. A recent English translator describes the sermon as "a deliberate 'filibuster,' intended to keep his audience as long as possible in church, and so prevent them from rushing off to the wicked pagan jollifications which he was preaching against."[42] Augustine kept his flock in check for hours during the day, too entranced (or too bored?) to integrate themselves into the rhythms of "pagan" life outside.[43] Yet those rhythms could not be ignored: they lay beneath, and behind, Augustine's overpowering rhetoric as the other time that must be overcome.

Later in the fifth century, Maximus of Turin also attempted to inscribe temporal difference at the threshold of the New Year. Like John Chrysostom and the Judaizers in fourth-century Antioch, Maximus was apparently faced with Christians who wanted to celebrate with pagans: "I speak of those who, while celebrating the Lord's birthday with us, abandoned themselves to pagan feasts (*gentilium se feriis dediderunt*), and after that heavenly banquet made themselves a meal of superstition, so that those who before had taken delight in holiness afterward got drunk on emptiness."[44] For Maximus the choice should be clear, and the "Lord's Epiphany" must be totally separated from "kalends of Janus"; not only is the pagan celebration blasphemous (since Janus, Maximus teaches, was a human being and it is unlawful to worship a creature), but Christian and pagan festivals must maintain utterly distinct rhythms: "their delight is condemned by our restraint."[45] The Christianization of time cannot help but invoke the idea of non-Christian time, lurking outside the doors of the church. Although his primary theme is the danger of pagan revelry, Maximus also warns: "Not only that of the pagans, but also the company of the Jews (*Iudaeorum consortia*) we ought to avoid, for their conversation is highly contagious (*magna pollutio*)."[46] Maximus's warning is dire, but also tantalizing: even as they foreswear the contagious company of Jews and pagans, the Christian congregation is made to imagine that polluting consortium.

As Christianity become a public religion, the sweep of time—daily, weekly, annual, cosmic—became a site of distinction, where difference was highlighted (and thereby crystallized and preserved) as it was excluded. At the dawn of the fifth century, Christian festival time was a site of contention, and January 1 already allowed for the deliberate confrontation of Christian and non-Christian temporal communities.[47] By the sixth century, that day would become even more thickly textured with internalized difference, as the Christian commemoration of Jesus' Jewish circumcision.

Christ's Festival Life

From the fifth century onward, Christian churches saw a rise in the commemoration of events from the life of Jesus and his family, such as the "presentation" (February 2), the "annunciation" (March 25), and the "dormition" (on August 2).[48] Even the Feast of the Nativity, which was sparsely and diversely commemorated well into the fourth century, found new traction in both the East and West in the fifth century, distinguished from the adjacent Feast of the Epiphany (January 6, originally commemorating either Jesus' birth or his baptism or both).[49] Certainly these events from Jesus' and Mary's lives had already found narrative expression in "apocryphal" texts circulating from the second century onward, such as the infancy gospels;[50] now, in the fifth century, these imagined moments from Christ's life took public place alongside more established feasts, such as Easter. There are many possible explanations for the multiplication of festivals. The Mediterranean city had always been structured, spatially and temporally, by public religious celebration and procession. As Christianity became dominant in the cities, and bishops took the lead in urban life (or attempted to do so), Christian commemorations purposefully filled the time and space of the city.[51] Studies of the "Christianization of the city" often focus on the static forms of architecture, but time was similarly reshaped by episcopal efforts (sometimes unsuccessfully, as Augustine and Maximus complained).[52]

More than just the need for new and more Christian public festivals prompted the increased memorialization of the life of Jesus. We must also take account of the growing theological and scriptural focus on the person of Christ beginning in the fourth century. Already by the late fourth century the contemplation of Jesus' human activities crystallized for the congregated Christians the mystery of the spirit-in-flesh that defined their communion.

At the Festival of Pentecost, Gregory of Nazianzus invoked the majesty of the incarnation:

> We celebrate Pentecost, and the indwelling of the Spirit, and the ap-
> pointed time of promise, and the fulfillment of hope. And what a great
> mystery! How great and august! The bodily matters of Christ have
> reached an end . . . and the matters of the Spirit begin. But what are
> those matters of Christ? Virgin, birth, manger, swaddling, angels glorify-
> ing, shepherds running around, the star's path, worship and gift-giving
> of *magi*, the child-massacre of Herod, Jesus fleeing into Egypt, returning
> from Egypt, circumcised, baptized, testified to from above, tempted,
> stoned on our behalf . . . betrayed, nailed up, buried, raised, ascending:
> even now he suffers many things! . . . Such are the matters of Christ: and
> we shall see yet more glorious things that follow, and we shall be seen:
> the things of the Spirit.[53]

The Cappadocian bishop invokes the cosmic turn of history, as Christ's bodily dispensation ends and the advent of the Holy Spirit begins. In order to invoke this great mystery, Gregory parades before his audience the life of Christ in a manner that recalls the mosaic panels and altar paintings of later Byzantine churches: scene after scene, palpable in their bodiliness, all leading to the "things of the Spirit."[54] Gregory takes the occasion of the festival of the Spirit to adumbrate his Trinitarian theology, focusing his audience's attention on the multiply signifying bodily life of Christ to make his point. Among the Cappadocians, and their Greek-speaking successors, festival observance could condense and refract debate over Trinity, Christology, and other points of theology.[55]

If deep theological desire infused the public commemoration of events from the life of Christ, so too did the intensified focus on Scripture in this period. We have already seen how public preaching drew on Luke's scene of the circumcision, whether as part of a series of homilies (such as those of Ambrose or Cyril of Alexandria) or as stand-alone homilies (such as those of Ephrem or Proclus). It is interesting to note how easily these exegetical homilies became incorporated into festival collections: Ephrem's homily that harmonizes the creation and nativity accounts has been collected as part of his homilies "on the feast of the Nativity"; Proclus of Constantinople's homily on Luke 2:21–14 is embedded in the manuscript tradition as a homily *de circumcisione domini*, to be preached on the day of that festival.[56] Scripture generated festival contemplation, even as Christian festivals became highly textualized: some of our earliest "calendars" of Christian festivals are, in fact, lectionaries, lists of scriptural, homiletic, and hagiographic texts to be read at particular festivals.[57]

These elements—the reconfigured urban space, the increased theological and scriptural attention to Jesus' earthly life—coalesce in the so-called presentation, or *hypapante*, which was being commemorated in the East by the mid-fifth century.[58] Evidence indicates that the Feast of the Presentation entered into common Christian commemoration before the Feast of the Circumcision: it may be indicated already in the fifth-century record of Jerusalem liturgical readings known as the *Armenian Lectionary*.[59] Certainly it has been established as part of the Jerusalem calendar by the time of Hesychius, a prominent preacher in the holy city who flourished in the first decades of the fifth century.[60] Two of his homilies on the Feast of the Presentation survive among his collected festal homilies, in which the preacher dilates on the mysteries of the incarnation and Christ's submission to human flesh and Law.[61] In the first homily, Hesychius declares: "The festival is called the Purification (καθαρσίων), but one would not be mistaken to call it the 'festival of festivals,' the 'Sabbath of Sabbaths,' or the 'holy of holies': for the entire mystery of Christ's incarnation is summarized in it, the entire advent (παράστασις) of the Only-Begotten Son is described in it."[62] The "mystery" that is summarized is one of complexity and contradiction, in which the events that Luke narrates do not really happen for the characters themselves (Jesus and Mary), since neither of them was in need of purification. Rather, the audience should imagine themselves receiving the benefit of these mysteries: "Christ was circumcised on our behalf, he was baptized for us, for us the purifications of the Law were accomplished. If he wept, he washed out [our] nature; if he was flogged, he freed us from captivity; if he was raised up on the cross, he lifted up the yoke of our sin."[63] Christ is the subject of these actions, but the audience is the object of them. Yet we should note how these actions are subtly transformed on Christ's body: Christians are not lifted on a cross, rather their yoke is lifted up; they are not beaten (like a slave), but freed from their (metaphorical) slavery. So too, we must assume, the circumcision and the Temple sacrifices in which Christians participate on the Feast of the Presentation mean otherwise, as well.

Hesychius, preaching near the ruins of the Temple,[64] transforms Jewish festival time into something radically Christian, even anti-Jewish. Hesychius explains what Symeon (the Jewish prophet in the Jewish Temple) meant when he prophesied about an "opposing sign" (σημεῖον ἀντιλεγόμενον [Luke 2:34]): "This is the cross; for while the Jews were crucifying him, the sun was setting: the synagogue falsely accused, and the earth shook. The people shouted, 'Crucify him!' but the stones, not bearing the weight of their blasphemy, broke apart."[65] The earth resists the blasphemy of the Jews, and Hesychius reconfigures the Jewish sacrifice of Jesus conducted to the rhythms of the Jewish calendar (the Feast of the Presentation was also known as the "Forty Days" feast, from the Levitical commandment being observed in Luke 2:22–24). Christian time gazes—here, in Hesychius's Jerusalem, quite literally and no doubt to great effect—upon the devastated time and space of the other.

Throughout the fifth century and into the sixth, the Feast of the Presentation offered Christians the opportunity to gaze upon—even step into—Jewish time, protected by the circumcised body of Christ. This other time transformed before them, but never lost its taste of otherness. A later homily on the presentation preserved mistakenly under John Chrysostom's name makes this absorption of Jewish time clear:

> For the Law commands circumcision on the eighth day, and if the eighth day arrives, the doctor comes among them and he brandishes the iron and he practices his craft: and the Sabbath is delayed on account of circumcision [cf. John 5:18]. Let's ask the Jews now: the Sabbath is loosened, the day of perfect rest: for what reason does the eighth override the seventh? Why is the eighth more important than the seventh? But Jews don't know about Jewish things (Ἰουδαῖοι μὲν τὰ Ἰουδαϊκὰ οὐκ οἴδασιν): but Christ's church knows Christ and Jewish teachings. For the child is circumcised on the eighth day since the resurrection was going to be on the eighth day, that is, the dominical circumcision of the whole world.[66]

The time of circumcision remains indisputably Jewish (after all, it is part of *judaica*) but can only be understood through Christ's life, the cosmic time of resurrection and salvation ("the whole world's circumcision"). Likewise, in the sixth century, Jacob of Serugh expands the Jewish temporality of the Law into a cosmic time frame: the circumcision recalls the creation of "humanity" in the flesh, and the animals offered for Jesus in the Temple recall his creation of "winged" and "swarming" creatures.[67] Christians are invited to contemplate Jewish time, and see their own cosmic—even imperial—time reflected back at them. We should not be surprised that, in several of these homilies on the presentation, we find the circumcision of Christ at work in this partial absorption of Jewish time. Of all the moments of Christ's life, this one paradoxical scene could condense for Christians the allure and fascination of other time.

Preaching Difference: The Feast of the Circumcision

I turn, now, to the Feast of the Circumcision, as it survives to us, primarily in festival homilies that were collected and catalogued throughout the medieval and Byzantine periods.[68] I focus on two textual sources, which may be the earliest sermons devoted explicitly to the festival of the circumcision of Jesus: one in Latin, one in Greek. Sermons, as homiletic historians have been telling us of late, provide an important window into the lives of ancient Christians:[69] in a society in which rhetoric was prized, and rhetorical performance believed to shape speaker and audience at once, ritualized liturgical speeches give us precious evidence for the varied articulations of religious identity. Both of these sermons are inflected by their original milieux: the Latin homily is marked by an Augustinian emphasis on love and humility, while the Greek sermon (which is also dedicated to Basil of Caesarea, whose feast day fell on January 1) generates a sense of orthodox triumphalism. These sermons have much in common, too. Their composers are unknown, and ascription has varied. The Latin homily has been attached to various figures, sometimes Augustine and Jerome, eventually settling into the manuscript tradition as the work of Fulgentius of Ruspe, a monk-turned-bishop who flourished in the early sixth century.[70] The Greek homily was ascribed to Amphilochius of Iconium, the cousin of Gregory of Nazianzus and theological ally of the Cappadocian fathers.[71] Both homilies use the rhythms of Christian time to contemplate the otherness that swirls around—and occasionally rests within—Christian ritual life. The event of Christ's circumcision is made manifest, discursively repeated, even taken up by the assembled congregants. These homilies considered together give us glimpses into the ways in which difference was ritualized, problematized, and inscribed within the Christian community.

Ps.-Fulgentius of Ruspe: Humilitas

The Latin sermon from North Africa is the shorter and probably earlier of the two, dating to the late fifth century.[72] The homily begins on a note of obedient unworthiness,[73] highlighting the stark difference between divinity and humanity that arguably undergirds much Christian ritual: "The mystery of the divine incarnation, the excellent sacrament of our reconciliation, is celebrated and honored by us at the New Year, so that the commemoration might show how great was the kindness which was paid out for us in our unworthiness, and alert us how much thanks we owe."[74] Above all, throughout this homily, the preacher seeks to locate his congregants—not only as a body of believers, but as individuals—squarely in the salvation history so brightly illuminated by Christ's first human actions. They are to look in the mirror of Christ's humiliation, and see their own shame. First, the shame of their own flesh and bodies which Christ has taken upon himself, "the humiliation of true flesh and true death."[75] But even more poignantly, each individual will feel the shame of his or her own unworthiness: "So pay attention, human being, to the honor of such great kindness, so that you may humbly render your thanksgiving!"[76] Certainly the homilist feels the influence of Augustine's theology keenly: "Let us give thanks, brothers, since we earned punishment but received grace."[77] With every step of Christ's abasement—descending from the "bread of angels" to "milk from a woman's breast"[78]—the congregants are pressed to reimagine their own fleshly abasement as a locus of both humiliation and redemption.

Yet as soon as the preacher configures his audience's human lowliness in the person of Christ, he makes that incarnate human strange to them by dislocating it from Christian time and space: "Not only did the creator of all flesh see fit to be born from the flesh of a virgin, according to the true nature of flesh, and God who made humanity to become a true human born of a human; but also to be wrapped in swaddling clothes, laid in the most confining crib, *circumcised on the eighth day,* and hefted in human hands *to his own Temple.* . . . That one, as a small child, was nursed by his mother, he who, in his vastness, created a mother for himself. He was carried as a tiny boy by parents *to his own Temple,* he who, as great God, was sought by holy men *in that same Temple.*"[79] I have indicated the phrases I think would have jarred (we might even imagine the orator adjusting his tone on these very phrases: certainly the repetition suggests emphasis), where the imagery shifts from the everyday rhythms of childhood (swaddling, crib, nursing) to the alien rhythms of Judaism.

That this imagery is meant to sound strange is clear from the way the homilist insists on its veracity: "you do not render honorable praise but rather shameful abuse for the divine gift, if you begin to doubt the magnitude of such a kindness," he says early on,[80] and soon after explains: "Indeed, dear ones, this integrity of Christ's faith has always customarily been held: that if we read or hear that something was done according to the narrative of the canonical gospel-writers, by Christ or in Christ himself, we should first believe that the story is true without any doubt, and then we should seek in the historical truth also the spiritual understanding."[81] No hiding behind metaphor or allegory is allowed: the congregants must believe their ears, and so conjure up before them Christ's tiny body conveyed into the Temple, offering sacrifice, circumcised. Yet here we, outside the communal context of this homily, feel a bit of confusion. Presumably a congregation gathered for the Feast of the Circumcision is already prepared to accept this mysterious and circumcised Christ. So why does the homilist invoke this "doubt"?

One reason, it seems, is so that he can also conjure the specter of disbelief, embodied in unworthy and condemned heretics: "since the text of the divine story is believed to be true, the Manichean is confounded in his narrowness (*severitate*)."[82] As we have already seen, in Augustine's debate with Faustus the Manichean in Chapter 3, we should be prepared to hear in these condemnations the allure of the heretic, the teasing error that haunts the interior borders of orthodoxy: "For [the Manichean] does not want to believe that human flesh was formed by God, nor that the circumcision of the flesh was ordained by God for our holy fathers."[83] That Christ's circumcision proved his fleshliness refutes the dualistic Manichean rejection of materiality, a potentially tempting dualism (how long did it take Augustine to overcome it?) that has now been safely spoken aloud, contemplated, and contained.

Once the preacher has allowed his audience to flirt with the rejection of Christ's materiality, he can also remind them of their scriptural ties to this alien Jewish past—the age of "our holy fathers" who circumcised and offered sacrifice: "when that wretched person deprecates the sacred history of the Old Testament, he denies himself also that cure found in the New Testament."[84] Having considered, and dispensed with, such scriptural error, the audience can now proudly embrace both Law and flesh (with humility, as we have seen, and shame). Indeed, these two points of Catholic pride—flesh and law—are intimately related, and deliberately performed by Christ in order to refute Manichean heresy: "Because the holy evangelist recounts it, we know that Christ, the Son of God, was born a real human being; Christ the Son of God was truly circumcised; a sacrifice of flesh was offered on behalf of Christ, the Son of God, according to the custom of the divine institution at that time (*tunc*); for both the circumcision of the flesh and the rules of animal sacrifice are known to be rules established in the Old Testament."[85] These two events— the circumcision and naming of Jesus (Luke 2:21) and the purification offering in the Temple (Luke 2:22–39)—share an emphasis on flesh (the infant flesh of Jesus and the sacrificial flesh of a pair of birds) and are regulated by the Old Testament. For the homilist, Christ's participation in carnal legalities therefore affirms the authority of the Old Testament, and counters the scriptural arguments of the Manichean. The fleshly laws of the Jews must have divine significance: why else would Jesus himself endorse them at his birth?[86] The Manichean who denies both flesh and the Old Testament, then, is defeated.[87] The Manichean temptation of the pious congregation is subtly acknowledged, but firmly set aside.

Both flesh and Law, in this homily, are also acutely temporal. Christ is, after all, obeying the Law "of the time" (*tunc*). Time (*tempus*) looms large in the sermon: "Why then should not God be believed to have caused the circumcision of the flesh to be commanded at the right time (*congruo tempore*) in order to signify something, since the Son of God caused it to be commemorated on himself? Why moreover should our God not have commanded the Jewish people in times past (*praeterito tempore*) to offer animal sacrifices to him, when the Only-Begotten God himself, born at that time from the Jews (*ex Iudaeis temporaliter natus*), saw fit to offer himself for our sins according to the flesh?"[88] The foreignness of Jewish time—"then," "their time," "times past"—structures Christian time here and now, the time of festival, ritual, the commemoration of the mystery of the incarnation. As we have seen, the invocation of Jewish time cuts in two directions: on the one hand, it creates distinction. *Our* time is not *their* time; our ritual, Law, and sacrifice stand in contradistinction. And yet this juxtaposition of temporalities is intimate: *our* time makes sense through *their* time, Jewish time creeps in to create the distinctiveness of Christian festivity. Which time do the assembled Christians inhabit? Having rejected the atemporality of the Manicheans, cut off from sacred history, which temporality do these Catholic Christians share with Christ circumcised? Is it not, after all, a Jewish time?

Having used Christ's circumcision to bound off (but leave visible) the Manichean heresy, the homilist has blurred this crucial distinction of late ancient Christianity. Despite his careful language—saying that Jesus was born "from the Jews of the time" and not "as a Jew"—the homilist has, by his focus on "flesh" and "Law" as the touchpoints of orthodoxy, brought his pious flock ever closer to Judaism. Both carnality and legality were the hallmarks of the Jews, contrasted by the orthodox with spirituality and grace, as Daniel Boyarin notes: "This accusation against the Jews, that they are indisputably carnal, was a topos of much Christian writing in antiquity."[89] Judaism itself, as we have seen in Chapter 4, became intimately intertwined with heresy, articulating desires that inhabited the tantalizing margins of acceptable Christian thought.[90] To inhabit that Judaism fully, to not only visualize but participate in the carnality of Jewish Law, was to create precisely those perilous religious links the Manicheans decried.

As if sensing that the assertion of one difference has problematized another, the homilist pulls back from his unadulterated praise of flesh and Law at this point. He makes clear how Jewish time has been converted on Christ's body, and how the congregated Christians participate in that festival conversion. Just as Jewish sacrifice becomes Christian ritual, so Jewish flesh becomes Christian spirit. The homilist lauds Christ's circumcision for its beneficial fashioning of "Christian customs, so that we might consider what was done bodily in him for our salvation, and we might imitate it *spiritually*."[91] Even though Christ's participation in Christian humanity was all too real and physical, the Christians' participation in Christ's ritual acts is fully spiritual. Indeed, the imitation of all of his infant acts is spiritualized. Christ was born a "little boy" to teach humility; he was "subject to his parents in the flesh" to teach Christians to "honor father and mother"; he was "wrapped in a cheap cloth so that rich Christians would learn not to love earthly riches," and so on.[92]

The homilist can now apply well-established spiritual interpretations of circumcision to the specific case of Jesus: "Through the circumcision that the Son of God received in the flesh, he previewed the circumcision of our hearts in the spirit."[93] Now, after a lengthy—and potentially Judaizing—paean to the flesh, the homilist has returned to the more comfortable, and comfortably Christian, realm of the spirit. He cites the "blessed apostle's" distinction between the "outward Jew" and the "inward Jew," and between "outward" (that is, fleshly) circumcision and "inward circumcision of the heart" (Rom 2:28–29).[94] He exhorts: "Just so Christ had a circumcision in the body, so that a Christian might have it spiritually in his heart. On this account that one, who could not have any sin whatsoever, gave up the foreskin of his flesh, so that we might abjure our depraved desires. So Christ was carried by hand to the Temple, so that a Christian might aspire to good works in heaven. Christ wanted a sacrifice offered for his sake, so that a Christian might offer himself to the Lord's altar."[95] "Inward circumcision" is understood in a moral, even ascetic sense: the "stripping away" of "depraved desires." In this the homilist follows a long tradition of reading the rituals of the Old Testament as exhortations to Christian ascetic behaviors.[96] The sermon continues to interpret the specific sacrifices offered for Jesus (according to Luke 2:24: "a pair of turtledoves and two young doves") in similarly allegorical fashion: "in the dove is understood love (*caritas*) and in the turtledove is found chastity (*castitas*)."[97] Renunciation of desire, embrace of charity and chastity: common themes of post-Augustinian Latin Christianity, serving, perhaps, to redraw that blurred line between the carnal rituals of the Jewish past and the spiritual aspirations of the Christian present.

Somewhere in the middle, caught between Jewish literalism and Christian figuralism (as well, perhaps, between Catholic earthliness and Manichean fantasy) is the body of Christ, the object of Christian imitation in this festal homily. For Christ quite explicitly models the "inward Christian" with the body of the "outward Jew," giving proper spiritual guidance through an inimitably fleshly ritual—a ritual in which the homilist's audience is called upon to participate. What's more, Christ's participation in these rituals is doubly unnecessary, and therefore doubly gracious: according to the homilist, he no more needed his "depravity" stripped away than he did his foreskin.

At the end of the homily the preacher returns to his concern at the beginning: the threat of heresy, now expanded. Not just Manicheans but Arians and Donatists threaten the Catholic fold. If the dove and the turtledove represent Catholic love and chastity, heretical beliefs are "evil birds of prey . . . who hunt the dove's love and execrate the turtledove's chastity: whomever they are able they devour with their mouths, or they shred with their talons—that is, they defile with their speech or they torture with their persecutions."[98] They are warded off by these symbols of the old Law, these birds of offering, refurbished among orthodox Christians. The old Law itself is deflected in the same gesture by its spiritualization and transformation.

The doubled gesture of the homilist—Judaizing against the heretic, spiritualizing against the Jew—is not terribly different from the common, equally paradoxical strategies of other texts from this period that I have examined in the previous chapters. The difference lies in its explicitly ritualized context: the homilist brings his congregation communally to the very precipice of Jewishness, embracing the legalized flesh of Christ "from the Jews," circumcised just like the Jews, carried with him to the threshold of the Jewish Temple, before pulling back into a spiritualizing mode.[99] The perplexing remainder of otherness is eradicated on neither side, and the discourse of difference is deferred.

The century following the festival commemoration of our Latin homilist witnessed the growing observance of the Feast of the Circumcision in the West.[100] We have already seen it attested as a previously known custom at the Council of Tours, in the mid-sixth century. We also have a sermon

On the Circumcision of the Lord preached by Caesarius of Arles in the early sixth century; although the sermon does not mention a festival occasion, it was collected (seemingly by Caesarius himself) with other sermons delivered on January 1.[101] Caesarius, like our anonymous Latin homilist before him, conforms Jewish time to Christian morality, highlighting at once their overlap and incommensurability: Christ was circumcised, Caesarius preaches, "so that he wouldn't be different from the fathers, from whose offspring he was engendered (*procreatus*); and so that the Jews could not excuse themselves and say, 'You're different from our fathers, so we don't want to believe you!'"[102] Ritual distinction ironically meant to show kinship now reinscribes difference: Christ's Jewish circumcision sets him (and his followers, gathered to commemorate this day) apart from the Jews. Instead of focusing on birth and infancy, the assembled Christians are now asked to contemplate "the day of our death," and through Christ's wounded genitalia consider "all the wounds of sin."[103] Embedded firmly in the Latin Christian context,[104] festival contemplation of and identification with Christ's circumcision open worshipers up to the multifarious differences of time, place, and belief that shape, and threaten, and inform their devotional life.

Ps.-Amphilochius of Iconium: Mnēmosunē

A Greek sermon of unknown provenance (catalogued by the Bollandists as Bibliotheca Hagiographica Graeca 261), usually ascribed to Amphilochius of Iconium, cousin of Gregory of Nazianzus, survives in several Byzantine *menologia* (saints' calendars).[105] It is my belief that this sermon dates to the late fifth or sixth century, and therefore constitutes our earliest evidence for the festival commemoration of Christ's circumcision in the eastern Mediterranean (I discuss my dating arguments in an excursus, below). The sermon combines thoroughgoing biblical typology and allegory with a kind of orthodox triumphalism, culminating in praise of Basil the Great, whose feast day also fell on January 1 by the sixth century.[106] Certainly the idea of typology—the reading of the New Testament into the Old, of Jewish letter into Christian spirit—is not novel here; but we should not lose sight of its ritual context. The homilist is not merely preaching the fulfillment of the "old" in the "new": it is impossible for the congregated Christians to lose sight of real, physical, and literal circumcision precisely because this is a Feast of the Circumcision of Christ.

The Greek homilist begins by drawing a sharp, even cutting distinction between Christian and Jewish time; the former is a time of illumination, the latter lies in darkness. Elaborating on Hebrews' images of the "Law as a shadow," the homilist exhorts his audience to "disregard the rest of the legal types, and the shadows; let us have regard instead for the finely etched form of the things themselves."[107] Yet the image of shadow and light is also an image of analogy and likeness: the "things themselves" must continue to bear an uncanny, if uneven, relationship with "legal types, and the shadows." Christ, by his circumcision, inhabits both the shadowy past and the brilliant present, delineating the type and antitype at the same time. Christians, who are called on not only to "contemplate" but to "perform" the Law (albeit in a "spiritual manner"),[108] also inhabit this dual time of Jewish past and Christian present (and, as shall see, heretical time that cuts across sacred history).

Like the Latin homilist, and Caesarius after him, the Greek homilist takes hold of the life-cycle rhythms suggested by the ritual of circumcision and subjects them to a kind of typological and allegorical inversion. To gaze upon the infant Christ is to aspire to spiritual maturity: "let us speak and discern and reason not like children—in the manner of the child-minded, or mindless, Jews."[109] The Jewish Law is shadowy and unformed—childlike—but Christ, in his childhood adherence to that Law, points to a different sense of time: "For this did the Lord God reveal himself to us as a child: so that which is childish and imperfect in our intellect may be transformed into perfect and suitably virile mind."[110] To look at Christ, the child keeping Jewish Law, is to learn how to leave behind "legal servitude and childish behavior (*politeia*)."[111]

Cosmic time is invoked alongside individual time. The homilist asks his audience to envision the grand sweep of sacred history and contemplate the shift from "old" to "new" Law. Of course, like the imagery of shadow and light, the idea of "former" and "latter" creates distinction and connection at once. The old flows into the new, and Christ embodies both:

> The former remained imperfect and functioned ineffectively [and so] he annulled it and put a stop to it: now Jesus is circumcised according to his own eight-day Law, not so that he might teach us to be circumcised, but so that he might put a stop to circumcision; indeed, so that he might divest us of the preconception of the old, useless [Law], and reveal the power of the new and salvific one; so that he might abolish [circumcision] according to the flesh, and cause it to sprout anew according to the spirit; for Christ is circumcised in a refutation of the former [Law's] weakness and in an affirmation of the latter [Law's] strength.[112]

Through participation in the ritual, Jesus both affirms and negates it. The Law of circumcision belongs to him, it is "his own eight-day Law," as the homilist affirms later: "He did not come to abolish the Law as if it were foreign, but rather he came fulfilling it by this deed, as his own and having been established by himself, as his own doctrine and commandment of God."[113] Christ in the past, the time of shadow, instituted the Law he displayed on his own incarnate body; yet by observing his own law, he changes it, makes it "new." This new law contains and covers over the old law, transforming "weak" flesh into "strong" spirit.

The ritual of Jewish infancy, on Christ, indicates the ritual of Christian maturity, "the greater circumcision, that which is in baptism."[114] Christians, as we have seen in earlier chapters, slowly came to understand the rite of circumcision as a typological placeholder for the ritual of baptism. (The circumcisions performed by Joshua on the Israelites crossing the Jordan River provided an exemplary intertext for this transtestamental interpretation.) The rhythms of the Christian calendar would likely encourage this identification, since the Feast of the Circumcision falls just five days before Epiphany. Not only did Epiphany commemorate Jesus' baptism, it was also the occasion at which bishops would begin calling for the enrollment of new catechumens to prepare for springtime baptism.[115] The invocation of baptism therefore emplots circumcision in simultaneous temporalities: "so circumcision according to the flesh outlines not only a remission of sins, and the circumcision of Christ in baptism, but indeed also subtly, and in shadows, it describes the resurrection and alteration of all, according to which all carnal discernment of human beings is circumcised and excised, and transformed into another living being."[116] Multiple streams of time intersect: historic time, articulated in the biblical narrative; individual time, which begins, in Christ, at baptism; communal time, punctuated by festivals and commemorations; and cosmic time, culminating in the utter transformation of being in the final resurrection.

Time preoccupies the homilist, as we might expect at such a precisely calibrated festival. Invocation of the final resurrection leads him to consider the eight days of circumcision. "Circumcision according to the flesh is like some obscure and shadowy prototype," he muses; "on this account, too, the former eight-day period was put into Law."[117] The limited time of one week explodes into the infinite time of the eschaton, "the eternal and future octave."[118] Once more the shadows of the past are contrasted with the illumination of the present, and the emphasis remains on ritual time: "it was necessary, at the rising of the sun, for the moon and the stars to grow dim and shrink; and when the true circumcision and ministry were laid bare, it was necessary for the shadowy perceptions of the truth and the types to withdraw."[119] What was purely animal ("circumcision in the flesh and animal sacrifices")[120] Christ shows to be incomplete and imperfect; yet only by assuming this animal imperfection can Christ set them aside: "Because of this, accordingly, God the Word formerly became flesh, and on this the eighth day today was bodily circumcised."[121] Christians feel the synchronicity: that eighth day is "today" (σήμερον); they stand with Christ and look backward to shadow and forward to the light.

Having overlaid Christian truth on top of Jewish Law and carnal ritual, the Greek homilist then redeploys these tropes—in appropriately transformed fashion—in order to create an ultimate marker of Christian distinction. Here, the figure of cocelebrand Basil of Caesarea intervenes, and the time of Christian festival expands even more. Basil, like Jesus, illuminates the shadows of the past and of error: a "firebrand of the Catholic church, renowned sun of the gospel truth, setting ablaze the entire earth with the rays of his theology."[122] Like Jesus also, Basil "put a stop to circumcision" by nobly "preaching circumcision in the spirit, and the divine baptism."[123] Much of Basil's praise comes in his defeat of heresy and his triumphant defense of orthodoxy against heresiarchs and erring emperors; yet his honor, it seems, comes in the day on which he died. I quote the homilist at length here:

> Thus also the dissolution of his body and his migration from the earth to God did not just happen to coincide with the same day as the circumcision of Jesus, as someone might irrationally suspect, between the divine birth of Christ and the baptism; but, by proclamation, as an exaltation of Christ's birth, his baptism, his circumcision in the spirit, exalted by that most blessed one on its sacred commemoration, then was he deemed worthy to be exalted in his passing alongside Christ. And it was decided that he would be honored on the very same day as these annual commemorations and celebrations: so as the universal church of all the saints in every part of the world celebrates and magnifies his most saintly and sacred commemoration, it also sings praises and extols Christ, who is glorified with his holy and most divine appropriate praises by all his saints; since, through him, it has been delivered from every heresy, confirmed in all piety through doctrines; and since it has been differentiated from every strange-thinking and heterodox teaching, and brought near to the Master's faith and teaching alone.[124]

Basil's death is as carefully calibrated as the day of circumcision, and the preacher's audience are reminded that they, too, have gathered on this selfsame day to participate in the death of a saint and the circumcision of the Lord. The two events are linked by their illuminating quality: just as Jesus (in his circumcision and, we presume, the rest of his earthly activity) overwrote and cast away Jewish ignorance, so too Basil (in his teaching and other episcopal duties) defeated the error of heretics. Basil himself becomes a kind of temporal marker: of the rhythms of the Christian calendar (dying between Nativity and Epiphany), and also of the way in which those rhythms cover over, but do not erase, the imperfect rhythms of "the other" (Jews then, heretics now). The old "Law" transmuted on Jesus in his circumcision reappears as *orthodoxia*, the "celestial and divinely perfect laws" enforced by Basil.[125] Times intersect through the crucial "culture-making" activity of memory and memorialization:[126] memory, as Elizabeth Castelli has shown us, is a multilayered activity that both constructs and sustains communities, but is also "shaped by notions of difference and practices of power."[127] The ritualization of memory (μνημοσύνη) creates a paradoxical time, a *heterochronia*, containing past and present at once.

Near the end of his sermon, the homilist charges his audience to honor Basil: "How shall we honor him? Let us be circumcised! Not according to the flesh of our foreskins, as that Old Israel does, but let us circumcise the interior person of the heart: stripping away all of the hidden passions of the soul and of the mind, or killing them."[128] If such a call for his congregation to "be circumcised" might astonish the apostle Paul, at least it is clearly a spiritual circumcision. Until the homilist continues: "Let us now permit circumcision *according to the flesh*," clarifying, "let us rise up to baptism! Let us run from the shadow, and let us run to the truth; let us run from Moses, and let us come out to John."[129] What began as a fleshly sign of distinction spiritualized—Jewish circumcision nullified on Jesus' body—rematerializes as a spiritual sign of distinction in the flesh. Of course, it is still "spiritual," insofar as baptism also signifies "something else" (citing Col 2:12): "[dying] together with Christ, and having been crucified with him and buried with him in the shedding of the body of sinful flesh."[130] But it is also irrefutably, and fundamentally, corporeal: the materiality of Christ's circumcision leading into his material baptism. The temporal juxtaposition is also fixed on the Christian festival calendar, collapsing Christ's life into a single week between the Feast of the Circumcision on January 1 and Epiphany, commemorating Jesus' baptism, on January 6: "Now Jesus after his circumcision in the flesh on the eighth day according to the Law comes to John at the age of thirty, to be baptized in the water, so that, bringing a halt to the immature circumcision of the letter, he might establish as law perfection in the spirit."[131] This temporal overlap will not allow the assembled Christians to forget that the body submerged in the Jordan River by John the Baptist remains a circumcised body: when they rise from the baptismal waters with him, are not these Christians also participating in that former circumcision "according to the flesh"?

How is it that our Greek homilist, preaching to a Christian audience in (probably) the sixth century, feels so comfortable proclaiming, "Let us be circumcised according to the flesh"? His Latin counterpart, while evincing some ambivalence about the flesh and Law, likewise fulsomely called upon his congregation to participate ritually in the incontrovertibly carnal sign of Jewish circumcision on Jesus' body. What differences are being invoked, erased, elided, or reinstated by this call to be circumcised with Christ?

Mature Christianity has grown from a private movement, anticipating the end of the world and the erasure of distinction between "Jew and Greek," into a public religion demonstrating constant concern for the articulation of communal boundaries. Yet this manner of defining self through the difference with the "other" is, as we can see in these festival homilies, not a matter of simple rejection: it is through appropriation and management of the difference with the "other" that Christianity demonstrates its "triumph," over Jews and heretics alike. For this reason, distinction—ostensibly the goal of such "boundary-making" rituals of orthodoxy—remains ultimately deferred: "Law" and "flesh," the obsolete counterparts of "grace" and "spirit," must be recuperated and retained. Heretics are summoned as witnesses to orthodox truth, lingering like the shadows of the past. Distinction and boundaries are suggested, but never fully realized. The highly charged sign of circumcision—real, physical, on Jesus' body—becomes a mark that erodes as it creates distinction.

Christians in the Greek-speaking East continued to find, at the commemoration of Christ's circumcision, an opportunity to contemplate, and even internalize, the time of others from multiple angles. As "shadow," as precursor, as contrast, or as foundation, Jewish ritual time (sometimes doubled and refracted by the rhetorical invocation of heretics) continued to haunt the margins of Christian festival time in the East. John Duffy has recently made public a homily on the Feast of the Circumcision delivered by Sophronius, patriarch of Jerusalem during the eventful decade of the 630s.[132] The surviving fragments of this homily were preserved precisely because of their ruminations on time and difference. Fragments from this sermon were preserved in a catalogue of sources having to do with "issues of time and dating," with Sophronius contributing insight into the origin and significance of "the Lord's Day" in Christianity.[133] It seems that in the year 635, the Feast of the Circumcision fell on a Sunday (as did the Nativity a week earlier, on December 25, 634). Sophronius also claims that the original Nativity fell on a Sunday: that is, Christ was born on Sunday, thus doubly sanctifying the day on which he also was reborn. As proof of this, Sophronius adduces two previously unknown fragments from the *Dialogue of Jason and Papiscus*, which he attributes to the evangelist Luke.[134]

Unmentioned in this fragment—but perhaps also made explicit in the portions of Sophronius's homily which have not survived—is that, if Christ was born on a Sunday, he was also circumcised on a Sunday. Three times, then, Christ dislodged the Jewish Sabbath with his own body: as Sophronius points out, the day was "previously known as the 'first of the Sabbath' (μία δὲ σαββάτων αὕτη τὸ παλαιόν)" but is now known as "the Lord's Day" (κυριακή). Born, circumcised, and resurrected, Christ Christianized time, erasing the Sabbath—at least, partially. It remains, ready to be summoned as the shadow of days past, in the preaching of a Christian bishop. Yet Christ performs this temporal alchemy through Jewish ritual time: his own Sunday circumcision, doubly punctuating, as our anonymous Greek homilist might say, the time of "shadows" and the time of "illumination" (Sophronius likewise refers to the divine circumcision as "illuminating"). That Sophronius should also cite a Jewish-Christian dialogue—that is, a text that places the Jewish voice on the Christian page in an act of polemical rhetorical appropriation— underscores this double-time act. That he believes the same author who wrote of Christ's circumcision in his gospel narrative also penned this anti-Jewish dialogue makes the appropriation of other voices, rituals, and temporalities even clearer.

Sophronius, preaching in Jerusalem in the year 635, seized the occasion of Christ's commemorated circumcision to ponder the powerful effects of Christian time; his own historical context adds a final layer to our contemplation of the Feast of the Circumcision. For circumcision was soon to acquire a new dimension in Christian thought: as the mark of a new "other," a new outsider, the circumcised Muslims who, even as Sophronius preached, were occupying sacred sites in Palestine.[135] The triumph of Christian time, its ability to enfold the ritual time of the other, would soon be dealt a serious blow.

Communal Bodies and the Commemoration of the Name

Andrew of Crete, preaching on the joint Feast of the Circumcision and Basil in the early eighth century, was one of those Christians who must surely have looked with fresh eyes on the distinctive mark of Christ's circumcision. Born and raised in Islamic Damascus and Jerusalem, Andrew moved to Constantinople as a young man, whence he was appointed (at some point in the early 700s) bishop of Gortyna, on Crete. His rather long homily on the Feast of the Circumcision does not mention the Arabs, except at the very end of his exhortation, and even there we find no direct reference to Islamic circumcision.[136] Nor, for that matter, does Andrew dwell much on Jews and Jewish error, like our Greek and Latin homilists before him.[137] He chooses to preach on a different theme at the commemoration of Christ's circumcision: the question of names.

Andrew marvels not only at the miracle of Christ's becoming human and fleshly but at the particular way that God at the circumcision became "known now clearly through naming (δι' ὀνομασίας)."[138] Of course, Andrew discusses the circumcision itself, and uses it to contemplate time: the "eight days" of circumcision signal individual perfection and historical culmination, as Andrew outlines the "eight stages" of the Law from Adam until Christ.[139] But before turning to praise Basil, Andrew dwells upon the miracle of Christ's name and the way in which it announces God's presence on earth: " 'Jesus' (τὸ Ἰησοῦς) is chanted together by the angelic voice;[140] now Jesus is interpreted as the one effecting all things salvifically through an affective dispensation (οἰκονομίαν συμπαθῶς ἐργασάμενος). This gives me the occasion (καιρός), and the power of the day effects it, raising me up from grace to grace, and uniting me to knowledge, and illuminating me with a great light, a lightning-flash of thanksgiving (χαριστήριον ἔλλαμψιν)."[141] The presence of God's name in the world has transformed Andrew, brought light and knowledge (γνῶσις). The Word incarnate makes himself known through the Name, and ushers in a new age of Christian illumination. "God is in his appellation (ἐν κλήσει θεός)," Andrew solemnly announces at the outset of his homily. Just as the circumcision marks Christ's body, so too his name marks the Christian soul: "he will become lawmaker to the whole world . . . anointing and perfecting all things in the Holy Spirit and calling them 'anointed' by his own name."[142] Christian time and community are thus doubly marked and punctuated.

Scholars assume that the naming of Jewish boys took place simultaneously with their circumcision throughout antiquity, although late ancient rabbinic sources do not explicitly link circumcision and naming.[143] In fact, the circumcisions and namings of John the Baptist and Jesus in the Gospel of Luke are taken as our earliest "source" for this custom, otherwise not explicitly attested until the ninth century. An anonymous text from the first century (which may have been written by a Jew, a gentile, or some combination thereof) is therefore our earliest source for the idea of the circumcision as the occasion for a double mark: of covenant community and personal identity. Likewise, two anonymous (eventually pseudonymous) texts from the fifth and sixth centuries constitute our earliest witnesses to the Christian participation in the Jewish rite of circumcision inscribed on the divine body of Jesus. What are we to make of this tangle of names and anonymity, of Jewish and Christian communal formations, of divine and human bodies?

Elliot Wolfson has traced the emergence of a trope in mystical Jewish writing that sees, in circumcision, the inscription of God's name on the male, Jewish body (forming the *yod* that either marks the last letter of *Shaddai*, or the first letter of the Tetragrammaton YHWH).[144] Much like Andrew of Crete's celebration of the name of Jesus on the Feast of the Circumcision, the covenant integration of infant boys was viewed as connecting two planes of reality on a human body, creating a physical mark of a transcendent spiritual truth. As the child receives his own name, he receives God's Name as well. Not only is this a double mark on the body, it is a double mark in time: the cosmic time articulated and contemplated through kabbalistic mysticism and the human time of an individual life, whose covenantal clock starts ticking on the eighth day of life. "Circumcision is not simply an incision of the male sex organ," Wolfson writes, "but is an inscription, a notation, a marking."[145] But what does it mark? Whose name are we meant to read there?

In a different context, Jacques Derrida asked what Sigmund Freud's circumcision might indicate, what notations it might contain: "is it an archive?" he asks playfully. Is it "an exterior mark?"[146] What and how does circumcision signify? Where and when does it signify? For the Jews and Christians of antiquity and the early Middle Ages, circumcision became a punctuated mark of distinction, carving out the communal body (of Jews and Christians, but never at the same time or in quite the same way) in space and time. Yet this mark pointed inevitably outward, signifying the other in/on the self: "the cut that opens the word or the heart or the ear to the other, to the *tout autre*."[147] Placed on Christ's body, this outward mark became almost impossibly capacious, containing a Jewish past, a heretical present, a transformed future. The

Christian Feast of the Circumcision, no less than the Jewish eight-day rite of circumcision, became a shifting archive that signified identity while always containing otherness.

Rituals are those performances that suggest, but finally defer, difference, in which gestures of distinction turn against themselves and "otherness" can be identified and—at the same time—reinternalized. Catherine Bell, writing on the role of power and boundary making in poststructuralist interpretations of "ritual," notes: "Ritualization and ritual mastery are not only circular; they are also an exercise in the endless deferral of meaning *and* purpose. The effectiveness of exercising ritual mastery as strategic practice lies precisely in this circularity and deferral."[148] This circularity and deferral of difference is central to the Christian appropriation of circumcision through the festival commemoration on January 1. The ritual mastery allows the congregations simultaneously to imagine and transcend difference and otherness on numerous levels. That this assertion and persistence of difference should be projected onto the divinized flesh of Christ—also at the heart of Christian ritual life, through the Eucharist—makes such a commemoration apt, but no less remarkable in scholarly attempts to understand how ancient Christians constructed, and deconstructed, the distance between "self" and "other." The participation in Christ's circumcision among early Christians allows us to explore the ways in which difference—once mobilized through ritual action—never again stands still, but continues to move through the discourses of identity.

Excursus: Dating Ps.-Amphilochius, *In circumcisionem et Basilium*

As I mentioned above, I believe that the homily on the Feast of the Circumcision and Basil, ascribed to Amphilochius of Iconium, dates from the late fifth or early sixth century and so constitutes our earliest witness to the Feast of the Circumcision in the Greek East. I think it is worthwhile to include here some of my arguments for this belief.

A dozen manuscripts of this homily survive; the earliest dates from the eleventh or twelfth century and the latest from the seventeenth century.[149] All of the copies come from menological collections—readings appropriate to the festivals and saints' days of the Christian calendar, which begin to coalesce in the early and middle Byzantine periods.[150] These collections include a great deal of "classical" patristic material, as well as a significant amount of sixth- and seventh-century (and later) writings, some transmitted under the names of earlier Church Fathers. This particular homily usually bears the title "Discourse on the Eight-Day Circumcision of Our Lord Jesus Christ and a Brief Praise of Basil the Great." A close reading of the homily suggests that the discourse on the circumcision and the praise of Basil were composed as a single unit for the feast day, and not grafted together from preexisting works: both sections of the homily share imagery of type and fulfillment, law and grace, shadow and light, and discipleship and orthodoxy. The homily seems to have circulated in a healthy manner throughout the Middle Ages,[151] and is presently found in libraries from Italy to Moscow.[152] I have looked at three copies of this homily: facsimiles of two of the oldest surviving manuscripts, from the twelfth century,[153] and the only published copy: a fourteenth-century version printed in 1644 by François Combefis as part of the collected works of Amphilochius and others.[154] There are very few differences between these three versions of the homily, suggesting a relatively uneventful diffusion.

In most (although not all) of the dozen surviving manuscripts the homily is ascribed to Amphilochius of Iconium.[155] Amphilochius was cousin to the more famous Gregory of Nazianzus, and metropolitan bishop of Iconium from 373 until his death sometime in the late 390s.[156] As a well-known correspondent and theological ally of Basil of Caesarea, Amphilochius would surely praise Basil—as does this homilist—as "the sublime and pre-eminent pillar of God's church."[157] Furthermore, as we have seen in Chapter 3, Amphilochius did discuss the circumcision of Christ in a refutation of overly zealous Christian ascetics who had decided to abstain from meat.[158] On first blush, therefore, Amphilochius seems a likely candidate to author a sermon *In circumcisionem et Basilium*. Indeed, some recent scholars have used the homily as direct evidence for the date of Basil's death.[159] More generally, however, scholars tends to discount this ascription to Amphilochius, for several reasons.[160]

Nowhere does the homilist refer to himself as Basil's friend Amphilochius (or provide any identifying information) and in the course of praising Basil makes no mention of any personal relationship. Reference is made to Gregory of Nazianzus's more famous encomium: "I suppose all of these things have been sufficiently philosophized and psalmodized in the sacred speeches of the divine Gregory, and I have already undertaken to speak at too much length about them."[161] Comparison with Gregory's speech makes clear that this homily *In circumcisionem* is not a funerary oration but rather a speech in memoriam: "let us glorify today the memory of our God-bearing father."[162] It is unclear from the homily's praise of Basil, which takes up roughly the last third of the sermon, whether Basil is even in living memory at the time the homily was delivered. The homilist extols: "This is the exalted Basil, not only of the church of Caesarea, of which he was proclaimed bishop: and not only in his own time, and in his own generation, but in all the lands and cities of the world, and for all of eternity, useful to all people, he is declared the most salvific teacher to Christians."[163] Such a statement could be made soon after Basil's death, to be sure, but would be more effective rhetorically delivered not "in his own generation."[164]

References to fourth-century heresies also provide little support for an early date. In the homily we see Basil defeating Arius, Eunomius, Sabellius, Macedonius "who raged against the Holy Spirit," and Apollinarius "the mindless."[165] Basil can only be said to have fought figuratively against Arius and Sabellius, emblematic of opposite poles of Trinitarian error. He certainly opposed Eunomius, and his later writings likewise took to task the theological positions associated with Apollinarians and Macedonians.[166] We might imagine our homilist caught up in similar sorts of Trinitarian and early christological controversies—and therefore place this homily in the fourth century, even on Amphilochius's own desk—but for the very static nature of this heresiological list. The first canon of the Council of Constantinople, for instance, condemns, among others, Eunomians, Sabellians, Arians, Macedonians, and Apollinarians, creating a stereotypical list of heresies defeated by the Cappadocians.[167] Furthermore, the homilist goes on to comment that "as many [heresies] as a long period of time before [Basil] brought to light, so many has the period after his death continued to bring to light; but all of them have been cast into the fire of Basil's divine theology, set afire and consumed."[168] More important than heresiological current affairs, for this homilist, is the continuing efficacy of Basil's theological legacy.[169]

It is understandable that the homily *In circumcisionem* should eventually fall under Amphilochius's name, as it is but one of several works linking Basil to Amphilochius during their lives and after their deaths.[170] As one of Basil's staunchest allies in the theological and political controversies of the later fourth century, Amphilochius corresponded frequently with his friend and mentor (although only Basil's letters survive). Other works about Basil later came to be ascribed to Amphilochius. An encomium written in honor of Basil survives (probably falsely) under Amphilochius's name in a Syriac translation.[171] A more popular *Vita et miraculi sancti Basilii* was likewise attributed to Amphilochius. The discrete elements of this *Life* began to bubble up in the East in the sixth and seventh centuries, coalescing into the Greek vita in the eighth century.[172] This later, hagiographic Basil differs in multiple respects from his Cappadocian original: he makes pilgrimages to Jerusalem, converts many Jews (even the Jewish doctor present at his deathbed), enjoys a miraculous meeting with Ephrem the Syrian,[173] and is blessed with countless divine visions.

In many menological collections, our homily *In circumcisionem* is paired with this so-called *Life of Basil*. Quite possibly a kind of hagiographic drift has led to Amphilochius's name landing on top of so much Basilian *spuria*: a convenient Cappadocian on the spot, from whom otherwise nothing to or about Basil survives, becomes a likely figure on whom to pin a growing corpus of Basilian praise. The homily on the circumcision is quite different in tone from the Syriac encomium and the Greek vita. Its particular style, content, and context, I think, make it at least highly likely that it was composed relatively early—toward the end of the sixth century, say—in an ecclesiastic or monastic festival setting.[174]

The homily *In circumcisionem* is much shorter than the Syriac encomium and much less florid—and more vague—in its depictions of Basil than the Greek vita. The Greek is clear and simple, a plain style that could have been used for much of the Byzantine period; it is light on biblical citations, only explicitly citing some fragments of Paul, primarily in the opening passages, and loosely alluding to Scripture elsewhere.[175] The homily begins with a discussion of the "Law as shadow,"[176] full of types that were fulfilled by Christ's advent: by participating in the "old Law" of Moses (which, as the divine lawgiver, Christ himself instituted), Jesus demonstrated the truth of the "new and salvific Law."[177] A discussion of Christ as lawgiver and high priest leads to the praise of Basil, who left behind the pale shadows of paideia and philosophy for the true wisdom of God.[178] Basil's biography is thin, with brief references to his secular education, his confrontations with heresiarchs, and his "struggles with emperors and engagements with lawless governors."[179] As we have seen, the homilist insists on the divinely ordained significance of Basil's death on the anniversary of Christ's circumcision.

The particular attention to Basil—vague on details and yet insistent, even defensive, on his calendrical significance—suggests that the dual commemoration of Basil's death and the divine circumcision was a recent innovation for the community in which the homily was preached. We might identify some other indicators that this homily emerges from an early commemoration of the circumcision. The language is typical patristic Greek of a simple rhetorical style. One of the few distinguishing characteristics of the homilist's language is a cluster of compound words, little used before the sixth century, related to divine knowledge and priesthood: words such as *thearchia, hierognōsia, alēthognōsia*,[180] almost all of which appear first in the writings of Ps.-Dionysius. Stylistically, our homilist also shares with other sixth-century writers a Platonic fondness for language of shadow, image, and portraiture (*skiagraphia*), although these tropes reach back to the fourth century, as well.[181]

The simplicity of language and ideas in this homily stands out most clearly when we compare it to the earliest complete datable Greek homily on the circumcision and Basil: that of Andrew of Crete, which I have already mentioned above.[182] Andrew's homily *In circumcisionem et Basilium* is much longer than our homily, and delivered in a markedly higher scriptural and intellectual register.[183] After expounding in great depth on names and numbers (particularly the octave),[184] Andrew turns to discuss Basil, "nearer than others" to Christ's image.[185] Unlike our homilist, who mentions only the encomium of Gregory of Nazianzus, Andrew refers to homilies by both Gregory of Nazianzus and Gregory of Nyssa, as well as Ephrem, the Syrian deacon.[186] A homily in Greek survives in Ephrem's name, perhaps inspired by the legends (included in that eighth-century vita) of the two fathers' miraculous meeting (or, perhaps, vice versa).[187] Clearly by Andrew's time a *dossier Basilien* has come together that is more fulsome than what was available to our homilist.

One of the most striking differences between Andrew and our homilist, however, is the level of theological sophistication.[188] It is true, Andrew of Crete is a complex thinker and it may be that our anonymous homilist simply didn't work at his level. Nonetheless, the simple "antiheretical" flavor of our homily *In circumcisionem* contrasts remarkably with the christological specificity of Andrew's discussion of "natures" (φύσεσι), "wills" (θελήσεις), and "energies" (ἐνεργείας).[189] Our homilist, by contrast, is happily orthodox but evinces no deep interest in the nuances of christological, or Mariological, truths.[190]

There are probably several ways to explain the comparative lack of linguistic and theological sophistication, coupled with a lack of knowledge of the corpus of Basilian hagiographa. Perhaps our homilist came late to the sermonizing game, and stitched together generalities on Trinitarian orthodoxy and the shadows of the Law when pressed for a festival homily. Or, perhaps, a longer homily came, in the Middle Byzantine period, to be whittled down to make room in the already crowded January menology. It is also possible that we are looking at a relatively early example of a January 1 homily on the circumcision and Basil, underdeveloped in many of the themes that would be nourished in the hands of later exponents such as Andrew. If this is the case, we should seek a likely time frame to expect such a homily to be delivered.

The commemoration of Christ's circumcision on January 1 does not seem to have caught on as quickly in the Greek East as in the Latin West. The date seems first to have attracted the commemoration of Basil, as we can see in some January 1 homilies by Severus of Antioch that memorialize Basil,[191] but make no mention of the circumcision of Christ (which, as we have seen, Severus does discuss in other contexts).[192] Yet it would make sense that eastern Christians would begin to attend to this date as an annual festival of Christ's life some time in the sixth century.

The separation of Christmas and Epiphany into distinct festivals—which is clear in the homily *In circumcisionem*—spread unevenly throughout the Greek East from the fourth through seventh centuries. While the *Armenian Lectionary* does not commemorate the Nativity on December 25 (but knows of churches that do), and has no readings or festivals on January 1 (see my discussion above), the later *Georgian Lectionary*, from the seventh or eighth century, does mark January 1 as the feast of the circumcision and of Basil.[193] The earliest synaxaries preserved in Syriac have a festival for Basil on January 1, and later include the Feast of the Circumcision.[194] All of this evidence suggests that, some time in the sixth century in the Greek- and Syriac-speaking East, a January 1 memorial day for Basil the Great also became a date for commemorating the circumcision of Christ. Our homily, eventually attributed to Amphilochius of Iconium, is quite possibly the earliest surviving witness to that dual commemoration.

Conclusion

Passing Fancies

In a 1997 essay that asked how Jewish feminist scholarship might be applied to "issues other than the explicitly gendered,"[1] Susannah Heschel described Jesus as a theological transvestite: "Just as gender may be seen to be performative, so too Jesus and even Christianity and Judaism can be seen as constructs of the modern period, which exist by the virtue of performative activity. The anxiety over the self-definition of the two religions, and over the boundaries between them, comes into relief through discussions of the jewishness of the historical figure of Jesus. Jesus, I argue, functions as a kind of theological transvestite, calling into question the constructions of Christianity and Judaism and destabilizing the boundaries between them."[2] Heschel draws on the work of Marjorie Garber and Judith Butler to articulate the "category crisis" that Jesus represented for modern, German Jews and Christians eager to secure their religious identities: "As a Jew and the first Christian," Heschel writes, "yet neither a Jew nor a Christian, Jesus is the ultimate theological transvestite."[3] The impossibility of Jesus' religious identity, Heschel concludes, ultimately "queers . . . the 'boundaries' between Judaism and Christianity."[4] Heschel focused on modernity, the age in which "the quest for the historical Jesus" emerged to make sense of post-Enlightenment religious subjectivities. But Jesus as a queer figure, poised between yet rendering impossible the boundaries of religious identity, illuminates the context of ancient religion, as well.

Throughout this book, I have been exploring how some gentile Christians from the second century onward attempted to understand their religious identity by deploying a contradictory symbol that—to use Heschel's phrase—"queer[ed] . . . the 'boundaries' between Judaism and Christianity." Once located on the body of the Christian savior, in the hands of a predominantly non-Jewish community, Jesus' circumcision both constructed and confounded the very categories of religion ostensibly signified on and by Christ's body. In her work on modern Germany, Heschel appropriated the gender-bending idea of transvestism to imagine how and why Jesus could queer religious bound-aries. Here, in the conclusion of my study, I want to look to a related and, perhaps, more expansive figure of troublesome boundary crossing: the trope of *passing*.

Passing emerged first as a narrative of racial camouflage in the literature of the nineteenth century, when "race" as a category acquired its patina of scien-tific inevitability.[5] Primarily accounts of passing portrayed a black individual "passing" for white, reinforcing the binary nature of U.S. racial politics;[6] but "passing" has been read into a diverse array of deceptive identities beyond race.[7] Passing both necessitates and undermines the imposition of stable, mu-tually exclusive categories (categories of race, gender, sexuality, and so on). Like transvestism, narratives of passing institute an unstable "optical economy of identity,"[8] emerging in social settings that rely on what Amy Robinson and others have called "specular identification."[9] The interior qualities of a person must be, in some way, legible on the body's surface; the surface of the skin conveys deeper, more ingrained and essential aspects of identity. We have already seen, in Chapter 1, how circumcision functioned as part of a Roman cultural economy of signs that made legible and therefore in some sense Ro-manized (but never made Roman) a host of "others" within the boundaries of the Roman Empire. The ability to read those signs was arrogated to the Romans themselves; the possibility of sign failure—of passing—lurked, often unspoken, within that web of cultural stereotypes.

To "pass" from one category to another calls the link between exterior surface and interior essence into question. How meaningful can "white" be as an essential category if a black person can mimic it so perfectly as to "pass"? How meaningful can "black" be as an essential category if a black woman—as philosopher and artist Adrian Piper recounted in a 1992 essay—has to remind or even insist to friends and colleagues that she is not "really" white?[10] The pass over the racial boundary calls that boundary—and the essential catego-ries it supposedly divides—into question. Yet in the logic of passing, those essences are also paradoxically affirmed: the notion of interior essence is never evaporated, it is temporarily dissociated from the surface of the passer's skin. To successfully pass as white, the "real person" (underneath? within?) must—somehow, in some fashion—remain not white, or else they are not "pass-ing" (they are simply white). As Elaine Ginsberg writes, "One cannot pass for something one *is not* unless there is some other, prepassing identity that one *is*."[11] Valerie Rohy concurs, "passing insists on the 'truth' of racial iden-tity . . . framing its resistance to essentialism in the very rhetoric of essence and origin."[12] Passing creates a situation in which the building blocks of identity are revealed to be a fantasy, constantly under invention, but still powerful and even real in their way.[13]

I'm drawn to the trope of passing in my exploration of Jesus' circumcision because of what it might help us say about the fractured and impossible nature of ancient religious subjectivity, precisely within the cultural economy that made circumcision meaningful to begin with. The awareness of passing and the anxiety over categories that it articulates neatly reflect the kind of anxieties about identity and fixity that I argue Christians adopted from the imperial strategies Rome used to articulate its others. The heretic is that individual who seems orthodox, but must be revealed by a superior "optical economy" as theologically counterfeit. Similarly: by the second century, an increasing number of Christians are beginning to insist on the real, total, and essential distinction between the Old Israel—Jews—and the New Israel—Christianity. To clarify this distinction they must constantly, repetitively, anxiously reiterate how a Jew is not a Christian. The instruction on how to tell the difference, the discursive reiteration of boundaries, tells us that the difference was not obvious, that essence and surface did not always match: that Jews, Christians, orthodox, and heretics were constantly "passing," even unknowingly.

Like Heschel's metaphor of transvestism, passing relies on a variety of overlapping discourses of performativity and knowledge that can never really be sorted out or untangled. Like Lacan's child gazing into the mirror, the subject who "passes" from one category to another embodies the fantasy of identity. Several essays in a 1996 collection on *Passing and the Fiction of Identity* make the connections clearly. Marion Rust writes: "Passing is merely one more indication that subjectivity involves fracture—that no true self exists apart from its multiple simultaneous enactments."[14] In the same volume, Samira Kawash writes: "identity does not originate in some internal core of the self, but rather emerges in the distance between the self and the other."[15] The narratives of passing teach us that all identities involve a form of "passing": "a performance," Valerie Rohy remarks in this same volume, "in which one presents oneself as what one is not."[16] The trope of passing captures the anxiety of identity, and narratives of the pass emerge at those cultural moments when identity is under intense scrutiny. We imagine the possibility of passing when we feel our categories of identity are in crisis, when our fantasies of identity feel both exquisitely necessary and under intense challenge: when the difference between "self" and "other" must be asserted and yet, finally, can never alleviate the dissonance between what one is and what one imagines.

Jesus Passes

Certainly, Jesus is already a figure who "passes." In many varieties of early Christianity, he is a divine figure "passing" for human. Those Christians labeled "docetists" by their opponents even believed that all of Jesus' material existence was a deception, a mirage that perfectly fooled all but the elect (we might even translate *dokēsis* as "passing").[17] Those Christians who eventually became the "orthodox," grounding their understanding of Christianity in the writings of Paul and the canonical gospels, also believed that Christ "who was in the form of God" nonetheless "took the form of a servant" and was "born in the likeness of humanity" (Phil 2:6–7). As in more modern examples of passing, Jesus' human pass reaffirms the essential natures of "humanity" and "divinity" even as it confounds them.

Arguably, Jesus is unique in his ability to be God and "pass" for human in early Christian thought. But as we have seen throughout this book, Jesus' unique ability to be both-and, neither-nor expanded outward in antiquity to provide a template for the increasingly complex production of interlocking, contradictory identities known as "Christianity." When Christians contemplated Christ circumcised, I have been arguing, they were allowing themselves to imagine the impossible: essential, unchangeable identities that could shift, mutate, and incorporate their "other" opposites.

What all of the varied treatments of Jesus' circumcision I have explored in this book have in common is their desire to simultaneously reject and reincorporate the essence of "the other." Christ circumcised provided a legend for this paradoxical formation of the self: true and false at the same time. His circumcision, I suggest, was the misleading surface that allowed Jesus to pass: it was his white skin, his American accent, his macho swagger, his penciled-in five o'clock shadow. I want to look at two arenas in which circumcised Jesus passed: first, as a Jew, and second, as a male. To explore Jesus passing, I shall reintroduce some passages that have appeared earlier in the book, presented from a new angle.

Jesus the Jew

One prominent way in which Jesus' circumcision allows him to pass, as we might guess, is as a Jew. Tertullian, refuting Marcion's truncated nativity in the second century, claimed that Jesus' circumcision gave him entry into "the most sacred places" of the Jews.[18] Ambrose of Milan, in the fourth century, borrowed a line from the apostle Paul and remarked that Jesus "was fashioned (*factus est*) under the Law so that he might win those who were under the Law."[19] That this "fashioning" was mere fashion and not fact Ambrose makes clear when he cites Paul even more creatively: "For those who are under the Law, as if he himself were under the Law (although he is not under the Law), he was circumcised, so that he might acquire those who are under the Law."[20] A century later, Maximus of Turin imagines the same rationale for the circumcision: "so that the Jewish people, brought up in circumcision (*alumna circumcisionis plebs Iudaica*), would not reject him as a foreigner."[21] All three agree that Jesus' Jewish disguise permitted him to pass unmolested among the Jews to spread his word; they all likewise assume that Jesus' disguise was effective and he was taken for a Jew by other Jews.

That Jesus' passing mission among the Jews was not intended to affirm Judaism becomes clear in the writings of Epiphanius, in his refutation of the Ebionites. "Christ was circumcised," we are told they claimed, "so you should be circumcised!"[22] From the orthodox perspective, however, the Ebionites have been duped: they are successfully fooled by Christ's Jewish passing, to the point where they emulate his disguise and think it is real. Epiphanius, however, is not fooled: he knows that Christ's circumcision gave him a Jewish appearance, but meant something else. It was, he insists, entirely real: "he set things up," Epiphanius writes, "so that he would be truly circumcised, and not merely in appearance, on the eighth day." His disguise, in order words, was perfect. But in Epiphanius's refutation of the Ebionites we begin to see why this disguise was perpetrated at all. Ambrose had said that Jesus came "like" a Jew to win the Jews. Epiphanius is a bit more precise: "[He was circumcised] in order to affirm that the circumcision which had been given in ancient times was justly ordained until his own arrival, and so that the Jews would not have any defense (*apologia*). For if he were not circumcised, they would have been able to say, 'We cannot accept an uncircumcised messiah.'"[23] Epiphanius affirms a little further on: "Having perfect humanity, he was circumcised, arranging everything truly, so that the Jews, as I said before, would be defenseless (*anapologēta*)."[24] Epiphanius makes explicit what is only implicit in Tertullian, Ambrose, or Maximus: Jesus may have come to "win" the Jews, and fashioned the perfect disguise to get the job done, but the Jews still rejected him (and continue to do so). The division between Jew and Christian, even when muddled on Christ's own body, cannot help but reassert itself.

Part of the paradoxical logic of passing in modern accounts is the affirmation of essentialism: "black" and "white" are destabilized by racial passing, but affirmed as "real" categories of race (to and from which one can pass). The Jewish passing of Jesus, ultimately, engineers the same confusion and reaffirmation of categories: "as if . . . under the Law, [but] not under the Law," Ambrose wrote. In the circumcision "justly ordained until his own arrival," Epiphanius affirmed. Jesus' circumcision is unquestionably Jewish—so Jewish even the Jews are fooled!—and in this way recognizes and affirms the category of "Jew," as distinct from Christian. And yet his disguise is so perfect, so admirable, that our Christian authors must take care to point out what every good Christian should already recognize: it is a ruse.

After all, some Christians are being fooled as well. The Ebionites believe that Jesus did not come just to "fulfill the Law"—which, for "orthodox" Christians contemplating the circumcision, means he "paid it in full," rendering its actual practice unnecessary. These "heretical" Christians have themselves become "dupes," believing they can maintain the strange admixture of essences they think they see on Jesus' earthly body: faithful to the Law and members of the Christian community. They have mistakenly believed what they see. Yet Epiphanius also believes that Christ's circumcised body gives him special insight into the relationship between Judaism and Christianity. Christ's "passing" provides a model for Epiphanius, as well, who can get inside and understand Judaism even as he repudiates it. Christ circumcised allows Epiphanius to gauge the narrow (indeed, illusory) distance between self and other, Jew and Christian, to locate himself, like Christ, momentarily in that "in-between" space where the fantasy of Christian identity is, for a second, unveiled.

Jesus the Male

Other fundamental boundaries of identity are affirmed and destabilized on Christ's passing body, such as sexuality and gender. We see this vividly in the debates over ascetic merit between Jovinian and Jerome in the later fourth century. Jovinian insisted on the specular fidelity of Christ's body and actions, which positively endorsed sexuality and reproduction. He cited Jesus' presence at the wedding at Cana to argue that the savior must have approved of the institution of marriage to bless it with his presence. Elsewhere, he gestured to the human body itself as evidence, saying (according to Jerome), "And why were genitals created, and why were we made in this way by our most wise creator, such that we suffer such burning desire for each other, and we delight in this natural coupling?" Jovinian believes what he sees when he looks at Christ's human life: a man, like other men, serving as a willing witness to human marriage and sexuality.[25]

Jerome, however, is not fooled: where Jovinian sees a sexed male, Jerome sees Christ passing as one. Jovinian is the dupe, Jerome the orthodox Christian whose specular acumen can reveal the truth. Jerome first addresses the point of Christ's physical nature: "Our Lord and Savior, who, although he was in the form of God, lowered himself to assume the form of a slave, having been made obedient to his Father even unto death, a death on the cross, why was it necessary that he should be born into these body parts which he did not use? Indeed, he who was circumcised so that he could demonstrate his sex. Why did he castrate John the apostle and the baptist with desire, whom he caused to be born as men? We therefore who believe in Christ, we follow his example!"[26] Here, Christ's circumcision performs two functions: on the one hand, it reveals the truth of Christ's sex. He was, indeed, a biological male. The seemingly irrefutable and essential categories of sexual identity are affirmed. But his maleness is immediately undermined: these were, after all, "body parts *which he did not use.*" Likewise the two Johns—the baptist and evangelist— were sexed (and circumcised) males who followed Christ's lead and lived as if they had been "castrated." Jesus' circumcision demonstrates the reality of his sex and renders it moot. He passed as a sexualized male in order to provide a model to asceticized Christians.

Jerome also refutes Jovinian's scriptural example, revealing, once again, Christ passing at the wedding at Cana: "I shall respond to this most briefly: just as he who was circumcised on the eighth day . . . sanctioned Jewish custom so that he would not seem to ascribe to them just cause to have him killed as one who destroyed the Law and condemned nature; just so this too was for us. He who came once to a wedding, taught that you should be married only once. For at that time it was possible to hinder virginity, if we did not place marriage after virginity, and chaste widowhood in the third rank."[27] Jerome begins with the assumption that Jesus' Jewishness was a clever ruse, a "pass," that allowed him to move among the Jews. And, like Epiphanius, he points out that because Jesus was perfectly passing, his rejection by the Jews lacked "just cause."

Jerome then points out that, in a similar manner, Christ was "passing" as a wedding-goer. His attendance at the wedding was no more sincere than his male sex. Both are misleading surfaces through which the orthodox Christian must look in order to perceive the truth. (Jovinian, like Epiphanius's Ebion-ites, is sadly fooled.) Christ's wedding attendance was not an endorsement of marriage, but rather a hint toward the higher calling of sexual renunciation (if one marriage is better than two, wouldn't *no* marriages be even better?). For those with eyes to see, those who have mastered the "optical economy" at work, Jesus' earthly actions reveal a higher sanctity.

Both Jovinian and Jerome apply an optical epistemology to Jesus, ren-dering his earthly activities—and his very body—legible according to their own ideas of what it meant to be Christian. Jerome, however, believed that the appearance of that body could deceive the uninitiated. Jerome sees in Christ the man and Christ the wedding guest the advocate of sexlessness, the despiser of matrimony. Amy Robinson, in her influential article on "passing," describes the "triangular theater of the pass," in which the deceptive relation-ship between "passer" and "dupe" is made real only by the knowing eye of a third party: the member of the "in group" who can see past the pass, who is not duped and so underscores the significance of the passing event.[28] That is, passing creates a multilayered epistemology of the self.

Christ passes—as Jewish, as ascetic, as human, even—only insofar as the orthodox Christian "perceives" his passing state (and heretics and Jews are fooled). What makes Christ circumcised *un*-Jewish is Ambrose's perception that his Jewishness is fashion, not fact; what makes Christ the man sexless is, likewise, Jerome's knowing glance that pierces the surface and gazes at the truth within. To posit Jesus as passing is to imagine a regime of knowledge and recognition that both constructs and fragments the foundations of reli-gious identity. The Christian gaze perceives the other—the Jew, the heretic—perfectly, and in that act of perfect perception recognizes himself. To see the savior as passing is to imagine the fracture of identity, but never quite make it whole again. Having observed Jesus passing as a Jew and a male, I pause here to ask: what are the limits of this specular play on the body of Christ?

Jesus the Antichrist

In the third century, Hippolytus was embroiled in theological and political controversies that wracked the Christian community in the city of Rome. After accusing the Roman bishop of heresy, Hippolytus became the leader of a splinter group of Christians.[29] Much of his life and writings remain shrouded in mystery, but we do possess fragmentary commentaries and theological treatises. In several of these works, Hippolytus envisions the end of Christian history, when a figure will arise who will try to usurp the faith of Christians by disguising himself as Christ's second coming.

> Now while the Lord, our savior Jesus Christ the Son of God, was preached of as being like a lion for his majesty and nobility, in the same way the Scriptures predict that the Antichrist will be like a lion for his tyranny and violence. For in all things the Deceiver wishes to make himself like the son of God. So Christ is a Lion, and the Antichrist is a Lion. Christ is a King, and the Antichrist is an earthly king. The savior was shown as lamblike, so he likewise will show himself as lamblike, while being a wolf on the inside. Circumcised came the savior into the world, so likewise that one will come. . . . The Lord appeared in the form of a human being. And that one will come in the form of a human being. . . . And we will make clear all of his artful deceits one by one.[30]

In Hippolytus's reckoning, the Antichrist himself will try to pass in all of Christ's guises: as a lion, a king, a lamb, a circumcised Jew, and a human being. Only the gaze of the Christian will perceive the counterfeit, see the wolf in sheep's clothing. The artful deceits of the Antichrist will be unveiled ultimately to all when Christ returns and destroys his evil sham.[31]

But if the Antichrist is passing, it is only because Jesus taught him how: Christ, too, passed as a "human being," clothed his divinity in the likeness of a mighty lion, a meek lamb, and a circumcised Jew. The disguise of the Antichrist calls into question Christ's own passing figure, building disguise upon disguise: who is "the Deceiver" here and who is authentically what he seems?[32] Hippolytus's perceptive eye can tell the difference, but even the momentary slippage of identities, the circular play in which, for a moment, Christ and Antichrist pass as each other, might give early Christians pause.[33]

Two centuries later, Augustine certainly resisted what so many other Christians delighted in: the play of Christ passing. For Augustine, the surface of Christ's body and its interior must reveal the same person no matter what the consequences. In his protracted debates with Jerome over how to interpret the Judaizing conflict between the apostles Peter and Paul (Gal 2), Augustine angered Jerome by remarking casually that "Paul was a Jew."[34] In reply to Jerome's anger, Augustine modified his opinion only slightly, conceding that the apostles' observance of the Jewish Law was sincere but limited to their own time. So too, he adds—whether in the interest of consistency or to needle Jerome further—was Jesus' observance: "Nor, moreover, do I think that the Lord himself was insincerely (*fallaciter*) circumcised by his parents. Perhaps someone might object on account of his age. Well, I don't think that he insincerely said to the leper. . . : 'Go and offer for yourself a sacrifice because Moses commanded it as a covenant for them' [Mark 1:44]. Nor did he go up insincerely (*fallaciter*) on the festival day, since he wasn't showing off for other people: rather, he went up secretly, not openly [John 7:10]."[35] Augustine refuses to imagine Jesus acting *fallaciter*, "falsely" or "insincerely." Jesus' circumcision cannot be a charade to pass among Jews, it must rather be a sincere gesture of faith in the Jewish covenant. Of course, Augustine asserts here and elsewhere, Jesus rendered the Jewish sacraments moot;[36] but in his time, in his life, on his body, they were real and they signified an interior state that matched the exterior appearance.

Augustine displays, throughout his life, an acute anxiety over signs and their meanings, seeking stability and fixity where others enjoyed variety and diversity.[37] He also famously mistrusts human perception, making popular the innovative idea that the human will has been so twisted by sin that it can never, on its own, correctly perceive God. The two intersect in Augustine's famous account of the lure of the theater, where the sights and sounds of the arena arouse Augustine and make his companion Alypius "drink in madness."[38] Whatever the reason for Augustine's refusal to see Jesus passing, he stands almost alone in his fear that, when the time comes, his eye might not be able to distinguish the disguise of Christ from that of the Antichrist. That he, too, will be a dupe.

Passing the Bounds of Empire

The Roman Empire was a careful mosaic of cultures and populations only lightly assimilated into any common language or system of values. Romans had long distinguished themselves from the Greeks—rightly or wrongly—because their power emerged out of the absorption of diverse "other" peoples into the Roman state. Romans delighted in the danger of the exotic, imported into the city and made legible by a cultural economy of signs. By gazing on the others whom they had conquered, whom they now knew so perfectly, Romans were looking at their own power and authority.[39] By sorting and categorizing the populations under their dominion, deploying an economy of stereotypical signs, they circulated and reproduced that power.

The power to "read" others under Roman command meant that Romans had to be adept at decoding the performance of identity: their own, and others'. In a pathbreaking study in 1995, classicist Maud Gleason drew attention to the ways in which the public personae of elite males was constantly under inspection for gender "slips," and how Roman gentlemen were trained to convey what came naturally to them: their masculinity. That masculinity should be in their essential nature, and yet require training and intense scrutiny, shows how deeply Roman elites internalized their own specular economy of power.[40] Mastery entailed self-mastery; the performance of both required the possibility of resistance, of failure, of slippage between masterful self and mastered other.

In the early centuries of their existence, Christians learned first to operate as objects of Roman specular power. Tertullian and Hippolytus in the third century imagined a world in which they, like Jesus, could move effortlessly—powerfully—through the Roman economy of power through the masterful performance of otherness. To imagine that performative power in their hands is to create a scene of fantasy and resistance. Jerome, Ambrose, and Epiphanius more than a century later learned to arrogate fully that specular power to themselves. They enjoy the danger in the pass, the hair's breadth that separates the orthodox heresiologist from the Judaizing heretic, the celibate monk from the oversexed male: they imagined their power in an imperial speculum, a shifting mirror into which they could look and see themselves and their others reflected back. The momentary danger of the pass—the thrill of the other—signals for them, perhaps, the passer's power.[41]

Augustine, however, was writing on the edge of an empire, on the hinge of history as the barbarians truly began to break in. Roman and orthodox Christian power disintegrated, and Augustine could not look in that mirror in the same way. He points us away from the early Christian era, to the foreclosing of horizons that we will call the Middle Ages.

Notes

Non-Christian ancient sources (including Josephus and Philo) are cited from the editions of the Loeb Classical Library. Rabbinic texts are cited from the most commonly available texts and translations.

English translations are listed in the bibliography where available; unless noted, translations are my own. The following abbreviations are used for critical editions:

CCG	Corpus Christianorum, series Graeca. Turnhout: Brepols, 1977– .
CCL	Corpus Christianorum, series Latina. Turnhout: Brepols, 1954– .
CSCO	Corpus scriptorum christianorum orientalium. Louvain: Secretariat du Corpus CSCO, 1903– .
CSEL	Corpus scriptorum ecclesiasticorum latinorum. Vienna: Akademie, etc., 1866– .
GCS (n.f.)	Grieschichen christlichen Shriftsteller (neue folge). Leipzig: J. C. Hinrichs, etc., 1899– .
PG	Patrologia Graeca. Ed. J.-P. Migne. Paris: Migne, 1857–66.
PL	Patrologia Latina. Ed. J.-P. Migne. Paris: Migne, 1844–65.
PO	Patrologia Orientalis. Paris, Brepols: Firmin-Didot, etc., 1904– .
SC	Sources chrétiennes. Paris: Cerf, 1943– .

PREFACE

Note to epigraph: Guibert of Nogent, *De pignoribus sanctorum* 2.1.1 (PL 156:629). Guibert claims the "great Origen" said this; he seems to be basing this on an otherwise lost fragment preserved by Pamphilus (whose work defending Origen was, in turn, preserved in Latin by Rufinus of Aquileia), where Origen says: "This circumcision of his, however, sufficiently constrains the heretics (*ex diverso*). For how could a spiritual body be circumcised with earthly iron? On account of this some of them did not blush to publish books even concerning the foreskin of his circumcision in which they attempted to show that it ended as a spiritual substance" (Pamphilus, *Apologia pro Origene* 113 [SC 464:184–86]). Whatever books Origen (or Pamphilus, or Rufinus) may be referring to do not, alas, survive.

1. See Amy Remensnyder, *Remembering Kings Past*, 172–82. For a brief, but competent, summary of the veneration of Christ's foreskin, see Johan J. Mattelaer, Robert A. Schipper, and Sakti Das, "The Circumcision of Jesus Christ," *Journal of Urology* 178 (2007): 31–34.

2. Jacobus de Voragine, *Legenda aurea* 13; text in Th. Graesse, *Legenda aurea*, 86.

3. See also the roughly contemporaneous discussion of the circumcision of Christ by Thomas Aquinas, *Summa Theologiae* 3a.37, 1; text and facing English translation in Roland Potter, *St. Thomas of Aquinas: Summa Theologiae*, vol. 52: *3a. 31–37, the Childhood of Christ*, 142–45.

4. Guibert of Nogent, *De pignoribus sanctorum* 2.1.1 and 2.2.1 (PL 156:629, 631–32, 651–52). For information on Guibert and this work, see the introduction of Thomas Head, "Guibert of Nogent, *On Saints and Their Relics*," in *Medieval Hagiography*, 399–404.

5. For a brief but provocative overview, see Marc Shell, "The Holy Foreskin; or, Money, Relics, and Judeo-Christianity," in Jonathan Boyarin and Daniel Boyarin, *Jews and Other Differences*, 345–59, expanded from Shell, *Art and Money*, 30–44. On artistic representations of Christ's maleness, see Leo Steinberg, *The Sexuality of Christ in Renaissance Art and Modern Oblivion*, particularly his discussion of the circumcision on 50–71; and Carolyn Walker Bynum, "The Body of Christ in the Later Middle Ages: A Reply to Leo Steinberg," in *Fragmentation and Redemption*, 86–87.

6. See Catherine of Siena, *Letter* 221 (to Suor Bartolomea della Seta), Italian text in Niccolo Tommaseo, *Le lettere di S. Caterina da Siena*, 3:247. Catherine, Agnes Blannbekin, and Birgitta of Sweden (see below) are all discussed by Caroline Walker Bynum, "The Female Body and Religious Practice in the Later Middle Ages," in *Fragmentation and Redemption*, 185–86. When Bynum writes that Catherine received the foreskin ring in a vision, she seems to be extrapolating from this letter to a nun, where Catherine equates a virgin's ring with the foreskin, and Catherine's own vision of receiving an invisible wedding ring from Christ (see Thomas McDermott, *Catherine of Siena*, 246). It seems a fair inference.

7. Agnes Blannbekin, *Life and Revelations* 37, translated and cited in Ulrike Wiethaus, *Agnes Blannbekin, Viennese Beguine*, 35.

8. Birgitta of Sweden, *Revelationes* 6.112 text in Birger Bergh, *Sancta Birgitta: Revelaciones, Book VI*, 272; see Bynum, "Body of Christ," 86 and 330n.11; and id., "Female Body," 186 and 369–70n.22. Like Agnes, Birgitta is also sometimes described as ingesting a part of the Holy Foreskin in her *Revelationes*. The source for this seems to be Marc Shell, who gives the citation as *De praeputio Domini* 37 ("Holy Foreskin," 346–47). This is, however, a misreading of Felix Bryk, *Circumcision in Man and Woman*, 28, where he cites Alphons Müller, who in turn is actually citing Agnes Blannbekin (who is then quoted by Shell as Birgitta).

9. Voltaire, who elsewhere ridicules the veneration of "le saint prépuce" (see, among other places, *Dictionnaire philosophique*, s.v. *Superstition*, chapter 1), also ironically prefers

its veneration to the other teachings of the monks and bishops "to detest and persecute our brothers" (*Traité sur la tolérance*, chapter 20). See, more recently, David Farley, *An Irreverent Curiosity*.

10. See, generally, Mary Douglas, *Natural Symbols*.

11. Innocent III, *De sacro altaris mysterio* 4.30 (PL 217:876–77).

12. Miri Rubin, *Gentile Tales*.

13. See the unpublished essay of Virginia Burrus, "Sexing Jesus in Late Antiquity" (2001): "To make matters worse, as a historian of late antiquity, I am feeling just a bit inadequate, even perhaps *envious*: what do *I* have to 'show'? how can the late antique Christ possibly compete with the protruding penises, bleeding breasts, and wandering wombs of which later Jesuses boast?" (1).

14. Such has been the contribution of the so-called Third Quest for the historical Jesus. See, among recent treatments, Paula Fredriksen, *Jesus of Nazareth, King of the Jews*. The premillennial forefather of this Third Quest common sense is typically taken to be E. P. Sanders, *Jesus and Judaism*. For a recent overview, see Craig Evans, "Assessing Progress in the Third Quest of the Historical Jesus," *Journal for the Study of the Historical Jesus* 4 (2006): 35–54.

15. Bart D. Ehrman, *Jesus*, 98.

16. Cyril of Alexandria, *Glaphyra in Exodum* 1.7 (PG 69:404–5).

INTRODUCTION

1. Rebecca Lyman, "2002 NAPS Presidential Address: Hellenism and Heresy," *Journal of Early Christian Studies* 11 (2003): 209–22, at 211. See also Karen L. King, "Which Early Christianity?" in Susan Ashbrook Harvey and David Hunter, *The Oxford Handbook of Early Christian Studies*, 66–84, at 66: "diversity would continue to characterize Christianity, even in the face of powerful claims to unity and uniformity."

2. An excellent, concise narrative of these models and their development can be found in Bart D. Ehrman, *The Orthodox Corruption of Scripture*, 1–15.

3. Indeed, we see this attempt at framing Christian difference already in the writings of the apostle Paul, who laments the proliferation of "gospels" passing under the names of various apostles (including himself: Gal 1; 1 Cor 1).

4. F. Winkelmann, *Euseb von Kaisareia*.

5. H. E. W. Turner, *The Pattern of Christian Truth*, is a classic example of a historical application of this traditional model.

6. We might describe the early, popular works influenced by the Nag Hammadi finds in this way, such as Elaine Pagels's early books: *The Gnostic Gospels* and *Adam, Eve, and the Serpent*.

7. Walter Bauer, *Orthodoxy and Heresy in Earliest Christianity*. In the same year appeared the very influential work of James M. Robinson and Helmut Koester, *Trajectories Through Early Christianity*, which operated from similar intellectual ideas.

8. The term "proto-orthodox" was coined by Ehrman, *Orthodox Corruption*, 13.

9. Lewis Ayres, "The Question of Orthodoxy," *Journal of Early Christian Studies* 14 (2006): 395–98, at 395.

10. Ayres, "Question of Orthodoxy," 395–96.

11. Especially influential was Fredrik Barth's introduction to *Ethnic Groups and Boundaries*; Barth has reconsidered his own work (emphasizing the cognitive aspects of identity formation) in "Boundaries and Connections," in Anthony Cohen, *Signifying Identities*, 17–36. A catalogue of Barth's use in early Christian and ancient Jewish studies would exceed reasonable space, but in the 1990s and early 2000s alone he was cited (incidentally and substantively) in the works of Sacha Stern, Lawrence Wills, Philip Esler, Halvor Moxnes, Mark Nanos, Vernon Robbins, Gay Byron, and Denise Kimber Buell. For recent examples of the use of Barth, see Aaron Johnson, "Identity, Descent, and Polemic: Ethnic Argumentation in Eusebius' *Praeparatio Evangelica*," *Journal of Early Christian Studies* 12 (2004): 25–56, at 30; and Judith Lieu, *Christian Identity in the Jewish and Greco-Roman World*, 100–101. See also the very nuanced discussion of Thomas Sizgorich, *Violence and Belief in Late Antiquity*, 8–9.

12. See the decades of essays recently collected in Jonathan Z. Smith, *Relating Religion*.

13. For a still serviceable introduction to the translation of psychoanalytic theory from therapeutic to theoretical (literary and historical) contexts, see Terry Eagleton, *Literary Theory*, 131–68. Several of the progenitors of contemporary postcolonial criticism, such as Louis Althusser and Frantz Fanon, were influenced by Lacan's account of the subject: see Ania Loomba, *Colonialism/Postcolonialism*, 35–38 and 142–48. Homi Bhabha make significant use of aspects of Lacanian thought (transferring its psychosexual implications, more or less, to questions of race): see the overview of Bart Moore-Gilbert, *Postcolonial Theory*, 114–51.

14. See Virginia Burrus, *The Sex Lives of Saints*; id., *Saving Shame*; Erin Felicia Labbie, *Lacan's Medievalism*; and Dyan Elliott, *Fallen Bodies*, whose explicitly post-Freudian lens has been described by David Brakke ("The Early Church in North America: Late Antiquity, Theory, and the History of Christianity," *Church History* 71 [2002]: 473–91, at 489n.37) as "a chastened form of psychoanalysis." Elizabeth A. Clark, *History, Theory, Text*, does not treat psychoanalytic theory with the same depth as other French theories (see 193n.1), but notes at several places (19, 44, 55, 121) the underlying influence of psychoanalysis on structuralist and poststructuralist thought.

15. It is a brief, but dense essay: Jacques Lacan, "The Mirror Stage as Formative of the Function of the I as Revealed in Psychoanalytic Experience," in *Écrits*, 1–7.

16. Eagleton, *Literary Theory*, 143 (emphasis in the original).

17. Loomba, *Colonialism*, 144.

18. The illusory and contingent nature of a subjective self does not, of course, mean "I" am not real or responsible as a moral agent, as philosopher Judith Butler patiently explains: *Giving an Account of Oneself*.

19. Judith Butler, *Gender Trouble*, points out that this instability inheres not only in "gender" but in sexual identity as well. See now Georgia Warnke, *After Identity*.

20. Christopher Lane's introduction to *The Psychoanalysis of Race*, 1–37, outlines both

the racialized assumptions of the founders of psychoanalysis as well as the profitable ways in which the discourses of racism/racialism can be analyzed through psychoanalytic concepts such as hybridity, fantasy, and displacement.

21. See the discussion in Moore-Gilbert, *Postcolonial Theory*, 140–51.

22. Anne McClintock, *Imperial Leather*, 73.

23. See McClintock, *Imperial Leather*, 8, 72, 184 on this term and 71–74 in general.

24. Anthropological models of "ethnicity" (which derive, to some extent, from the work of Fredrik Barth mentioned above) heavily inform the work of Edith Hall, *Inventing the Barbarian*; and Jonathan Hall, *Ethnic Identity in Greek Antiquity* and *Hellenicity*.

25. Judith Perkins, *Roman Imperial Identities in the Early Christian Era*, 17–28.

26. See Catherine Chin, *Grammar and Christianity in the Late Roman World*, esp. 11–38 on "Latinity" as constructed out of visibly fragmentary and partially reassembled elements; Joseph Farrell, *Latin Language and Latin Culture*; and the persuasive survey of J. N. Adams, "'*Romanitas*' and the Latin Language," *Classical Quarterly* 53 (2003): 184–205.

27. Latin grammar, for instance, still recognized the category of the "barbarism" (*barbarismus*), defined (as by Donatus in his *artes minores*) as a "bad part of speech" (*una pars orationis vitiosa*). Donatus's grammatical definition of *barbarismus* is notable in two ways, however: first, it appropriates Greek grammatical and lexical categories (such as aspiration and tone) into a treatise on Latin grammar; second, it begins with examples of "barbarism" that are in fact non-Latin words that have become common in Latin speech: L. Holtz, *Donat et la tradition de l'enseignement grammatical*, 137 and 150 (Donatus, *Artes grammaticae*); and see Raija Vainio, "On the Concept of *Barbarolexis* in the Roman Grammarians," *Arctos* 28 (1994): 129–40.

28. Greg Woolf, *Becoming Roman*, 48–76; Perkins, *Roman Imperial Identities*, 25–27.

29. Jeremy Schott, *Christianity, Empire, and the Making of Religion in Late Antiquity*, 161.

30. For general discussion, see the works of Edith Hall and Jonathan Hall cited above. Also still useful is Elias J. Bickerman, "Origines gentium," *Classical Philology* 47.2 (1952): 65–81; more recently, see Aaron P. Johnson, *Ethnicity and Argument in Eusebius' "Praeparatio Evangelica."*

31. Emma Dench, *Romulus' Asylum*; and Gary Farney, *Ethnic Identity and Aristocratic Competition in Republican Rome*.

32. There are marked differences between this speech in Tacitus and the version preserved in bronze in ancient Lugdunum (the so-called Lyons Tablet): see M. Griffin, "The Lyons Tablet and Tacitean Hindsight," *Classical Quarterly* 32 (1982): 404–18; and id., "Claudius in Tacitus," *Classical Quarterly* 40 (1990): 482–501. My point is not about Claudius specifically, but rather the growing sense of Roman imperial dominion. See Woolf, *Becoming Roman*, 64–65.

33. On Roman political ideologies, see Clifford Ando, *Imperial Ideology and Provincial Loyalty in the Roman Empire*.

34. For Juvenal, see Catharine Edwards, *Writing Rome*.

35. Martial, *Spec.* 3.11–12: "vox diversa sonat populorum, tum tament una est, / cum

verus patriae diceris esse pater"; see the commentary of Kathleen M. Coleman, *M. Valerii Martialis Liber Spectaculorum*, 37–53; and discussion of Farrell, *Latin Language*, 3. The arena, as container of exotic combatants and spectators, thereby replicates Roman imperial ideology, on which see Alison Futrell, *Blood in the Arena*; and more recently Catharine Edwards, *Death in Ancient Rome*, 53–55.

36. Catharine Edwards and Greg Woolf, "Cosmopolis: Rome as World City," in id., *Rome the Cosmopolis*, 7.

37. See Peter Brown, "In Gibbon's Shade," in *Society and the Holy in Late Antiquity*, 49–62.

38. For a defense of the more traditional notion of barbarian incursion and the "fall" of the empire, see Bryan Ward-Perkins, *The Fall of Rome and the End of Civilization*.

39. C. R. Whittaker, *Frontiers of the Roman Empire*, 1–10 on the historiography of "frontiers" and 192–242 on the ideology and reality of the frontiers in the later Roman Empire. He notes on 197 the "ideological tension between the Greek concept of an empire surrounded by fortified frontiers to separate provincials from the irredeemable savagery of the barbarian exterior and the more Roman vision of universal rule [that] also continued in the later Empire."

40. Compare Mary Louise Pratt, *Imperial Eyes*, 1–11, on the notion of the "contact zone."

41. Postcolonial criticism on hybridity itself draws on Marxism, literary criticism, and psychoanalytic theory: see Robert Young, *Colonial Desire*.

42. Homi K. Bhabha, *The Location of Culture*, 162.

43. See Greg Woolf, "Becoming Roman, Staying Greek: Culture, Identity, and the Civilizing Process in the Roman East," *Proceedings of the Cambridge Philological Society* 40 (1994): 116–43; and Tim Whitmarsh, *Greek Literature and the Roman Empire*, 1–38, who describes the Roman "possession of Greek education ('possession' implying imperialistic dominance in addition to ownership)" (14).

44. Cicero, *Verr.* 2.1.59, cited by Catharine Edwards, "Incorporating the Alien: The Art of Conquest," in *Rome the Cosmopolis*, 58; see now also Margaret M. Miles, *Art as Plunder*, which takes Cicero's *Verrines* as its centerpiece. I thank Laura Nasrallah for first bringing this Cicero passage to my attention.

45. Cicero is also, famously, ambivalent about Roman appropriation (both material and intellectual) of Greek culture: see Whitmarsh, *Greek Literature*, 14n.56; and Edwards, "Incorporating the Alien," 52 and 55.

46. Whitmarsh, *Greek Literature*, 15.

47. Bhabha, *Location of Culture*, 121–31.

48. This is the basic argument of Whitmarsh, *Greek Literature*; see also id., *The Second Sophistic*. See also the essays in Simon Goldhill, *Being Greek Under Rome*.

49. McClintock relies on the theoretical and historical survey of William Pietz, "The Problem of the Fetish, I," *Res* 9 (1985): 5–17; "The Problem of the Fetish, II: The Origin of the Fetish," *Res* 13 (1987): 23–45; and "The Problem of the Fetish, IIIa: Bosman's Guinea and the Enlightenment Theory of Fetishism," *Res* 16 (1988): 105–23.

50. McClintock, *Imperial Leather*, 181–203 on fetishism and the scene of colonialism and 368–89 on the "national fetish" in postcolonial South Africa.

51. McClintock, *Imperial Leather*, 184.

52. Patricia Cox Miller, "Jerome's Centaur: A Hyper-Icon of the Desert," *Journal of Early Christian Studies* 6 (1998): 209–33, citing Mitchell's *Picture Theory*, 49.

53. Patricia Cox Miller, "Is There a Harlot in This Text? Hagiography and the Grotesque," *Journal of Medieval and Early Modern Studies* 33 (2003): 419–35, citing Harpham's *On the Grotesque*. Miller's essay was reprinted in Dale B. Martin and Patricia Cox Miller, *The Cultural Turn in Late Ancient Studies*, 87–102.

54. McClintock, *Imperial Leather*, 185.

55. McClintock, *Imperial Leather*, 185; see also 192 and 202 on "opening up" the restrictive universalism of fetishism to historical analysis.

CHAPTER 1. CIRCUMCISION AND THE CULTURAL ECONOMY OF DIFFERENCE

Note to epigraph: Joan Wallach Scott, "Gender as a Useful Category of Historical Analysis," in *Gender and the Politics of History*, 43.

1. The verb either indicates prosecution (being "turned over" to the courts) or, more likely, "snitching" (*delatio*), an interesting glimpse into the dynamics of "multicultural" life in the ancient city.

2. On this incident, see Martin Goodman, "Nerva, the *fiscus iudaicus*, and Jewish Identity," *Journal of Roman Studies* 79 (1989): 40–44; Shaye J. D. Cohen, *Beginnings of Jewishness*, 42–43; and Marius Heemstra, *The* Fiscus Judaicus *and the Parting of the Ways*.

3. Most of the texts typically cited were compiled by Menahem Stern, "The Jews in Greek and Latin Literature," in Shemuel Safrai, Menahem Stern, and David Flusser, *The Jewish People in the First Century*, 1101–59, with discussion of Latin literature at 1144–58; the expanded version of this essay is Stern's compendious three-volume *Greek and Latin Authors on Jews and Judaism*.

4. The most recent surveys, covering the early Roman to Christian periods, are Shaye J. D. Cohen, "'Those Who Say They Are Jews and Are Not': How Do You Know a Jew in Antiquity When You See One?" in Shaye J. D. Cohen and Ernest Frerichs, *Diasporas in Antiquity*, 1–45, repr. in Cohen, *Beginnings of Jewishness*, 25–67; Pierre Cordier, "Les romains et la circoncision," *Revue des Études Juives* 160 (2001): 337–55; Ra'anan Abusch, "Circumcision and Castration Under Roman Law in the Early Empire," in Elizabeth Wyner Mark, *The Covenant of Circumcision*, 75–86; Gillian Clark, "'In the Foreskin of Your Flesh': The Pure Male Body in Late Antiquity," in Andrew Hopkins and Maria Wyke, *Roman Bodies*, 43–53; and Simon Mimouni, *La circoncision dans le monde judéen aux époques grecque et romaine*, 290–321.

5. See Cohen, *Beginnings of Jewishness*, 40; Cordier, "Romains," 343–44; Clark, "Foreskin," 46; and Mimouni, *Circoncision*, 302–4.

6. Cohen, *Beginnings of Jewishness*, 41, 44, 351–57; Cordier, "Romains," 344–45; and Mimouni, *Circoncision*, 305–9.

7. Abusch, "Circumcision and Castration," 86.

8. That circumcision acquired stereotypical significance does not mean it had a static signification: see now Nina E. Livesey, *Circumcision as a Malleable Symbol.*

9. This is not to say that classical Greek literature did not indulge in stereotypical portraits of different "barbarian" populations, such as Persians, Egyptians, and Medes, some of which were even appropriated by Romans (and, ironically, applied to Greeks): see the essays in Benjamin Isaac, *The Invention of Racism in Classical Antiquity.*

10. Clifford Ando, *The Matter of the Gods.*

11. See also the overview of "cross-cultural exchange" in late ancient philosophy of Jeremy Schott, *Christianity, Empire, and the Making of Religion in Late Antiquity*, 15–28.

12. Michael Satlow comments on stereotyping in another context: "Stereotypes do not lump the Other into a single category; they parcel out fears and fantasies into different groups" ("Fictional Women: A Study in Stereotypes," in Peter Schäfer and Catherine Hezser, *The Talmud Yerushalmi and Graeco-Roman Culture III*, 225–43, at 226). See also Thomas Sizgorich, *Violence and Belief in Late Antiquity*, 46–80: "members of late Roman Christian communities, like all individuals in all societies, were required to arrange the experiential data which pours in from moment to moment in a manner which made the world they inhabited comprehensible" (48). In the case of imperial Rome (and, later, Christian Rome), I would add that the "manner" involved specific discourses of epistemic dominance.

13. Homi K. Bhabha, *The Location of Culture*, 107, and the entire essay ("The Other Question: Stereotype, Discrimination and the Discourse of Colonialism," in *Location of Culture*, 94–120). David Brakke applies Bhabha's work on stereotype effectively to the Egyptian monastic culture of the fourth and fifth centuries: *Demons and the Making of the Monk*, 157–81.

14. Benjamin Isaac, "Orientals and Jews in the *Historia Augusta*: Fourth-Century Prejudice and Stereotypes," in id., *The Near East Under Roman Rule*, 268–83; and Yasmin Syed, "Romans and Others," in S. J. Harrison, *A Companion to Latin Literature*, 360–71.

15. The sneering suggestion (by Giton) is in response to Encolpius's suggestion that they use ink to dye their skin and pass for Ethiopians. Not only is the ruse impractical, Giton responds (what if the color should wash off?), but they can't imitate all of the recognizable signs of an Ethiopian: thick lips, kinky hair, scarification, bowed legs, and "beard figured in foreign fashion" (*barbam peregrina ratione*). See the discussion in Cohen, *Beginnings of Jewishness*, 40; Abusch, "Circumcision and Castration," 83; and in conjunction with another Petronian fragment (fr. 37) Mimouni, *Circoncision*, 304–5.

16. Bhabha, *Location of Culture*, 95.

17. Cohen, *Beginnings of Jewishness*, 44–48. John Barclay, *Jews in the Mediterranean Diaspora*, 411–12, suggests that it was precisely its utility in private (sexual) circumstances that made circumcision valuable to Jews to ensure endogamy. Such a function still requires some regular public viewing of genitals, so that the Jewish women (or their fathers) charged with this religious gatekeeping could recognize the requisite marks of circumcision. On Roman clothing conventions in the republic and early empire, see *The World of Roman Costume*, ed. Judith Lynn Sebesta and Larissa Bonfante, especially Norma Goldman's

fascinating essay, "Reconstructing Roman Clothing," 213–37; the more focused cultural studies essays in *Roman Dress and the Fabric of Roman Culture*, ed. Jonathan Edmondson and Alison Keith; and on the later period (where pants come into regular use, in the northern provinces), see Annemarie Stauffer, "Clothing," in Glen Bowersock, Peter Brown, and Oleg Grabar, *Late Antiquity*, 381–82.

18. The maleness of the Jewish covenant mark is also the central question in Shaye J. D. Cohen, *Why Aren't Jewish Women Circumcised?*

19. I thank Laura Nasrallah for pressing me to think more critically about gender in this context.

20. Marjorie Garber, *Vested Interests*, 21–40.

21. Scott, "Gender," 42.

22. On the gendered gaze as a theoretical tool, see Blake Leyerle, "Chrysostom on the Gaze," *Journal of Early Christian Studies* 1 (1993): 159–74.

23. On Jewish appropriation and mimicry of this feminization, see Daniel Boyarin, "Homotopia: The *Fem*inized Jewish Man and the Lives of Women in Late Antiquity," *differences* 7 (1995): 41–81. The idea that (circumcised) Jewish males would persist as a trope into the modern period, racialized in modern Europe (see Sander Gilman, *The Jew's Body*) and appropriated into psychoanalysis by Sigmund Freud (see Jay Geller, *On Freud's Jewish Body*).

24. Bhabha, *Location of Culture*, 107.

25. Circumcision is not the only sign of Jewish identity in this Roman cultural economy, often appearing in tandem with Sabbath observance and dietary laws (on the latter, see now Jordan D. Rosenblum, " 'Why Do You Refuse to Eat Pork?' Jews, Food, and Identity in Roman Palestine," *Jewish Quarterly Review* 100 [2010]: 95–110).

26. On the origins of Abrahamic circumcision, see Howard Eilberg-Schwartz, *The Savage in Judaism*, 141–77; Eric Kline Silverman, *From Abraham to America*, 49–73; Lawrence Hoffman, *Covenant of Blood*, 27–48; and Cohen, *Why Aren't*, 8–21. Ulrich Zimmerman, *Kinderbeschneidung und Kindertaufe*, 18–40, provides a brief overview of the theological signification of circumcision in various Old Testament texts.

27. Literally, "they fashioned foreskins for themselves" (καὶ ἐποίησαν ἑαυτοῖς ἀκ—ροβυστίας). On epispasm in antiquity, see Robert Hall, "Epispasm and the Dating of Ancient Jewish Writings," *Journal for the Study of the Pseudepigrapha* 2 (1988): 71–86; and Mimouni, *Circoncision*, 113–28. For a modern, psychoanalytic reading of the procedure, see Sander Gilman, "Decircumcision: The First Aesthetic Surgery," *Modern Judaism* 17 (1997): 201–10.

28. The forced circumcision of the Idumeans under the Hasmonean John Hyrcanus is recounted by Josephus, *Antiquitates* 13.257–58; see Cohen, *Beginnings of Jewishness*, 109–39.

29. Josephus, *Antiquitates* 14.403; ἡμιιουδαίῳ is a play on "Idumean" ('Ιδουμαίῳ); see Cohen, *Beginnings of Jewishness*, 13–24.

30. Cohen, *Why Aren't*, 64.

31. Philo, *De migratione Abraham* 89–94. On these so-called antinomian opponents of Philo, see Maren R. Niehoff, "Circumcision as a Marker of Identity: Philo, Origen, and the

Rabbis on Gen 17:1–14," *Jewish Studies Quarterly* 10 (2003): 89–123, at 92–102. Mimouni, *Circoncision*, 140–44, discusses these passages from Philo in the context of Jews who "hide" or dissimulate in their circumcision.

32. Debate persists among scholars as to whether Philo even imagined circumcision as a necessary prerequisite for membership in Israel: see John J. Collins, "A Symbol of Otherness: Circumcision and Salvation in the First Century," in id., *Seers, Sibyls, and Sages in Hellenistic-Roman Judaism*, 211–35, at 218–24; and Mimouni, *Circoncision*, 143–44.

33. Daniel Boyarin, *A Radical Jew*, 26.

34. The account of Philo's role in a delegation to Rome is preserved in his *Legatio ad Gaium*: see the edition and introduction of Mary Smallwood, *Philonis Alexandrini Legatio ad Gaium*; and C. Kraus Reggiani, "I rapporti tra l'impero romano e il mondo ebraico al tempo di Caligula secondo la 'Legatio ad Gaium' di Filone Alessandrino," *Aufstieg und Niedergang der römischen Welt* II.21.1, 554–86; for important historical and social context, see Erich Gruen, *Diaspora*, 54–83.

35. Cohen, *Why Aren't*, 21. Much of my discussion of circumcision relies on Cohen, going back to my participation in an undergraduate seminar with him on circumcision in the mid-1990s.

36. Nissan Rubin, "*Brit Milah*: A Study of Change in Custom," in Mark, *Covenant of Circumcision*, 87–97, associates the institution of *peri'ah* with Jews "passing" as gentile following the Bar Kokhba revolt; see also Cohen, *Why Aren't*, 24–26.

37. Cohen, *Why Aren't*, 26.

38. Cohen, *Why Aren't*, 28. See also Daniel Boyarin, *Carnal Israel*, 7: "the rite of circumcision became the most contested site of this contention [between rabbinic Judaism and its Greek-speaking contenders], precisely because of the way that it concentrates in one moment representations of the significance of sexuality, genealogy, and ethnic specificity in bodily practice."

39. See now the important work of Laura Nasrallah, *Christian Responses to Roman Art and Architecture*.

40. See m. Ned. 3:11, cited by Cohen, *Why Aren't*, 26–27, with supplementary passages from t. Ned. 2:5–7. See also Cohen, *Beginnings of Jewishness*, 219n.46.

41. As Cohen argues in *Beginnings of Jewishness*, 209–11, of b. Yeb. 47b–48a.

42. The translation of b. Yeb. 47a–b consulted throughout this section is from Cohen, *Beginnings of Jewishness*, 199–202.

43. See Cohen, *Beginnings of Jewishness*, 210n.22.

44. The typically ethnographic Tacitus lists several common tropes of Jewish oddness: abstention from pork, observance of the Sabbath, misanthropy, lustfulness, circumcision, monotheism, and aniconism (*Hist.* 5.4–5).

45. הרי הוא כישראל (b. Yeb. 47b).

46. Bhabha, *Location of Culture*, 121–31.

47. Bhabha, *Location of Culture*, 95.

48. See generally Friedrich Wilhelm Horn, "Der Verzicht auf die Beschneidung im frühen Christentum," *New Testament Studies* 42 (1996): 479–505.

49. So Niehoff, "Circumcision," 102–3.

50. So Boyarin, *Radical Jew*, 116, speaks of "the conservative wing of the Jerusalem church."

51. See now also Pamela Eisenbaum, *Paul Was Not a Christian*.

52. Paula Fredriksen, "Judaism, the Circumcision of Gentiles, and Apocalyptic Hope: Another Look at Galatians 1 and 2," *Journal of Theological Studies* n.s. 42 (1991): 532–64, at 548.

53. Fredriksen, "Judaism," 532–43.

54. Paul's Pharisaism does not, of course, vanish in his experience of and preaching for Christ: indeed, Boyarin perceptively reads most of Romans 1–2 as "a sermon to which many if not most Pharisaic preachers as heirs of the prophets could have and would have assented" (*Radical Jew*, 92); see also Eisenbaum, *Paul*, 132–49.

55. See the salutary introductory chapters of Richard Horsley, *Paul and Empire*, 1–8, 10–24, 140–47. See also J. R. Harrison, "Paul and the Imperial Gospel at Thessaloniki," *Journal for the Study of the New Testament* 25 (2002): 71–96.

56. Horn, "Verzicht," 484–87.

57. It is interesting to note that Paul is our earliest example of an author using "circumcision" and "foreskin" as labels for populations (see Caroline Johnson Hodge, *If Sons Then Heirs*, 60–64). Paul's binary usage absorbs and reimagines the kind of particularist distinction that Roman stereotypes employed: "circumcision" still signifies "Jew," but now all of the rest of the nations are flattened (and indistinguishable) as "foreskin."

58. Boyarin, *Radical Jew*, 93, characterizes these verses as "a conclusion that would have shocked his Pharisaic teachers." Perhaps in the radicalness of Paul's formulation, but I suspect the more apocalyptic of those teachers might have laid the groundwork that allowed Paul to view circumcision through the lens of political resistance.

59. So I would nuance Cohen's fairly straightforward reading of Paul as "the most outspoken Jewish critic of Jewish circumcision in the first century" (*Why Aren't*, 68).

60. Much like Philo's opponents during roughly the same period in Alexandria: interestingly, Cohen (*Why Aren't*, 68) also links Paul to "Philo's opponents," but in a clearly negative vein (i.e., they both object to circumcision *tout court*).

61. On this count I think my reading of Paul and circumcision dovetails with Boyarin, *Radical Jew*, 106–35, in that Paul's universalism clearly drives and explains his variegated rhetoric with respect to circumcision and "the Law."

62. Daniel Marguerat, *The First Christian Historian*, 34: "History, for Luke, is the place where humanity and the divine meet. This conception of history is worlds away from apocalyptic." But see also Virginia Burrus, "The Gospel of Luke and the Acts of the Apostles," in Fernando F. Segovia and R. S. Sugirtharajah, *A Postcolonial Commentary on the New Testament Writings*, 133–55, who argues for a more politically subversive reading of Acts.

63. As Horn, "Verzicht," 480–81, points out: Jesus was more concerned with common issues of observance under sectarian debate in first-century Palestine, such as Sabbath observance and purity regulations. Although circumcision was a point of debate among Jews generally in late antiquity (see above), it seems not to have been part of the constellation

of issues (such as purity) argued among the major sects in Palestine before the destruction of the Temple. Jesus discusses circumcision in John 7:21–24, but even here (in a rather late text) the issue at hand is the Sabbath: see Zimmerman, *Kinderbeschneidung*, 42–43.

64. Paul does describe Jesus as "born of a woman, born under the Law (γενόμενον ἐκ γυναικός, γενόμενον ὑπὸ νόμου), in order to redeem those who were under the law (τοὺς ὑπὸ νόμου)" (Gal 4:4–5), so probably if pressed would have conceded that Jesus was circumcised. But Paul evinces very little interest in Jesus' human life: the fact that the question did not occur to him, but may have occurred to his later followers, is what interests me here.

65. The classification of Colossians as deutero-Pauline is by no means unanimous: see John Knox, "Philemon and the Authenticity of Colossians," *Journal of Religion* 18 (1938): 144–60; N. T. Wright, *Colossians and Philemon*, 31–39; Ben Witherington III, *The Letters to Philemon, the Colossians, and the Ephesians*, 100–107; and Mimouni, *Circoncision*, 221n.112. On arguments for pseudonymity—but by a companion of Paul's not long after his death—see Margaret Y. MacDonald, *Colossians and Ephesians*, 6–10; and James D. G. Dunn, *The Epistles to the Colossians and to Philemon*, 35–41. E. P. Sanders, "Literary Dependence in Colossians," *Journal of Biblical Literature* 85 (1966): 28–45, splits the difference by arguing for a later author for the first two chapters of Colossians (which will interest us here), leaving open the possibility that the last chapters are authentically Pauline.

66. Jerry L. Sumney, *Colossians*, 5. But see also T. D. Still, "Eschatology in Colossians: How Realized Is It?" *New Testament Studies* 50 (2004): 125–38.

67. On *Haustafeln* and their conventional (even imperial) outlook, see the summary of relevant literature in Carolyn Osiek and Margaret Y. MacDonald, *A Woman's Place*, 118–43. Scholars who defend Pauline authorship do not see so radical a break between, say, Galatians and Colossians: see, typically, Witherington, *Letters*, 30–35 and 181–96.

68. Of course, Paul had spoken approvingly of circumcision for Jews—as discussed above—and figurative "circumcision" for all Jesus believers. My point is that Colossians speaks in positive terms, without reservation, about circumcision here.

69. Witherington, *Letters*, 153: "This argument [Col 2:6–3:4] bristles with grammatical and exegetical difficulties."

70. Harry O. Maier, "A Sly Civility: Colossians and Empire," *Journal for the Study of the New Testament* 23 (2005): 323–49. As Maier's title suggests, he draws on Bhabha's concepts of hybridity and mimicry to suggest that this Christian text "echoes imperial-sounding ideals, it does not replicate them. Colossians twists Empire and makes it slip" (349).

71. Although it is unclear whether the author intends a direct parallel, as in later interpretation—whereby circumcision is a type of baptism—or whether the concatenation of events in Christ's life (circumcision, death, resurrection) are being analogically equated with events in a Christian's salvation (baptism and regeneration), the difference, which seems important to many interpreters of the letter, may be too fine to parse.

72. So, among others, Sumney, *Colossians*, 138, who asserts (with MacDonald, *Colossians and Ephesians*, 100) that this is "the first place where circumcision appears as a symbol

for baptism in extant early Christian writings." Zimmerman, *Kinderbeschneidung*, 56–58, follows suit through detailed comparison with Paul's letters (especially Romans). Dunn, *Epistle*, 157–59, dissents on this point.

73. Interestingly, however, after uniformly reading "circumcision" in Col 2:11–12 as figurative (in multiple ways), most modern commentators take the reference to uncircumcision in Col 2:13 to refer to the literal gentile status of the letter's recipients (so, somewhat grudgingly, MacDonald, *Colossians and Ephesians*, 101; more comfortably Sumney, *Colossians*, 141–42; and Dunn, *Epistle*, 163–64). I do not know if this is the case; certainly the entire chapter slips quite frequently between literal and figurative language, even in the same verse. I merely point out that we can just as fruitfully read *both* "circumcision" and "uncircumcision" as figurative.

74. MacDonald, *Colossians and Ephesians*, 100. See also F. F. Bruce, *The Epistle to the Colossians, to Philemon, and to the Ephesians*, 104: "The phrase may either mean the circumcision undergone by Christ or (preferably) the circumcision effected by Christ. If it bears the former meaning, the reference is not so much to his circumcision as a Jewish infant of eight days old (Luke 2:21) as to his crucifixion, of which his circumcision in infancy was at best a token anticipation."

75. Dunn, *Epistle*, 158; so also Witherington, *Letters*, 156; and Ralph P. Martin, *Ephesians, Colossians, and Philemon*, 115.

76. Even one apparent exception understands the circumcision performed on Christ as both literal but (more importantly) a symbol of cosmic sacrifice resonant with Jews, gnostics, and "orthodox" Christians: Michel van Esbroeck, "Col. 2, 11 «dans la circoncision du Christ»," in Julien Ries, *Gnosticisme et monde hellénistique*, 299–35.

77. Karl A. Kuhn, "The Point of the Step-Parallelism in Luke 1–2," *New Testament Studies* 47 (2001): 36–49. But see also the cautions of E. Galbiati, "La circoncisione di Gesù (*Luca* 2, 21)," *Bibbia e Oriente* 8 (1966): 37–45, at 37–38.

78. Modern exegetes nonetheless tend to minimize the significance of the circumcision in favor of the naming: so Erich Klostermann, *Das Lukasevangelium*, 41: "daß die Beschneidung dann tatsächlich efolgt ist, wird hier so wenig ausdrücklich erwähnt wie in der Parallele [Luke] 1 59; in beiden Fällen richtet sich das Interesse auf die Namengebung." See similarly Joseph A. Fitzmyer, *The Gospel According to Luke I–IX*, 420: "the stress falls on the naming rather than on the circumcision" (repeated at 424: "Stress is put here more on the naming of Jesus than on his circumcision"). This reluctance to face the circumcision head on is mentioned also by Jeffrey Keiser, "The Circumcision of Jesus (Luke 2:21) and the Formation of Luke's Infancy Narrative," paper delivered at the Society of Biblical Literature 2007 Annual Meeting (I think Mr. Keiser for sharing his paper with me). The only ancient Christians I have found who possibly accept this Lucan passage but read it as denying Jesus' physical circumcision are the sixth-century aphthartodocetists, discussed below in Chapters 4 and 6.

79. Two sustained treatments of the circumcision of Jesus in the Gospel of Luke stand out: Jacob Jervell, "The Circumcised Messiah," in *The Unknown Paul*, 138–45, originally published as "Den omskårne Messias," *Svensk Exegetisk Årsbok* 37–38 (1972–73): 145–55; and

Graham Ward, *Christ and Culture*, 166–72 and 175–80, drawn from his earlier "Uncovering the Corona: A Theology of Circumcision," in George J. Brooke, *The Birth of Jesus*, 35–46. Despite its title, Galbiati, "Circoncisione," treats the entire passage (circumcision and naming) in terms of its place in the structure of Luke 1–2; likewise, Keiser, "Circumcision," seeks out structural parallels (in Genesis) for the "step-parallelism" of Luke 1–2, only briefly treating the circumcision itself.

80. This Jewish ambiance is frequently combined with assertions of the "semitizing" language of these chapters: Raymond E. Brown, *The Birth of the Messiah*, 246; Jack T. Sanders, *The Jews in Luke-Acts*, 160–61; and Bradley S. Billings, "'At the Age of Twelve': The Boy Jesus in the Temple (Luke 2:41–52), the Emperor Augustus, and the Social Setting of the Third Gospel," *Journal of Theological Studies* n.s. 60 (2009): 70–89.

81. Dennis Hamm, "The Tamid Service in Luke-Acts: The Cultic Background Behind Luke's Theology of Worship (Luke 1:5–25; 18:9–14; 24:50–53; Acts 3:1; 10:3, 30)," *Catholic Biblical Quarterly* 25 (2003): 215–31; James Dawsey, "The Origin of Luke's Positive Perception of the Temple," *Perspectives in Religious Studies* 18 (1991): 5–22; and Cyprian Robert Hutcheon, "'God is with Us': The Temple in Luke-Acts," *St. Vladimir's Theological Quarterly* 44 (2000): 3–33.

82. Brown, *Birth of the Messiah*, 235; Luke Timothy Johnson, "Luke-Acts, Book of," in David Noel Freedman, *Anchor Bible Dictionary*, 4:403–20 at 405; and id., *The Gospel of Luke*, 3. One significant dissenting voice from this *sensus communis* is Jacob Jervell, discussed below. See also now Andrew Gregory, *The Reception of Luke and Acts in the Period Before Irenaeus*, 200–201.

83. On universal salvation in Luke, see S. G. Wilson, *The Gentiles and the Gentile Mission in Luke-Acts*; on Luke's style, see Loveday Alexander, *The Preface to Luke's Gospel*. That this view of Luke as "gentile"—in contrast to the more "Jewish" Gospel of Matthew—has roots in nineteenth- and twentieth-century politics is outlined by Joseph Tyson, *Luke, Judaism, and the Scholars*.

84. Paul Winter, "The Proto-Source of Luke 1," *Novum Testamentum* 1 (1956): 184–99; among the several denominated Hebrew sources laid out by Winter, Luke 2:21 belongs to a (relatively) later *Nazarene Adaptation* (186).

85. Redaction criticism displaced form criticism in the twentieth century as exegetes ascribed more theological creativity to the evangelists: see Robert H. Stein, "What Is Redaktionsgeschichte?" *Journal of Biblical Literature* 88 (1969): 45–56; and Gail P. C. Streete, "Redaction Criticism," in Stephen Haynes and Steven McKenzie, *To Each Its Own Meaning*, 105–24. We should keep in mind, however, the warning of the Bible & Cultural Collective: "the source critic and the redaction critic propose their hypotheses in response to their own experience of reading the Gospel. Sometimes they report their reading experience in explicit terms, but usually it is disguised as claims for the discovery of putative sources and redactions" (*The Postmodern Bible*, 22).

86. François Bovon, *Luke 1*, 6–8 (note that Bovon, *Luke 1*, 86 and 96, discusses Luke 2:21 out of order, with the birth scene in Luke 2:7). Despite its ubiquity in studies of late Second Temple Judaism and the Jesus movement, "god-fearers" is not an obvious or

unproblematic category: for some recent discussion, see Dietrich-Alex Koch, "The God-Fearers Between Fact and Fiction," *Studia Theologica* 60 (2006): 62–90; for a general discussion of God-fearers and circumcision, see Collins, "Symbol of Otherness," 228–32.

87. Brown, *Birth of the Messiah,* 237. Compare Sanders, *Jews,* 161: "In every way possible Luke informs us that Christianity did not seek an exodus out of Judaism but was rather squeezed out by the Jews. The infancy narratives play their part in the pattern, for they show how totally immersed the Christian beginnings were in good Jewish piety." On Sanders's rather strong understanding of Lucan supersessionism, see Tyson, *Luke, Judaism, and the Scholars,* 113–22.

88. Brown, *Birth of the Messiah,* 26: "Both in the lateness of their incorporation into the written Gospels and in their very origins the infancy narratives are unusual." Brown draws on, and tempers, the supersessionist theological reading of Luke established by Hans Conzelmann, *The Theology of Saint Luke.* See also the useful analysis of François Bovon, *Luke the Theologian,* 14–33, who places Conzelmann in conversation with his subsequent critics and continuators.

89. John Knox, *Marcion and the New Testament,* esp. 77–139 on the Gospel of Luke and Acts (some of this material appeared earlier as "On the Vocabulary of Marcion's Gospel," *Journal of Biblical Literature* 58 [1939]: 193–201); and Joseph Tyson, *Marcion and Luke-Acts.* Knox's and Tyson's larger point—that Marcion's textual collection stimulated the idea of a New Testament canon—is perhaps just a stronger version of the *sensus communis* of early Christian and canon studies: see, briefly, Harry Y. Gamble, "Marcion and the 'Canon,'" in Margaret M. Mitchell and Frances M. Young, *The Cambridge History of Christianity,* vol. 1: *Origins to Constantine,* 195–213. Recent detailed text-critical arguments have been made by Matthias Klinghardt, "Markion vs. Lukas: Plädoyer für die Wiederaufnahme eines alten Falles," *New Testament Studies* 52 (2006): 484–513; see the refutation of Christopher Hays, "Marcion vs. Luke: A Response to the *Plädoyer* of Matthias Klinghardt," *Zeitschrift für die Neutestamentliche Wissenschaft* 99 (2008): 213–32. The basic proposition—that Marcion possessed an earlier version of the gospel than the final version of the Gospel of Luke—dates in some respect to the nineteenth century: see Matthias Klinghardt, "The Marcionite Gospel and the Synoptic Problem: A New Suggestion," *Novum Testamentum* 50 (2008): 1–27, at 5–10; with important corrections by Dieter Roth, "Marcion's Gospel and Luke: The History of Research in Current Debate," *Journal of Biblical Literature* 127 (2008): 513–27.

90. See my discussion in Chapter 3.

91. Knox, *Marcion,* 111–12. Part of Knox's argument relies on the late attestation of Acts and the assumption that Luke and Acts were produced and circulated in tandem (but see Hays, "Marcion," 215–16 and 228–30). The late dating of Acts (and also, perhaps, Luke) has gained momentum in recent years, particularly with respect to the Marcionite challenge: Shelly Matthews, *Perfect Martyr,* 43–47; following Gregory, *Reception of Luke,* 173–210. Relatedly, Tyson, *Marcion and Luke Acts,* 31, suggests that Marcion's views could have been known (and required redactional response) as early as the 120s.

92. Knox, *Marcion,* 87.

93. Indeed, as Knox himself later declares (*Marcion,* 155): "It is more than probable

that the substance of the Third Gospel was 'the Gospel' in Pontus or elsewhere in Asia Minor, as well as for Marcion, who probably brought it to Rome."

94. Tyson, *Marcion*, 120.

95. Tyson, *Marcion*, 90, 98, drawing in part on his own previous scholarship: *Images of Judaism in Luke-Acts*.

96. Tyson, *Marcion*, 99. As we shall see in Chapter 3, Tertullian in his refutation of Marcion eagerly exploits this "offensiveness."

97. Jacob Jervell, "The Divided People of God: The Restoration of Israel and Salvation for the Gentiles," in *Luke and the People of God*, 41–74. On Jervell's scholarship, see Tyson, *Luke, Judaism, and the Scholars*, 91–109.

98. Jervell, "Circumcised Messiah," 145. Discussed more briefly in "The Law in Luke Acts," in *Luke and the People of God*, 133–51, at 138.

99. Ward, *Christ and Culture*, 168: Jervell "refuses a supersessionist reading of the covenant."

100. Ward, *Christ and Culture*, 162–80. I treat Ward's theology of the circumcision of Christ more fully in Chapter 3.

101. Ward, *Christ and Culture*, 172.

102. Ward, *Christ and Culture*, 175. In his earlier essay, Ward specified that Luke's inclusion of circumcision "appears to be a gesture of resistance to the cultural hegemony of Hellenism" ("Uncovering the Corona," 44).

103. Burrus, "Gospel of Luke," 134.

104. Paul Walaskay, *"And So We Came to Rome,"* 46: "The Lucan writings bear witness to the importance that the city of Jerusalem holds for early Christians. Not only was it the place of Jesus' circumcision and consecration, but the goal of his pilgrimage and place of his death." Luke does not, of course, specify that Jesus was circumcised in Jerusalem (indeed, a close reading of the text makes this unlikely), but often Luke 2:21 is drawn into the gravitational pull of the subsequent verses of Luke 2, which take place in Jerusalem and at the Temple.

105. Luke also displays an interest in the monetary economy of empire (see Burrus, "Gospel of Luke," 140–44): certainly, the control of commercial and cultural forces are intertwined in the Roman context, as Suetonius's anecdote demonstrates.

106. Bovon, *Luke 1*, 9. See also Loveday Alexander, "The Acts of the Apostles as an Apologetic Text," in Mark Edwards, Martin Goodman, and Simon Price, *Apologetics in the Roman Empire*, 15–44, who surveys several ways of reading Acts (and, more broadly, Luke-Acts), in an apologetic context, and notes: "By far the commonest reading of Acts is the view that the book was written to provide a defence against political charges brought before a Roman tribunal" (18).

107. Walaskay, *"And So We Came to Rome,"* 25. See now also Matthews, *Perfect Martyr*, 37–43.

108. Bhabha, *Location of Culture*, 100.

109. See the similar reading of Revelation offered by Christopher Frilingos, *Spectacles of Empire*.

110. Gary Gilbert, "The List of Nations in Acts 2: Roman Propaganda and the Lukan Response," *Journal of Biblical Literature* 121 (2002): 497–529, at 523–24.

111. Laura Nasrallah, "The Acts of the Apostles, Greek Cities, and Hadrian's Panhellenion," *Journal of Biblical Literature* 127 (2008): 533–66, at 534. See now also her *Christian Responses*.

112. James D. G. Dunn, *Paul and the Mosaic Law*, 27, sympathetically frames the distance between Luke and Paul: "We should not be too critical if [Luke's] understanding of Paul was inadequate. Students often fail to understand their teachers, as we often find in the history of theology."

113. Of course, the sages around the same period referred to themselves and their covenant community as "Israel," and only rarely used the term "Jew": see Cynthia Baker, "When Jews Were Women," *History of Religions* 45 (2005): 114–34. Conversely, Augustine (*Epistula* 196 [CSEL 57:216–30]) expresses concern that some (presumably orthodox) Christians in his own day want to go so far as to claim the name *Iudaeus* (cited by Cohen, *Beginnings of Jewishness*, 26–27). Generally see Graham Harvey, *The True Israel*.

114. See, generally, Mimouni, *Circoncision*, 247–90.

115. Arguments for dating tend to assume close temporal proximity to the Bar Kokhba revolt: see James Carleton Paget, *The Epistle of Barnabas*, 9–30; and Reidar Hvalvik, *The Struggle for Scripture and Covenant*, 17–34.

116. *Epistula Barnabae* 9.1 Text and translation (which I have modified) in Bart D. Ehrman, *The Apostolic Fathers*, 2:42. Early Christian authors deploying this metaphorical circumcision were assisted in this by Paul's metaphorical use of "inward circumcision" in Rom 2, as well as Philo's allegorical readings of covenant law. See generally Everett Ferguson, "Spiritual Circumcision in Early Christianity," *Scottish Journal of Theology* 41 (1988): 485–97.

117. *Epistula Barnabae* 9.4 (Ehrman, *Apostolic Fathers*, 2:44).

118. James Carleton Paget, "Barnabas 9:4: A Peculiar Verse on Circumcision," *Vigiliae Christianae* 45 (1991): 242–54, cited at 251.

119. *Epistula Barnabae* 9.6 (Ehrman, *Apostolic Fathers*, 2:44).

120. Another contender for earliest Christian gematria is the "Beast" of Revelation, whose number is 666. Reidar Hvalvik, "Barnabas 9.7–9 and the Author's Supposed Use of Gematria," *New Testament Studies* 33 (1987): 276–82, does not want to describe the letter's transposition of letters, numbers, and meanings as gematria in the classical rabbinic sense (in which an entire name should equate to a number, and vice versa), but does point out the significance of this passage as an early attestation of Christian *nomina sacra*, scribal abbreviations of common Christian terms (such as ιησοῦς as ι̅η̅).

121. He actually combines the mention of "318 trained men" in Gen 14:14 and assumes their circumcision is narrated in Gen 17:23, 27.

122. *Epistula Barnabae* 9.7–8 (Ehrman, *Apostolic Fathers*, 2:44).

123. Justin Martyr, *Dialogus cum Tryphone* 1.3; text in Miroslav Marcovich, *Iustini Martyris Dialogus cum Tryphone*, 70. On Justin and circumcision in the *Dialogue*, see Nina E. Livesey, "Theological Identity Making: Justin's Use of Circumcision to Create Jews and Christians," *Journal of Early Christian Studies* 18 (2010): 51–79.

124. This casus belli is proffered by both the *Historia Augusta* and rabbinic sources, all of which are, naturally, much later: see the discussion of E. Mary Smallwood, *The Jews Under Roman Rule*, 429–31; and Hanan Eshel, "The Bar Kochba Revolt, 132–35," in Steven T. Katz, *The Cambridge History of Judaism*, vol. 4: *The Late Roman-Rabbinic Period*, 105–27, at 107–8. Daniel Schwartz, "On Barnabas and Bar-Kokhba," in *Studies in the Jewish Background of Christianity*, 147–54, tries to use the *Epistle of Barnabas* to bolster the claim that a ban on circumcision preceded the war.

125. Justin Martyr, *Dialogus cum Tryphone* 16.2–3 (Marcovich, *Dialogus*, 96); see also *Dialogus* 18–29 (Marcovich, *Dialogus*, 99–100).

126. This reference to "cursing" Christians in synagogues in often taken to be early evidence for the *birkat ha-minim*, or "benediction against heretics" attested in much later rabbinic liturgies: see the discussion of Daniel Boyarin, *Border Lines*, 67–73.

127. Justin Martyr, *Dialogus cum Tryphone* 16.4 (Marcovich, *Dialogus*, 96–97).

128. Justin Martyr, *Dialogus cum Tryphone* 113.6 (Marcovich, *Dialogus*, 264–65).

129. Justin Martyr, *Dialogus cum Tryphone* 114.4 (Marcovich, *Dialogus*, 266).

130. Justin Martyr, *Dialogus cum Tryphone* 24.2 (Marcovich, *Dialogus*, 109). On the "ethnic reasoning" in Justin's thought, see Denise Kimber Buell, *Why This New Race?* 94–115.

131. The association with the number eight is mentioned by Justin in *Dialogus cum Tryphone* 24.1 (Marcovich, *Dialogus*, 109), but not explicitly tied to the resurrection and circumcision until later.

132. Justin Martyr, *Dialogus cum Tryphone* 41.4 (Marcovich, *Dialogus*, 138).

133. Zimmerman, *Kinderbeschneidung*, 87–88, assumes the correlation.

134. Justin Martyr, *Dialogus cum Tryphone* 18.2 (Marcovich, *Dialogus*, 99).

135. Justin Martyr, *Dialogus cum Tryphone* 43.2 (Marcovich, *Dialogus*, 140).

136. See J. P. T. Hunt, "Colossians 2:11–12, the Circumcision/Baptism Analogy, and Infant Circumcision," *Tyndale Bulletin* 41 (1990): 227–43, at 236 on Justin: "Spiritual circumcision is effected 'through baptism' in an extended sense, in that a person's response to Christian teaching reaches its climax in the baptismal ceremony, perhaps in response to the baptismal interrogations."

137. See the thorough survey of Zimmerman, *Kinderbeschneidung*, 70–127.

138. Origen, *Homiliae in Josue* 5.6 (SC 71:170).

139. Origen, *Homiliae in Josue* 1.7 (SC 71:112–13). See Everett Ferguson, "Baptism According to Origen," *Evangelical Quarterly* 78 (2006): 117–35, esp. 128–29 (on circumcision and baptism); and id., "Spiritual Circumcision," 489–97. The metaphorical Christian appropriations of circumcision are catalogued by Hervé Savon, "Le prêtre Eutrope et la 'vraie circoncision,'" *Revue de l'Histoire des Religions* 199 (1982) : 273–302, 381–404, at 288–302.

140. See Cyprian, *Epistula* 64.2.1 (in Migne's collation [PL], this is *Epistula* 59). Text in La Chanoine Bayard, *Saint Cyprien*, 2:214. Fidus was apparently also adducing arguments concerning the general "uncleanness" of newborn infants in addition to the circumcision law of Gen 17 (*Epistula* 64.4.1 [Bayard, *Saint Cyprien*, 2:215]), on which see G. W. Clarke, "Cyprian's *Epistle* 64 and the Kissing of Feet in Baptism," *Harvard Theological Review* 66

(1973): 147–52. On the letter in the context of debates over "infant baptism," see now Zimmerman, *Kinderbeschneidung*, 81–84.

141. Cyprian, *Epistula* 64.4.3 (Bayard, *Saint Cyprien*, 2:215).

142. Cyprian, *Epistula* 64.5.1 (Bayard, *Saint Cyprien*, 2:215–16).

143. An interesting parallel also emerges in the third century concerning the application of levitical purity regulations to the taking of the Christian Eucharist: see Shaye J. D. Cohen, "Menstruants and the Sacred in Judaism and Christianity," in Sarah B. Pomeroy, *Women's History in Ancient History*, 287–90; and Charlotte Fonrobert, *Menstrual Purity*, 160–210.

144. See further discussion in Hunt, "Colossians 2:11–12," 231–32; and Everett Ferguson, *Baptism in the Early Church*, 370–72.

145. See the perceptive essay of Blake Leyerle, "Blood Is Seed," *Journal of Religion* 81 (2001): 26–48; and Elizabeth A. Clark, *Reading Renunciation*, 225–30.

CHAPTER 2. (DE-)JUDAIZING CHRIST'S CIRCUMCISION

Note to epigraph: Mikhail Bakhtin, "From Notes Made in 1970–1971," in *Speech Genres and Other Late Essays*, 132–59, at 147.

1. Robert A. Markus, "The Problem of Self-Definition: From Sect to Church," in E. P. Sanders, *Jewish and Christian Self-Definition*, vol. 1: *The Shaping of Christianity in the Second and Third Centuries*, 1–15, at 3.

2. Judith Lieu, " 'Impregnable Ramparts and Walls of Iron': Boundary and Identity in Early 'Judaism' and 'Christianity,' " *New Testament Studies* 48 (2002): 297–313, at 299. See id., *Image and Reality* and *Christian Identity in the Jewish and Graeco-Roman World*.

3. Lieu, "Impregnable Ramparts," 309.

4. Lieu, "Impregnable Ramparts," 313; see also on 301–2: "The creation of apparent homogeneity and unchangeability is, of course, part of the seduction of the idea of boundaries." See also Averil Cameron, *Christianity and the Rhetoric of Empire*, 31.

5. Terry Eagleton, *The Idea of Culture*, 96. See also Homi K. Bhahba on the "hybrid location of cultural value" (*The Location of Culture*, 248).

6. Mikhail Bakhtin, "Discourse in the Novel," in *The Dialogic Imagination*, 259–422, at 288. Eagleton does not explicitly invoke Bakhtin in his text, but see his much earlier discussion in "Wittgenstein's Friends," *New Left Review* 135 (September–October 1982): 64–90, esp. 74–81. Bakhtin's dialogics is elaborated in an explicitly postcolonial cultural register by Bhabha, *Location of Culture*, 176–79.

7. Bakhtin, "Discourse in the Novel," 358. See also Michael Mayerfeld Bell, "Culture as Dialogue," in Michael Mayerfeld Bell and Michael Gardiner, *Bakhtin and the Human Sciences*, 49–62.

8. See Dale E. Peterson, "Response and Call: The African American Dialogue with Bakhtin and What It Signifies," in Amy Mandelker, *Bakhtin in Contexts*, 89–98, at 91: "The long and the short of it, and by far the most culturally influential side of it, is that

Bakhtinian discourse analysis presumes that utterances come into the world showing and voicing the fact that they are sites of cultural contestation. Texts display themselves as linguistic arenas in which perceptible cultural conflicts are acting out or acting up."

9. My use of Bakhtin's notions of "dialogue" has been sharpened by the philosophical considerations of Dmitri Nikulin, "Mikhail Bakhtin: A Theory of Dialogue," *Constellations* 5 (1998): 381–402. Many thanks to R. Michael Feener, Hendrik Maier, and Justin T. McDaniel for drawing my attention to this article.

10. Dale B. Martin, *The Corinthian Body*, 133, defines *heteroglossia* as "the capacity of language to reflect several different discourses," a useful gloss that I would infuse, in the late ancient context, with clearer political, even colonizing, implications.

11. My integration of strong notions of power into my dialogical readings differs from more optimistically multicultural postmodern applications of Bakhtin's ideas: see Fred Evans, "Bakhtin, Communication, and the Politics of Multiculturalism," *Constellations* 5 (1998): 403–23.

12. As Lieu points out ("Impregnable Ramparts," 301–4), such reimagination also embeds the development of early Christian culture more securely in the sociopolitical worlds of the Roman Empire.

13. Daniel Boyarin, *Socrates and the Fat Rabbis*, 39–42, points out that the dialogue format does not create "dialogism" in a Bakhtinian sense: indeed, he argues, both Plato and the rabbis in the Babylonian Talmud produce hegemonic and monological dialogues. Nonetheless (as Boyarin also details), dialogic traces persist in the margins and interstices of these monologic texts.

14. Nikulin, "Mikhail Bakhtin," 385: "The other person becomes an integral and most intimate 'part' of myself."

15. For a similar historical analysis of projection in early Christian monasticism, see David Brakke, *Demons and the Making of the Monk*, 157–212.

16. Compare the discussions of these questions with respect to Justin Martyr in Tessa Rajak, "Talking at Trypho: Christian Apologetic as Anti-Judaism in Justin's *Dialogue with Trypho the Jew*," in her *The Jewish Dialogue with Greece and Rome*, 512–33, at 526–31; Miroslav Marcovich, *Iustini Martyris Dialogus cum Tryphone*, 64–65; and Timothy J. Horner, *Listening to Trypho*, who represent the range of opinions.

17. Certainly some of our ancient sources make references to public dialogues: Tertullian's *Adversus Iudaeos* begins with a mention of a recent debate between Jews and Christians that has prompted his writing (*Adversus Iudaeos* 1.1, text in Hermann Tränkle, *Q. S. F. Tertulliani Adversus Iudaeos mit Einleitung und kritischem Kommentar*, 3). See also Origen's comments cited in n. 45.

18. The *locus classicus* for this interpretation is Adolf von Harnack, *Die Altercatio Simonis Iudaei et Theophili Christiani nebst Untersuchungen über die antijüdische Polemik in der alten Kirche*. For recent discussion of the context and impact of this argument, see David M. Olster, *Roman Defeat, Christian Response, and the Literary Construction of the Jew*; and Stephen J. Shoemaker, "'Let Us Go and Burn Her Body': The Image of the Jews in the Early Dormition Traditions," *Church History* 68 (1999): 775–823.

19. Claudia Setzer, *Jewish Responses to Early Christian History and Polemics,* 129–46, for instance, emphasizes Justin's rhetorical production while still insisting we can mine the text for sociohistorical clues to early Jewish-Christian relations.

20. Ancient Christians refer to other "dialogue" texts that do not survive (such as the *Dialogue of Jason and Papiscus*), or are absorbed into much later redactions (such as the *Dialogue of Timothy and Aquila*): see the overview and references of William Varner, *Ancient Jewish-Christian Dialogues,* 1–15 (*Altercatio Simonis et Theophili*); and the survey of Lawrence Lahey, "Evidence for Jewish Believers in Christian-Jewish Dialogues Through the Sixth Century (Excluding Justin)," in Oskar Skarsaune and Reidar Hvalvik, *Jewish Believers in Jesus: The Early Centuries,* 581–639.

21. In addition to the *Dialogue with Trypho*, Justin composed two *Apologies* and a (lost) heresiological text. For a concise overview of Justin's writings and his context, see David Rokéah, *Justin Martyr and the Jews,* 1–11. On Justin's role in the "invention" of heresiology, see Alain Le Boulluec, *La notion de l'hérésie dans la littérature grecque,* 64–92 and 110–12: "Il revient à Justin d'avoir inventé l'hérésie" (110); and Daniel Boyarin, "Justin Martyr Invents Judaism," *Church History* 70 (2001): 427–61, at 449–61.

22. Horner, *Listening to Trypho,* 7, remarks that the *Dialogue* "is far and away the longest Christian document we have from the second century." But Bart D. Ehrman, *Lost Christianities,* 149, makes the same claim for the *Shepherd of Hermas.*

23. Rajak, "Talking at Trypho," notes that modern scholars often gloss over Justin's sharp antagonism.

24. See similarly Rebecca Lyman, "The Politics of Passing: Justin Martyr's Conversion as a Problem of 'Hellenization,'" in Kenneth Mills and Anthony Grafton, *Conversion in Late Antiquity and the Early Middle Ages,* 36–60; and Laura Nasrallah, "Mapping the World: Justin, Tatian, and the Second Sophistic," *Harvard Theological Review* 98 (2005): 283–314.

25. Rajak, "Talking at Trypho," 513.

26. Horner, *Listening to Trypho,* 155: "The thread which keeps Trypho in the dialogue once he discovers that Justin is a Christian is a question which embodies his chief reservation about the Christian claim. Simply put: Trypho is not convinced that Jesus is the messiah."

27. Shaye J. D. Cohen, *Why Aren't Jewish Women Circumcised?* 74–76, examines Justin's more general arguments against circumcision and Jewish Law. See also Judith Lieu, "Circumcision, Women, and Salvation," *New Testament Studies* 40 (1994): 358–70, who takes one of Justin's critiques as her hermeneutical launching point; and Maren R. Niehoff, "Circumcision as a Marker of Identity: Philo, Origen and the Rabbis on Gen 17:1–14," *Jewish Studies Quarterly* 10 (2003): 89–123, at 105–8.

28. Justin Martyr, *Dialogus cum Tryphone* 67.5; text in Marcovich, *Dialogus,* 185.

29. Justin Martyr, *Dialogus cum Tryphone* 67.7 (Marcovich, *Dialogus,* 185–86).

30. It is not clear whether the dispensation (οἰκονομία) in this passage being "brought to fulfillment" is the old covenant of the Jews or the new covenant of the Christians: the ambiguity is telling.

31. Horner, *Listening to Trypho*, 162, picks up on the tepidness of Justin's responses here; he assigns this portion of chapter 67 to the "Trypho Text," which he argues derives from the original *acta* of Justin's encounter with Trypho decades earlier. We would therefore not expect Justin automatically to counter all of Trypho's arguments.

32. Justin Martyr, *Dialogus cum Tryphone* 67.7 (Marcovich, *Dialogus*, 186).

33. Justin Martyr, *Dialogus cum Tryphone* 67.8, 10 (Marcovich, *Dialogus*, 186).

34. Justin Martyr, *Dialogus cum Tryphone* 46.5 (Marcovich, *Dialogus*, 145–46).

35. Justin Martyr, *Dialogus cum Tryphone* 47.1 (Marcovich, *Dialogus*, 146).

36. Justin Martyr, *Dialogus cum Tryphone* 47.1 (Marcovich, *Dialogus*, 146).

37. Justin Martyr, *Dialogus cum Tryphone* 47.2 (Marcovich, *Dialogus*, 147). The term ὁμοσπλάγνος may have a literal meaning ("of the same guts," i.e., "born of the same family") or a metaphorical one ("of the same heart" or "disposition"). On Justin's deliberate and ambiguous invocation of racial-ethnic language see Denise Kimber Buell, "Rethinking the Relevance of Race for Early Christian Self-Definition," *Harvard Theological Review* 94 (2001): 449–76, at 464–66 and 472; id., *Why This New Race?*

38. So we can interpret Ignatius of Antioch's warning that "it is better to learn Christianity from a man who is circumcised than to learn Judaism from a man with a foreskin" as apprehension about blurring the boundaries between Judaism and Christianity (*Epistula ad Philadelphios* 6.1 [SC 10:144]); see Shaye J. D. Cohen, "Judaism Without Circumcision and 'Judaism' Without 'Circumcision' in Ignatius," *Harvard Theological Review* 95 (2002): 395–415.

39. A marked difference from later Jewish-Christian dialogues, in which the Jewish interlocutor is moved to convert by the experience, as we see below in the *Altercation of Simon and Theophilus*.

40. For a different, but complementary, reading of the "dialogical process" and incongruity in the *Dialogue*, see Boyarin, "Justin Martyr," 455–56 and the boundary-destabilizing conclusions on 460–61; as well as his treatment of Justin Martyr in *Border Lines*, 37–73.

41. Joseph W. Trigg, *Origen*, 214–39; Robert Wilken, *The Christians as the Romans Saw Them*, 94–125; Michael Frede, "Celsus' Attack on the Christians," in Jonathan Barnes and Miriam Griffen, *Philosophia Togata II*, 218–40; id., "Origen's Treatise Against Celsus," in Mark Edwards, Martin Goodman, and Simon Price, *Apologetics in the Roman Empire*, 131–55. On the philosophical contexts of Celsus and Origen, see Silke-Petra Bergjan, "Celsus the Epicurean? The Interpretation of an Argument in Origen, *Contra Celsum*," *Harvard Theological Review* 94 (2001): 181–206.

42. An argument made by Carl Andresen, *Logos und Nomos*, 308–11 and 345–72; referenced by Wilken, *Christians as the Romans*, 101. Even if the correlation between Justin's and Celsus's understanding of the Logos and history is due more to common Platonic roots than direct influence (as suggested by Robert Grant, "Review of *Logos und Nomos*," *Journal of Religion* 36 [1956]: 270–72), Celsus himself makes mention of the now-lost *Dialogue of Jason and Papiscus* (παπίσκου τινὸς καὶ Ἰάσονος ἀντιλογίαν): see Origen, *Contra Celsum* 4.52 (SC 136:318), suggesting a sense of ongoing interreligious "dialogue."

43. On the polemical attempt to absorb the philosophical knowledge of one's

opponents in late antiquity and outperform them, see the discussion of Jeremy Schott, *Christianity, Empire, and the Making of Religion in Late Antiquity*, 45–51.

44. Origen, *Contra Celsum* 1.28, 32–44, 56–71, and 2.1, 3–79 (SC 132:150–52, 162–92, 228–74, 276–80, 268–476).

45. See my discussion and references in *Remains of the Jews*, 60–67, esp. 61–62. At several points in his refutation of "Celsus's Jew," Origen disputes Celsus's characterization by referring to his own more authoritative experience in public debate with "real" Jews (*Contra Celsum* 1.45, 1.55 [SC 132:192–94, 224–28]), even going so far as to sneer at Celsus's inauthentic Jew, who cites Greek mythology "like some Greek" (*Contra Celsum* 1.67 [SC 132:264]).

46. Origen, *Contra Celsum* 1.22 (SC 132:132).

47. Earlier in the treatise, Origen had deferred defense of "the reason of circumcision . . . which was begun by Abraham and hindered by Jesus, who did not want his disciples to do it" (*Contra Celsum* 1.22 [SC 132:130–32]).

48. Origen, *Contra Celsum* 5.41 (SC 147:120–22). The rest of this section details the banality of the Jews' religion.

49. Origen, *Contra Celsum* 5.43 (SC 147:126). On Origen's long-standing argument on the chronological and ontological priority of "Hebrew" wisdom over Greek philosophy, see my discussion and references in " 'Solomon's Salacious Song': Foucault's Author Function and the Early Christian Interpretation of the *Canticum Canticorum*," *Medieval Encounters* 4 (1998): 1–23.

50. Of course, Origen believes his Jewish contemporaries had abandoned their "greater wisdom" when they turned on Jesus; but the blueprint of the "holy nation," he insists, outshines that of Plato's "city of philosophy": "If only they hadn't sinned by their lawlessness, in former times by killing the prophets and of late by plotting against Jesus: we would have a model of the heavenly city, which even Plato strove to describe; but I don't know if he could achieve as much as Moses and those after him wrought, rearing a 'chosen people' and a 'holy nation' [1 Pet 2:9] set aside for God, through teachings purified from all superstition" (*Contra Celsum* 5.43 [SC 147:127]). On later Christian writings on "Platonopolis," see Jeremy M. Schott, "Founding Platonopolis: The Platonic πολιτεία in Eusebius, Porphyry, and Iamblichus," *Journal of Early Christian Studies* 11 (2003): 501–31.

51. Compare my discussion of circumcision as a quintessential sign of "Jewishness" in the Roman cultural economy in Chapter 1: I would suggest that, far from decrying this collection of cultural signs, Celsus takes upon himself the authority to rearrange and reassort them like a good imperial Roman.

52. Origen, *Contra Celsum* 5.44–45 (SC 147:128–32).

53. Origen, *Contra Celsum* 5.47 (SC 147:134).

54. Origen, *Contra Celsum* 5.48 (SC 147:48).

55. In other contexts Origen lays out more substantive arguments against Jewish circumcision: see Niehoff, "Circumcision as a Marker," 108–14. As Niehoff points out, Origen's discussions of circumcision were not uniformly negative.

56. Origen, *Contra Celsum* 5.48 (SC 147:138). Origen may be elaborating the argument

of the *Epistle of Barnabas* that circumcision was ordained by an evil angel (see my discussion in Chapter 1).

57. This incident, of course, continues to arouse exegetical and scholarly curiosity: from very different perspectives, see William H. Propp, "That Bloody Bridegroom (Exodus IV 24–6)," *Vetus Testamentum* 4 (1993): 495–523; Seth D. Kunin, "The Bridegroom of Blood: A Structuralist Analysis," *Journal for the Study of the Old Testament* 70 (1996): 3–16; and Bonna Devora Haberman, "Foreskin Sacrifice: Zipporah's Ritual and the Bloody Bridegroom," in Elizabeth Wyner Mark, *The Covenant of Circumcision*, 18–29. See now also my "Blood Will Out: Jesus' Circumcision and Early Christian Readings of Exodus 4:24–26," *Henoch* 30 (2008): 310–32.

58. Origen, *Contra Celsum* 5.48 (SC 147:138–40). The crucial "not" (μή) has been inserted by all modern translators, and the critical edition: see SC 147:138n48.

59. On early Christian conflation of angels and idolatry, see Annette Yoshiko Reed, "The Trickery of the Fallen Angels and the Demonic Mimesis of the Divine: Aetiology, Demonology, and Polemics in the Writings of Justin Martyr," *Journal of Early Christian Studies* 12 (2004): 141–71. On the apotropaic function of circumcision, intertextualizing Exodus 4 with the Passover account, see the sources and comments of Cohen, *Why Aren't*, 16–18 and 229–30.

60. See Arthur Droge, *Homer or Moses?* 152–67 (on Origen); Peter Pilhofer, *Presbyteron Kreitton*, 221–84 (on Christian authors following their pagan and Jewish predecessors); Daniel Ridings, *The Attic Moses*; and Schott, *Christianity*, 30–44.

61. See also Origen, *Contra Celsum* 2.7 (SC 132:296), where Origen seemingly refers to Christ's rejection of the significance of physical circumcision. "Celsus' Jew" claimed that Jesus was "impious," prompting Origen to reply: "Is it impiety to renounce bodily circumcision and bodily Sabbath and bodily festivals and bodily new moons and clean and unclean, to turn the mind toward a Law worthy of God, both true and spiritual?" So Origen claims that Jesus "renounced" circumcision even as he underwent the ritual.

62. On Origen's highly incarnational Christology, see Henri Crouzel, "Le Christ Sauveur selon Origène," *Studia Missionalia* 30 (1981): 87.

63. To take but one example, the interpretation of prophecy: "Celsus's Jew" prompts Origen both to defend the veracity of Jewish prophecy over against pagan criticism (*Contra Celsum* 1.36 [SC 132:174–76]) and to justify Christian interpretation of Jewish prophecy over against Jewish criticism (*Contra Celsum* 2.28 [SC 132:356–58]).

64. Harnack argued in *Altercatio* that we could recover the lost Greek *Dialogue of Jason and Papiscus* from the *Altercatio Simonis et Theophili*. See now Lahey, "Evidence for Jewish Believers."

65. Varner, *Ancient Jewish-Christian Dialogues*, 87–88 and notes.

66. Gennadius, *De virus inlustribus* 51 (text in E. C. Richardson, *Hieronymus liber de viris inlustribus*, 79). The chapter in full reads: *Evagrius alius scripsit altercationem Simonis Iudaei et Theophili Christiani, quae paene omnibus nota est*. Presumably Gennadius is distinguishing this Evagrius (*alius*) from the monk of Pontus (*de viris inlustribus* 11 [Richardson, *Hieronymus liber*, 65]).

67. *Altercatio Simonis et Theophili* 2.10, 3.11, 5.20 (CCL 64:261, 273). Citations from the Corpus Christianorum text are given according to the chapter and paragraph numbers of Varner's translation.

68. *Altercatio Simonis et Theophili* 3.11 (CCL 64:261): *loqueris quasi Iudaeus*. Of course, a Christian of this period could direct such a sneering response equally to an uninformed believer or a heretic. More straightforwardly, Theophilus generally addresses Simon as "Jew" (*Iudaee*: *Altercatio* 1.6, 2.7, 5.19, 6.22, 6.24, 7.28 [CCL 64:259, 260, 273, 280, 282, 299]), and repeatedly tells him, "You're wrong, Jew" (*erras, Iudaee*: *Altercatio* 2.8, 2.9, 3.12, 3.13 [CCL 64:260, 265]). On two occasions only, Theophilus addresses Simon by his name (*Altercatio* 4.17, 7.28 [CCL 64:271, 299]).

69. *Altercatio* 8.29 (CCL 64:300).

70. *Altercatio* 3.14 (CCL 64:269).

71. The argument appears in Tertullian, *Adversus Marcionem* 3.13 (text in Ernest Evans, *Tertullian*, 1:206–10); and in *Adversus Iudaeos* 9 (Tränkle, *Adversus Iudaeos*, 20–23), which takes up much of the argument of the anti-Marcionite tractate. On the relationship of these two texts, see Tränkle, *Adversus Iudaeos*, liii–lix. Tertullian does not, however, bring Christ's circumcision into this part of his argument in those works. Harnack, *Altercatio*, 91–96, briefly surveys the places he sees comparison with Tertullian's *Adversus Iudaeos*, and concludes that both Tertullian and the *Altercatio* relied on an older, Greek dialogue.

72. I mean that Theophilus ascribes no apparent Jewish significance to the act here— covenantal or ritual significance, for example—apart from his assumption of circumcision as a routine aspect of Jesus' (Jewish) infancy.

73. See Justin, *Dialogus cum Tryphone* 66, 77–78 (Marcovich, *Dialogus*, 183–84, 203–6).

74. *Altercatio* 4.15 (CCL 64:269–70): "Bene quidem per omnia interrogationibus meis patefacis mysteria, et quia Christum deum, dei filium, ore dei prolatum, verbo genitum et ex virgine natum probasti." As often throughout the *Altercation*, Simon the Jew sounds remarkably like a catechumen.

75. *Altercatio* 5.18 (CCL 64:272). Simon's language here—"superius professus es"— recalls Trypho's mention of the circumcision of Christ to Justin (σὺ γὰρ ὡμολόγησας ἡμῖν), which, as I noted, was in fact not preceded by such a "confession." The interlocutory doublet may suggest a common source for both Justin and "Evagrius," such as the lost *Dialogue of Jason and Papiscus*.

76. *Altercatio* 5.18 (CCL 64:273). This concluding phrase, along with the general argument about circumcision and "salvation" (*salus*), is also found in the late-fourth-century exegesis of Gregory of Elvira, *Tractatus Origenis* 4 (CCL 69:27–34), a possible source for "Evagrius."

77. *Altercatio* 5.19 (CCL 64:273). Simon cites the Exodus passage according to the Latin version of the Septuagint: "Stet sanguis circumcisionis pueri." That is, Simon suggests that Moses' son was literally "saved" by being circumcised.

78. *Altercatio* 5.19 (CCL 64:273).

79. *Altercatio* 8.29 (CCL 64:300).

80. See the sympathetic reading of Demetrios Trakatellis, "Justin Martyr's Trypho,"

Harvard Theological Review 79 (1986): 289–97, who prefers to see the *Dialogue* as "beyond the stereotyped classification of anti-Jewish or anti-Christian . . . dominated by a consuming shared passion for the truth revealed in Scriptures" (297).

81. Celsus's Jew is used to corroborate and date talmudic accusations against Jesus by Peter Schäfer, *Jesus in the Talmud*, 18–21.

82. See, for instance, William Horbury, *Jews and Christians in Contact and Controversy*, 170 and 205.

83. See Harnack, *Altercatio*; and now the discussion of Lahey, "Evidence for Jewish Believers," 587–96, who takes a more optimistic approach to this text as evidence for authentic Jewish criticism of Christianity.

84. See Adam H. Becker and Annette Yoshiko Reed, "Introduction: Traditional Models and New Directions"; and my "The Lion and the Lamb: Reconsidering Jewish-Christian Relations in Antiquity"; both in Adam H. Becker and Annette Yoshiko Reed, *The Ways That Never Parted*, 1–33 and 95–118.

85. On the ancient novel, see Stefan Tilg, *Chariton of Aphrodisias and the Invention of the Greek Love Novel*; and the classic essay of Bakhtin, "Discourse in the Novel." On the gospel, see Jonathan Z. Smith, "Good News Is No News: Aretalogy and Gospel," in *Map Is Not Territory*, 190–207; followed by Patricia Cox, *Biography in Late Antiquity*, 3–4, 46–65.

86. The classic study remains the six-part publication of Gustave Bardy, "La littérature patristique des 'quaestiones et responsiones' sur l'Écriture Sainte," *Revue Biblique* 41 (1932): 210–36, 341–60, 515–37; 42 (1933): 14–30, 211–29, 328–52 (cited as Bardy, "Littérature patristique I–VI"). Bardy, "Littérature patristique I," 211–12, briefly notes that the genre seems to emerge out of philosophical pedagogy, but also remarks, "Il est inutile d'insister sur les origines du genre" (211). Bardy's yeoman's work of cataloguing is now supplemented by the collected essays in Annelie Volgers and Claudio Zamagni, *Erotapokriseis*; and Yannis Papadoyannakis, "Instruction by Question and Answer: The Case of Late Antique and Byzantine *Erotapokriseis*," in Scott Fitzgerald Johnson, *Greek Literature in Late Antiquity*, 91–105.

87. Bardy, "Littérature patristique I," 212–17; Peder Borgen and Roald Skarsten, "Quaestiones et solutiones: Some Observations on the Form of Philo's Exegesis," *Studia Philonica* 4 (1976–77): 1–16; and Pieter W. van der Horst, "Philo and the Rabbis on Genesis: Similar Questions, Different Answers," in Volgers and Zamagni, *Erotapokriseis*, 55–70.

88. See the overview and references of Claudio Zamagni, "Une introduction méthodologique à la littérature patristique des questions et réponses: Le cas d'Eusèbe de Césarée," in Volgers and Zamagni, *Erotapokriseis*, 7–24, who distinguishes between a question-and-answer process (evident from Aristotle onward) and a question-and-answer genre, which he asserts originates with Eusebius. On this technical (but not unimportant) point, Bardy seemed already in some agreement, saying of Eusebius's περὶ τῶν ἐν εὐαγ–γελίοις ζητημάτων καὶ λύσεων: "pour la première fois, dans la littérature patristique, nous rencontrons le titre exact qui caractérise le genre littéraire dont nous nous occupons ici" ("Littérature patristique I," 228).

89. On Augustine's several texts, see Bardy, "Littérature patristiques III"; and the

much more expansive catalogue of Ronald J. Teske, S.J., "Augustine of Hippo and the Quaestiones et Responsiones Literature," in Volgers and Zamagni, *Erotapokriseis*, 127–44.

90. See Bakhtin, "Discourse in the Novel," 282–84 on "internal dialogism" and 324–28 on "double-voicedness." See also the critical discussions of Evans, "Bakhtin, Communication," 405–6 on "intentional and nonintentional" dialogues; and Nikulin, "Mikhail Bakhtin," 399: "Rejoinders of the inner dialogue (with oneself) and of the outer dialogue (with the other) are not really separable, but always intersect; they both interrupt and support each other."

91. Such topics were staples of adversus Iudaeos and Christian apologetic texts, and also appear regularly in Christian erotapokriseis. See, for example, the discussion of Augustine's "question-and-answer" texts alongside his polemical treatises (such as the *Contra Faustum*) in Teske, "Augustine of Hippo."

92. Bardy, "Littérature patristique V," 215, points out that the possibly fourth-century Greek Ps.-Justin, *Quaestiones ad orthodoxos*, recycled issues raised by Celsus, Porphyry, and the emperor Julian in their respective anti-Christian treatises.

93. See Alexander Souter, *A Study of Ambrosiaster*; and, for more recent bibliography and discussion, Annelie Volgers, "Ambrosiaster: Persuasive Powers in Progress," in Volgers and Zamagni, *Erotapokriseis*, 99–125; Sophie Lunn-Rockliffe, *Ambrosiaster's Political Theology*, 12–86; and David Hunter, "2008 NAPS Presidential Address: The Significance of Ambrosiaster," *Journal of Early Christian Studies* 17 (2009): 1–26.

94. Different MSS contain various numbers of questions: see the "Prolegomena" in Alexander Souter, *Pseudo-Augustini quaestiones veteris et novi testamenti CXXVII*, vii–xxxv. I am following Souter's critical edition, which lists forty-seven "Old Testament" questions and eighty "New Testament" questions (although questions 100–127 are an Old-New Testament catch-all). See Souter, *Study*, 161–74; and Lunn-Rockliffe, *Ambrosiaster's*, 33–62, on Ambrosiaster's likely date of composition (366–82 CE) and location (Rome).

95. The editor of the critical edition, Alexander Souter, notes in the *apparatus criticus* that he inserted the individual "chapter titles" before each question: "Singulorum capitulorum sectiones ipse constitui" (CSEL 50:13).

96. See Volgers, "Ambrosiaster," 99–100; and Andrew Cain, "In Ambrosiaster's Shadow: A Critical Re-Evaluation of the Last Surviving Letter Exchange Between Pope Damasus and Jerome," *Revue des Études Augustiniennes* 51 (2005): 257–77, esp. 268–75, who persuasively gauges Ambrosiaster's literary impact in late fourth-century Roman Christianity.

97. Many of the "questions" and "answers" are highly polemical, aimed at the Jews and pagans of Ambrosiaster's milieu (late fourth-century Rome). On his polemical interests, see Franz Cumont, "La polémique de l'Ambrosiaster contre les païens," *Revue d'Histoire et de Littérature Religieuses* 8 (1903): 417–40; Lydia Speller, "Ambrosiaster and the Jews," *Studia Patristica* 17.1 (1982): 72–78; Souter, *Study*, 180–83; and Cain, "In Ambrosiaster's Shadow."

98. Despite the questionless title, quaestio 44 (CSEL 50:71–81) is actually framed as a scriptural "answer" to the meaning of the location of the "house" of God in Isa 56:7.

99. Jeffrey S. Siker, *Disinheriting the Jews*.

100. Ambrosiaster, *Liber quaestionum* 108.2 (CSEL 50:522). On contemporary opinion, see Jerome, *Liber Hebraicorum quaestionum in Genesim* 1.10.24 (CCL 72:14): "Heber, a quo Hebraei." On modern scholarly opinion, see Francis Brown, *The New Brown-Driver-Briggs-Gesenius Hebrew and English Lexicon*, 720. Some of this discussion on the Hebrew language is repeated in Ambrosiaster's *Commentary on Paul's Letters*.

101. Ambrosiaster, *Liber quaestionum* 108.2 (CSEL 50:252). Throughout the chapter, Ambrosiaster provides philological arguments for lost gutturals, transposed consonants, and shifting vowels.

102. Ambrosiaster, *Liber quaestionum* 108.6–7 (CSEL 50:255–56).

103. Ambrosiaster, *Liber quaestionum* 108.7 (CSEL 50:256). The passage is somewhat confusing, as Ambrosiaster seems about to concede that Jews still speak Hebrew: "denique neque terram aliquam habet inter homines, ut ceterae linguae, neque gentem exceptis Iudaeis, quia primo homini data est in paradiso."

104. Ambrosiaster, *Liber quaestionum* 108.8 (CSEL 50:256).

105. This is made even clearer in the more fulsome discussion of Ambrosiaster's *Commentarius in Philippienses* 3:5/7 (CSEL 81.3:152–53); see my discussion in "A Jew's Jew: Paul and the Early Christian Problem of Jewish Origins," *Journal of Religion* 86 (2006): 258–86, at 265–67. Joshua Papsdorf, "Ambrosiaster's Theological Anthropology," 96n.235, takes great issue with my argument there.

106. Ambrosiaster, *Liber quaestionum* 49 (CSEL 50:95–96).

107. Ambrosiaster, *Liber quaestionum* 49.1 (CSEL 50:95).

108. Ambrosiaster, *Liber quaestionum* 50 (CSEL 50:96–97).

109. Ambrosiaster, *Liber quaestionum* 50 (CSEL 50:96).

110. On "difference in times" as a strategy of ancient Christian exegesis, see Elizabeth A. Clark, *Reading Renunciation*, 145–52 and 225–30 on circumcision in particular.

111. Compare *Liber quaestionum* 12 (CSEL 36–39): "quare Abraham fidei suae signum circumcisionem accepit?" Ambrosiaster understands Abraham's circumcision as the ultimate sign of trust in God (he draws the interesting parallel with Achior at the end of the book of Judith). The circumcision is an unequivocally positive sign, and also points ahead to "futurus Christus."

112. Ambrosiaster, *Liber quaestionum* 50 (CSEL 50:96–97).

113. By "spiritual circumcision" Ambrosiaster seems to indicate a moral "excision" of fleshly "blindness," and not a typology for baptism: see, for instance, *Liber quaestionum* 12.2 (CSEL 50:37): "nebula carnis circumcidi haberet a cordibus hominibus per fidem Christi, quia carnalis error obstabat caliginem praestans humanis cordibus, ne cognoscerent creatorem."

114. See, for instance, Ambrosiaster, *Liber quaestionum* 44.10 (CSEL 50:77): "idcirco autem nova lex data est, id est spirtualis, ut cessarent carnalia." As I noted above, quaestio 44 in the MS is labeled "Adversus Iudaeos."

115. Discussed by Volgers, "Ambrosiaster," 100.

116. See the texts surveyed in Volgers and Zamagni, *Erotapokriseis*; and Bardy, "Littérature patristique."

117. Bardy, "Littérature patristique VI," 328–32; and Robert G. Hoyland, *Seeing Islam as Others Saw It*, 96–97 and nn.142–46.

118. Hoyland, *Seeing Islam*, 96, says it is "in part at least a product of the seventh century"; Olster, *Roman Defeat*, 133, to "the last quarter of the seventh century." The composite, and evolving, nature of the text, however, makes dating something of an impossible task since versions of the *Quaestiones* could have been circulating for a century or more before it took on its present form in the post-Islamic period.

119. Olster, *Roman Defeat*, 123–25.

120. Bardy, "Littérature patristique VI," 332.

121. Bardy, "Littérature patristique VI," 332, coolly remarks: "Inutile de nous arrêter sur ces chaînes; qu'il nous suffise d'opposer leur médiocrité à l'intérêt des ouvrages homogènes qui peuvent se recommander du nom d'un auteur unique."

122. Olster, *Roman Defeat*, 116–37, places the *Quaestiones ad Antiochum* in conversation with other anti-Jewish sources of the period, and notes that the *Quaestiones* itself seems to have made fulsome use of explicitly anti-Jewish source material.

123. Ps.-Athanasius, *Quaestiones ad Antiochum Ducem* 37 (PG 28:620): τίνος χάριν τοῦ Χριστοῦ περιτμηθέντος, οὐ περιτεμνόμεθα καὶ ἡμεῖς, ὡς αὐτός;

124. Olster, *Roman Defeat*, 123, translates this section as follows: "Thus, we thereby know clearly that all the circumcised are races that are alien to Christ, whether faithful or unfaithful, Jews or pagans, since they puff themselves up with the Mosaic law, and do not follow Christ." His translation of ἀλλότριος as "of an alien race" and Ἕλληνες as "pagans" helps him emphasize the utility of this passage in addressing the "far more important implications [in the seventh century] that circumcision had for the Arabs, their victories, and the question of God's favor" (124).

125. Ps.-Athanasius, *Quaestiones ad Antiochum Ducem* 37 (PG 28:620–21). The reference to a "bloodless sacrifice" is likely meant to contrast the Eucharist with Old Testament sacrifice. Nonetheless, the invocation of the crucifixion in the same passage problematizes the "bloodlessness."

126. On the long "gamut of interpretations" (they list nine) for Matt 5:17, see William D. Davis and Dale Allison, *Matthew 1–7*, 484–87.

127. See, for example, Cyril of Alexandria, *Homilia 12 in Lucam (in occursum Domini)* (PG 77:1041), which I discuss more fully in Chapter 5.

128. Boyarin, *Socrates and the Fat Rabbis*, 140–61, argues similarly for the dialectic monologic of the Babylonian Talmud.

129. See the concluding section of Daniel Boyarin and Virginia Burrus, "Hybridity as Subversion of Orthodoxy? Jews and Christians in Late Antiquity," *Social Compass* 52 (2005): 431–41.

130. Robert Young, *Colonial Desire*, 53.

CHAPTER 3. HERESY, THEOLOGY, AND THE DIVINE CIRCUMCISION

Note to epigraph: Julia Kristeva, *Powers of Horror*, 17.

1. Vincentius of Lerins, *Commonitorium* 1.2.5 (CCL 64:149).

2. Thomas Guarino, "Vincent of Lerins and the Hermeneutical Question: Historical and Theological Reflections," *Gregorianum* 75 (1994): 491–523, attempts to reconcile the seemingly static theological canon of Vincentius (especially his "second canon" [*In eodem scilicet dogmate, eodem sensu eademque sententia*] from *Commonitorium* 1.23.4 [CCL 64:178]) with the progressive (even, to Guarino, postmodern) historical development of Catholic dogma, arguing (with Vincentius) that "incorporation of 'otherness' . . . in no way militates against organic and homogeneous development" (520–21).

3. Vincentius himself is deeply embedded in the cultural politics of vanishing Roman imperialism in the West as "Peregrinus" (his pseudonym), the provincial *collator* of a "classical" theology: see Mark Vessey, "Peregrinus Against the Heretics: Classicism, Provinciality, and the Place of the Alien Writer in Late Roman Gaul," in *Cristianesimo e specificità regionali nel Mediterraneo latino (sec. IV–VI)*, 529–65.

4. So John B. Henderson, *The Construction of Orthodoxy and Heresy*, 42: "But once having created a dichotomy between heresy and orthodoxy, and having identified the latter with specific ideas and principles, the early heresiologists were obliged to give a more stable and positive content to orthodoxy." For a cogent description of the anthropological-sociological sources of this binary sensibility, as well as some sense of its limitations, see Shaye J. D. Cohen, *The Beginnings of Jewishness*, 5–10.

5. Kristeva is explicitly indebted to, and in dialogue with, Mary Douglas: Kristeva, *Powers of Horror*, 65–66.

6. For a slightly different use of Kristeva and abjection, see Virginia Burrus, *Saving Shame*, 44–80.

7. Elizabeth Grosz, "The Body of Signification," in John Fletcher and Andrew Benjamin, *Abjection, Melancholia, and Love*, 80–103, at 86.

8. Kristeva's classic examples are excrement and the corpse, both of which simultaneously create a sense of the bounded body (from which and to which these abjections refer) but call that secure boundedness into question: *Powers of Horror*, 108–9.

9. Kristeva, *Powers of Horror*, 9.

10. Kristeva, *Powers of Horror*, 9.

11. Kristeva, *Powers of Horror*, 90–134.

12. Kristeva, *Powers of Horror*, 67.

13. Anne McClintock, *Imperial Leather*, 71.

14. On the context of abjection in the early Roman Empire, see Judith Perkins, *Roman Imperial Identities in the Early Christian Era*, 90–91; Perkins's analysis focuses primarily on the horror of the abject (as on 93 and 99), with less attention to the possibilities of jouissance that Kristeva intimates at the site of abjection.

15. See the helpful comments of Catharine Edwards and Greg Woolf, "Cosmopolis: Rome as World City," in id., *Rome the Cosmopolis*, 1–20, which maps the imperial

strategies I am discussing onto the city of Rome itself: "Everywhere in the city elements of the conquered world had been appropriated and recontextualized; the city had absorbed the world" (2).

16. See Jeremy Schott, "Heresiology as Universal History in Epiphanius's *Panarion*," *Zeitschrift für Antikes Christentum* 10 (2006): 546–63.

17. See Kristeva, *Powers of Horror*, 8: "A deviser of territories, languages, works, the *deject* [the one who exists in abjection] never stops demarcating his universe whose fluid confines . . . constantly question his solidity and impel him to start fresh."

18. On our historiographic replication of this via media, see Karen L. King, "Which Early Christianity?" in Susan Ashbrook Harvey and David G. Hunter, *The Oxford Handbook of Early Christian Studies*, 66–84; and Virginia Burrus, "Hailing Zenobia: Anti-Judaism, Trinitarianism, and John Henry Newman," *Culture and Religion* 3 (2002): 163–77.

19. David Dawson, *Allegorical Readers and Cultural Revision in Ancient Alexandria*, 127–82, gives a particularly nuanced reading of Valentinus's exegetical and theological affinities with his Jewish and "orthodox" Christian predecessors and contemporaries.

20. Irenaeus, *Adversus haereses* 1.8.1, 1.9.1 (SC 264:112–16, 136–38).

21. Dawson, *Allegorical Readers*, 176, describes Valentinus's interpretation of sacred history as a "sublimation and transformation of Jewish covenantal monotheism."

22. See Dawson, *Allegorical Readers*, 132–45; and Karen L. King, *The Secret Revelation of John*. See also King's insightful exploration of how modern scholarship on "Gnosticism" fundamentally reproduces ancient Christian discourses of categorization: *What Is Gnosticism?*

23. On Marcion in his historical and historiographic context, see Gerhard May and Katharina Greschat, *Marcion und seine kirchengeschichtliche Wirkung*.

24. Irenaeus, *Adversus haereses* 1.27.2 (SC 264:350). See, though, my discussion in Chapter 1 on the possibility that the circumcision verse was added to a more primitive version of Luke as a response to Marcion's version of the gospel.

25. Quoted by Tertullian, *De carne Christi* 2.1 (SC 216:212–24).

26. Tertullian, *Adversus Marcionem* 2.17.4–19.4; text in Ernest Evans, *Tertullian*, 1:134–40.

27. Tertullian, *Adversus Iudaeos* 3; text in Hermann Tränkle, *Q. S. F. Tertulliani Adversus Iudaeos mit Einleitung und kritischem Kommentar*, 6–9. On the surprising amount of overlap between Tertullian's treatises against Jews and Marcion, see Tränkle, *Tertulliani*, liii–lix.

28. On the still vexed question of Tertullian's "anti-Judaism," see Geoffrey D. Dunn, "The Universal Spread of Christianity as a Rhetorical Argument in Tertullian's *adversus Iudaeos*," *Journal of Early Christian Studies* 8 (2000): 1–19; id., "Tertullian and Rebekah: A Re-Reading of an 'Anti-Jewish' Argument in Early Christian Literature," *Vigiliae Christianae* 52 (1998): 119–45; id., "*Pro temporum condicione*: Jews and Christians as God's People in Tertullian's *adversus Iudaeos*," in Pauline Allen et al., *Prayer and Spirituality in the Early Church*, 2:315–41; and now id., *Tertullian's "Adversus Iudaeos."*

29. Tertullian, *Adversus Marcionem* 4.7.2, 5 (Evans, *Adversus Marcionem*, 2:276, 278).

30. Tertullian, *Adversus Marcionem* 4.7.6–7 (Evans, *Adversus Marcionem*, 2:278). The forcefulness of Tertullian's defense here is made all the more notable, again, by contrast with his treatise *Adversus Iudaeos*, where his description of Christ as the "mountain" "sine manibus concidentium praecisus" may be a blending of Dan 2:34 (a "stone cut away without hands") with Col 2:11 ("a circumcision performed without hands") that diminishes the significance of Christ's circumcision (*Adversus Iudaeos* 3 [Tränkle, *Tertulliani*, 8]).

31. Luke 16:16, cited by Tertullian, *Adversus Marcionem* 4.33.7–8 (Evans, *Adversus Marcionem*, 2:446).

32. C. R. Whittaker has been at the fore of a historiographic rereading of Roman *limites* not as "boundaries" but as "frontier zones of interaction": see *Frontiers of the Roman Empire* and *Rome and Its Frontiers*.

33. Willamien Otten, "Christ's Birth of a Virgin Who Became a Wife: Flesh and Speech in Tertullian's *De Carne Christi,*" *Vigiliae Christianae* 51 (1997): 247–60, argues that rhetorical analysis fails to adequately address Tertullian's theology; but see also rhetorico-theological analyses of Geoffrey D. Dunn in "Mary's Virginity *in partu* and Tertullian's Anti-Docetism in *De carne Christi* Reconsidered," *Journal of Theological Studies* n.s. 58 (2007): 467–84; and in Dunn's response to Otten in "Rhetoric and Tertullian's *de virginibus velandis,*" *Vigiliae Christianae* 59 (2005): 1–30.

34. On Augustine, Jews, and heresy see Paula Fredriksen, "*Excaecati Occulta Iustitia Dei*: Augustine on Jews and Judaism," *Journal of Early Christian Studies* 3 (1995): 299–324; and id., *Augustine and the Jews*, esp. 105–21 on Augustine's Manichean "phase" and 213–89 on Augustine's *Contra Faustum*.

35. On the manner in which Manicheans of Augustine's time—and perhaps Mani's own—configured their Christian community, see Michel Tardieu, "Une définition du Manichéisme comme *secta christianorum,*" in A. Caquot and P. Canivet, *Ritualisme et vie intérieure*, 167–77.

36. Literature on Mani and the Manicheans has undergone a renaissance in recent decades: an indispensable starting point remains Samuel Lieu, *Manichaeism in the Later Roman Empire and Medieval China*.

37. For a concise overview of Augustine's Manichean background and foreground, see Gregor Wurst, "Manichäismus um 375 in Nordafrika und Italien," in Volker Henning Drecoll, *Augustin Handbuch*, 85–92. The degree to which Manicheism became embedded in the social and theological circles of otherwise "orthodox" Christians is clear in the post-Constantinian West: see Harry O. Maier, "'Manichee!' Leo the Great and the Orthodox Panopticon," *Journal of Early Christian Studies* 4 (1996): 441–60.

38. The *Contra Faustum* was one of several works explicitly or implicitly directed against the Manicheans following his baptism into Catholic Christianity in 386. A first spate of works (such as *On the Morals of Manicheans* and *On Genesis Against the Manicheans*) appeared in the late 380s, in the period preceding Augustine's ordination as a priest. A second spate of works, including his *Answer to Simplicianus* and *Contra Faustum* appeared around the time of his ordination as bishop in the 390s. On the question of the "anti-Manichean"

character of his *Confessiones*, see Annemarré Kotzé, "The 'Anti-Manichaean' Passage in *Confessions* 3 and Its 'Manichaean Audience,'" *Vigiliae Christianae* 62 (2008): 187–200; on Augustine's desire to defend himself to Catholics against charges of crypto-Manicheism, see now Jason D. BeDuhn, "Augustine Accused: Megalius, Manichaeism, and the Inception of the *Confessions*," *Journal of Early Christian Studies* 17 (2009): 85–124.

39. Augustine, *Confessiones* 5.3, 6 (CCL 27:58, 61).

40. On Faustus's text, see Gregor Wurst, "Bemerkungen zu Struktur und *genus litterarium* der *Capitula* des Faustus von Mileve," in Johannes von Oort, Otto Wermelinger, and Gregor Wurst, *Augustine and Manichaeism in the Latin West*, 307–24. An analysis of the *Contra Faustum* lies at the heart of Fredriksen, *Augustine and the Jews*: I am, throughout this section, indebted to Professor Fredriksen's work.

41. Augustine, *Contra Faustum Manichaeum* 1.1 (PL 42:207).

42. We can compare the quasi-dramatic format of the *Contra Faustum* with Augustine's use of *serminocatio* to speak "for" Paul in many of his sermons: see Thomas F. Martin, "*Vox Pauli*: Augustine and the Claims to Speak for Paul, an Exploration of Rhetoric at the Service of Exegesis," *Journal of Early Christian Studies* 8 (2000): 237–72. See also my discussion of dialogues and dialogism in Chapter 2.

43. "Proximate other" is the felicitous phrase of Jonathan Z. Smith, "What a Difference a Difference Makes," in Jacob Neusner and Ernest S. Frerichs, "*To See Ourselves as Others See Us,*" 3–48; now reprinted in *Relating Religion*, 251–302.

44. On this comparison—which also draws on Tertullian's anti-Marcionite writings—see Fredriksen, *Augustine and the Jews*, 223–27.

45. Manicheans, like gnostics, were a thoroughly scripturalized movement: see Julien Ries, "La bible chez saint Augustin et chez les manichéens," *Revue des Études Augustiniennes* 7 (1961): 231–43; 9 (1963): 201–15; 10 (1964): 309–29, esp. "Bible III," 320–25; and the brief discussion of Johannes van Oort, "*Secundini Manichaei Epistula*: Roman Manichaean 'Biblical' Argument in the Age of Augustine," in von Oort, Wermelinger, and Wurst, *Augustine and Manichaeism*, 161–73. On the appeal of Manicheism to Augustine the young reader, see Brian Stock, *Augustine the Reader*, 43–53.

46. Augustine, *Contra Faustum* 4.1 (PL 42:217): *misera . . . et corporalis*.

47. Augustine, *Contra Faustum* 1.2 (PL 42:207).

48. Augustine, *Contra Faustum* 32.6 (PL 42:500).

49. Augustine, *Contra Faustum* 32.7 (PL 42:500–501).

50. In the 390s Augustine wrote a treatise *De mendacio* (on the context of which, see BeDuhn, "Augustine Accused," 103–7); near the end of his life, he wrote a second treatise *Contra mendacium*, written specifically in response to the question of whether or not an orthodox Christian could go "undercover" to reveal the falsehoods of heretics. Augustine raises the issue of orthodox and scriptural falsehood (*mendacium* or *fallacium*) throughout his life, notably (described below) in his correspondence with Jerome. See Boniface Ramsey, "Two Traditions of Lying and Deception in the Ancient Church," *Thomist* 49 (1985): 504–33 (504–15 specifically on Augustine).

51. Augustine refers here—in some form—to the dualistic cosmology of the

Manicheans: see a concise summary (based on multiple sources from North Africa to China) in Lieu, *Manichaeism*, 7–32.

52. Augustine, *Contra Faustum* 32.22 (PL 42:510).

53. Augustine, *Contra Faustum* 22.2 (PL 42:402).

54. Augustine, *Contra Faustum* 22.6 (PL 42:404).

55. On "difference in times" as an exegetical strategy, see Elizabeth A. Clark, *Reading Renunciation*, 145–52.

56. I have discussed this correspondence in my *Remains of the Jews*, 89–96. On these letters in the context of Augustine's emerging thought, see Fredriksen, *Augustine and the Jews*, 290–302.

57. Augustine, *Epistula* 82.18 (CSEL 34.2:370). The insinuation of scriptural "lying" here probably betrays Augustine's Manichean fears. For a discussion of "falsehood" in the context of this debate, see Alfons Furst, "Hieronymus über die heilsame Täuschung," *Zeitschrift für Antikes Christentum* 2 (1998): 97–112.

58. Augustine, *Epistula* 82.18 (CSEL 34.2:370).

59. The treatise is directed against Marcion, Apelles, and Valentinus, insofar as they share a "docetic" Christology: see Jean-Pierre Marré, *Tertullien (De carne Christi)*, SC 216:27–112.

60. Tertullian, *De carne Christi* 2.2 (SC 216:214). On Tertullian, flesh, shame, and abjection, see the thoughtful analysis of Burrus, *Saving Shame*, 52–57.

61. See Tertullian, *De carne Christi* 5.3 (SC 216:228), where the incarnation is the "necessary disgrace of faith" (*dedecus necessarium fidei*).

62. Tertullian, *De carne Christi* 5.1 (SC 216:226). Jennifer Glancy, "The Law of the Opened Body: Tertullian on the Nativity," *Henoch* 30 (2008): 45–66, shows how Tertullian adopts an almost Marcionite disgust for the body in order to elevate the significance of Christ's incarnation; see her *Corporal Knowledge*, 81–136, on Jesus' and Mary's bodies *in partu* more broadly.

63. See Tertullian, *De carne Christi* 5.7 (SC 216:230): "So the measure of both substances showed him human and God: the one born, the other unborn; one fleshly, the other spiritual; one weak, the other very strong; one dying, the other living. The particularity (*proprietas*) of these states, divine and human, is kept distinct by the true equality of each of its natures, by the same faith of spirit and of flesh; the miracles (*virtutes*) of God's spirit prove him God, the sufferings (*passiones*) prove his human flesh."

64. On this phrase, and Tertullian's "rational" use of paradox in general in *De carne Christi*, see Eric Osborn, *Tertullian, First Theologian of the West*, 48–64: "For Tertullian, almost anything worth saying can be expressed in a paradox" (63).

65. Burrus, *Saving Shame*, 44–80, discusses flesh—particularly the corruptible quality of humanity assumed by Christ—in her analysis of early Christian abjection. Her excellent discussion overlaps, naturally, with my own articulation of human essence itself as abject in ancient Christologies and asceticisms. The problem of early Christian bodies and flesh also preoccupies Perkins, *Roman Imperial Identities*, 45–61, 90–106, and 144–71.

66. According to Élie D. Moutsoulas, "La lettre d'Athanase d'Alexandrie à Epictète,"

in Charles Kannengeisser, *Politique et théologie chez Athanase d'Alexandrie*, 313–33, the letter was written "in 371 or a little earlier" (133).

67. It is preserved by Epiphanius in his chapter on the Apollinarians (also called "Dimoirites"); but it was likely written after Athanasius received the minutes of various European synods in the early 360s and does not seem to represent any recognizable positions of Apollinarius of Laodicea. Hans Lietzmann, *Apollinaris von Laodicea und seine Schule*, 11–12, accepted it as an authentic critique of Apollinarius; and Charles Raven, *Apollinarianism*, 103–10, argued for an early dating of the letter (before 362) and rejected the idea that Athanasius is arguing against Apollinarius or his followers at all, preferring instead varied and confused groups of pro-Nicene "docetists." Moutsoulas, "Lettre," acknowledges that the argument about Christ's divine body does not "come from Apollinarius," but asserts nonetheless that it emerges from "Apollinarian circles" that likely misinterpreted Apollinarius (322–25).

68. Athanasius, *Epistula ad Epictetum* 2, in Epiphanius, *Panarion* 77.4.4 (GCS 37:419).

69. Athanasius, *Epistula ad Epictetum* 2, in Epiphanius, *Panarion* 77.4.3, 6.5 (GCS 37:419, 421).

70. Athanasius, *Epistula ad Epictetum* 4, 11, in Epiphanius, *Panarion* 77.6.4, 6.7, 12.6 (GCS 37:421, 426).

71. My thanks to James Ernest for pointing out the ambiguity of the first references to "circumcision" in this text.

72. Athanasius refers several times to the ὑπομνήματα that have come into his possession: *Epistula ad Epictetum* 2, 3, 12, in Epiphanius, *Panarion* 77.4.1, 5.1 (GCS 37:418, 420).

73. Athanasius, *Epistula ad Epictetum* 2, in Epiphanius, *Panarion* 77.4.4 (GCS 37:419).

74. The Nicene and Post Nicene Fathers translation renders the word "circumcised" (Philip Schaff and Hery Wace, *Athanasius*, 570); Frank Williams, in his English translation of Epiphanius's *Panarion*, translates it as "curtailed" (*The Panarion of Epiphanius of Salamis*, 2:570).

75. Burrus, *Saving Shame*, 76 and 72–78 on Athanasius generally.

76. Athanasius, *Epistula ad Epictetum* 5, in Epiphanius, *Panarion* 77.7.4 (GCS 37:422).

77. Athanasius, *Epistula ad Epictetum* 5, in Epiphanius, *Panarion* 77.7.5 (GCS 37:422), referring to Luke 2:21, 2:28, and 2:40.

78. Athanasius, *Epistula ad Epictetum* 5, in Epiphanius, *Panarion* 77.7.7 (GCS 37:422–23).

79. Athanasius, *Epistula ad Epictetum* 10, in Epiphanius, *Panarion* 77.12.5 (GCS 37:426).

80. Athanasius, *Epistula ad Epictetum* 6, in Epiphanius, *Panarion* 77.8.6–7 (GCS 37:423).

81. Indeed, he notes at the close of his letter that all of the various disputes in Epictetus's congregations had been settled: "But thanks be to the Lord that, as much as we grieved reading the minutes, so much did we rejoice at their conclusion: for afterwards they left in concord and made peace on the confession of pious and orthodox faith!" (Athanasius, *Epistula ad Epictetum* 12, in Epiphanius, *Panarion* 77.13.4–5 [GCS 37:427])

82. Athanasius notes at the outset how surprised he is that such controversies can still arise after Nicaea (*Epistula ad Epictetum* 1, in Epiphanius, *Panarion* 77.3.1 [GCS 37:417]); the closing burst of "joy" at resolution lets us know that such fears are unfounded, that Nicaea does indeed triumph in the end, even without Athanasius's intervention.

83. Nestorius, *Epistula 2 ad Cyrillum* 8; text in˙F. Loofs, *Nestoriana*, 179.

84. Aloys Grillmeier, *Christ in Christian Tradition*, 2.2:80–128, provides a lucid summary of this debate; see also Pauline Allen and C. T. R. Hayward, *Severus of Antioch*, 46–49. To Severus's supreme irritation, Julian claimed that he could base his theology in part on Severus (as well as their shared hero, Cyril of Alexandria).

85. Severus of Antioch, *Epistula* 97 (PO 14.1:194/369), translation of E. W. Brooks, who includes two versions of this letter in the Patrologia Orientalis. A very similar Greek fragment is found in extant versions of Titus of Bostra's *Scholion in Lucam*, although the editors are not sure whether Severus found this argument in Titus or a later editor inserted it into Titus's commentary. Given the relatively late appearance of Christ's foreskin, in sixth-century Syrian theologians, the latter seems more likely. See Joseph Sickenberger, *Titus von Bostra*, 149–51 (the Greek fragment is found on 150 and was printed in PG 106:1188).

86. Such a reading of Luke 2:21 may explain why later, Syriac infancy gospels deny Christ's circumcision: see my discussion below in Chapter 5.

87. Severus, *Epistula* 97 (PO 14.1:196/366).

88. Severus, *Epistula* 97 (PO 14.1:196/366).

89. Severus, *Epistula* 97 (PO 14.1:197/367).

90. See Roberta C. Chesnut, *Three Monophysite Christologies*, 51–55.

91. John Chrysostom, *De cruce et latrone homilia 1* 1 (PG 49:400).

92. See the citation of Tertullian at n.62; the comparison is also found in Justin Martyr and Ambrose.

93. The foreskin of Christ appears in other Syrian, anti-Chalcedonian literature of the period: see my discussion of Philoxenus of Mabbug (Severus's elder contemporary) in Chapter 5. The only earlier reference I have found to the foreskin appears in a fragment of Origen preserved by Pamphilus of Caesarea (in turn preserved by Rufinus of Aquileia in the fourth century): Pamphilus, *Apologia pro Origene* 115 (SC 464:184–86), where Origen claims that gnostic heretics refuted by Christ's circumcision tried to write whole volumes about his foreskin. For speculation on what Origen might be talking about (or if this passage is even authentically Origenian), see the note of the Source Chrétiennes editors: René Amacker and Éric Junod, *Apologie pour Origène suivi de Sur la falsification des livres d'Origène*, SC 464:186–87n.2.

94. On Amphilochius, see Karl Holl, *Amphilochius von Ikonium in seinem Verhältnis zu den grossen Kappadoziern*, 1–115; and the introduction of C. Datema, *Amphilochii Iconiensis Opera*; on his rhetorical advancement, see the brief discussion of Jaclyn Maxwell, *Christianization and Communication in Late Antiquity*, 33–39. As Maxwell points out (36–37n.108), modern scholarship has paid relatively little attention to Amphilochius.

95. Amphilochius claims his opponents "call themselves Encratites" (*Contra haereticos* 13 [CCG 3:197, 199]) or sometimes "Encratites and Apotactites" (*Contra haereticos* 17, 21

[CCG 3:201, 206]), but these labels long predate Amphilochius's context and, by the late fourth century, had become stereotypical labels. That Amphilochius's opponents might be associated with the Syrian monastic groups lumped together by their opponents as "Messalians" is suggested by later orthodox treatises that cite Amphilochius: see the citations of Daniel Caner, *Wandering, Begging Monks*, 140–41. On Messalian asceticism and theological debates, see Susanna Elm, *"Virgins of God,"* 189–99.

96. An exegetical strategy not unknown to a variety of ascetic Christians in this period: see Elizabeth A. Clark, "Antifamilial Tendencies in Ancient Christianity," *Journal of the History of Sexuality* 5 (1995): 356–80; and my " 'Let Him Guard *Pietas*': Early Christian Exegesis and the Ascetic Family," *Journal of Early Christian Studies* 11 (2003): 265–81.

97. Amphilochius, *Contra haereticos* 23 (CCG 3:208).

98. Amphilochius compares his opponents to "Manicheans and Marcionites": *Contra haereticos* 21 (CCG 3:206), whose docetism likewise misrepresented Scriptures (see above, 77–82).

99. Amphilochius, *Contra haereticos* 23 (CCG 3:208).

100. Amphilochius also briefly ties circumcision to food and the Law, and the paradox of Christ's human form, in a sermon defending virginity and the married state. Most of this homily is an exposition of Luke 2:22–52 (known as "on the Presentation," and preserved with later collections of festal homilies), in which Amphilochius can praise virginity and the family at once: "Do you not see this child sucking at the breast, taking from the teat, resting in his mother's bosom, his feet not yet walking the earth, circumcised on the eighth day? This one laid the foundations of the ages, laid the vaults of heavens, stretched the earth, bounded the sea with sand" (*Homilia 2 [in occursum]* 6 [CCG 3:55]).

101. For an important reevaluation of Jovinian's goals in his treatise, particularly his anti-Manichaeism, see David G. Hunter, "Resistance to the Virginal Ideal in Late-Fourth-Century Rome: The Case of Jovinian," *Theological Studies* 48 (1987): 45–64.

102. Fear of—and popularity of—Manicheism in fourth-century Rome pervades all sides of the "Jovinianist" controversy: see now David G. Hunter, *Marriage, Celibacy, and Heresy in Ancient Christianity*, 22–24, 141–46.

103. On Jerome's motives in involving himself in this debate, see David G. Hunter, "Rereading the Jovinianist Controversy: Asceticism and Clerical Authority in Late Ancient Christianity," *Journal of Medieval and Early Modern Studies* 33 (2003): 453–70, esp. 462–66; and id., *Marriage, Celibacy, and Heresy*, 234–42.

104. On various aspects of this debate, see Yves-Marie Duval, *L'affaire Jovinien*.

105. On the "problem" of Jesus' sexed body, see Elizabeth A. Clark, "The Celibate Bridegroom and His Virginal Brides: Metaphor and the Marriage of Jesus in Early Christian Ascetic Exegesis," *Church History* 77 (2008): 1–25, at 18–20. Clark places Jerome's argument against Jovinian in an exegetical trajectory stretching back (at least) to Origen: see Origen's *Homilia 9 in Leviticum* 2 (SC 287:76–80), which interprets the Levite's "linen tunic and bands" (Lev 16:4) as Christ's incarnate flesh. Origen, like Jerome later, will undermine the reality of Jesus' sex by insisting here that "only one [bodily] act did he not perform, that which pertains to the body's 'privates' (*quod ad pudenda corporis pertinet*)."

106. Interestingly, the Nicene and Post-Nicene Fathers editors translate *castravit* as "made a eunuch"—a less graphic way of indicating the metaphor of sexual renunciation (Philip Schaff and Henry Wace, *Jerome*, 374). See Mathew Kuefler, *The Manly Eunuch*, 178–81 (on Jerome and Jovinian) and 245–82 (on the language of castration in general).

107. Jerome, *Adversus Iovinianum* 1.36 (PL 23:260–61).

108. Dale B. Martin provides a survey of ideological (including patristic) views of Jesus' "ambiguous sexuality": *Sex and the Single Savior*, 91–102.

109. Jerome, *Adversus Iovinianum* 1.40 (PL 23:269).

110. I discuss the broader implications of Christ's "passing" in the concluding chapter.

111. Including that of Jesus, who rose "in the same sex in which he died" (Jerome, *Epistula* 108.24.2 [CSEL 55:342]).

112. Caroline Walker Bynum, *The Resurrection of the Body in Western Christianity*, 86–94, following closely upon Elizabeth A. Clark, "The Place of Jerome's *Commentary on Ephesians* in the Origenist Controversy: Apokatastasis and Ascetic Ideals," *Vigiliae Christianae* 41 (1987): 154–71.

113. Bynum, *Resurrection*, 91: "what Jerome feared was change itself." See also Peter Brown, *The Body and Society*, 383–85.

114. Launched by Graham Ward, John Milbank, and Catherine Pickstock, *Radical Orthodoxy*. On its tangled roots in, through, and against postmodernism (in various forms), see D. Stephen Long, "Radical Orthodoxy," in Kevin J. Vanhoozer, *The Cambridge Companion to Postmodern Theology*, 126–46.

115. Graham Ward, "The Displaced Body of Jesus Christ," in Ward, Milbank, and Pickstock, *Radical Orthodoxy*, 163–81, at 164–65. Ward also discusses the circumcision in "Uncovering the Corona: A Theology of Circumcision," in George J. Brooke, *The Birth of Jesus*, 35–44 and 125–26 (notes), most of which is reprinted in *Christ and Culture*, 159–80.

116. Ward, "Displaced Body," 165, concatenates the incarnation, circumcision, transfiguration, and ascension of Jesus.

117. Ward, "Displaced Body," 177.

118. Ward, "Displaced Body," 163. He singles out Rosemary Radford Ruether's query, "Can a male Saviour save women?" for rebuke: see her *Sexism and God-Talk*, 116–38.

119. Addressed more directly—but in the exact same fashion—by Ward, *Christ and Culture*, 162: "Furthermore, how do we read the Jewish maleness of Jesus Christ when we do not have the body itself, only a body of writings?"

120. Ward, "Displaced Body," 176. See similarly Ward, *Christ and Culture*, 2–3: "Every statement about Christ cannot be reduced to, but is, nevertheless, a statement about ourselves and the times and cultures we inhabit."

121. Virginia Burrus, "Radical Orthodoxy and the Heresiological Habit: Engaging Graham Ward's Christology," in Rosemary Radford Ruether and Marion Grau, *Interpreting the Postmodern*, 36–53, at 37: "Why does Ward's 'radically orthodox' Christology . . . apparently need to represent itself as both preceding and superseding the assertions of identified 'heretics,' whether wrong-headed 'feminist' or pathological 'sado-masochists'?"

122. Grosz, "Body of Signification," 87.

123. Burrus, "Radical Orthodoxy," 37.

124. Burrus, *Saving Shame*.

CHAPTER 4. DUBIOUS DIFFERENCE

Note to epigraph: Robert J. C. Young, *Colonial Desire*, 4.

1. Its coinage (as *Judenchristen*) is usually traced to the New Testament criticism of Ferdinand Christian Baur, "Die Christuspartei in der korinthischen Gemeinde, der Gegensatz des petrinischen und paulinischen Christentums in der ältesten Kirche, der Apostel Petrus in Rom," *Tübinger Zeitschrift für Theologie* (1831). See James Carleton Paget, "Jewish Christianity," in W. D. Davies and William Horbury, *Cambridge History of Judaism*, vol. 3: *The Early Roman Period*, 731–75, at 731; and id., "The Terms *Jewish Christian* and *Jewish Christianity* in the History of Research," in Oskar Skarsaune and Reidar Hvalvik, *Jewish Believers in Jesus*, 22–52, at 23–30. For an attemt to resuscitate the term, see now Edwin K. Broadhead, *Jewish Ways of Following Jesus*, 1–3 and 56–57 for a new "working definition."

2. Daniel Boyarin, "Rethinking Jewish Christianity: An Argument for Dismantling a Dubious Category (to Which Is Appended a Correction of My *Border Lines*)," *Jewish Quarterly Review* 99 (2009): 7–36, at 7.

3. Karen L. King, "Which Early Christianity?" in Susan Ashbrook Harvey and David G. Hunter, *The Oxford Handbook of Early Christian Studies*, 66–84, at 74; Carleton Paget, "Jewish Christianity," 733–42, seems hopeful that a "working definition" can be crafted; but Carleton Paget seems less sanguine in "Terms," 51–52. The "classificatory imprecision" attendant upon distinguishing Judaism from Christianity persists at the level of the earliest New Testament documents: see Dale B. Martin, "Paul and the Judaism/Hellenism Dichotomy: Toward a Social History of the Question," in Troels Enberg-Pedersen, *Paul Beyond the Judaism/Hellenism Divide*, 29–61.

4. Among the more recent studies (both of which are discussed in Boyarin's *JQR* essay): Skarsaune and Hvalvik, *Jewish Believers in Jesus*; and Matt Jackson McCabe, *Jewish Christianity Reconsidered*.

5. Such a view of religious evolution has been subject to critique in recent years: see the essays in Adam H. Becker and Annette Yoshiko Reed, *The Ways That Never Parted*; following such earlier forays as Judith Lieu, "The Parting of the Ways: Theological Construct or Historical Reality?" *Journal of the Study of the New Testament* 56 (1994): 101–19.

6. The reconstruction of such Judeophile gentile Christians resonates with the similarly ethnic trappings of modern "messianic Judaism," comprising (ethnic) gentiles who fold traits of Eastern European Jewish culture (language, cuisine, and so forth) into their syncretistic religious communities: see Dan Cohn-Sherbok, "Modern Hebrew Christianity and Messianic Judaism," in Peter Tomson and Doris Lambers-Petry, *The Image of Judaeo-Christians in Ancient Jewish and Christian Literature*, 287–98, esp. at 290–91.

7. Bemoaned by Patrick Henry, "Why Is Contemporary Scholarship So Enamored of Ancient Heresies?" *Studia Patristica* 17.1 (1982): 123–26; and reconsidered a bit more broadly

by Elizabeth A. Clark, "From Patristics to Early Christian Studies," in Harvey and Hunter, *Handbook*, 7–41, at 22–23. See also Virginia Burrus, *The Making of a Heretic*, 1–2.

8. Peter Tomson, "The Wars Against Rome, the Rise of Rabbinic Judaism and of Apostolic Gentile Christianity, and the Judaeo-Christians: Elements for a Synthesis," in Tomson and Lambers-Petry, *Image of Judaeo-Christians*, 1–31, at 25.

9. See, e.g., A. F. J. Klijn and G. J. Reinink, *Patristic Evidence for Jewish Christian Sects*; A. F. J. Klijn, *Jewish-Christian Gospel Tradition*; Ray A. Pritz, *Nazarene Jewish Christianity*; and Simon Mimouni, *Le judéo-christianisme ancien*.

10. Bart D. Ehrman, *Lost Christianities*, frames his subject as primarily a canonical process so that "Marciontes" and "Ebionites" stand at "polar ends of the spectrum" with respect to the valorization of the Hebrew Bible (95).

11. Bellarmino Bagatti, *L'église de la circoncision*; but see Joan E. Taylor, *Christians and the Holy Places*; and Carleton Paget, "Jewish Christianity," 732n.6.

12. See Joan E. Taylor, "The Phenomenon of Early Jewish-Christianity: Reality or Scholarly Construct?" *Vigiliae Christianae* 44 (1990): 313–34; the comments and references of Stephen Shoemaker, *Ancient Traditions of the Virgin Mary's Dormition and Assumption*, 212–14, 229–31; and several of the essays in Becker and Reed, *Ways That Never Parted*, especially David Frankfurter, "Beyond 'Jewish Christianity': Continuing Religious Sub-Cultures of the Second and Third Centuries and Their Documents," 131–43; and Annette Yoshiko Reed, " 'Jewish Christianity' After the 'Parting of the Ways': Approaches to Historiography and Self-Definition in the Pseudo-Clementines," 189–231.

13. On classificatory systems (particularly that of Linnaeus), see Mary Louise Pratt, *Imperial Eyes*, 24–37; and David Chidester, *Savage Systems*, 59: "Conceptually, the Linnaean taxonomy was a scheme of global order."

14. Daniel Boyarin, *Border Lines*, 1–27, outlines this complex and highly rewarding thesis regarding the construction of Christian and rabbinic orthodoxies.

15. Boyarin, *Border Lines*, 16.

16. Boyarin, *Border Lines*, 207.

17. See Rebecca Lyman, "The Politics of Passing: Justin Martyr's Conversion as a Problem of 'Hellenization,' " in Kenneth Mills and Anthony Grafton, *Conversion in Late Antiquity and the Early Middle Ages*, 36–60.

18. Young, *Colonial Desire*, 4.

19. Young, *Colonial Desire*, 53. On "culture as hybridity," see Homi K. Bhabha, *The Location of Culture*. Theoretical critiques have been leveled against the critical force of "hybridity": it risks unintentionally reifying the "real" and "pure"; it becomes so universalized ("all culture is hybrid") as to lose critical traction altogether; it celebrates a colonial "strategy" that may, in reality, be more submissive than subversive (see Bart Moore-Gilbert, *Postcolonial Theory*, 129–30, 192–95; see also Boyarin, *Border Lines*, 234n.65). While I concede that the danger of celebrating a "liberatory" rhetorical strategy risks ceding "real" political ground, I am more optimistic concerning the promise found in analyzing the irruption of hybridities within sociopolitical (and, obviously, religious) discourses explicitly grounded in "purity" and totalizing unity (such as late ancient *orthodoxia*). While it may be true

(and, if true, politically inexpedient) to claim that "all culture is hybrid," it strikes me that there is a vast gulf between the "hybridity" to be found in a political regime constituted through strategies of "multiplicity" and that emerging in a regime that lauds singularity and exclusion.

20. Among modern scholars, as well, who in the nineteenth and twentieth centuries frequently dubbed primitive Jewish Christianity in general as "Ebionism," see the discussion of F. C. Baur's *De Ebionitarum origine et doctrina ab Essenis repetenda* in Glenn Alan Koch, "A Critical Investigation of Epiphanius' Knowledge of the Ebionites," 14–15; and Gregory C. Finley, "The Ebionites and 'Jewish Christianity,'" 12–16.

21. For a recent thorough survey of Ebionites in ancient and modern scholarship, see Koch, "Critical Investigation," 5–107; Finley, "Ebionites," 11–74; Richard Bauckham, "The Origin of the Ebionites," in Tomson and Lambers-Petry, *Image of the Judaeo-Christians*, 162–81; Oskar Skarsaune, "The Ebionites," in Skarsaune and Hvalvik, *Jewish Believers*, 419–62; and Broadhead, *Jewish Ways*, 188–212. I leave aside in this chapter discussion of the historiographically fraught Pseudo-Clementine writings, which have been associated with the Ebionites since F. C. Baur (see n.20), although see the discussion in Reed, "Jewish Christianity," 197–201. Finley's dissertation has as one of its central questions the relation between Ebionites and the Ps.-Clementine literature, and it is often assumed that Epiphanius knew some forms of the Ps.-Clementines and used them as a source for *Panarion* 30; see also Koch, "Critical Investigation," 268–315.

22. Irenaeus, *Adversus haereses* 1.26.2 (SC 264:346): "Moreover they only use the Gospel according to Matthew, and they deny the apostle Paul, saying that he was an apostate from the Law." The scriptural deficiencies of the Ebionites also preoccupy Eusebius, who tends to mention the Ebionites in relation to the "impoverished" biblical translation of Symmachus and the other post-Septuagintal biblical translators: see, e.g., *Historia ecclesiastica* 6.16 (GCS 9.2:552–54); and *Demonstratio evangelica* 7.1.33 (GCS 23:304).

23. Tertullian, *De praescriptione haereticorum* 33.5 (SC 46:132–33), in contrast to the docetism of the Marcionites; and *De carne Christi* 14.5 (SC 216:270–72), in contrast to heretics who claim Christ took on a superior, angelic nature.

24. Origen, *Contra Celsum* 2.1 (SC 132:276–78); see also *Contra Celsum* 5.61 (SC 147:166): "Let it be established that there are some also who accept Jesus, such that from this they boast that they are Christians, yet they wish to live according to the Law of the Jews, like the majority of Jews: these are the two-fold Ebionites."

25. Notably Jean Daniélou argued for a more theological understanding of Jewish Christianity, yet still separated the Ebionites as primarily defined by their adherence to the Mosaic Law: *The Theology of Jewish-Christianity*, 55–64, discussed by Finley, "Ebionites," 47–48. Skarsaune, "Ebionites," 462, explicitly ties Law observance to imitatio Christi.

26. Irenaeus, *Adversus haereses* 1.14 (SC 264:346). Skarsaune, "Ebionites," 437–38, connects the "singular" (*curiosus*) interpretation with the Jewish practices.

27. Tertullian, *De praescriptione haereticorum* 33.5 (SC 46:132–33).

28. Origen, *Homilia 3 in Genesim* 5 (SC 7*bis*:128).

29. Origen links Ebionite observance of the Passover with Jesus' observance, one of

a handful of sources we have that Jesus' Jewishness was seen as fit for imitatio Christi: *Commentariorum series in Matthaeum* 79 (PG 13:1728): "Someone uneducated (*aliquis imperitorum*) might fall into Ebionism (*ebionismum*)—from the fact that Jesus celebrated the Passover bodily, in a Jewish fashion (*more Iudaïco*), as well as the first day of the Feast of the Unleavened Bread and Passover—and say that it is fitting for us, as *imitatores Christi*, to do the same." See also my discussion of John Chrysostom below.

30. That Epiphanius had some loose structure in mind for a heresiological treatise is clear already in *Ancoratus* 12.7–13.8 (GCS 25:20–22), which comprises a bare list of the eighty heresies of the *Panarion* (more or less).

31. Aline Pourkier, *L'hérésiologie chez Épiphane de Salamine*; Averil Cameron, "How to Read Heresiology," *Journal of Medieval and Early Modern Studies* 33 (2003): 471–92; Frank Williams, *The Panarion of Epiphanius of Salamis*, 1:ix–xxvii; and Young Richard Kim, "The Imagined Worlds of Epiphanius of Cyprus."

32. See my *Remains of the Jews*, 44–51; Kim, "Imagined Worlds"; and Jeremy Schott, "Heresiology as Universal History in Epiphanius's *Panarion*," *Zeitschrift für Antikes Christentum* 10 (2006): 546–63. On "totalizing" discourse in early Christianity, see Averil Cameron, *Christianity and the Rhetoric of Empire*, 87–88.

33. Epiphanius, *Panarion* 28.8.5 (GCS 25:372), referring to the Cerinthians, the first of the three groups, followed by the Nazoraeans and the Ebionites. On Jewish-Christian heresies in Epiphanius, see Koch, "Critical Investigation"; and Joseph Verheyden, "Epiphanius on the Ebionites," in Tomson and Lambers-Petry, *Image of the Judaeo-Christians*, 182–208.

34. On the placement and structure of this chapter against the Ebionites along with the other chapters against Jewish-Christian heresies, see Verheyden, "Epiphanius," 184–86.

35. At one point Epiphanius notes that he must restrain himself, "lest I render the treatise too bulky" (*Panarion* 30.20.11 [GCS 25:361]); see also *Panarion* 30.30.1 (GCS 25:374), where he laments that he "lacks time for a discussion of the full demonstration of the truth."

36. Koch, "Critical Investigation," 191–267 (Koch lists Epiphanius's unique information on the Ebionites on 211–15).

37. Epiphanius, *Panarion* 30.1.1 (GCS 25:333).

38. Epiphanius, *Panarion* 30.1.2–3 (GCS 25:333). See also Verheyden, "Epiphanius," 186–87.

39. Epiphanius, *Panarion* 30.1.4 (GCS 25:333–34).

40. Epiphanius, *Panarion* 30.17.1 (GCS 25:355).

41. Eusebius and Origen, for instance, understand the root of the label "Ebionite" to derive from the Biblical Hebrew term *'ebyôn* ("poor [person]") (see Eusebius, *Historia ecclesiastica* 3.27.6 [GCS 9.1:256]; and Origen, *Contra Celsum* 2.1 [SC 132:276]; and *De principiis* 4.3.8 [SC 268:370]). The Latin tradition, following Tertullian, speaks of an eponymous founder named Ebion (see, among others, Hilary of Poitiers, *De trinitate* 1.26 [SC 443:248]; Filastrius, *De haeresibus* 37 (in *Diversarum hereseon liber*) [CSEL 38:20]; Jerome, *Epistula* 112.13.1 [CSEL 55:381]). In Greek, the only author before Epiphanius to speak of an individual named Ebion is Hippolytus, *Refutatio omnium haeresium* 7.35 (text in Miroslav Marcovich, *Hippolytus*, 318). See also Bauckham, "Origin of the Ebionites," 177–80.

42. Epiphanius, *Panarion* 30.17.2–3 (GCS 25:356).

43. Stated succinctly a little later by Jerome, *Epistula* 112.13.2: "quid dicam de Hebionitis, qui Christianos esse se simulant?. . . dum volunt et Iudaei esse et Christiani, nec Iudaei sunt nec Christiani" (CSEL 55:381–82).

44. Epiphanius, *Panarion* 30.3.1 (GCS 25:335).

45. Epiphanius, *Panarion* 30.3.6 (GCS 25:337).

46. Epiphanius, *Panarion* 30.17.1 (GCS 25:355).

47. Epiphanius, *Panarion* 30.17.6 (GCS 25:356–57).

48. See the brief summary of Carleton Paget, "Jewish Christianity," 766–67; and earlier R. McL. Wilson, "Jewish Christianity and Gnosticism," *Recherche de Sciences Réligieuses* 50 (1972): 261–72.

49. Epiphanius, *Panarion* 30.3.7 (GCS 25:337–38). Epiphanius acknowledges that Matthew wrote in Hebrew, but also notes that various translations from Greek to Hebrew of New Testament books exist in "secret" Jewish treasuries (*Panarion* 30.3.8–9 [GCS 25:338]); this inside information leads to Epiphanius's digression on Count Joseph of Tiberias, which I discuss below.

50. Epiphanius, *Panarion* 30.13.2 (GCS 25:349).

51. Epiphanius, *Panarion* 30.14.1 (GCS 25:351).

52. Epiphanius, *Panarion* 30.14.3 (GCS 25:351).

53. Epiphanius, *Panarion* 30.14.6 (GCS 25:352).

54. Epiphanius, *Panarion* 30.2.3–6 (GCS 25:334–35); on forced marriage among the Ebionites, see *Panarion* 18.3 (GCS 25:357); on multiple baptisms, see also *Panarion* 30.21.1–2 (GCS 25:361).

55. Epiphanius, *Panarion* 30.15.3–4 (GCS 25:352–53); see also *Panarion* 30.13.4–5 (GCS 25:350), where John the Baptist's food is changed from "locusts" to "honey," presumably to support Ebionite vegetarianism.

56. Epiphanius, *Panarion* 30.16.1 (GCS 25:353). See Andrew McGowan, *Ascetic Eucharists*, 145–47.

57. Epiphanius, *Panarion* 30.17.4 (GCS 25:356).

58. For a recent reading of one of Epiphanius's more colorful heresies on this score, see Stephen J. Shoemaker, "Epiphanius of Salamis, the Kollyridians, and the Early Dormition Narratives: The Cult of the Virgin in the Fourth Century," *Journal of Early Christian Studies* 16 (2008): 371–401.

59. Verheyden, "Epiphanius," 205.

60. Epiphanius, *Panarion* 30.18.4 (GCS 25:357–58).

61. Epiphanius's canon—four "pentateuchs" that roughly follow the present-day Christian canonical ordering of the Old Testament—separates the historical books ("hagiographa") from the prophetic books: *De mensuris et ponderibus* 4 (this text survives principally in Syriac with Greek fragments: see James Elmer Dean, *Epiphanius's Treatise on Weights and Measures*, 19 [English]; 89 [Syriac]). Epiphanius also embeds a canon list in *Panarion* 8.6 (GCS 25:191–92), on the Epicureans. On the establishment of the tripartite Jewish canon, see James A. Sanders, "The Canonical Process," in Steven T. Katz, *The Cambridge History of*

Judaism, vol. 4: *The Late Roman-Rabbinic Period*, 230–43; on some of the problems involved in determining canonicity in late antiquity, see Daniel Stökl Ben Ezra, "Canonization—A Non-Linear Process? Observing the Process of Canonization through the Christian (and Jewish) Papyri from Egypt," *Zeitschrift für Antikes Christentum* 12 (2008): 193–214.

62. Epiphanius, *Panarion* 30.18.7 (GCS 25:358–359). Klijn and Reinink, *Patristic Evidence,* 37, connect this with similar culling of the Torah referred to in the Pseudo-Clementine *Homilies* (cf. *Hom.* 2.41, 3.50 [GCS 42:52, 75]). Klijn and Reinink believe this demonstrates a social relation between the Ebionites and the Jewish-Christian producers and readers of the Pseudo-Clementines, although it is just as likely that Epiphanius has adduced these arguments himself from the literature; see on this also Bauckham, "Origin of the Ebionites," 164–71.

63. Epiphanius, *Panarion* 30.18.2 (GCS 25:357).

64. ματαιόφρων, used repeatedly of Ebion and the Ebionites: *Panarion* 30.26.7, 30.30.1, 30.32.1, 30.34.1 (GCS 25:369, 374, 377, 380). "Lame-brained" is the felicitous translation of Frank Williams (see n.31).

65. Epiphanius, *Panarion* 30.20.8 (GCS 25:360–61).

66. Epiphanius, *Panarion* 30.14.1 (GCS 25:351).

67. Epiphanius had already ascribed this defense of circumcision as imitatio Christi to Cerinthus (*Panarion* 28.5.1–3 [GCS 25:317]), taken there to be the "troublemaker" of Acts 21:28 who has Paul arrested for "polluting" the Temple with his uncircumcised companion Titus. But see Charles E. Hill, "Cerinthus, Gnostic or Chiliast? A New Solution to an Old Problem," *Journal of Early Christian Studies* 8 (2000): 135–72, who posits that Epiphanius's description of Cerinthus as a Judaizer constitutes a (willful or otherwise) misreading of Irenaeus, and concludes that Cerinthus was, in fact, a thoroughly de-Judaized Christian predecessor of Marcion. This would mean that the use of Matt 10:25 and call to Jesus' example for circumcision was retrojected backward (two chapters) by Epiphanius, and explains why his serious refutation of the example of Christ's circumcision waits until his chapter against the Ebionites. It also calls into question whether anyone—Cerinthian, Ebionite, or otherwise—ever made such an exegetical argument relating Matt 10:25 to an account of Jesus' circumcision, or whether it derived entirely from Epiphanius's imagination.

68. Epiphanius, *Panarion* 30.26.1–2 (GCS 25:368). The reference to the Cerinthians' "silly reasoning" (ληρώδη λόγον) may be a punning allusion to the Jewish Christians' defective understanding of Christ (the Logos).

69. Epiphanius, *Panarion* 30.27.2 (GCS 25:370). Epiphanius cites Matt 5:27 here, an exegetical proof text that—by the fourth century—carried the sense of "fulfillment" as "brought to fullness," understood by anti-Judaizing Christians as abrogation of the Law.

70. Epiphanius, *Panarion* 30.28.4 (GCS 25:371).

71. Epiphanius, *Panarion* 30.28.5 (GCS 25:371).

72. Epiphanius, *Panarion* 30.28.6–8 (GCS 25:371–72).

73. The failure to understand the truth about their own Law and prophets character-izes the "heresy" of Judaism, according to Epiphanius: *Panarion* 8.7.1 (GCS 25:193): "since then they were guided by the type and did not achieve the perfection which has been

preached through the Law and the prophets and the others, and every book, they were cast out of the pasture."

74. I discuss this scene, and other early Christian interpretations along similar lines, more fully in "Blood Will Out: Jesus' Circumcision and Early Christian Readings of Exodus 4:24–26," *Henoch* 30 (2008): 310–32.

75. Epiphanius, *Panarion* 30.27.3 (GCS 25:370). Epiphanius is citing Exod 4:25 according to the Septuagint.

76. This is, of course, an entirely baffling pericope that continues to engender much speculation among biblical scholars: see my discussion in "Blood Will Out."

77. Epiphanius, *Panarion* 30.32.11–12 (GCS 25:379). Epiphanius's nearly halachic reasoning here is, perhaps, meant to sound rabbinic, a rhetorical nuance that adds to his knowledge of "real" Judaism against the counterfeit knowledge of the Ebionites. The question of Sabbath circumcision is raised in m. Shab. 19:1–6, and launches myriad discussion of Sabbath priorities and other details of circumcision in b. Shab. 130a–137b. The permissibility of Sabbath circumcisions is merely a "given" in these discussions, which focus much more on what ancillary work (carrying implements, bathing the child, and so forth) are permissible on the Sabbath. As for the cutting itself, the Bavli relates (b. Shab. 132a): "Now, the Rabbis disagree with R. Eliezer only in respect of the preliminaries of circumcision; but as for the circumcision itself, all hold that it supersedes the Sabbath. Whence do we know it? Said 'Ulla: It is a traditional law (*halachah*); and thus did R. Isaac say: It is a traditional law."

78. Epiphanius, *Panarion* 30.32.9 (GCS 25:378).

79. Epiphanius, *Panarion* 30.33.4 (GCS 25:380), the most obvious of Epiphanius's various puns on cutting and excising and curtailing in this selection: τοῦ Χριστοῦ περιτομῆς τῆς ἐν αὐτῷ καλῶς περιτμηθείσης καὶ δι' αὐτοῦ καταλυθείσης.

80. Epiphanius, *Panarion* 30.26.3–7 (GCS 25:368–69). The self-cutting here both draws on the (incomplete) language of boundary transgression in the preceding lines and puns on the act of the circumcision. The reference to God's "natural boundaries" draws on Job 38.

81. Boyarin, *Border Lines*, 209.

82. Epiphanius, *Panarion* 30.28.2–4 (GCS 25:371).

83. Epiphanius discusses this teaching on Christ's "divine body" in *Panarion* 72: see my discussion in Chapter 3 of Athanasius's letter to Epictetus on "Apollinarian" teaching.

84. Epiphanius, *Panarion* 30.28.9 (GCS 25:372).

85. Boyarin, *Border Lines*, 2–17; see also Averil Cameron, "Jewish and Heretics—A Category Error?" in Reed and Becker, *Ways That Never Parted*, 345–60.

86. Epiphanius, *Panarion* 30.4.1–12.9 (GCS 25:338–48); Boyarin, *Border Lines*, 211–14, likewise draws out the significance of this "digression" within the larger argument of *Panarion* 30. See Stephen Goranson, "The Joseph of Tiberias Episode in Epiphanius"; and id., "Joseph of Tiberias Revisited: Orthodoxies and Heresies in Fourth-Century Galilee," in Eric M. Meyers, *Galilee Through the Centuries*, 335–43. .

87. Epiphanius, *Panarion* 30.4.5–7, 9.2–6, 5.7 (GCS 25:339, 344, 340).

88. Epiphanius, *Panarion* 30.33.2 (GCS 25:379). On Justin Martyr's similar critique of the gender limitations of circumcision, see Judith Lieu, "Circumcision, Women, and Salvation," *New Testament Studies* 40 (1994): 358–70.

89. Epiphanius, *Panarion* 30.34.2 (GCS 25:380–81).

90. On the connections between circumcision and baptism in early Christian sacramental theology, see my discussion in Chapter 1.

91. See my discussion in Chapter 3.

92. Epiphanius, *Panarion* 30.26.9 (GCS 25:369). The casual remark that it was Mary who circumcised Christ is attested nowhere else that I have found. It seems possibly confirmed also in Epiphanius's excursus on the advent of Christ after *Panarion* 20, where Epiphanius comments that "he was born in Bethlehem [and] circumcised in the cavern" (*De Incarnatione* 1.4 [GCS 25:228]), where presumably (eight days after the Nativity) the Holy Family still remained alone (the magi arrive two years later: *De Incarnatione* 1.5 [GCS 25:228]). It is intriguing to imagine Epiphanius here once more combining a pretense at knowledge of Jewish law and custom (whereby it was the father's responsibility to circumcise his son) with a good Christian theology of the Virgin Birth (whereby Jesus had no earthly "father," and so this ritual responsibility fell to his mother). This may also be an echo of Zipporah's circumcision of her son, which follows soon after in the text: that is, Epiphanius may have thought it "natural" for a holy woman to circumcise her child. I am grateful to Susan Weingarten for drawing the significance of this passage to my attention.

93. Epiphanius, *Panarion* 30.27.1–2 (GCS 25:370). Koch, "Critical Investigation," in his otherwise meticulous study, misreads this portion of Epiphanius's argument when he concludes that Epiphanius's "rebuttal of circumcision argues that Jesus did not advocate circumcision and had no control over his own circumcision" (234, see also 166n.28). The logic of Epiphanius's christological argument—concerning Jesus' divinity—must operate in exactly the opposite fashion: Jesus *must* have had control over his own circumcision because he never lost his divinity and was never a "mere man" as the Ebionites claim.

94. Koch, "Critical Investigation," very much set the stage for this reading of *Panarion* 30, but the focus on "sources" (and their legitimacy or fabrication) reflects a larger discomfort with Epiphanius and his work in the academy.

95. Epiphanius, *Panarion* 30.13.6 (GCS 25:350). On Epiphanius's various "fragments" of the Gospel of the Ebionites, and their sources and parallels, see Koch, "Critical Investigation," 316–58; more recently, see Bauckham, "Origin of the Ebionites," 163–64; Verheyden, "Epiphanius," 188–200; and James R. Edwards, "The *Gospel of the Ebionites* and the Gospel of Luke," *New Testament Studies* 48 (2002): 568–86.

96. See Burrus, *Making of a Heretic*, 16: "the alliance of Christianity with empire resulted in an innovative technology of orthodoxy."

97. See Young, *Colonial Desire*, 161. Despite Young's misgivings about applying postcolonial criticism to premodern cultural contexts (articulated already in *Colonial Desire*, 164–65; and repeated in *Postcolonialism*, 56–58), I find this to be a remarkably trenchant formulation of the complexities of late ancient Roman identity. On the inherently doubleedged processes of Roman imperialization, see (among other recent treatments), Clifford

Ando, *Imperial Ideology and Provincial Loyalty in the Roman Empire*; and Greg Woolf, *Becoming Roman*.

98. The rise of the "monk-bishop-saint" is charted by Claudia Rapp, *Holy Bishops in Late Antiquity*.

99. Socrates, *Historia ecclesiastica* 6.14 (GCS n.f. 1:335–36); the story is also told by Sozomen, *Historia ecclesiastica* 8.15 (GCS n.f. 4:369–70). Michael Gaddis, *There Is No Crime for Those Who Have Christ*, 225, discusses the incident in which two acknowledged holy men curse each other and, due to their holiness, must have their respective curses honored by God.

100. John Chrysostom, *Adversus Iudaeos* 1.1.4 (PG 48:844). Most of the homilies were delivered around the time of the Jewish New Year in 386 and 387: on dating and occasion, see now Wendy Pradels, Rudolf Brändle, and Martin Heimgartner, "The Sequence and Dating of the Series of John Chrysostom's Eight Discourses *Adversus Iudaeos*," *Zeitschrift für Antikes Christentum* 6 (2002): 90–116. *Homilia* 3, on the "true Passover," was not originally part of this series but collected with the other seven homilies later (Pradels, Brändle, and Heimgartner, "Sequence," 91).

101. See Christine C. Shepardson, "Controlling Contested Places: John Chrysostom's *Adversus Iudaeos* Homilies and the Spatial Politics of Religious Controversy," *Journal of Early Christian Studies* 15 (2007): 483–516; drawing on Isabella Sandwell, *Religious Identity in Late Antiquity*.

102. John Chrysostom, *Adversus Iudaeos* 1.3.4 (PG 48:847).

103. John Chrysostom, *Adversus Iudaeos* 4.4.2 (PG 48:876).

104. John Chrysostom, *Adversus Iudaeos* 4.4.1 (PG 48:876).

105. So Robert Wilken, *John Chrysostom and the Jews*, says that "judaizing practices had *cut into* the Church's life" in Antioch (76, emphasis added), but also notes that "I am inclined to see the Judaizers in Antioch not as unlettered and uneducated Christians, 'half-Christians' who indiscriminately mixed Jewish and Christian elements" (94). Marcel Simon, *Verus Israel*, 322, considers these fourth-century "Judaizing Christians" as a "spontaneous and popular movement [which] does not embody any tradition going back to the origins of Christianity."

106. Shepardson, "Controlling Contested Places"; see also Thomas Sizgorich, *Violence and Belief in Late Antiquity*, 51–56.

107. On festivals as sites of polemical self-differentiation, see Daniel Stökl Ben Ezra, "'Christians' Observing 'Jewish' Festivals of Autumn," in Tomson and Lambers-Petry, *Image of the Judaeo-Christians*, 53–73; and my extended discussion in Chapter 6.

108. John Chrysostom, *Adversus Iudaeos* 3.3.9 (PG 48:866). John, like some modern commenters, conflates Luke 2:21 with the passages that follow and here envisions Jesus' circumcision in the Temple in Jerusalem.

109. So Wilken, *John Chrysostom*, 93, citing the examples of Origen and Epiphanius. See also now Joshua Garroway, "The Law-Observant Lord: John Chrysostom's Engagement with the Jewishness of Christ," *Journal of Early Christian Studies* 18 (2010): 591–615.

110. John Chrysostom, *Adversus Iudaeos* 3.4.1 (PG 48:866).

111. Bhabha, *Location of Culture*, 13.

CHAPTER 5. SCRIPTURAL DISTINCTIONS

Note to epigraph: Michel Foucault, "The Discourse on Language," in *The Archaeology of Knowledge and the Discourse on Language*, 221.

1. At issue is the positive citation of Origen in Jerome's *Commentary on Ephesians*, but Rufinus also notes the approving citation of such heretics as Eusebius of Caesarea and Apollinarius of Laodicea. See Elizabeth A. Clark, "The Place of Jerome's Commentary on Ephesians in the Origenist Controversy: Apokatastasis and Ascetic Ideals," *Vigiliae Christianae* 41 (1987): 154–71; and id., *The Origenist Controversy*, 11–42, 121–51, and 159–93.

2. Jerome, *Apologia adversus Rufinum* 1.16 (SC 303:44). See the commentary of Pierre Lardet, *L'apologie de Jérôme contre Rufin*, 81–84; and Catherine M. Chin, *Grammar and Christianity in the Late Roman World*, 76–87.

3. Note the advice of Paul Griffiths, *Religious Reading*, 78: "Acts of commentary, like other acts of religious reading, are usually performed within a tradition, and this suggests that those who engage in them will often have thought about what they are doing and why, about what can and cannot be a proper commentarial object, and about what properties a commentarial work should have. Therefore it will often, though not always, be possible for the student of acts of commentary to find explicit statements by those who perform them about these matters."

4. The destabilizing dissonance of inscribing multiple voices within Christian commentary writing is further compounded by the introduction of non-Christian voices, a feature of the commentaries of (for instance) Eusebius of Caesarea (see Michael J. Hollerich, *Eusebius of Caesarea's "Commentary on Isaiah,"* 147–53) and Jerome himself (see my *Remains of the Jews*, 67–83).

5. On the unifying *skopos* of Scriptures, see Frances M. Young, *Biblical Exegesis and the Formation of Christian Culture*, 20–45.

6. Augustine, *Confessiones* 12.32.43 (CCL 27:241).

7. Augustine, *De doctrina christiana* 3.27.38 (CCL 32:99–100), cited by Elizabeth A. Clark, *Reading Renunciation*, 6. See also Chin, *Grammar and Christianity*, 93–109, on various methods of reading "excess" from the biblical text.

8. Martin Irvine, *The Making of Textual Culture*, 260–71, discusses the "semiotic anxiety" that emerges from this interpretive multiplicity.

9. On the earliest appearance of Christian commentaries, see Bart D. Ehrman, "Heracleon, Origen, and the Text of the Fourth Gospel," *Vigiliae Christianae* 47 (1993): 105–18; and, despite their very specific titles, the important context provided by Wilhelm Geerlings, "Die lateinisch-patristischen Kommentare"; and Hildegund Müller, "Zur Struktur des patristischen Kommentars: Drei Beispiele aus Augustins *Enarrationes in psalmos*"; both in Wilhelm Geerlings and Christian Schulze, *Der Kommentar in Antike und Mittelalter*, 1–14 and 15–31 respectively. On religious commentaries more generally, see Griffiths, *Religious Reading*, 77–97.

10. Young, *Biblical Exegesis*, 18–19; and my "The Disorder of Books: Priscillian's Canonical Defense of Apocrypha," *Harvard Theological Review* 93 (2000): 135–59.

11. Clark, *Reading Renunciation*, 8. Clark draws on Roland Barthes, Jacques Derrida, Foucault, Edward Said, and Fredric Jameson to explore the paradoxical inscriptions of "original meaning" bound up in commentarial practice (5–10).

12. Chin, *Grammar and Christianity*, also considers the ways Roman aesthetics are instantiated in territory, religion, and culture.

13. On Roman imperialism as appropriation of otherness, see my discussion in the Introduction.

14. See the discussion of Mary Beard, John North, and Simon Price, *Religions of Rome*, volume 1: *A History*, esp. 245–363; and Clifford Ando, *The Matter of the Gods*.

15. Michael Roberts, *The Jeweled Style*; Chin, *Grammar and Christianity*, 170; Patricia Cox Miller, "'Differential Networks': Relics and Other Fragments in Late Antiquity," *Journal of Early Christian Studies* 6 (1998): 113–28; and Anthony Grafton and Megan Williams, *Christianity and the Transformation of the Book*.

16. On lemmatization see Christina Shuttleworth Kraus, "Introduction: Reading Commentaries/Commentaries as Reading," in Christina Shuttleworth Kraus and Roy K. Gibson, *The Classical Commentary*, 10–16.

17. I am not suggesting that Luke 1–2 have not provided sufficient grist for biblical critical mills, but as even ancient commentators have noted (see Ambrose below), the Lucan nativity is remarkable for its narrative clarity and tidy rhetorical construction: see Karl A. Kuhn, "The Point of the Step Parallelism in Luke 1–2," *New Testament Studies* 47 (2001): 38–49.

18. Of course, biblical commentary was not the sole domain of Christians in this period. Philo's philosophical commentaries on the Torah provided important basis for later Platonic Christian commentaries, and rabbinic midrash likewise emerges from within and in dialogue with Roman literary and cultural aesthetics: see Daniel Boyarin, *Intertextuality and the Reading of Midrash*; on the common themes and strategies of Christian and Jewish biblical interpretation, see Gilles Dorival, "Exégèse juive et exégèse chrétienne," in Geerlings and Schulze, *Kommentar*, 131–50.

19. Didymus the Blind's surviving "commentaries" are more properly lecture notes, including questions from students: see Richard Layton, *Didymus the Blind and His Circle in Late-Antique Alexandria*.

20. Gregory of Nyssa's homilies on the Song of Songs were collected and published as a "commentary": see Alden Mosshammer, "Gregory of Nyssa as Homilist," *Studia Patristica* 37 (2001): 212–39.

21. The necessity to refer in some manner to a base text may be a particular constraint of Western (Christian, Jewish, Greco-Roman) commentaries, in cultures that valued written (and, ultimately, fixed) textual traditions. For a very different context of religious commentary and spiritual formation, see Justin T. McDaniel, *Gathering Leaves and Lifting Words*.

22. Irvine, *Making of Textual Culture*, uses the term "metatext" (121); Griffiths, *Religious Reading*, uses the term "metawork" (81 and 86–88), and roughly defines commentary as a "metawork" with "overt signs of the presence of another work . . . [in which] these

signs outweigh . . . other elements in the work . . . and [in which] the structure and order of the work is largely given to it by those of the other work" (85).

23. On Origen's Luke homilies in general, see William Rusch, "Some Comments on Origen's *Homilies on the Gospel According to Luke*," in L. Perrone, ed., with P. Bernardino and D. Marchini, *Origeniana Octava*, 727–32; and the introduction of Joseph Lienhard (*Homiliae in Lucam*), *Origen*, xxiv–xxxviii.

24. See, among other sympathetic biographers, Joseph W. Trigg, *Origen*, about whom Mark J. Edwards comments (positively): "In the work of Joseph Trigg indeed [Origen] becomes almost a Protestant, beholden to no authority but the Bible" (*Origen Against Plato*, 1).

25. Origen's homilies and commentaries were both highly intellectual and spiritualized products: he did not "dumb down" his interpretation for church audiences, nor did he squirrel away his more speculative theologies in recondite commentaries. See the comments of R. P. C. Hanson, *Allegory and Event*, 184.

26. Greek fragments also survive, preserved especially in *catenae* (see below).

27. Origen, *Homilia 14 in Lucam* 10 (SC 87:230).

28. Origen, *Homilia 14 in Lucam* 6 (SC 87:224).

29. Similarly, see Virginia Burrus's reading of Origen in *Saving Shame*, 64–72; and that of John David Dawson, *Christian Figural Reading and the Fashioning of Identity*.

30. Dawson, *Christian Figural*, 65.

31. A point Origen makes in his early speculative treatise *De principiis* 4.2–3 (SC 268:292–298).

32. Burrus, *Saving Shame*, 65–66.

33. Origen, *Homilia 14 in Lucam* 4 (SC 87:220).

34. Origen, *Homilia 14 in Lucam* 7 (SC 87:224).

35. Origen, *Homilia 14 in Lucam* 4 (SC 87:220).

36. The two statements are *propter nos* and *pro nobis*: Origen, *Homilia 14 in Lucam* 1 (SC 87:216).

37. Origen, *Homilia 14 in Lucam* 1 (SC 87:216).

38. Origen, *Fragmenta in Lucam* fr. 41 (in *Homiliae in Lucam*) (SC 87:492).

39. Origen, *Homilia 14 in Lucam* 1 (SC 87:216).

40. Origen, *Homilia 14 in Lucam* 7 (SC 87:226).

41. Burrus, *Saving Shame*, 65.

42. On the (lack of) distinction between Epiphany and Christmas in the East, see my discussion in Chapter 6.

43. See the introductory comments in Kathleen McVey, *Ephrem the Syrian*; and Paul Russell, "The Image of the Infant Jesus in Ephrem the Syrian," *Hugoye* 5.1 (2002).

44. Because of its biblical structure and lack of clear festival context, I find it more fitting to discuss *Hymn 26* in this chapter than in Chapter 6.

45. Stanza 2 certainly deals with Matt 2 (mention of the magi, the massacre of the innocents, and other details). Stanza 1 may refer to John 1:1 (as well as, of course, Gen 1:1) with the phrase "in the beginning" or may echo the end of Matt 1:25 by referring to the day as "firstborn" (Ephrem, *Hymnus 26 de nativitate* 2 [CSCO 186:133]).

46. Ephrem, *Hymnus 26 de nativitate* 11 (CSCO 186:136); tr. McVey, *Ephrem*, 208–9.

47. The so-called Diatessaron ("through the four [gospels]"), traditionally ascribed to Tatian: see William Peterson, *Tatian's Diatessaron*. On the ascription to Tatian, see now Naomi Koltun-Fromm, "Re-Imagining Tatian: The Damaging Effects of Polemical Rhetoric," *Journal of Early Christian Studies* 16 (2008): 1–30, esp. 18–26.

48. A commentary on the Diatessaron survives under Ephrem's name (without comment on the circumcision of Jesus), but Christian Lange, *The Portrayal of Christ in the Syriac Commentary on the Diatessaron*, concludes that "an Ephraemic 'school' extended the 'basic' authentic material by inserting their own statements" (162). As far as we can tell, the Diatessaron combined both nativity accounts and included a version of Luke 2:21 (it appears in the early Arabic version: A.-S. Marmardji, *Diatessaron de Tatien*, 18–19); Ephrem's commentary, however, does not discuss it (see Carmel McCarthy, *Saint Ephrem's Commentary on Tatian's Diatessaron*, 66–67).

49. Ephrem, *Hymnus 5 de crucifixione* 5 (CSCO 248:60); translation of Christine Shepardson, *Anti-Judaism and Orthodoxy*, 103; Shepardson also notes references to Jesus' circumcision in Ephrem's *Hymns on Virginity* 37.7 and his *Sermon on the Lord* 7: see her discussion on 98–104.

50. Shepardson, *Anti-Judaism*, 104.

51. A useful summary of Ambrose's writings is found in Boniface Ramsey, *Ambrose*, 56–68. Ramsey translates the prologue to the *Expositio evangelii secundam Lucam* on 161–65; see also the detailed analysis of Thomas Graumann, *Christus Interpres*.

52. Graumann, *Christus*, 166–71.

53. S. M. Oberhelman, "Jerome's Earliest Attack on Ambrose: *On Ephesians*, Prologue (ML 26:469D-70A)," *Transactions of the American Philological Association* 121 (1991): 377–401; Richard Layton, "Plagiarism and Lay Patronage of Ascetic Scholarship: Jerome, Ambrose, and Rufinus," *Journal of Early Christian Studies* 10 (2002): 489–522; and David G. Hunter, "Fourth-Century Latin Writers," in Frances Young, Lewis Ayres, and Augustine Casiday, *The Cambridge History of Early Christian Literature*, 310–11. The crux of Jerome's criticism rests on the idea of "borrowing" and translation: he criticizes Ambrose's seamless interweaving of previous commentary and opinion as a kind of plagiarism. See my discussion in "'What Has Rome to Do with Bethlehem?' Cultural Capital(s) and Religious Imperialism in Late Ancient Christianity," *Classical Receptions Journal* 3 (2011): 29–45.

54. Ramsey, *Ambrose*, 59.

55. Ambrose, *Expositio evangelii secundum Lucam* praef. 1 (CCL 14:1), which we might also translate "he [Luke] was a historian"; see also praef. 4: "holy Luke possessed a certain historical order (*historicum ordinem*)" (CCL 14:3).

56. Ambrose, *Expositio evangelii secundum Lucam* praef. 7 (CCL 14:5).

57. In discussing the relative popularity of "noncanonical" gospels, Bart D. Ehrman, *Lost Christianities*, 22, notes the sparse references to Mark in the literary and archaeological record.

58. Ambrose, *Expositio evangelii secundum Lucam* praef. 6 (CCL 14:5).

59. Ambrose, *Expositio evangelii secundum Lucam* 2.54 (CCL 14:54).

60. Ambrose, *Expositio evangelii secundum Lucam* 2.55 (CCL 14:54).

61. Jesus' actions are also notably sacrificial: Gillian Bonney, "The Exegesis of the Gospel of Luke in the *Expositio evangelii secundum Lucam* of Ambrose and in the *In Lucae evangelium expositio* of Bede as Observed in the Figure of Elisabeth," *Zeitschrift für Antikes Christentum* 5 (2001): 50–64, at 52: "The third Gospel above all narrates the *sacrificium sacerdotale* of Jesus Christ."

62. Ambrose, *Expositio evangelii secundum Lucam* 2.55 (CCL 14:54).

63. Ambrose, *Expositio evangelii secundum Lucam* 2.56 (CCL 14:55).

64. Ambrose, *Expositio evangelii secundum Lucam* 4.6 (CCL 14:107).

65. On Ambrose's literary production of orthodoxy, see Virginia Burrus, *"Begotten, Not Made,"* 134–83.

66. Burrus, *Begotten*, 180, describes Ambrose as modeling "a transvestite masculine subjectivity," by which he parodies gender roles and reinstates them simultaneously in his theology.

67. Other Greek writers composed commentaries on Luke between Origen and Cyril. Angelo Mai published Eusebius's *Commentary on Luke* (now found in PG 24:529–605), on which see D. S. Wallace-Hadrill, "Eusebius of Caesarea's *Commentary on Luke*: Its Origin and Early History," *Harvard Theological Review* 67 (1974): 55–63. Mai excerpted the *Commentary* from the eleventh-century catena of Nicetas of Heraclea. Fragments of homilies on Luke by Titus, bishop of Bostra (d. ca. 378), are also included in later catenae (see n.83).

68. For a narrative chronology of Cyril's life and writings, see Norman Russell, *Cyril of Alexandria*, 3–58. On Cyril as scriptural interpreter, see now Lois M. Farag, *St. Cyril of Alexandria, a New Testament Exegete*; on 155–56 Farag points out the more clearly homiletical context of Cyril's *Commentary on Luke*.

69. See Robert Wilken, *Judaism and the Early Christian Mind*; and id., "Cyril of Alexandria as Interpreter of the Old Testament," in Thomas G. Weinandy and Daniel A. Keating, *The Theology of St. Cyril of Alexandria*, 1–21. Of course, Cyril's rhetorical violence was too often matched by physical violence against pagans, heretics, and Jews in Alexandria.

70. Wilken, *Judaism*, 56–67.

71. Parts of the Syriac translation, Greek homilies, and catena fragments are translated together in R. Payne Smith, *Gospel of Saint Luke by Cyril of Alexandria* (*Commentarius in Lucam* [5]). The homilies on Luke 2:21–39 (the circumcision and presentation), numbered as *Homilies 3* and *4* of the *Commentary on Luke*, and as *Homily 12* in the *Homiliae diversae* edited by J. P. Migne, have been independently transmitted: see the discussion of the Greek catenae in general by Michel Aubineau, "Les 'catenae in Lucam' de J. Reuss et Cyrille d'Alexandrie," *Byzantinische Zeitschrift* 80 (1987): 29–47; and on *Homiliae 3* and *4* particularly on 40, as well as the brief notice by Aubineau, "Deux homélies de Cyrille d'Alexandrie *de hypapante* (*BHG* 1958w et 1963)?" *Analecta Bollandiana* 90 (1972): 100. The comments on this part of Luke 2 are not found in the Syriac edition, although J.-M. Sauget, "Nouvelles homélies du Commentaire sur l'Évangile de s. Luc de Cyrille d'Alexandrie dans leur traduction syriaque," in *Symposium Syriacum I*, 439–56, describes several unedited fragments of these homilies that corroborate fragments of the Greek catenae (although, as far as I know,

these fragments remain unpublished). I cite the Greek from the Patrologia Graeca (the catenae are found in PG 72; the surviving homilies in PG 77).

72. The structural parallels with classical rabbinic discourse are notable in this respect, also preserving a mode of dissonant dialogue that defers resolution: but see now Daniel Boyarin, *Socrates and the Fat Rabbis.*

73. The beginning of the homilies refers to a "festival" (ἑορτή) at which the sermon is being delivered (see PG 77:1041A), but it is unclear whether this is a celebration of the "presentation" (in February) or an early witness to the Feast of the Circumcision (in January); it is equally likely that a later redactor added this phrase. I address the problem of dating the Feast of the Circumcision in Chapter 6.

74. Cyril of Alexandria, *Homilia 12 in Lucam* (PG 77:1041C = PG 72:496C). Significant portions of the passages cited here are also found in the catenists catalogued by Joseph Reuss, *Lukas-Kommentare aus der griechischen Kirche*, 56–57 (Cyril I, fr. 7–8 [*Commentarius in Lucam* (5)]); and also in the Vatican catenae compiled by Cardinal Mai (and edited by Migne) in PG 72.

75. Cyril of Alexandria, *Homilia 12 in Lucam* (PG 77:1041C). This passage is not found in the catenae.

76. Cyril, like most ancient Christians, did not consider Jesus Jewish in a modern, historical-critical sense: see below, and my discussion in Chapter 1.

77. Cyril of Alexandria, *Homilia 12 in Lucam* (PG 77:1041B).

78. Cyril of Alexandria, *Homilia 12 in Lucam* (PG 77:1044A). For a somewhat briefer version of this passage, see Reuss, *Lukas-Kommentare*, 57, and PG 72:497A.

79. Wilken, *Judaism*, 227, notes that "Paul provided the key to Cyril's reading of the Scriptures." As this one example shows, the intertextual play moves in many directions.

80. The homily reads ὁ μετὰ Μωσέα στρατηγός; the catenae read ὁ μετὰ Μωυσέα στρατηγήσας.

81. Cyril of Alexandria, *Homilia 12 in Lucam* (PG 77:1044B; cf. Reuss, *Lukas-Kommentare*, 57, and PG 72:497B).

82. The typological reading of Joshua's circumcision of the Israelites and the mystical number "eight" as a sign of the resurrection are found before Cyril (see, among others, Hilary of Poitiers, *Tractatus super psalmos 118* prol. 5 [SC 344:98]). The concatenation of all of these sources, directed specifically at interpreting Christ's circumcision, is of note in Cyril's commentary.

83. Cyril of Alexandria, *Commentarius in Lucam (in catena)* (PG 72:499–500). This passage follows immediately upon the citation from the homily quoted above, with an intervening passage that comes from Origen's *Homilia 14 in Lucam*, which may also have been included in Cyril's commentary. Reuss, *Lukas-Kommentare*, 281, notes the Origenian passage briefly (Cyril III, section fr. 14), but does not include the cited fragment as verifiably Cyrillian. A very similar passage is ascribed to Titus of Bosra (see n.67), and edited as such by Joseph Sickenberger, *Titus von Bostra*, 149–50. It is certainly possible that this comment on the circumcision comes from Titus in the fourth century; it is also possible that Cyril knew Titus's commentary and incorporated the idea into his own commentary; finally, it is possible

that Cyril originated this comment, which was later incorporated (as other parts of Cyril's corpus were) into the Ps.-Titus catena. The logic of the passage certainly fits with Cyril's other discussions of Jesus' Jewishness and the circumcision. It is symptomatic of the modes of commentary production and dissemination that these threads are so difficult to disentangle.

84. In his comments on Luke 2:22–39 (sometimes preserved as a separate homily "on the presentation"), Cyril momentarily contextualizes Jesus' submission to the Law (here, in the Temple) as a sincere gesture to save Jews: "Therefore Christ became a light for the revelation of gentiles, but also for the glory of Israel. For even if some of them became proud and unpersuaded, and possessed a mind rife with stupidity, nevertheless the remnant will be saved and made glorious by Christ." Cyril goes on, however, to suggest that this "remnant" is found most clearly (and, perhaps, uniquely) among the "divine disciples" (PG 77:1048B–C). A version of this passage is found in the catenae edited by J. A. Cramer, *Catenae graecorum patrum*, 2:23 (*Commentarius in Lucam* [3]).

85. Most scholars date Cyril's *Commentary on Luke* to his "post-Nestorian" phase, that is, the early 430s: see Daniel Keating, *The Appropriation of Divine Life in Cyril of Alexandria*, 17 and n.53. Proclus's homily is dated by Michel Aubineau to his archepiscopacy (434–46; see below n.86), although he preached in the capital city for the greater part of the early 400s: see Jan H. Barkhuizen, "Proclus of Constantinople: A Popular Preacher in Fifth-Century Constantinople," in Mary B. Cunningham and Pauline Allen, *Preacher and Audience*, 179–200; and the introduction to Proclus's life and works in Nicholas Constas, *Proclus of Constantinople and the Cult of the Virgin Mary in Late Antiquity*, 7–124. Michel Aubineau, "Emprunts de Proclus de Constantinople à Cyrille d'Alexandrie dans son Homélie XXII, In illud 'et postquam consummati dies octo . . .' (Lc. 2,21)," in C. Laga, J. Munitz, and L. van Rompay, *After Chalcedon*, 23–34, proposes that Proclus directly borrowed from Cyril in his homily and, further, that Proclus delivered this homily at the Feast of the Presentation (February 2; I discuss this festival further in Chapter 6).

86. The Greek text of the homily appears in PG 65:836–40 (*De circumcision domini* [1]), but has more recently been edited and translated, with brief commentary, by Michel Aubineau, "Proclus de Constantinople, In illud: 'et postquam consummati sunt dies octo' (*Lc* 2,21)," in E. Lucchesi and H. D. Saffrey, *Mémorial André-Jean Festugière*, 199–207 (text on 202 [*De circumcision domini* (2)]).

87. Barkhuizen, "Proclus," 191, describes Proclus's homilies as more "thematic" than "exegetical" (as contrasted with, for example, John Chrysostom, who often proceeds verse by verse in his homilies). By this he seems to indicate that Proclus does not proceed through Scripture chapter by chapter, but rather draws on particular scriptural passages to illuminate a particular topic or festival occasion.

88. Proclus, *De circumcisione domini* 1.1. Citations refer to Aubineau's chapter and line numbers (see n.86).

89. Proclus, *De circumcisione domini* 2.1–3.

90. Proclus, *De circumcisione domini* 2.5–6.

91. Proclus, *De circumcisione domini* 2.8–10.

92. Proclus, *De circumcisione domini* 3.1–2.

93. Proclus, *De circumcisione domini* 3.2–4.

94. Proclus also quickly treats the presentation and sacrifice at the Temple (Luke 2:22–24) in similar fashion: Proclus, *De circumcisione domini* 3.4–10.

95. On the slave tattoo and its incorporation (at various semantic levels) into early Christian thought, see Susanna Elm, "'Pierced by Bronze Needles': Anti-Montanist Charges of Ritual Stigmatization in Their Fourth-Century Context," *Journal of Early Christian Studies* 4 (1996): 409–39; and Virginia Burrus, "Macrina's Tattoo," *Journal of Medieval and Modern Studies* 33 (2003): 403–18; also in Dale B. Martin and Patricia Cox Miller, *The Cultural Turn in Late Ancient Studies*, 103–16.

96. A similar exegetical move is found in a fragment of Eustathius of Antioch preserved in later catenae and in Theodoret of Cyrus's *Eranistes* 2.21 (text in Gérard Ettlinger, *Eranistes*, 158–59; there it is identified as part of an exegesis of Prov 8:22). Eustathius understands Luke 2:21–24 as an elaboration of Gal 4:4–5, commenting that "God did not submit to the Law . . . rather he is the Law," but by taking the Law on himself God freed all others from "the judgment of ruin": Eustathius of Antioch *Fragment* 70 (CCG 51:141–42).

97. Edmund Beck, "Philoxenos und Ephräm," *Oriens Christianus* 46 (1962): 61–76; and André de Halleux, *Philoxène de Mabbog*, esp. 318, with n.30.

98. Philoxenus was an older contemporary and ally of Severus of Antioch, whose attention to the circumcision of Jesus I discuss in Chapter 3. Work on Philoxenus has lagged behind that of Severus, but see de Halleux, *Philoxène*; Roberta C. Chesnut, *Three Monophysite Christologies*, 57–112; David Michelson, "Practice Leads to Theory"; and now the double issue of *Hugoye* 13.1–2 (2010), edited by Michelson.

99. On Philoxenus's education, see de Halleux, *Philoxène*, 22–30; Michelson, "Practice," 3–7; and Adam Becker, *Fear of God and the Beginning of Wisdom*, 41–76, on the "school of the Persians."

100. Philoxenus was intensely interested in biblical textual criticism, and as bishop of Mabbug commissioned a (now lost) Syriac version of the New Testament: see de Halleux, *Philoxène*, 117–25; Sebastian Brock, *The Bible in the Syriac Tradition*, 18–20, 35–36, 49–50; and Daniel King, "New Evidence on the Philoxenian Versions of the New Testament and the Nicene Creed," *Huyoge* 13.1 (2010): 9–30.

101. On Philoxenus's attitudes toward Ephrem, see Lucas van Rompay, "*Mallpânâ dilan Suryâyâ*: Ephrem in the Works of Philoxenus of Mabbog: Respect and Distance," *Hugoye* 7.1 (2004).

102. The colophon is found in BL Add. 17126, which was probably written in Mabbug during Philoxenus's episcopacy: see de Halleux, *Philoxène*, 129; and Michelson, "Practice," 76–77; the text of the colophon is found J. W. Watt, *Philoxenus of Mabbug*, CSCO 392:93n.4 (*Commentary on Matthew and Luke* [1]).

103. Watt, *Philoxenus of Mabbug*. For de Halleux's reconstruction of the fragments, see *Philoxène*, 134–50.

104. Douglas J. Fox, *The "Matthew-Luke Commentary" of Philoxenus*, 30 (*Commentary on Matthew and Luke* [2]).

105. Fox, *Commentary*, 187; see also 190.

106. For a comparison of the two editions of Philoxenus, including a response to Fox's discussion of commentary (on 27–30), see André de Halleux, "Le commentaire de Philoxène sur *Matthieu* et *Luc*: Deux éditions récentes," *Le Muséon* 93 (1980): 5–35.

107. The wide-ranging social implications of scriptural interpretation in shaping the lives of early Christians have been exquisitely traced by Philip Rousseau, "Homily and Exegesis: Reflection on Their Intersection," plenary lecture delivered at the Annual Meeting of the North American Patristics Society (May 27, 2010); I am grateful to Professor Rousseau for sharing his talk with me.

108. De Halleux, *Philoxène*, 423–45, explores Philoxenus on "contemplation," including the influence of Evagrius. See now also Michelson, "Practice," 55–72.

109. On the triangulation of imitatio Christi, Scripture, and monastic ethics in Evagrius, see David Brakke, "Making Public the Monastic Life: Reading the Self in Evagrius' *Talking Back*," in David Brakke, Michael Satlow, and Steven Weitzman, *Religion and the Self in Antiquity*, 222–33; and id., *Evagrius of Pontus*, 3–30.

110. See the useful analysis of Columba Stewart, "Imageless Prayer and the Theological Vision of Evagrius Ponticus," *Journal of Early Christian Studies* 9 (2001): 173–204; and William Harmless, *Desert Christians*, 311–58.

111. On the particular theological (particularly christological) resonances of the commentary, see Barbara Aland, "Monophysitismus und Schriftauslegung: Der Kommentar zum Matthäus- und Lukasevangelium des Philoxenus von Mabbug," in Peter Hauptmann, *Unser ganzes Leben Christus unserm Gott überantworten*, 142–66.

112. The so-called second Origenist controversy was already brewing in Philoxenus's lifetime: see Daniël Hombergen, *The Second Origenist Controversy*; and id., "Barsanuphius and John of Gaza and the Origenist Controversy," in Brouria Bitton-Ashkelony and Aryeh Kofsky, *Christian Gaza in Late Antiquity*, 173–81.

113. Michelson, "Practice," 90.

114. Michelson, "Practice," 91–108.

115. These four fragments appear together in the same eighth-century manuscript (see CSCO 392:13*), where they are identified as coming from a "discourse" on Luke 2:6–7, in which Philoxenus speaks "about the circumcision of our Lord."

116. Philoxenus, *Commentary on Matthew and Luke* fr. 39 (CSCO 392:38–39 [Syr.], 393:33–34 [Eng.]). Numbering of the fragments follows de Halleux as organized by Watt in his edition (CSCO 392) and translation (CSCO 393). The text is cited from Watt's edition, and my translation is modified from his.

117. Philoxenus, *Commentary on Matthew and Luke* fr. 40 (CSCO 392:39 [Syr.], 393:34 [Eng.]).

118. Philoxenus, *Commentary on Matthew and Luke* fr. 41 (CSCO 392:39 [Syr.], 393:34 [Eng.]).

119. Boyarin, *Intertextuality*, 16.

120. Watt translates *qenumâ* here (probably rightly) as *hypostasis*.

121. Philoxenus, *Commentary on Matthew and Luke* fr. 42 (CSCO 392:39 [Syr.], 393:34 [Eng.]).

122. Fox, *Commentary*, 133, translates "its subjection" and "its curse" as "His obedience" and "His becoming accursed," reading the suffix as referring to Jesus and not "the Law." De Halleux, "Commentaire," 14–17, prefers Watt's translation to Fox's.

123. Philoxenus, *Commentary on Matthew and Luke* fr. 51 (CSCO 392:72 [Syr.], 393:61–62 [Eng.]). Fox, *Commentary*, 57 (Syr.) and 133 (Eng.), numbers passages as part of fragment 2.

124. The order of recensions and their Severan context are discussed by Clemens Leonhard, "Die Beschneidung Christi in der syrischen *Schatzhöhle*: Beobachtungen zu Datierung und Überlieferung des Werks," in Martin Tamcke, *Syriaca II*, 11–28.

125. *Cave of Treasures* 29.10–11, in Andreas Su-Min Ri, *La caverne des trésors*, CSCO 486:222–29 (Syriac) and CSCO 487:86–89 (French); and the brief note in id., *Commentaire de la "Caverne des Trésors,"* 363–64.

126. Although the *Infancy Gospel of Thomas* notably deals with issues of Jews and Judaism (see Christopher Frilingos, "No Child Left Behind: Knowledge and Violence in the *Infancy Gospel of Thomas*," *Journal of Early Christian Studies* 17 [2009]: 27–54), the text has nothing about Jesus' nativity, but begins when he is five years old. The *Protevangelium of James* also deals with issues of Judaism, particularly in Mary's Temple service (see, among other treatments, Timothy J. Horner, "Jewish Aspects of the *Protoevangelium of James*," *Journal of Early Christian Studies* 12 [2004]: 313–35), but likewise does not mention Jesus' circumcision.

127. See the general introduction of James K. Elliott, *The Apocryphal New Testament*, 84–87. Elliott does not translate the chapter with the mention of the circumcision, since it is part of a section based on the *Protevangelium of James*; the latter text, however, does not mention the circumcision.

128. *Pseudo-Matthaei evangelium* 15; text in Constantine Tischendorf, *Evangelia apocrypha*, 77. Tischendorf's main text reads "octavo vero die circumcidentes puerum," which is closer to the inflected infinitive of Luke 2:21; an alternate version reads less equivocally "ubi octavo die circumciderunt puerum." *Ps.-Matthew*'s nonchalant reference to the circumcision may, nonetheless, be a response to aphthartodocetism, especially considering the previous silence concerning the circumcision in infancy gospels and the prominence of the circumcision of Christ in aphthartodocetic debates. The modern editor of the (probably) seventh-century Anglo-Saxon Christian chronicle known as the *Laterculus Malalianus* posits that the inclusion of the circumcision of Christ in this text (*Laterculus Malalianus* 16) may "be best understood as reacting *against* eastern ideas" of "Docetism" (Jane Stevenson, *The "Laterculus Malalianus" and the School of Archbishop Theodore*, 205 [text on 142–43]).

129. On this text, see Elliott, *Apocryphal New Testament*, 100–102. Elliott again omits the nativity passages, since they are (loosely) based on second-century sources.

130. *Evangelium infantiae arabicum* 5; Latin text in Tischendorf, *Evangelia*, 173. The Arabic text can be found in J. Giles, *Codex Apocryphus Novi Testamenti*, 13; my translation is adapted from the Ante-Nicene Fathers (8:405–6).

131. *Armenian Infancy Gospel* 2; translation from Abraham Terian, *The Armenian Gospel of the Infancy*, 60; see also xviii–xxvi for Terian's argument for a sixth-century date (based, in part, on its Julianist Christology).

132. On the Syriac manuscript as a site of ambiguous gaps, see Michael Penn, "Moving Beyond the Palimpsest: Erasure in Syriac Manuscripts," *Journal of Early Christian Studies* 18 (2010): 261–303.

133. Clark, *Reading Renunciation*, 255, citing Michel Foucault, "The Order of Discourse," in Robert Young, *Untying the Text*, 58.

134. Chin, *Grammar and Christianity*, 82–93. Chin compares Jerome's interpretation of the "foreign captive" of Deuteronomy 21 (which he appropriates from Origen, even as Origen himself is being configured as "heretical" and "foreign") and Augustine's reading of the "spoiling of the Egyptians" (Exod 3) as strategies for articulating and eliding the "otherness" of non-Christian ("pagan") knowledge.

135. Several of the Greek writers who comment on Colossians knew this verse with an early, common variant: τοῦ σωμάτος τῶν ἁμαρτιῶν τῆς σαρκός (see the critical apparatus in Barbara Aland and Kurt Aland, *Novum Testamentum Graece*, 526).

136. Before Origen, Clement of Alexandria cited Col 2:11 along with Col 3:1–5 and 8–10, in a passage exhorting the stripping away of passions (while avoiding overly strict, heretical asceticism): Clement of Alexandria, *Stromateis* 3.5.43 (GCS 15:215–16). As in much of the *Stromateis*, Clement freely cites this passage without context or elaboration.

137. Jerome, *Epistula* 33.4.5 (CSEL 54:257), refers to Origen's commentary on Colossians: "in epistolam ad Colossenses libros II." It is not clear whether Jerome saw this commentary or simply knew of its existence.

138. Elaine Pagels, *The Gnostic Paul*.

139. Margaret Mitchell, *The Heavenly Trumpet*, 5n.19, 66–67.

140. Mitchell, *Heavenly Trumpet*.

141. John Chrysostom, *Homilia 6 in epistolam ad Colossenses* 2 (PG 62:339–40).

142. Theodore of Mopsuestia, *Commentarius in epistula ad Colossenses* 2:11; text in H. B. Swete, *Theodori Episcopi Mopsuesteni in Epistulas B. Pauli Commentarii*, 1:287. Swete also includes a Greek fragment on Col 2:13 in this section (from the Greek catena) in which Theodore again calls circumcision "the removal of mortality" (περιτομὴν τὴν ἀφαίρεσιν ἐκάλεσεν τῆς θνητότητος). The reading of "Christ's circumcision" in Col 2:11 as "shedding mortality" is also found in the Latin tradition already as early as Tertullian, *De resurrectione mortuorum* 7.6 (CCL 2:929–30). The text has been reissued as *Theodore of Mopsuestia: The Commentaries on the Minor Epistles of Paul*, Writings from the Greco-Roman World 26, ed. and tr. Rowan Greer (Atlanta: SBL Press, 2010).

143. Theodore of Mopsuestia, *Commentarius in epistula ad Colossenses* 2:11 (Swete, *Theodori*, 1:287; Greer, *Theodore*, 404–5).

144. Theodore of Mopsuestia, *Commentarius in epistula ad Colossenses* 2:12–13 (Swete, *Theodori*, 1:288–89; Greer, *Theodore*, 406–9).

145. Severian of Gabala's commentary also survives only in fragments in catenae: K. Staab, *Pauluskommentar aus der griechischen Kirche aus Katenenhandshriften gesammelt*, 322 col. 2.

146. Ambrosiaster, *Commentarius in epistula ad Colossenses* 2:11–12 (CSEL 81:184). Ambrosiaster is one of the earliest Latin writers to comment on all of Paul's letters, after

Marius Victorinus (whose comments on Colossians are not extant). Pelagius also, in the late fourth century, executed a commentary on all of Paul's letters; his comments on Col 2:11 are minimal, however.

CHAPTER 6. "LET US BE CIRCUMCISED!"

Note to epigraph: Jacques Derrida, *Archive Fever*, 12.

1. Jonathan Z. Smith, *To Take Place*, 109 and 112. See also id., "What a Difference a Difference Makes," in Jacob Neusner and Ernest S. Frerichs, *"To See Ourselves as Others See Us,"* 3–48, and in Smith, *Relating Religion*, 251–302.

2. I distinguish, of course, between late ancient reception of Paul as a more or less anti-Jewish writer and recent work on the "historical" Paul: see, for instance, John Gager, *Reinventing Paul*, 77–100 on the Letter to the Galatians, and specifically 98 on this passage: "Taken out of context, these words of Paul lead to the view that the law has been annulled for Israel. But read within this letter, they merely reiterate . . . [that] gentiles are now redeemed from the curse of the law by Christ."

3. Second Council of Tours (567 C.E.), canon 17 (CCL 148a:182). The first part of the canon suggests attempts by the clergy to restrain celebration of the New Year, on which see below.

4. See, for instance, F. Cabrol, "Circoncision (Fête de la)," *Dictionnaire d'archéologie chrétienne et de liturgie* 3.2 (1914): 1718–28, at 1718: "On remarquera aussi que le concile ne parle pas de cette institution comme d'une nouveauté, mais plutôt comme d'une coutume ancienne."

5. The Feast of the Circumcision still exists in Orthodox Christian calendars; following the calendrical reforms of the Second Vatican Council, however, the Roman Catholic feast of January 1 was renamed the Feast of the Solemnity of Mary, as explained by Pope Paul VI in *Marialis Cultus*, chapter 1, paragraph 5: see the discussion of Thomas A. Thompson, "Mary in Western Liturgical Tradition," *Liturgical Ministry* 6 (Winter 1997): 1–10; and the website "Marian Feasts Past and Present" maintained by the International Marian Research Institute at the University of Dayton, http://campus.udayton.edu/mary/resources/dogmas.html (accessed March 20, 2011). Many thanks to Maureen Tilley for directing me to this resource.

6. Michael Penn, *Kissing Christians*, 53, and see also 123–24; and id., "Performing Family: Ritual Kissing and the Construction of Early Christian Kinship," *Journal of Early Christian Studies* 10 (2002): 151–74.

7. Daniel Stökl Ben Ezra, "An Ancient List of Christian Festivals in *Toledot Yeshu*: Polemics as Indication for Interaction," *Harvard Theological Review* 102 (2009): 481–96, at 481.

8. A famous definition of "festival" comes from Alessandro Falassi: "a periodically recurrent, social occasion in which, through a multiplicity of forms and a series of coordinated events, participate directly or indirectly and to various degrees, all members of a whole community, united by ethnic, linguistic, religious, historical bonds, and sharing a world-view" (*Time out of Time*, 2).

9. See Denis Feeney, *Caesar's Calendar*.

10. On provincial calendars in the early imperial period, see Chris Bennett, "The Early Augustan Calendars in Rome and Egypt," *Zeitschrift für Papyrologie und Epigraphik* 142 (2003): 221–40; on Roman time, which was multilayered by the Christian period, see Michele Renée Salzman, *On Roman Time*.

11. Michel Foucault, "Of Other Spaces," tr. Jay Miskowiec, *Diacritics* 16 (1986): 22–27.

12. Foucault, "Of Other Spaces," 26.

13. Feeney, *Caesar's Calendar*, 196.

14. Feeney, *Caesar's Calendar*, 196, draws an apt comparison between Caesar's regulation of time and his regularization of Latin grammar in his *De analogia*. On scientific systematization and empire, see Mary Louise Pratt, *Imperial Eyes*, 15–37.

15. Feeney, *Caesar's Calendar*, 210.

16. See, for instance, the discussion of the Jewish calendar under Rome by Sacha Stern, *Calendar and Community*, 42–45.

17. Feeney, *Caesar's Calendar*, 197. The horologium was not, as is often supposed, a sundial, but rather a solar meridian used to mark time from solstice to solstice: see Peter Heslin, "Augustus, Domitian, and the So-called Horologium Augusti," *Journal of Roman Studies* 97 (2007): 1–20.

18. *Didache* 8.1; text in Bart D. Erhman, *The Apostolic Fathers*, 1:428.

19. On the complex relationship between the "Lord's Day" and the Jewish Sabbath, see the overview of Gerard Rouwhorst, "The Reception of the Jewish Sabbath in Early Christianity," in *Christian Feast and Festival*, 233–66.

20. Marcello del Verme, *Didache and Judaism*, 143–88, like many recent commentators on the *Didache*, understands the calendrical debate here as witness to friction between various Jewish, Christian Jewish, and Christian gentile groups in flux.

21. See *Didascalia apostolorum* 21 (CSCO 407:203–18); *Constitutiones apostolorum* 5. 13, 19 (SC 329:246, 266–68); and *Traditio apostolica* 33 (SC 11*bis*:116).

22. On these debates, see the fine summary of Susan K. Roll, *Toward the Origins of Christmas*, 87–164.

23. See the overview, and critique, of Robert Taft, "Historicism Revisited," *Studia Liturgica* 14 (1982): 97–109; the theory of post-Constantinian "historicism" was posited by Gregory Dix, *The Shape of the Liturgy*, 347–60.

24. This syncretistic understanding of Christianity (not limited to liturgiology) predominated among the Religionsgeschichtliche Schule in late nineteenth- and early twentieth-century Europe, as in Hermann Usener, *Das Weihnachtsfest*. See Hans Förster, *Die Anfänge von Weihnachten und Epiphanias*, 4–25, for a critique of the most prominent of such theories regarding Christmas and Epiphany.

25. Two classic, and influential, studies remain Paul F. Bradshaw, *The Search for the Origins of Christian Worship*; and Thomas Talley, *The Origins of the Liturgical Year*. On Jews, Christians, and festivals, see now also Oskar Skarsaune, *In the Shadow of the Temple*, 377–97.

26. John Chrysostom, *Adversus Iudaeos* 1.5 (PG 48:851): "For after you worship

according to our own customs Christ who was crucified by them, then you chase down and do honor to their customs!"

27. See, generally, Clemens Leonhard, *The Jewish Pesach and the Origins of the Christian Easter*, 270–72; and Israel Yuval, *Two Nations in Your Womb*, 56–90.

28. Setting the dates for festivals according to the Jewish calendar seems to have been very much a local, varied affair for much of late antiquity: see Stern, *Calendar and Community*; and Joseph Tabory, "Jewish Festivals in Late Antiquity," in Steven Katz, *The Cambridge History of Judaism*, vol. 4: *The Late Roman-Rabbinic Period*, 556–72. For a consideration of the possible social contacts between Jews and Christians around Passover-Easter, see David Brakke, "Jewish Flesh and Christian Spirit in Athanasius of Alexandria," *Journal of Early Christian Studies* 9 (2001): 453–81, at 464–67.

29. Stephen G. Wilson, *Related Strangers*, 238.

30. So Stökl Ben Ezra, "Ancient List," sees the comparison of Jewish and Christian festivals as evidence of polemical interaction in late antiquity. See also the observation of the so-called Piacenza Pilgrim, who mentions nearly simultaneous Christian and Jewish festivals at Mamre: *Itinerarium Antonini Placentini* 30 (CCL 175:144), with my discussion in *Remains of the Jews*, 130.

31. On public festivals as polemics, see Elliott S. Horowitz, *Reckless Rites*.

32. Alistair Stewart-Sykes, *The Lamb's High Feast*. That Melito was a Quartodeciman derives from a notice in Eusebius (*Historia ecclasiastica* 5.24.5–6 [GCS 9.1:492]), a notice Stewart-Sykes accepts and amplifies with literary and social evidence. Not all modern scholars accept this theory: see, among recent studies, Lynn Cohick, *The Peri Pascha Attributed to Melito of Sardis*.

33. In another article, Alistair Stewart-Sykes argues that Melito was himself born Jewish, and that this accounts (in some fashion) for his anti-Judaism: "Melito's Anti-Judaism," *Journal of Early Christian Studies* 5 (1997): 271–83.

34. For a similar study of Yom Kippur and Christian festival time, see Daniel Stökl Ben Ezra, *The Impact of Yom Kippur on Early Christianity*.

35. There are of course references to some festivals—principally Easter (although Holy Week and Lent develop more slowly)—in the pre-Constantinian period, but little sustained attention: see Bradshaw, *Search for the Origins*, 178–91.

36. I discuss much of this evidence below, which comprises primarily sermons but also late ancient lectionaries, early medieval canons, and Byzantine menologies.

37. See the discussion of John F. Baldovin, "The Empire Baptized," in Geoffrey Wainwright and Karen B. Westerfield Tucker, *The Oxford History of Christian Worship*, 77–130, at 112–17.

38. Marie-Anne Vannier, "L'apport du *Sermon Dolbeau 26*," *Studia Patristica* 38 (2001): 331–27; and François Dolbeau's introduction to the text, *Vingt-six sermons au peuple d'Afrique*, 70–89.

39. The sermon—perhaps the longest we have of Augustine's—was discovered with other sermons in the modern period and published by Dolbeau, *Vingt-six sermons*, 90–141. Fragments of this sermon existed previously, preserved by Bede (and numbered as

Sermo 198); it is also entitled "Dolbeau 26"; "Mayence 62"; and *Contra paganos* in modern studies.

40. Augustine, *Sermo* 198.6 (Dolbeau, *Vingt-six sermons*, 95). John Scheid, "Les réjouissances des calendes de janvier d'après le *sermon* Dolbeau 26: Nouvelle lumières sur une fête mal connue," in Goluven Madec, *Augustin prédicateur*, 353–65, attempts to use the sermon to reconstruct pagan New Year's rites in Carthage during this period.

41. Augustine spends a great deal of time discussing the origins of the pagan gods, as well as the true nature of creation and the angels: *Sermo* 198.27–41 (Dolbeau, *Vingt-six sermons*, 110–22). Clifford Ando, *The Matter of the Gods*, 39–41, places these comments in the context of Augustine's larger critique of idolatry.

42. *Sermons*, part 3, vol. 11 (*Sermo 198*): *Newly Discovered Sermons*, 180–237, at 229.

43. On boredom as pedagogy, see Catherine M. Chin, *Grammar and Christianity in the Late Roman World*, 118–23.

44. Maximus of Turin, *Sermo* 63.1 (CCL 23:266), translation modified from Boniface Ramsey, *The Sermons of Maximus of Turin*, 155–56. The sermon is listed as *Sermo 6* in the Patrologia Latina (PL 57:543–44).

45. Maximus of Turin, *Sermo* 63.2 (CCL 23:266).

46. Maximus of Turin, *Sermo* 63.3 (CCL 23:267).

47. Robert A. Markus, *The End of Ancient Christianity*, 103–6.

48. See, for instance, one of our earliest extant lectionary calendars, *Armenian Lectionary*, from Jerusalem, which lists the following festivals from Christ's life: 1: Epiphany (January 6), 13: Presentation (February 14), 18–51: Lent and Easter, 55: Massacre of the Innocents (May 9), 57–58: Ascension and Pentecost, 64: Dormition (August 15) (PO 36.2 [168]: 210–11 [72–73], 228–29 [90–91], 231–323 [100–185], 334–35 [196–97], 336–39 [198–99], 354–55 [216–17]).

49. See Roll, *Toward the Origins of Christmas*; Talley, *Origins*, 117; and Everett Ferguson, "Preaching at Epiphany: Gregory of Nyssa and John Chrysostom on Baptism and the Church," *Church History* 66 (1997): 1–17. The *Armenian Lectionary* (see n.48) notes the Feast of the Nativity on December 25, but also explains that it is not observed in Jerusalem but is "in other cities"; see the discussion of Athanase Renoux, *Le codex Arménien Jérusalem 121*, vol. 1, PO 35.1 (163): 73–78 (on Christmas), and vol. 2, PO 36.2 (168): 182–83 (on Epiphany).

50. See Averil Cameron, *Christianity and the Rhetoric of Empire*, 96–106; Stephen J. Shoemaker, *Ancient Traditions of the Virgin Mary's Dormition and Assumption*, 25–32; and my discussion of later infancy gospels in Chapter 5.

51. For example, John R. Curran, *Pagan City and Christian Capital*, 221–24, who discusses festivals. On the role of bishops in reshaping cities, see J. H. W. G. Liebeschuetz, *Decline and Fall of the Roman City*, 137–66.

52. As Mark Humphries remarks, in the context of an Italian town: "And just as the building itself was becoming a more visible feature in the landscape of Aquileia, so too the liturgy celebrated within was no longer shielded from the prying eyes of the urban community as a whole" (*Communities of the Blessed*, 194). On the broader context (with a

focus on Jerusalem, Rome, and Constantinople), see John Baldovin, *The Urban Character of Christian Worship*.

53. Gregory of Nazianzus, *Oratio* 41.5 (PG 36:436).

54. See, generally, Robin Jensen, *Understanding Early Christian Art*, 94–129. One early example of this parade of scenes from Christ's life is found in the so-called Arian church of San Apollinare Nuovo in Ravenna: for discussion, see Deborah Mauskopf Deliyannis, *Ravenna in Late Antiquity*, 152–73.

55. The separate observance of Christmas as distinct from Epiphany seems to have been promoted among the Cappadocians early on, only later spreading through the Greek- and Latin-speaking Christian world: see Beth Elise Dunlop, "Earliest Greek Patristic Orations on the Nativity," 1–10. Dunlop closely follows Talley, *Origins*, 134–47 (on Christmas and Epiphany). See also Roll, *Toward the Origins of Christmas*, 189–95; and Förster, *Anfänge von Weihnachten*.

56. See my discussion of these texts in Chapter 5.

57. Harry Gamble, *Books and Readers in the Early Church*, 217–18.

58. Nicholas Denysenko, "The *Hypapante* Feast in Fourth to Eighth Century Jerusalem," *Studia Liturgica* 37 (2007): 73–97. The feast is called hypapante after the holy family's encounter (originally from ὑπαντάω, which becomes in reduplicated form ὑπαπαντή; in Latin, *occursus*) with Anna and Symeon. It is also known as the Feast of the Purification and Candlemas.

59. *Armenian Lectionary* 13 (PO 36.2 [168]: 228–29 [90–91]); see Denysenko, "*Hypapante*," 77–80.

60. Although a great number of his festival homilies survive, we possess little concrete biographical information about Hesychius: see Robert Pittman, "The Marian Homilies of Hesychius of Jerusalem," 1–10; Job Getcha, "The Unity of the Mystery of Salvation According to the Festal Homilies of Hesychius of Jerusalem," *Studia Patristica* 37 (2001): 472–81; and Cornelia Horn, *Asceticism and Christological Controversy in Fifth-Century Palestine*, 370–72.

61. The homilies are edited and translated by Michel Aubineau, *Hesychius: Les homélies festales*, vol. 1: *Les homélies i–xv*, 24–75. See also Denysenko, "*Hypapante*," 80–85.

62. Hesychius, *In hypapante* 1.1 (Aubineau, *Homélies*, 24).

63. Hesychius, *In hypapante* 1.2 (Aubineau, *Homélies*, 28).

64. In his introduction, Aubineau, *Homélies*, lxii and 3, asserts that Hesychius would have preached this homily in the Martyrion (based, in part, on the notation of the *Armenian Lectionary*: see above n.48), part of the complex of the Holy Sepulcher opposite the Temple Mount.

65. Hesychius, *In hypapante* 1.8 (Aubineau, *Homélies*, 40).

66. Ps.-Chrysostom, *In occursu domini* (PG 50:807–8).

67. Jacob of Serugh, *Homiliae* 165 (*On the Presentation*) ll. 25–30; text in P. Bedjan, *Homiliae selectae Mar-Jacobi Sarugensis*, 5:448–49; translation in Thomas Kollamparampil, *Jacob of Serugh*, 142.

68. Pauline Allen, "The Sixth-Century Greek Homily: A Reassessment," in Mary B.

Cunningham and Pauline Allen, *Preacher and Audience*, 201–25 at 209; id., "Severus of Antioch and the Homily: The End of the Beginning?" in Pauline Allen and E. M. Jeffreys, *The Sixth Century—End or Beginning?*, 167–75, at 165; and Mary Cunningham, "The Sixth Century: A Turning Point for Byzantine Homiletics?" in Allen and Jeffreys, *Sixth Century*, 176–86, at 178–79.

69. See the essays in Cunningham and Allen, *Preacher and Audience*.

70. Fulgentius has not drawn a great deal of attention from contemporary scholarship: the fullest modern treatment remains G. G. Lapeyre, *Saint Fulgence de Ruspe*.

71. I discuss Amphilochius's biography more fully in my excursus below.

72. G. Morin, *Miscellanea agostiniana*, vol. 1: *Sancti Augustini sermones post mauritios reperti*, 747: "Auctoris est antiqui profecto, et Afri, nec prorsus ineruditi, qui contra sui temporis haereticos Arrianos, Donatistas quoque, praecipue vero Manichaeos disputat. Merito advertit Cailau quamdam similitudinem in esse huic sermoni cum alio, qui incipit *Temporalis secundum carnem filii dei*, quemque pariter ad Fulgentium fortasse pertinere suo loco observari."

73. It is possible that the homily (at least as it preserved) was originally delivered in a monastic context, as it is addressed to "brothers" (*fratres*). But this could be a biblicism or a scribal alteration.

74. Ps.-Fulgentius, *Sermo dubius II* 1 (CCL 91A:953).

75. Ps.-Fulgentius, *Sermo dubius II* 1 (CCL 91A:953).

76. Ps.-Fulgentius, *Sermo dubius II* 2 (CCL 91A:953).

77. Ps.-Fulgentius, *Sermo dubius II* 2 (CCL 91A:953). On Augustine and shame, see now Virginia Burrus, *Saving Shame*, 116–33. Augustine had specifically preached against the "pride" (*superbia*) of pagans in his tremendous New Year's sermon, discussed above: see Claude Lepelley, "L'aristocratie lettrée païenne: Une menace aux yeux d'Augustin (à propos du sermon Dolbeau 26–Mayence 62)," in Madec, *Augustin prédicateur*, 327–42.

78. Ps.-Fulgentius, *Sermo dubius II* 1 (CCL 91A:953).

79. Ps.-Fulgentius, *Sermo dubius II* 2 (CCL 91A:954).

80. Ps.-Fulgentius, *Sermo dubius II* 1 (CCL 91A:953).

81. Ps.-Fulgentius, *Sermo dubius II* 3 (CCL 91A:954).

82. Ps.-Fulgentius, *Sermo dubius II* 3 (CCL 91A:954).

83. Ps.-Fulgentius, *Sermo dubius II* 3 (CCL 91A:954).

84. Ps.-Fulgentius, *Sermo dubius II* 3 (CCL 91A:954).

85. Ps.-Fulgentius, *Sermo dubius II* 4 (CCL 91A:955).

86. It is, of course, never a question for these homilists but that Jesus—even in his infancy—acted with the due deliberation of the Godhead.

87. Ps.-Fulgentius, *Sermo dubius II* 4 (CCL 91A:955–56).

88. Ps.-Fulgentius, *Sermo dubius II* 4 (CCL 91A:955).

89. Daniel Boyarin, *Carnal Israel*, 1–10, at 10.

90. See also Averil Cameron, "Jewish and Heretics—A Category Error?" in Annette Yoshiko Reed and Adam H. Becker, *The Ways That Never Parted*, 345–60.

91. Ps.-Fulgentius, *Sermo dubius II* 5 (CCL 91A:956), emphasis added.

92. Ps.-Fulgentius, *Sermo dubius II* 5 (CCL 91A:956).

93. Ps.-Fulgentius, *Sermo dubius II* 6 (CCL 91A:956).

94. Ps.-Fulgentius, *Sermo dubius II* 6 (CCL 91A:956–57). The homilist also cites Jer 4:4 on "circumcising the foreskin of your heart," but interestingly says it is "legal speech" (*legalis sermo*) from Moses.

95. Ps.-Fulgentius, *Sermo dubius II* 6 (CCL 91A:957).

96. Elizabeth A. Clark, *Reading Renunciation*, 204–32; Clark discusses the ascetic ritualization of circumcision specifically on 225–30.

97. Ps.-Fulgentius, *Sermo dubius II* 6 (CCL 91A:957). The same interpretation for the dove and turtledove is offered by Ambrose, *De Abraham* 2.8.53 (PL 14:479).

98. Ps.-Fulgentius, *Sermo dubius II* 7 (CCL 91A:958).

99. The attraction to and fear of Judaism elicited by this festival perhaps accounts for its inclusion among feasts on which Jews are not permitted to work in Visigothic Spain: *Lex Visigothorum* 12.3.6 (text and translation from Amnon Linder, *The Jews in the Legal Sources of the Early Middle Ages*, 294–95). My thanks to Mark Handley who first posted this text to the LT-ANTIQ listserv (October 16, 1997).

100. For the later Latin period, see the brief but helpful survey of Eva Castro Caridad, "The Hispanic Texts *In Diem Circumcisionis Domini*," in Susana Zapke, *Hispania Vetus*, 127–39.

101. Caesarius's biographer, Cyprian of Toulon, records that Caesarius "delivered sermons (*praedicationes*) suitable for seasons and feast days" and that these sermons "suited to particular feast and passages" were collected by Caesarius and distributed to visitors and sent to other bishops in Gaul and Germany (*Vita Caesarii Primi* 15, 42 [PL 67:1008, 1021]).

102. Caesarius of Arles, *Sermo* 191.1 (CCL 104:778).

103. Caesarius of Arles, *Sermo* 191.2 (CCL 104:778).

104. The festival appears regularly in Latin lectionaries and sacramentaries in the West: see Yitzhak Hen, *Culture and Religion in Merovingian Gaul*, 62; Mario Righetti, *Manuale di storia liturgica*, vol. 2: *L'anno liturgico il brevario*, 73–81 on January 1's "strana compenetrazione di parecchie ricorrenze," including the circumcision. More recent discussion on the western festival can be found in the introductory matter to Els Rose, *Missale Gothicum*, 216–22.

105. See my discussion below.

106. I have consulted three versions of this homily. The first, a fourteenth-century MS (Paris, Bibliothèque Nationale, Ancien gr. 1551, 121–124v), was transcribed and published by François Combefis, *SS. Patrum Amphilochii Iconiensis, Methodii Patarensis, et Andreae Cretensis*. The second (Florence, Biblioteca Medicea-Laurenziana, Ms. gr. IV.4, 227–232) is an eleventh- or twelfth-century MS, which I have transcribed from microfilm; the third is a twelfth-century MS (Venice, Biblioteca Nazionale Marciana, Ms. gr. VII.25 [972], 142–146v.), also transcribed from microfilm. I shall refer to the text of the Florentine MS (by page, folio, column, and line number), as that seems to be the oldest, but I shall provide cross-references to the Combefis edition (by page number) since that is the only published copy available. Any significant differences between the two texts, or with the Venetian

manuscript, will be noted. Because the homily is difficult to acquire, I cite the Greek in full in the notes. More details on the manuscript tradition of BHG 261 can be found in the excursus below.

107. Ps.-Amphilochius, *In circumcisionem et Basilium* 228r1.20–24: ἀμελῶμεν λοιπὸν τῶν νομικῶν τύπων, καὶ τῶν σκιῶν; αὐτῆς δὲ τῆς τῶν πραγμάτων ἐκτυπωτερας ἐπιμελώμεθα μορφῆς (Combefis, *SS. Patrum*, 11).

108. Ps.-Amphilochius, *In circumcisionem et Basilium* 228r2.10: διὰ τοῦ πνευματικῶς τὸν αὐτοῦ νόμον καὶ ποιεῖν καὶ θεωρεῖν (Combefis, *SS. Patrum*, 12).

109. Ps.-Amphilochius, *In circumcisionem et Basilium* 228r2.2–5: μηδὲ ὡς νήπιοι λαλῶμεν ἢ φρονῶμεν, ἢ λογιζώμεθα· κατὰ τους νηπιόφρονας Ἰουδαίους ἢ ἄφρονας (Combefis, *SS. Patrum*, 12).

110. Ps.-Amphilochius, *In circumcisionem et Basilium* 228r2.13–19: εἰς τοῦτο θεὸς κύριος νηπιάσας ἐπέφανεν ἡμῖν· ἵνα τὸ νηπιῶδες καὶ ἀτελὲς τῆς ἡμετέρας διανοιας φρόνημα καὶ ἀνδροπρεπὲς μεταποιήσῃ (Combefis, *SS. Patrum*, 12).

111. Ps.-Amphilochius, *In circumcisionem et Basilium* 228r2.27–29: τῆς νομικῆς πάσης δουλείας, καὶ νηπιοπρεποῖς πολιτείας ἐλευθερώσας (Combefis, *SS. Patrum*, 12).

112. Ps.-Amphilochius, *In circumcisionem et Basilium* 228v1.19–228v2.4: ὡς ἀτελῆ λοιπὸν ταύτην, καὶ ἀνωφελῶς ἐνεργουμένην, κατήργησε καὶ κατεπαυσε· περιτεμνεται τοίνυν ὁ Ἰησοῦς, κατὰ τὸν αὐτου νόμον ὀκταήμερος, οὐχ ἵνα διδάξῃ περιτέμνεσθαι, ἀλλ᾽ ἵνα καταπαύσῃ περιτομήν· μᾶλλον δὲ, ἵνα τῆς παλαιᾶς μὲν καὶ ἀνωφελοῦς, ἐκτίλῃ τὴν πρόληψιν, τῆς νέας δὲ καὶ σωτηριώδους τὴν δύναμιν ἀποκαλύψῃ, ἵνα τὴν κατὰ σάρκα μὲν καταργήσῃ, τὴν κατὰ πνεῦμα δὲ ἀναθηλήσῃ· καὶ τῆς μὲν, τὸ ἀδρανὲς ἐλέγξῃ· τῆς δὲ, παραδείξῃ τὸ ἰσχυρόν, περιτέμνεται ὁ Χριστός (Combefis, *SS. Patrum*, 13).

113. Ps.-Amphilochius, *In circumcisionem et Basilium* 228v2.4–10: οὐ γὰρ ἦλθε καταλῦσαι τὸν νόμον ὡς ἀλλότριον· ἀλλ᾽ ὡς οἰκεῖον καὶ παρ᾽ ἑαυτοῦ συντεταγμένον, ἔργῳ τοῦτον ἦλθε πληρώσων, ὡς ἴδιον δόγμα καὶ θεοῦ ἐντολήν (Combefis, *SS. Patrum*, 13).

114. Ps.-Amphilochius, *In circumcisionem et Basilium* 228v1.16–18: εἶτα τὴν κρείττων περιτομὴν ἀναδείξας τὴν ἐν τῷ βαπτίσματι (Combefis, *SS. Patrum*, 13).

115. Thomas Finn, *From Death to Rebirth*, 196–97; and Maxwell Johnson, "The Apostolic Tradition," in Wainwright and Westerfield Tucker, *Oxford History of Christian Worship*, 32–76, at 40.

116. Ps.-Amphilochius, *In circumcisionem et Basilium* 228v2.22–229r1.2: καὶ γὰρ ἡ κατὰ σάρκα περιτομὴ, οὐ τὴν τῶν ἁμαρτιῶν μόνον ἀπόθεσιν σκιαγραφεῖ, καὶ τὴν ἐν τῷ βαπτίσματι τοῦ Χριστοῦ περιτομὴν, ἀλλὰ δὴ καὶ αὐτὴ ἠρέμα καὶ ὡς ἐν σκιαῖς διαγράφει τοῦ παντὸς ἐξανάστασιν καὶ ἀλλοίωσιν, καθ᾽ ἣν πᾶν τὸ σάρκινον τῶν ἀνθρώπων φρόνημα περιτέμνεται καὶ ἐκκόπτεται, καὶ πρὸς ἑτέραν μεταστοιχειοῦται ζωήν (Combefis, *SS. Patrum*, 13–14). Combefis reads "restitution" or "reckoning" of sins (ἀπόδοσις) for "remission" (ἀπόθεσις), which both the Florentine and Venetian MSS have.

117. Ps.-Amphilochius, *In circumcisionem et Basilium* 229ΓΙ.2–7: ταύτης οἷον τις ἀμυδρὰ καὶ σκιώδης προτύπωσις, ἡ κατὰ σάρκα περιτομή. διὸ καὶ ὀκταήμερος πρῶτον νενομοθέτεται (Combefis, *SS. Patrum*, 14).

118. Ps.-Amphilochius, *In circumcisionem et Basilium* 229ΓΙ.7–9: τὸν ὄγδοον . . . αἰῶνα καὶ μέλλοντα (Combefis, *SS. Patrum*, 14).

119. Ps.-Amphilochius, *In circumcisionem et Basilium* 229Γ2.2–10: ἔδει, τοῦ ἡλίου ἀνίσχοντος, σελήνην καὶ τοὺς ἀστέρας ἀμυδροῦσθαι καὶ μειοῦσθαι, καὶ τῆς ἀληθινῆς παραγυμνουμένης περιτομῆς καὶ λατρείας, τὰ σκιώδη τῆς ἀληθείας ἰνδάλματα, καὶ τοὺς τύπους ὑποχωρεῖν (Combefis, *SS. Patrum*, 14). "Moon and stars" likely alludes to the Jewish festival calendar (cf. Gen 1:14).

120. Ps.-Amphilochius, *In circumcisionem et Basilium* 229ΓΙ.20–21: τῆς ἐν σαρκὶ περιτομῆς καὶ τῶν ζωοθυσιῶν (Combefis, *SS. Patrum*, 14).

121. Ps.-Amphilochius, *In circumcisionem et Basilium* 229Γ2.10–14: διὰ τὸ τοιγαροῦν ὁ θεὸς λόγος σὰρξ γενόμενος πρότερον, σήμερον ὀκταήμερος τὸ σωμάτιον περιτέτμηται (Combefis, *SS. Patrum*, 14–15).

122. Ps.-Amphilochius, *In circumcisionem et Basilium* 229v2.6–10: τῆς καθολικῆς ἐκκλησίας πυρσός· ὁ περιφανὴς τοῦ εὐαγγελίου τῆς ἀληθείας ἥλιος, ὁ πᾶσαν ταῖς τῆς αὐτοῦ θεολογίας ἀκτῖσι καταπυρσεύων τὴν γῆν (Combefis, *SS. Patrum*, 16).

123. Ps.-Amphilochius, *In circumcisionem et Basilium* 230Γ2.2–7: οὗτος, τὴν ἐν πνεύματι καὶ τῷ θείῳ βαπτίσματι τὴν μεγαλοφυῶς ἀνακηρύξας περιτομήν, σφόδρα περιφανῶς εἴπερ ἄλλος τις τῶν θεοσόφων, τὴν ἐν σαρκὶ καταπέπαυκεν περιτομήν (Combefis, *SS. Patrum*, 17).

124. Ps.-Amphilochius, *In circumcisionem et Basilium* 230Γ2.8–230vΙ.12: διὸ καὶ ἡ τοῦ τοῦ πρὸς τὸν θεὸν ἀπὸ τῆς γῆς, καὶ τοῦ σώματος λύσις καὶ μετανάστασις, οὐ μάτην οὐδὲ συντυχικῶς ὡς ἄν τις ἀλόγως ὑπονοῆσαι μεταξὺ τῆς θείας Χριστοῦ γενέσεως καὶ τῆς βαπτίσεως, τῇ τοῦ Ἰησοῦ σήμερον συνεδεδραμή– κει περιτομῇ· ἀλλ᾽ ὡς ἐν τῇ ἀναρρήσει καὶ ὑψώσις τῆς Χριστοῦ γενέσεως καὶ βαπτίσεως τὴν ἐν πνεύματι περιτομὴν ὁ μακαριώτατος ἀνυψωκώς, ἐν τῷ ἱερῷ μνημοσύνῳ ταύτης, καὶ αὐτὸς συνυψωθῆσαι τῇ ἀναλύσει τῇ πρὸς τὸν Χριστὸν κατηξίωται. καὶ ἐτησίοις κατὰ ταύτην τὴν ἡμέραν κέκριται τιμᾶσθαι μνημοσύ– ναις καὶ πανηγύρεσι· διὸ τὸ παναγιώτατον αὐτοῦ καὶ ἱερὸν μνημόσυνον, σή– μερον ἡ καθόλου τῶν ὅλων ἁγίων ἐκκλησία κατὰ πᾶν μέρος τῆς οἰκουμένης ἐπιτελοῦσα καὶ δοξάζουσα, θεοπρεπεστάταις αἰνέσεσι τὸν τοῖς ἁγίοις αὐτοῦ ἐνδοξαζόμενον, συνυμνωδεῖ καὶ συνδοξάζει Χριστόν· ὡς δι᾽ αὐτοῦ πάσης μὲν αἱρέσεως ἀπαλλαγεῖσαι· πάσης δὲ εὐσεβείας δόγμασι βεβαιωθεῖσα· καὶ ὡς παντὸς μὲν ἀλλοτριόφρονος ἑτεροδιδασκαλίας ἀλλοτριωθεῖσα, μόνῃ δὲ τῇ δεσποτικῇ προσοικειωθεῖσα πίστει καὶ διδαχῇ (Combefis, *SS. Patrum*, 17–18).

125. Ps.-Amphilochius, *In circumcisionem et Basilium* 231ΓΙ.23–24: καὶ νόμων οὐρανίων καὶ θεοτελῶν (Combefis, *SS. Patrum*, 20).

126. For memory and liturgy in hagiography, see Derek Krueger, *Writing and Holiness*, 116–32.

127. Elizabeth Castelli, *Martyrdom and Memory*, 4.

128. Ps.-Amphilochius, *In circumcisionem et Basilium* 231r2.31–231v1.6: τιμήσωμεν δέ πως; περιτμηθῶμεν· μὴ τὴν σάρκα τῆς ἀκροβυστίας ἡμῶν, ὡς ἐκεῖνος ὁ παλαιὸς Ἰσραὴλ, ἀλλὰ τὸν ἐντὸς ἄνθρωπον τῆς καρδίας περιτέμνωμεν· πάντα τὰ κρύφια τῆς ψυχῆς πάθη καὶ τοῦ νοὺς περιαιροῦντες, ἢ νεκροῦντες (Combefis, *SS. Patrum*, 21).

129. Ps.-Amphilochius, *In circumcisionem et Basilium* 231v1.19–25: ἐῶμεν τοίνυν τὴν κατὰ σάρκα περιτομήν· ἀναστῶμεν ἐπὶ τὸ βάπτισμα· τὴν σκιὰν παραδρα-μωμεν· τῇ ἀληθεια προσδράμωμοεν· τὸν Μωσῆν ὑπερίδωμεν· πρὸς τὸν Ἰωά νυην ἐξέλθωμεν (Combefis, *SS. Patrum*, 21), emphasis added. Combefis lacks the phrase "run from Moses."

130. Ps.-Amphilochius, *In circumcisionem et Basilium* 231v1.7–12: συννεκρούμενοι προθύμος Χριστῷ, καὶ συσταουρούμενοι καὶ συνθαπτόμενοι ἐν τῇ ἀπεκδύσει τοῦ σώματος τῶν ἁμαρτιῶν τῆς σαρκὸς (Combefis, *SS. Patrum*, 21). On this variant of Col 2:12, see my discussion in Chapter 5.

131. Ps.-Amphilochius, *In circumcisionem et Basilium* 231v2.6–13: νῦν Ἰησοῦς μετὰ τὸ περιτμηθῆναι σαρκὶ κατὰ τὸν νόμον ὀκταήμερος, ἔρχεται πρὸς Ἰωάννην τριακονταετὴς, βαπτισθῆναι τῷ ὕδατι· ἵνα τὴν νηπιώδη τοῦ γράμματος κατ-απαύσας περιτομὴν, τὴν ἐν πνεύματι τελειότατην νομοθετήσῃ (Combefis, *SS. Pa-trum*, 21–22).

132. For a lucid short biography of Sophronius, see Pauline Allen, *Sophronius of Je-rusalem and Seventh-Century Heresy*, 15–23. Sophronius surrendered Jerusalem to the Arab Muslim armies in 638, and died the next year.

133. I am tremendously grateful to John Duffy for sharing the manuscript of his paper, "New Fragments of Sophronius of Jerusalem and Aristo of Pella?" (delivered at the 2007 Oxford International Conference on Patristic Studies), which contains the full Greek text of the sermon fragment. The description of the contents of the manuscript (Sinaiticus grae-cus 1807) is Duffy's; the fragment from Sophronius's homily on the circumcision appears at folio pages 6r–7v. This sermon will be included in Professor Duffy's new critical edition of Sophronius's sermons, presently being completed for the Corpus Christianorum Greek series. I am especially grateful to Susan Holman, who heard the original paper delivered and led me to contact Professor Duffy.

134. All of this is carefully examined in Duffy's paper.

135. On the Islamic connotations of circumcision among early Byzantine Christians, see David Olster, *Roman Defeat, Christian Response, and the Literary Construction of the Jew*, 124.

136. Andrew of Crete, *In circumcisionem et Basilium* mentions "heathens" (ἔθνων) and "Hagarites" (ἀγαρηνῶν) (PG 97:932).

137. But see Andrew of Crete, *In circumcisionem et Basilium* (PG 97:921–23).

138. Andrew of Crete, *In circumcisionem et Basilium* (PG 97:913).

139. The "eight lawgivers" are Adam, Noah, Abraham, Moses, David, Ezra, John the Baptist, and Christ: Andrew of Crete, *In circumcisionem et Basilium* (PG 97:921).

140. Andrew refers to the harmonization of angelic pronouncements to Mary (Luke 1:31–32) and to Joseph (Matt 1:18–21) (PG 97:917)

141. Andrew of Crete, *In circumcisionem et Basilium* (PG 97:917).

142. Andrew of Crete, *In circumcisionem et Basilium* (PG 97:923).

143. See Shaye J. D. Cohen, *Why Aren't Jewish Women Circumcised?* 34 and 40–41.

144. Elliot Wolfson, "Circumcision and the Divine Name: A Study in the Transmission of Esoteric Doctrine," *Jewish Quarterly Review* 78 (1987): 77–112.

145. Elliot Wolfson, "Circumcision, Vision of God, and Textual Interpretation: From Midrashic Trope to Mystical Symbol," *History of Religions* 27 (1987): 189–215, at 191.

146. Derrida, *Archive Fever*, 12. On circumcision, marking, and publication see also Kathleen Biddick, *The Typological Imaginary*.

147. John Caputo, *The Prayers and Tears of Jacques Derrida*, 250.

148. Catherine Bell, *Ritual Theory, Ritual Practice*, 108.

149. Robert E. Sinkewicz, *Manuscript Listings for the Authors of the Patristic and Byzantine Periods.*

150. See the magisterial study of Albert Ehrhard, *Überlieferung und Bestand der hagiographischen und homiletischen Literatur der griechischen Kirche von den Anfängen bis zum Ende des 16. Jahrhunderts.* Much work on these homiletical and hagiographic collections was done by the Bollandist Hippolyte Delehaye: see, for instance, his overview essay, "Les ménologes grecs," *Analecta Bollandiana* 16 (1897): 311–29; and the several essays collected in *Synaxaires byzantines, ménologes, typica.*

151. This homily (recognizable by its incipit, Σκιὰν μὲν τῶν μελλόντων ἀγαθῶν) is also indicated in the table of liturgical readings for the eleventh- or twelfth-century *typikon* of the Constantinopolitan monastery of the Mother of God Evergetis: Ehrhard, *Überlieferung*, 1:42–45, at 44. There it follows the *miraculi Basilii* of Amphilochius (see below), and is listed without author. The typikon also instructs the community to read the encomium of Gregory of Nazianzus with this homily (if January 1 falls on a Sunday) or on the following Sunday (if it falls on a weekday).

152. Although it is not part of contemporary Greek Orthodox liturgical readings, the homily *In circumcisionem* seems to have been incorporated into modern Russian menologia after its publication by Combefis. It was not included in the Great Menology of Archbishop Makarii (sixteenth century, expanded in the eighteenth century by Dmitrii of Rostov), but fragments were included in menological guides published in the 1970s in Moscow. My thanks to Eugene Clay (Arizona State University) for his help in tracking down the Russian sources.

153. Florence, Biblioteca Medicea-Laurenziana, Ms. gr. IV.4, 227v–232; Venice, Biblioteca Nazionale Marciana, Ms. gr. VII.25 [972], 142–146v.

154. See n.106. The very few differences between Combefis's transcription and the Italian MSS give me no reason to doubt Combefis's accuracy. Ehrhard gives descriptions and contents of these three MSS: Cod. laur. Plut. 4.4 (Florence), a half-year menologion (September–March), Ehrhard, *Überlieferung*, 2:93–95; Cod. marc. 7.25 [972] (Venice), a three-month (December–February) menologion, Erhard, *Überlieferung*, 3:501–4; and the

MS published by Combefis, Cod. ancien grec 1551, a full-year menologion, Ehrhard, *Über-lieferung*, 3:222–23. On the dating of the Florentine homily to the twelfth century instead of the eleventh, see François Halkin, "Les manuscrits grecs de la Bibliothèque Laurentienne à Florence: Inventaire hagiographique," *Analecta Bollandiana* 96 (1978): 5–50, at 7–8). On the Paris MS, see further J. Darrouzès, "Manuscrits originaires de Chypre à la Bibliothèque Nationale de Paris," *Revue des Études Byzantines* 8 (1950): 162–96, at 189.

155. According to Sinkewicz, *Manuscript Listings*, a sixteenth-century MS presently in Greece attributes the homily to John Chrysostom.

156. The most complete biography of Amphilochius remains Karl Holl, *Amphilochius von Ikonium in seinem Verhältnis zu den grossen Kappadoziern*; on his life and works, see 1–83.

157. Ps.-Amphilochius, *In circumcisionem et Basilium* 230r1.6–7: οὗτος ὁ ὑψηλὸς καὶ ὑπερφερὴς τῆς ἐκκλησίας τοῦ θεοῦ στύλος (Combefis, *SS. Patrum*, 17).

158. Amphilochius, *Contra haereticos* 23 (CCG 3:208); see my discussion in Chapter 3. Amphilochius also (briefly) makes reference to Christ's circumcision in *Homilia 2 6* (CCG 3:52) in which, again, the polemical thrust of the text is to defend "fleshliness" (here motherhood and widowhood) against overly exuberant asceticism.

159. Timothy Barnes (who first pointed this text out to me at Oxford in 2003) cited this homily as evidence for the date of Basil's death (on January 1): "The Collapse of the Homoeans in the East," *Studia Patristica* 29 (1997): 6–13. On the dating of Basil's death, see below. Other scholars, even when acknowledging a relatively early institution of January 1 commemorations of Basil (see below), draw a distinction between a martyr's feast day—held on the date of the martyr's death—and a festival of commemoration: see, for instance, Élie D. Moutsoulas, "Le problème de la date de la mort de Basile de Césarée," *Studia Patristica* 33 (1997): 196–200, and sources cited there. In response to Barnes, see Pierre Maraval, "Retour sur quelques dates concernant Basile de Césarée et Grégoire de Nysse," *Revue d'Histoire Ecclésiastique* 99 (2004): 153–57.

160. Already the editors of the Patrologia Graeca, in compiling the prolegomena to the works of Basil, dismissed the homily *in circumcisionem* (along with the *vita*, on which more below) as spurious: PG 29:ccxcvn.1 ("hoc exordium Amphilochio inepte affictum"). On Amphilochius's works in general, see the entries (3230–54) in Maurice Geerard, *Clavis Patrum Graecorum*, 2:230–42; and C. Datema, *Amphilochii Iocniensis Opera*, ix–xxx (Amphilochius of Iconium).

161. Ps.-Amphilochius, *In circumcisionem et Basilium* 231r2.11–14: ταῦτα πάντα τοῖς ἱεροῖς τοῦ θείου Γρηγορίου λόγοις, ἀποχρόντως οἶμαι πεφιλοσοφῆσθαι καὶ ὑμνῆσθαι (Combefis, *SS. Patrum*, 20). For τοῖς ἱεροῖς τοῦ θείου Γρηγορίου λόγοις Cod. marc. 7.25 [972] has simply τοῖς ἱεροῖς θεολόγοις, perhaps acknowledging awareness of more than one encomium on Basil.

162. Ps.-Amphilochius, *In circumcision et Basilium* 231r2.16–18: ἡμεῖς δὲ δοξάσωμεν τὸ τοῦ θεοφόρου πατρὸς μνημόσυνον σήμερον (Combefis, *SS. Patrum*, 20).

163. Ps.-Amphilochius, *In circumcisionem et Basilium* 230v2.13–24: οὗτος ὁ ὑψηλὸς Βασίλειος, οὗ τῆς Καισαρέων ἐκκλησίας μόνον, ἧς καὶ ἐπίσκοπος ἀνηγόρευτο·

οὐδὲ τῷ κατ' αὐτὸν χρόνῳ μόνον· καὶ τῇ κατ' αὐτὸν γενεᾷ, ἀλλὰ καὶ πάσαις τῆς οἰκουμένης χώραις καὶ πόλεσι, καὶ ὅλῳ δὲ τῷ νῦν αἰῶνι, πᾶσιν ἀνθρώποις (deest Cod. marc. 7.25) ὠφέλιμος, καὶ σωτηριωδέστατος Χριστιανοῖς διδάσκαλος ἀποδείκνυται (Combefis, *SS. Patrum*, 19).

164. The homilist earlier refers to Basil as "great in his own time" (τὸν μέγαν Βασι—λειον, κατὰ τὸν αὐτοῦ καιρὸν): Ps.-Amphilochius, *In circumcisionem et Basilium* 229vi.17–19 (Combefis, *SS. Patrum*, 15).

165. Ps.-Amphilochius, *In circumcisionem et Basilium* 230vi.12–26 (Combefis, *SS. Patrum*, 18).

166. On Basil and Eunomius, see Philip Rousseau, *Basil of Caesarea*, 100–132. On Basil's more complicated relationship with Apollinarius: Rousseau, *Basil*, 245–54 and 313–15; G. L. Prestige, "Apollinaris; or, Divine Irruption" in id., *Fathers and Heretics*, 195–246; and id., *St. Basil the Great and Apollinaris of Laodicea*. Macedonius, sometime bishop of Constantinople until 360, was dead by the time Basil wrote his treatise *De spiritu sancto* and it is unclear what relationship the so-called *pneumatomachoi* actually had with the former patriarch. The link with Macedonius seems to emerge at the end of the fourth century, around the time of the Council of Constantinople.

167. Karl Joseph von Hefele and H. Leclerq, *Histoire des conciles d'après les documents originaux*, 2.1:10–21, which retains the variant "semi-Arians" for "Macedonians." On these variants, see Peter L'Huillier, *The Church of the Ancient Councils*, 111–15. It seems that this slightly variable list of "defeated" Trinitarian heresies coalesced in the wake of the council, as evident from various Theodosian and post-Theodosian antiheresy laws: see, for instance, *Codex Theodosianus* 16.5.11 (383), 16.5.12 (383), and 16.5.13 (384) (SC 497:248–52).

168. Ps.-Amphilochius, *In circumcisionem et Basilium* 230v2.3–9: καὶ ὅσας δὲ μετὰ τὴν αὐτοῦ πρὸς τὸν θεὸν ἐκδημίαν ὁ χρόνος ἔμελλεν ἐκφάναι, πᾶσαι τῷ τῆς θε—ολογίας Βασιλείου τοῦ θείου πυρὶ παρατιθέμεναι, ἐμπιπρανταί τε καὶ καταναλί—σκονται (Combefis, *SS. Patrum*, 19).

169. This draws a contrast with the heresiological uses of the Ps.-Fulgentius homily, which makes specific arguments against Manicheans through interpretation of the divine circumcision.

170. We might also consider Amphilochius's role in promoting festivals commemorating events from Christ's life, such as the Nativity: Dunlop, "Patristic Orations," 112–32 and 202–10, adduces one of Amphilochius's homilies as early evidence for a December 25 commemoration of the Nativity. Datema, *Amphilochii*, xii, thinks the homily comes from late in Amphilochius's episcopal career since it describes the festival as *pansebasmios*; see also J. H. Barkhuizen, "Amphilochius of Iconium: Homily 1 'On the Nativity,'" *Acta Patristica et Byzantina* 12 (2001): 1–23, for translation and brief commentary on this homily. Likewise, Amphilochius's *Homilia 2* has historically been read as very early evidence for the hypapante in Cappadocia, as by Holl, *Amphilochius*, 104–5. Datema, *Amphilochii*, xiii–xiv, interprets this as an exegetical homily on Luke 2 (along the same lines as the Proclus homily discussed in Chapter 5) that was later adapted as a festival sermon.

171. Apart from some Greek fragments, the only full copy survives in a Syriac

translation. Sometimes cited by scholars as evidence for Basil's life (as by Susan Holman, *The Hungry Are Dying*, 4, 29, 127), this encomium is generally considered spurious (see Geerard, *Clavis Patrum Graecorum* 3252 [2:241]). The Syriac text was published by K. von Zettersteen as "Ein Homilie des Amphilochius von Ikonium über Basilius von Caesarea," in Gustav Weill, *Festschrift Eduard Sachau*, 223–47; and translated into German by von Zettersteen under the same title in *Oriens Christianus* 31 (1934): 67–98.

172. The Greek text of the *vita* was published by Combefis in the same volume as the homily on the circumcision; a list of available Greek manuscripts and a full English translation of the *vita* can be found in Charles L. Harrell, "Saint Basil the Great as Icon," 163–71 and 175–225. John Wortley, "The Pseudo-Amphilochian *Vita Basilii*: An Apocryphal *Life* of Saint Basil the Great," *Florilegium* 2 (1980): 217–39, attempts to discern a plausible circumstance for the vita's composition. Harrell and Wortley both view the vita as the work of a creative editor compiling earlier traditions. See also Alexei Muraviev, "The Syriac Julian Romance as a Source of the Life of St. Basil the Great," *Studia Patristica* 38 (2001): 240–49.

173. On this meeting—which may figure in the traditions of Basil's festival below—see David G. K. Taylor, "St. Ephraim's Influence on the Greeks," *Hugoye* 1.2 (1998); Sidney H. Griffith, "A Spiritual Father for the Whole World: The Universal Appeal of St. Ephraem the Syrian," *Hugoye* 1.2 (1998); Sebastian Brock, "St. Ephrem in the Eyes of Later Syriac Liturgical Tradition," *Hugoye* 2.1 (1999); and O. Rousseau, "La rencontre de saint Ephrem et de saint Basile," *L'Orient Syrien* 2 (1957): 261–84, 3 (1958): 73–90. The tradition that Basil and Ephrem met appears already in the early sixth century in Severus of Antioch's *Contra impium grammaticum* (see the chronological table at the end of Brock, "St. Ephrem").

174. On Amphilochius's authentic homiletic style (which draws much more heavily on explicit biblical typologies), see J. H. Barkhuizen, "Homily 3 of Amphilochius of Iconium: 'On the Four-day [Dead] Lazarus,' An Essay in Interpretation," *Acta Patristica et Byzantina* 5 (1994): 1–9; id., "Amphilochius of Iconium"; and id., "Imagery in the (Greek) Homilies of Amphilochius of Iconium," *Acta Patristica et Byzantina* 13 (2002): 1–33.

175. Explicit citations of Scripture: Heb 10:1 (227v1.29–30 [Combefis, *SS. Patrum*, 10]); 1 Cor 13:8–10 (228r1.4–12 [Combefis, *SS. Patrum*, 11]); Phil 3:13 (228r1.25–30 [Combefis, *SS. Patrum*, 11]), joined directly to Eph 4:14, 13 (228r1.31–228r2.8 [Combefis, *SS. Patrum*, 12]). The homilist later alludes to Matthew, Isaiah, Hebrews, and 1 Kings.

176. As Georgia Frank has noted, late antique eastern Christian writing (particularly hagiography and liturgy) becomes permeated with imagery of shadow, image, and representation in the fourth through sixth centuries: "The Image in Tandem: Painting Metaphors and Moral Discourse in Late Antique Christianity," in Richard Valantasis, Deborah J. Hanynes, and James D. Smith III, *The Subjective Eye*, 33–47.

177. It is noteworthy that Basil is often compared positively to Moses as "lawgiver": Harrell, "Saint Basil the Great," 51–127, points out that both Gregory of Nazianzus and Gregory of Nyssa discuss Basil as "lawgiver" (65–68, 109–10); to these we may add Severus of Antioch, *Homilia 102* (PO 22.2:274–88). Andrea Sterk, "On Basil, Moses, and the Model Bishop: The Cappadocian Legacy of Leadership," *Church History* 67 (1998): 227–53, also draws out the Mosaic comparisons in the Gregories' depictions of Basil.

178. Ps.-Amphilochius, *In circumcisionem et Basilium* 230v2.24–31 (Combefis, *SS. Patrum*, 19).

179. Ps.-Amphilochius, *In circumcisionem et Basilium* 230v2.32–231r1.21 (Combefis, *SS. Patrum*, 19–20), at 231r1.16–18: καὶ βασιλεῦσι μὲν ἀσεβοῦσιν ἀνταγωνιζόμενος, ὑπάρχοις δὲ παρανομοῦσι συμπλεκόμενος.

180. θεαρχικώτατον: 229v1.24 (Combefis, *SS. Patrum*, 16); θεαρχία: 230r1.6 (Combefis, *SS. Patrum*, 17); ἱερογνωσία: 230r1.3 (Combefis, *SS. Patrum*, 16); ἀληθογ‐νωσίαν: 229v2.34 (Combefis, *SS. Patrum*, 16). The use of *tupos* language (ἀρχέτυπον, διατυποῦσιν, πρωτότυπον, ἐκτυπωτέρας: 227v1.32; 227v2.3, 7, 11, 15; 228r1.15, 23 [Combefis, *SS. Patrum*, 10–11]) also has a ring of Ps.-Dionysius, but is common in other late ancient authors (Christian and non-Christian) influenced by Platonism. One rare word in this homily, which the *Thesaurus Linguae Graecae* reports only in Photius and the late epitome of the *Acts of Philip* (found, coincidentally enough, in the same Paris MS from which Combefis published his version of the homily *in circumcisionem*), is θεορημοσύνη which, according to Photius's *Lexicon*, means "divine teaching or catechesis."

181. Apart from the many forms of σκιά, we find: σκιοειδῶς, σκιογραφία (Ps.-Amphilochius, *In circumcisionem et Basilium* 227v2.2, 6; Combefis, *SS. Patrum*, 11); σκιοεδῶν, σκιαγραφεῖ (228v2.23, 26; Combefis, *SS. Patrum*, 12); σκιώδη, σκιώδης (229r1.3–4, 229r2.8; Combefis, *SS. Patrum*, 14), all of which become common mainly in fourth-century Christian Greek.

182. Sophronius of Jerusalem's homily, if authentic as John Duffy persuasively argues, exists only in fragments and, so far as we know, does not mention Basil.

183. Cunningham, "Sixth Century," describes the (seeming) decline of homiletic production in the sixth century and its rise in the "long" eighth century (ca. 650–850); although there are (as she points out) exceptions, these later homilies are often characterized by rhythmic, almost poetic prose (180); much longer duration (183); a self-consciously "high-style" use of rhetorical figures (183); and a general "elevation to a higher literary style and more rigid structure after the end of the seventh century" due to a "deliberate rising of standards in preaching" (184). While Andrew's homily shares all of these characteristics, the Ps.-Amphilochius homily does not.

184. Andrew of Crete, *In circumcisionem et Basilium* (PG 97:918–22).

185. Andrew of Crete, *In circumcisionem et Basilium* (PG 97:924): καὶ οἱ μὲν, τῶν ἄλλων ἐγγύτεροι . . . Βασίλειός ἐστιν.

186. Andrew of Crete, *In circumcisionem et Basilium* (PG 97:928). Harrell's dissertation, "Saint Basil," compares the two Gregories' encomia in detail. The texts: Gregory of Nazianzus, *Oratio* 43 (PG 36:493–605); and Gregory of Nyssa, *In laudem fratris Basilii* (PG 46:788–817).

187. The text is found in Sylvio G. Mercati, *S. Ephraem Syri Opera*, 1.1:143–78 (Ps.-Ephrem). On the hagiographic relationship between Basil and Ephrem, see above.

188. There is also a much higher level of linguistic sophistication, as well: see Mary Cunningham, "Andrew of Crete: A High-Style Preacher of the Eighth Century," in Cunningham and Allen, *Preacher and Audience*, 267–94.

189. Andrew of Crete, *In circumcisionem et Basilium* (PG 97:929).

190. It is striking, for instance, that a later homilist would not use the term *Theotokos*—or refer to Mary at all—in a homily on the infant Jesus.

191. Several homilies commemorating Basil with Gregory of Nazianzus survive in Syriac translations. Severus explicitly mentions the date of the festival of these saints as the "first day of the first month . . . *januarius*": Severus of Antioch, *Homilia* 84 (PO 23.1:8–9); cf. *Homilia* 116 (PO 26.3:327), where Severus analogizes the New Year's festival of the Old Testament with the "beginning of the year" on which Basil and Gregory are commemorated. Susan Holman has also pointed out to me (private communication) Gregory of Nyssa's encomium on his brother in which he refers to several festival days in a row beginning with the Nativity (τῆς ἐκ Παρθένου γεννήσεως) followed by five saints (Stephen, Peter, James, John, and Paul), culminating in the commemoration of Basil, which would then fall on December 31/January 1 (Gregory of Nyssa, *In laudem fratris Basilii* 1 [PG 46:789A–B]). On this point, see also Margaret M. Hasluck, "The Basil-Cake of the Greek New Year," *Folklore* 38 (1927): 143–77, at 151; citing the earlier works of Martin Rade, *Damasus*, 114–15n.1; and J. Schäfer, *Basilius des Grossen Beziehungen zum Abendlande*, 30 (*non vidi*). Sterk, "On Basil," 231, assumes Gregory delivered his homily on January 1, 381, "an anniversary of Basil's death," and further speculates that the "text suggests that there was already a cult of Basil at an early date and that Gregory wished to honor his brother with a new feast day in the liturgical calendar" (231n.14).

192. See my discussion in Chapter 3.

193. *Georgian Lectionary*; Michel Tarchnishvili, *Le Grand Lectionnaire de l'église de Jérusalem (Ve–VIIIe siècle)*, secs. 65–73 (CSCO 188:12–14 [Georgian]; CSCO 189:17–18 [Latin]).

194. See the various calendars compiled by F. Nau (*Syriac Menologies*): PO 10.1:31, 36–37, 49, 53–54 (these oldest Jacobite menologies only mark the feast of Basil); 69, 94, 98, 103, 109, 117, 128 (these later calendars commemorate both Basil and the circumcision).

CONCLUSION

1. Susannah Heschel, "Jesus as a Theological Transvestite," in Miriam Peskowitz and Laura Levitt, *Judaism Since Gender*, 188–212, at 188.

2. Heschel, "Jesus as a Theological Transvestite," 191.

3. Heschel, "Jesus as a Theological Transvestite," 194. Heschel cites Marjorie Garber, *Vested Interests*, who defines "category crisis" as "a failure of definitional distinction, a borderline that becomes permeable, that permits of border crossing from one (apparently distinct) category to another: black/white, Jew/Christian, noble/bourgeois, master/servant, master/slave" (Garber, *Vested Interests*, 16); see also Judith Butler, *Gender Trouble*.

4. Heschel, "Jesus as a Theological Transvestite," 198.

5. As a literary phenomenon, "passing" appears in the 1853 novel by William Wells Brown (a former slave) entitled *Clotel; or, The President's Daughter* (about a slave daughter of Thomas Jefferson) and other midcentury fiction (as well as ambiguous memoirs).

Sometimes "the pass" is central to the plot, sometimes one of many complicating factors, as the passing of Eliza as a white man in *Uncle Tom's Cabin* (see Julia Stern, "Spanish Masquerade and the Drama of Racial Identity in *Uncle Tom's Cabin*," in Elaine K. Ginsberg, *Passing and the Fiction of Identity*, 103–30). Most recent studies of passing in novels focus on the twentieth century, especially Nella Larsen's 1929 novel *Passing*: see Catherine Rottenberg, "*Passing*: Race, Identification, and Desire," *Criticism* 45 (2003): 435–52.

6. One famous account of "passing" was of a white man as black: John Howard Griffin, *Black Like Me*; see Gayle Wald, "'A Most Disagreeable Mirror': Reflections on White Identity in *Black Like Me*," in Ginsberg, *Passing*, 151–77. Martha A. Sandweiss, *Passing Strange*, has recently argued that Clarence King, the nineteenth-century geologist and first head of the United States Geological Survey, passed as black in his clandestine common-law marriage to former slave Ada Copeland.

7. Elaine K. Ginsberg, "Introduction: The Politics of Passing," in Ginsberg, *Passing*, 1–18: "By extension, 'passing' has been applied discursively to disguises of other elements of an individual's presumed 'natural' or 'essential' identity, including class, ethnicity, and sexuality, as well as gender, the latter usually effected by deliberate alterations of physical appearance and behavior, including cross-dressing" (3). See also Valerie Rohy, "Displacing Desire: Passing, Nostalgia, and *Giovanni's Room*," in the same volume (218–33), who discusses passing on the "axis of sexuality."

8. One of many felicitous phrases from Amy Robinson, "It Takes One to Know One: Passing and Communities of Common Interest," *Critical Inquiry* 20 (1994): 715–36, at 719.

9. Robinson, "Takes One," 720.

10. Adrian Piper, "Passing for White, Passing for Black," *Transition* 58 (1992): 4–32; this essay has been reprinted multiple times, including in Piper's own collected works: *Out of Order, Out of Sight*, 1:275–307.

11. Ginsberg, "Introduction," 4 (emphasis in the original).

12. Rohy, "Displacing Desire," 226.

13. It is worth noting recent, postmodern attempts to appropriate the concept of "passing" as a positive mode of performativity that works to undermine all essentialism: see, for instance, Pamela L. Caughie, *Passing and Pedagogy*.

14. Marion Rust, "The Subaltern as Imperialist: Speaking of Olaudah Equiano," in Ginsberg, *Passing*, 21–36, at 35.

15. Samira Kawash, "*The Autobiography of an Ex-Coloured Man*: (Passing for) Black Passing for White," in Ginsberg, *Passing*, 59–74, at 65.

16. Rohy, "Displacing Desire," 219.

17. See G. Guy Stroumsa, "Christ's Laughter: Docetic Origins Reconsidered," *Journal of Early Christian Studies* 12 (2004): 267–88, who rightly points out that "in modern scholarly usage 'Docetism' does not refer to any clearly definable sect but rather to an attitude" (269). I would reply, however, that all versions of this "attitude" seem to agree that Christ's physicality was not what it seemed.

18. Tertullian, *Adversus Marcionem* 4.7; text in Ernest Evans, *Tertullian*, 2:278. Compare the reading of Jennifer Glancy, *Corporal Knowledge*, 103–4, on the nursing of the infant

Jesus in the *Ascension in Isaiah*, which takes place not out of nutritional need, but in order to convince the locals that he is a real baby.

19. Ambrose, *Expositio evangeli secundam Lucam* 2.55 (CCL 14:54).

20. Ambrose, *Expositio evangeli secundam Lucam* 4.6 (CCL 14:107).

21. Maximus of Turin, *Homilia* 35 (*homilia 7 de baptismo Christi*) (PL 57:299).

22. Epiphanius, *Panarion* 30.26.2 (GCS 25:368).

23. Epiphanius, *Panarion* 30.28.4 (GCS 25:371).

24. Epiphanius, *Panarion* 30.28.9 (GSC 25:372).

25. Jerome, *Adversus Iovinianum* 1.36 (PL 23:260). On Jovinian, see Yves-Marie Duval, *L'affaire Jovinien*; and now David G. Hunter, *Marriage, Celibacy, and Heresy in Ancient Christianity*, esp. 230–42 (on Jerome). Despite Jerome's heated rhetoric, we should not overestimate Jovinian's love of sexuality: much of his concern for ascetic elitism, as Hunter, *Marriage*, has shown, was driven by concerns over heresy (especially Manicheism).

26. Jerome, *Adversus Iovinianum* 1.36 (PL 23:260–61).

27. Jerome, *Adversus Iovinianum* 1.40 (PL 23:269–70).

28. Robinson, "Takes One," 723–24.

29. On Hippolytus in general, see Allen Brent, *Hippolytus and the Roman Church in the Third Century*.

30. Hippolytus, *De antichristo* 6; text in Enrico Norelli, *Ippolito*, 72–74. These lines are also taken up in the pseudo-Hippolytan *De consummatione mundi* 22. On the Antichrist in Hippolytus, see Bernard McGinn, *Antichrist*, 60–64.

31. Hippolytus, *De antichristo* 44 and 64 (Norelli, *Ippolito*, 114–16, 148–50); see also his *Commentarius in Danielem* (Gustave Bardy, *Commentaire sur Daniel*). On later traditions of the circumcised Antichrist, see Bonita Rhoads and Julia Reinhard Lupton, "Circumcising the Antichrist: An Ethno-Historical Fantasy," *Jouvert: A Journal of Postcolonial Studies* 3.1–2 (1999).

32. On traditions of Christ's shifting appearance in earliest Christianity, see Paul Foster, "Polymorphic Christology: Its Origins and Development in Earliest Christianity," *Journal of Theological Studies* n.s. 58 (2007): 66–99.

33. Although John Parker, *The Aesthetics of Antichrist*, 1–42, argues that early medieval Christianity "reveled" in the play of Christ-as-Antichrist.

34. See my *Remains of the Jews*, 89–96; Jerome responds to Augustine's offhand "*Iudaeus [Paulus] erat*" in his *Epistula* 112.14 (citing Augustine, *Epistula* 40.4 [CSEL 34.2:73]).

35. Augustine, *Epistula* 82.18 (CSEL 34.2:370).

36. See Augustine, *Epistula* 23.4 (CSEL 34.1:69), in which he debates baptism with Donatists. Just as circumcision was a valid *sacramentum* until Jesus' first coming, so baptism (Augustine argues) will be valid until Christ's second coming.

37. See Brian Stock, *Augustine the Reader*.

38. Augustine, *Confessiones* 6.8 (CCL 27:82–83).

39. Some studies that use "passing" to decode the logics of late Roman texts also suggest this: see Judith Perkins, "An Ancient 'Passing' Novel: Heliodorus' *Aithiopika*," *Arethusa* 32 (1999): 197–214; followed by Virginia Burrus, "Mimicking Virgins: Colonial

Ambivalence and the Ancient Romance," *Arethusa* 38 (2005): 49–88, at 82–83; and Rebecca Lyman, "The Politics of Passing: Justin Martyr's Conversion as a Problem of 'Helleniza-tion,'" in Kenneth Mills and Anthony Grafton, *Conversion in Late Antiquity and the Early Middle Ages*, 36–60.

40. Maud Gleason, *Making Men*.

41. An interesting comparison would be with John Howard Griffin's "passing" as a black man in the South in 1959 (see n. 6). Wald, "Disagreeable Mirror," 160–63, points out the ways in which Griffin's passing functions more as a gesture of "sovereignty" over the categories of race than a gesture of resistance.

Bibliography

PRIMARY SOURCES

Agnes Blannbekin, *Life and Revelations*. Text in *Leben und Offenbarungen der Wiener Begine Agnes Blannbekin (†1315)*. Göppinger Arbeiten zur Germanistik 419. Ed. Peter Dinzelbacher and Renate Vogeler. Göppingen: Kümmerle, 1994. Tr. Ulrike Wiethaus. *Agnes Blannbekin, Viennese Beguine: Life and Revelations*. Cambridge: D. S. Brewer, 2002.

Altercatio Simonis et Theophili. Text in *Liber contra Arrianos; De laude sanctorum; Libellus emendationis; Epistulae; Commonitorium. Excerpta ex operibus s. Augustini; Altercatio legis inter Simonem Iudaeum et Theophilum christianum*. CCL 64. Ed. R. Demeulenaere et al. Turnhout: Brepols, 1985. Tr. William Varner. *Ancient Jewish-Christian Dialogues: Athanasius and Zacchaeus, Simon and Theophilus, Timothy and Aquila: Introduction, Texts, and Translations*. Studies in the Bible and Early Christianity 58. Lewiston, N.Y.: Edwin Mellen Press, 2004.

Ambrose of Milan. *De Abraham*. PL 14:419–500.

———. *Expositio evangelii secundum Lucam*. Text in *Ambrosii Mediolanensis Opera*, pars IV. CCL 14. Ed. M. Adriaen. Turnhout: Brepols, 1957.

Ambrosiaster. *Commentarius in epistulas Paulinas*. CSEL 81.1–3. Ed. H. J. Vogels. Vienna: Tempsky, 1966–69.

———. *Liber quaestionum*. Text in *Pseudo-Augustini quaestiones veteris et novi testamenti CXXVII*. CSEL 50. Ed. Alexander Souter. Vienna: Tempsky, 1908.

Amphilochius of Iconium. *Contra haereticos*. Text in *Amphilochius Iconiensis: Opera*. CCG 3. Ed. C. Datema. Turnhout: Brepols, 1978. Pp. 185–214.

———. *Homilia 2 (in occursum)*. Text in *Amphilochius Iconiensis: Opera*. CCG 3. Ed. C. Datema. Turnhout: Brepols, 1978. Pp. 37–73.

Andrew of Crete. *In circumcisionem et Basilium*. PG 97:913–32.

Armenian Infancy Gospel. Tr. Abraham Terian. *The Armenian Gospel of the Infancy*. Oxford: Oxford University Press, 2008.

Armenian Lectionary. *Le codex Arménien Jérusalem 121*. 2 vols. PO 35.1 (163), PO 36.2 (168). Ed. Athanase Renoux. Turhout: Brepols, 1970.

Athanasius. *Epistula ad Epictetum*. In Epiphanius, *Panarion*. Tr. Philip Schaff and Henry Wace. *Athanasius: Select Works and Letters*. Nicene and Post Nicene Fathers Series 2, vol. 4. Grand Rapids, Mich.: Wm. B. Eerdmans, 1890. Pp. 570–74.

Augustine. *Confessiones*. Text in *Augustinus, Opera I.1*. CCL 27. Ed. L. Verheijen. Turnhout: Brepols, 1971.

———. *Contra Faustum Manichaeum*. PL 42:207–518.

———. *De doctrina christiana*. Text in *Augustinus, Opera VI.1*. CCL 32. Ed. Joseph Martin. Turnhout: Brepols, 1962.

———. *Epistulae*. Text in *Sancti Aureli Augustini Hipponiensis Episcopi Epistulae*. CSEL 34.1–2, 44, 57–58. Ed. A. Goldbacher. Vienna: Tempsky, 1895–1923.

———. *Sermo 198 = Contra paganos*. Text in François Dolbeau. *Vingt-six sermons au peuple d'Afrique*. Paris: Institut d'Études Augustiniennes, 1996. Pp. 90–141. Tr. *Sermons III/11: Newly Discovered Sermons*. The Works of Saint Augustine: A Translation for the 21st Century. Tr. Edmund Hill. Hyde Park, N.Y.: New City Press, 1997. Pp. 180–237.

Birgitta of Sweden. *Revelationes*. Text in *Sancta Birgitta Revelaciones*. Ed. Birger Bergh et al. Stockholm: Almqvist and Wiskell, 1971– .

Caesarius of Arles. *Sermones*. CCL 103–4. Ed. G. Morin. Turnhout: Brepols, 1953.

Catherine of Siena, *Letters*. Text in *Le lettere di S. Caterina da Siena*, 4 vols. Ed. Niccolo Tommaseo. Florence: G. Barbèra, 1860.

Cave of Treasures. Text in *La caverne des trésors: Les deux recensions syriaques*. Ed. Andreas Su-Min Ri. CSCO 486 (Syriac) and 487 (French). Louvain: Peeters, 1987.

Clement of Alexandria. *Stromateis*. GCS 15, 17. Ed. O. Stählin and L. Früchtel. Berlin: Akademie, 1960.

Codex Theodosianus 16. Text in *Les lois réligieuses des empereurs romains de Constantin à Théodose II (312–428)*. SC 497. Ed. M. Delmaire. Paris: Cerf, 2005.

Constitutiones apostolorum. Text in *Constitutions apostoliques*. SC 320, 329, 336. Ed. M. Metzger. Paris: Cerf, 1985–87.

Cyprian of Carthage. *Epistulae*. Text in *Saint Cyprien: Correspondance*, 2 vols. 2nd ed. Ed. La Chanoine Bayard. Paris: Belles Lettres, 1961.

Cyprian of Toulon. *Vita Caesarii Primi*. PL 67:1001–1024.

Cyril of Alexandria. *Commentarius in Lucam*. (1) *Homiliae 3* and *4* (= *Homilia diversa 12*): PG 77:1040–49. (2) *In catenis* a: PG 72:476–949. (3) *In catenis* b: J. A. Cramer. *Catenae graecorum patrum*. Vol. 2: *Catenae in evangelia s. Lucae et s. Joannis*. Oxford: Oxford University Press, 1841. (4) Collected fragments: J. Sickenberger. *Fragmente der Homilien des Cyrill von Alexandrien zum Lukasevangelium*. Texte und Untersuchungen 34. Leipzig: J. C. Hinrichs, 1909. (5) Additional fragments: Joseph Reuss. *Lukas-Kommentare aus der griechischen Kirche*. Texte und Untersuchungen 130. Berlin: Akademie, 1984. Tr. R. Payne Smith. *Gospel of Saint Luke by Cyril of Alexandria*. 1859; repr. New York: Studion, 1983.

———. *Glaphyra in Pentateuchum*. PG 69:9–677.

Diatessaron (Arabic). *Diatessaron de Tatien*. Ed. A.-S. Marmardji. Beirut: Imprimière Catholique, 1935.

Didache. Text and tr. in *The Apostolic Fathers*, vol. 1. Loeb Classical Library. Ed. Bart D. Ehrman. Cambridge, Mass.: Harvard University Press, 2003.

Didascalia apostolorum. Text in *The Didascalia Apostolorum in Syriac*, 2 vols. CSCO 401

(Scriptores Syri 175), CSCO 407 (Scriptores Syri 180). Ed. A. Vööbus. Louvain: CSCO, 1979.

Donatus. *Artes grammaticae.* Text in L. Holtz. *Donat et la tradition de l'enseignement grammatical: Étude sur l'Ars Donati et sa diffusion (IVe-IXe siècle) et édition critique.* Paris: CNRS, 1981.

Ephrem [?]. *Commentary on the Diatessaron.* Tr. *Saint Ephrem's Commentary on Tatian's Diatessaron: An English Translation of Chester Beatty Syriac MS 709. Journal of Semitic Studies* Supplement 2. Ed. and tr. Carmel McCarthy. Oxford: Oxford University Press, 1993.

Ephrem. *Hymns on the Crucifixion.* Text in *Des heiligen Ephraem des Syrers Paschahymnen (De Azymis, De Crucifixione, De Resurrectione).* CSCO 248–249 (Scriptores Syri 108–9). Ed. Edmund Beck. Louvain: CSCO, 1964

————. *Hymns on the Nativity.* Text in *Des heiligen Ephraem des Syrers Hymnen de Nativitate (Epiphania).* CSCO 186 (Scriptores Syri 82). Ed. Edmund Beck. Louvain: CSCO, 1959. Tr. *Ephrem the Syrian: Hymns.* Classics of Western Spirituality. Tr. Kathleen McVey. New York: Paulist Press, 1989.

Epiphanius. *Ancoratus.* Text in *Werke*, vol. 1. GCS 25. Ed. Karl Holl. Leipzig: J. C. Hinrichs, 1915. Pp. 1–149.

————. *De mensuris et ponderibus.* Text and tr. in *Epiphanius's Treatise on Weights and Measures: The Syriac Version.* Studies in Ancient Oriental Civilization 11. Ed. and tr. James Elmer Dean. Chicago: University of Chicago Press, 1935.

————. *Panarion.* Text in *Werke*, vols. 1–3. GCS 25:153–464; 31; 37. Ed. Karl Holl. Leipzig: J. C. Hinrichs, 1915–33. Tr. Frank Williams. *The Panarion of Epiphanius of Salamis.* 2 vols. Nag Hammadi Studies 35–36. Leiden: Brill, 1987–94.

Epistula Barnabae. Text and tr. in *The Apostolic Fathers*, vol. 2. Loeb Classical Library. Ed. Bart D. Ehrman. Cambridge, Mass.: Harvard University Press, 2003.

Eusebius of Caesarea. *Demonstratio evangelica.* Text in *Werke*, vol. 6. GCS 23. Ed. I. A. Heikel. Leipzig: J. C. Hinrichs, 1913.

————. *Historia ecclesiastica.* Text in *Werke*, vol. 2. GCS 9. Ed. Eduard Schwartz. Leipzig: J. C. Hinrichs, 1909.

Eustathius of Antioch. *Fragments.* Text in *Opera omnia.* CCG 51. Ed. J. H. Declerck. Turnhout: Brepols, 2002.

Evangelium infantiae arabicum. Arabic text: J. Giles. *Codex Apocryphus Novi Testamenti: The Uncanonical Gospels and Other Writings Referring to the First Ages of Christianity.* London: D. Nutt, 1852. Pp. 12–32. Latin text: Constantine Tischendorf. *Evangelia apocrypha.* Lipsius: Avenarius and Mendelssohn, 1853. Pp. 171–202. Tr. in *The Twelve Patriarchs, Excerpts and Epistles, The Clementina, Apocrypha, Decretals, Memoirs of Edessa and Syriac Documents, Remains of the First Ages.* Ante-Nicene Fathers, vol. 8. Ed. A. Coxe. Edinburgh: T & T Clark, 1885. Pp. 405–15.

Filastrius. *Diversarum hereseon liber.* CSEL 38. Ed. F. Marx. Vienna: Tempsky, 1898.

Gennadius. *De viris inlustribus.* Text in *Hieronymus liber de viris inlustribus: Gennadius liber de viris inlustribus.* Texte und Untersuchungen 14.1a. Ed. E. C. Richardson. Leipzig: J. C. Hinrichs, 1896.

Georgian Lectionary. Le Grand Lectionnaire de l'église de Jérusalem (Ve–VIIIe siècle). CSCO 188–89. Ed. Michel Tarchnishvili. Louvain: CSCO, 1959.

Gregory of Elvira. *Tractatus Origenis.* Text in *Gregorius Iliberritanus, Gregorius Iliberritanus (Ps.), Faustinus Luciferianus: Opera quae supersunt. Dubia et spuria; Opera.* CCL 69. Ed. V. Bulhart et al. Turnhout: Brepols, 1967.

Gregory of Nazianzus. *Oratio 41 (in pentecosten).* PG 36:428–52.

———. *Oratio 43 (funebris oratio in laudem Basilii Magni).* PG 36:493–605.

Gregory of Nyssa. *In laudem fratris Basilii.* PG 46:788–817.

Guibert of Nogent. *De pignoribus sanctorum.* PL 156:607–79.

Hesychius of Jerusalem. *Homiliae 2 in hypapante.* Text *Hesychius: Les homélies festales.* Vol. I: *Les homélies i–xv.* Subsidia Hagiographa 59. Ed. Michel Aubineau. Brussels: Société de Bollandistes, 1978. Pp. 24–75.

Hilary of Poitiers. *De trinitate.* Text in *La Trinité.* SC 443, 448, 462. Ed. P. Smulders. Paris: Cerf, 1999–2001.

———. *Tractatus super psalmos 118.* Text in *Commentaire sur le psaume 118.* SC 344, 347. Ed. M. Milhau. Paris: Cerf, 1988.

Hippolytus. *Commentarius in Danielem.* Text in *Commentaire sur Daniel.* SC 14. Ed. Gustave Bardy. Paris: Cerf, 1947.

———. *De antichristo.* Text in *Ippolito: L'anticristo.* Biblioteca Patristica. Ed. Enrico Norelli. Florence: Nardini Editore, 1987.

———. *Refutatio omnium haeresium.* Text in *Hippolytus: Refutation omnium haeresium.* Patristische Texte und Studien 25. Ed. Miroslav Marcovich. Berlin: De Gruyter, 1986.

Ignatius of Antioch. *Epistulae.* Text in *Lettres. Martyre de Polycarpe.* SC 10bis. Ed. P. Camelot. Paris: Cerf, 1945.

Innocent III. *De sacro altaris mysterio.* PL 217:773–915.

Irenaeus. *Adversus haereses.* Text in *Contre les hérésies.* SC 263–64, 293–94, 210–11, 34, 100, 152–53. Ed. P. Doutreleau et al. Paris: Cerf, 1952–69.

Itinerarium Antonini Placentini. Text in *Itineraria et alia geographica.* CCL 175. Ed. P. Geyer. Turnhout: Brepols, 1965. Pp. 129–53.

Jacob of Serugh. *Homiliae.* Text in *Homiliae selectae Mar-Jacobi Sarugensis.* 5 vols. Ed. P. Bedjan. Leipzig: Otto Harassowitz, 1905–1910. Tr. *Jacob of Serugh: Select Festal Homilies.* Ed. and tr. Thomas Kollamparampil. Bangalore: Dharmaram Publications, 1997.

Jacobus de Voragine. *Legenda aurea.* Text in *Legenda aurea.* 3rd ed. Ed. Th. Graesse. Breslau: Wilhelm Koebner, 1890.

Jerome. *Adversus Iovinianum.* PL 23:205–338. Tr. Philip Schaff and Henry Wace. *Jerome: Letters and Select Works.* Nicene and Post Nicene Fathers Series 2, vol. 6. Grand Rapids, Mich.: Wm. B. Eerdmans, 1892. Pp. 346–416.

———. *Apologia adversus Rufinum.* Text in *Apologie contre Rufin.* SC 303. Ed. Pierre Lardet. Paris: Cerf, 1983.

———. *Epistulae.* Text in *Sancti Hieronymi Eusebii Epistulae.* CSEL 54–56. Ed. I. Hilberg and M. Kamptner. Vienna: Österreichischen Akademie der Wissenschaften, 1996.

————. *Liber Hebraicorum quaestionum in Genesim.* Text in *Opera Exegetica.* CCL 72. Ed. P. de Lagard. Turnhout: Brepols, 1959. Pp. 1–56.

John Chrysostom. *Adversus Iudaeos.* PG 48:843–942. Tr. *John Chrysostom: Discourses Against Judaizing Christians.* Fathers of the Church 68. Tr. Paul Harkins. Washington, D.C.: Catholic University Press of America, 1979.

————. *De cruce et latrone homilia 1.* PG 49:399–408.

————. *Homiliae in epistolam ad Colossenses.* PG 62:299–392.

Justin Martyr. *Dialogus cum Tryphone.* Text in *Iustini Martyris Dialogus cum Tryphone.* Patristische Texte und Studien 47. Ed. Miroslav Marcovich. Berlin: De Gruyter, 1997.

Maximus of Turin. *Homiliae.* PL 57:221–530.

————. *Sermones.* Texts in *Sermonum collectio antiqua, nonnullis sermonibus extravagantibus adiectis.* CCL 23. Ed. A. Mutzenbecher. Tr. *The Sermons of Maximus of Turin.* Ed. and tr. Boniface Ramsey. Ancient Christian Writers 50. Mahwah, N.J.: Paulist Press, 1989.

Nestorius. *Epistula 2 ad Cyrillum.* Text in *Nestoriana: Die Fragmente des Nestorius.* Ed. F. Loofs. Halle: Niemeyer, 1905. Pp. 173–80.

Novum Testamentum Graece. 27 ed. Ed. Barbara Aland and Kurt Aland. Stuttgart: Deutsche Bibelgesellschaft, 1993.

Origen. *Commentariorum series in Matthaeum.* PG 13:1599–1800.

————. *Contra Celsum.* Text in *Contre Celse.* 5 vols. SC 132, 136, 147, 150, 227. Ed. Marcel Borret. Paris: Cerf: 1967–76. Tr. *Origen: Contra Celsum.* Ed. and tr. Henry Chadwick. Cambridge: Cambridge University Press, 1953.

————. *De principiis.* Text in *Traité des principes.* 5 vols. SC 252–53, 268–69, 312. Ed. Henri Crouzel and M. Simonetti. Paris: Cerf, 1978–84.

————. *Homiliae in Genesim.* Text in *Homélies sur la Genèse.* SC 7*bis*. Ed. L. Doutreleau. Paris: Cerf, 1943. Tr. *Homilies on Exodus and Genesis.* Fathers of the Church 71. Ed. and tr. Ronald E. Heine. Washington, D.C.: Catholic University of America Press, 2002.

————. *Homiliae in Josue.* Text in *Homélies sur Josué.* SC 71. Ed. Annie Jaubert. Paris: Cerf, 1960. Tr. *Homilies on Joshua.* Fathers of the Church 105. Tr. Barbara Bruce. Ed. Cynthia White. Washington, D.C.: Catholic University of America Press, 2002.

————. *Homiliae in Leviticum.* Text in *Homélies sur le Lévitique.* SC 286–87. Ed. Marcel Borret. Paris: Cerf, 1981. Tr. *Homilies on Leviticus.* Fathers of the Church 83. Tr. Gary Barkley. Washington, D.C.: Catholic University of America Press, 1990.

————. *Homiliae in Lucam.* Text in *Homélies sur S. Luc.* SC 87. Ed. Henri Crouzel. Paris: Cerf, 1962. Tr. *Homilies on Luke.* Fathers of the Church 94. Ed. and tr. Joseph Lienhard. Washington, D.C.: Catholic University of America Press, 1996.

Pamphilus. *Apologia pro Origene.* Text in *Apologie pour Origène.* SC 464–65. Ed. René Amacker and Éric Junod. Paris: Cerf, 2000–2001.

Philoxenus of Mabbug. *Commentary on Matthew and Luke.* (1) *Philoxenus of Mabbug: Fragments of the Commentary on Matthew and Luke.* CSCO 392–93. Ed. J. W. Watt. Louvain: CSCO, 1978. (2) *The "Matthew-Luke Commentary" of Philoxenus.* SBL Dissertation Series 43. Ed. Douglas J. Fox. Missoula, Mont.: Scholars Press, 1979.

Proclus of Constantinople. *De circumcisione domini.* (1) PG 65:836–840. (2) Michel Aubineau. "Proclus de Constantinople, In illud: 'et postquam consummati sunt dies octo' (*Lc* 2,21)." In *Mémorial André-Jean Festugière: Antiquité païenne et chrétienne.* Ed. E. Lucchesi and H. D. Saffrey. Geneva: Patrick Cramer, 1984. Pp. 199–207.

Ps.-Amphilochius. *In circumcisionem et Basilium.* (1) Paris, Bibliothèque Nationale, Ancien gr. 1551, 121–124v = François Combefis. SS. *Patrum Amphilochii Iconiensis, Methodii Patarensis, et Andreae Cretensis: Opera omnia quae reperiri potuerunt.* Paris: Simon Piget, 1644. Pp. 10–22. (2) Florence, Biblioteca Medicea-Laurenziana, Ms. gr. IV.4, 227–232. (3) Venice, Biblioteca Nazionale Marciana, Ms. gr. VII.25 [972], 142–146v.

Ps.-Athanasius. *Quaestiones ad Antiochum Ducem.* PG 28:597–708.

Ps.-Chrysostom. *In occursu domini.* PG 50:807–12.

Ps.-Clement. *Homilies.* Text in *Die Pseudoklementinen: Homilien.* GCS 42. Ed. Georg Strecker. Berlin: Akademie Verlag, 1992.

Ps.-Ephrem. *In Basilium magnum.* Text in *S. Ephraem Syri Opera.* Monumenta Biblica et Ecclesiastica. Ed. Sylvio G. Mercati. Rome: Pontificium Institutum Biblicum, 1915. Vol. 1.1, pp. 143–78.

Ps.-Fulgentius. *Sermo dubius II.* Text in *Sancti Fulgentii Episcopi Ruspensis Opera.* CCL 91A. Ed. J. Fraipont. Turnout: Brepol, 1968. Pp. 953–59.

Pseudo-Matthaei evangelium. Text in Constantine Tischendorf. *Evangelia apocrypha.* Lipsius: Avenarius and Mendelssohn, 1853. Pp. 50–105.

Severus of Antioch, *Epistulae.* Text in *A Collection of Letters of Severus of Antioch, from Numerous Syriac Manuscripts.* PO 12.2, 14.1. Ed. and tr. E. W. Brooks. Paris: Firmin-Didot, 1919–20.

———. *Homiliae.* Text in *Les homiliae cathedrales de Sévère d'Antioche.* PO 8.2, 12.1, 16.5, 22.2, 23.1, 25.1, 25.4, 26.3, 28.2, 29.1, 35.3, 36.1, 36.3, 36.4, 37.1, 38.2. Diverse editors. Paris, etc.: Firmon-Didot, etc., 1912–76.

Socrates. *Historia ecclesiastica.* Text in *Kirchengeschichte.* GCS n.f. 1. Ed. G. C. Hansen. Berlin: Akademie, 1995.

Sozomen. *Historia ecclesiastica.* Text in *Kirchengeschichte.* GCS n.f. 4. Ed. G. C. Hansen. Berlin: Akademie, 1995.

Syriac Menologies. Text in *Un martyrologie et douze Ménologes syriaques.* PO 10.1. Ed. F. Nau. Paris: Firmin-Didot, 1915.

Tertullian. *Adversus Iudaeos.* Text in *Q. S. F. Tertulliani Adversus Iudaeos mit Einleitung und kritischem Kommentar.* Ed. Hermann Tränkle. Wiesbaden: Franz Steiner Verlag GMBH, 1964.

———. *Adversus Marcionem.* Text in *Tertullian: Adversus Marcionem.* 2 vols. Ed. and tr. Ernest Evans. Oxford: Clarendon Press, 1972.

———. *De carne Christi.* Text in *La chair du Christ.* SC 216–17. Ed. Jean-Pierre Mahé. Paris: Cerf, 1975.

———. *De praescriptione haereticorum.* Text in *La préscription contre les hérétiques.* SC 46. Ed. François Refoulé. Paris: Cerf, 1957.

————. *De resurrectione mortuorum.* Text in *Opera Montanistica.* CCL 2. Ed. A. Gerlo et al. Turnhout: Brepols, 1996.

Theodore of Mopsuestia. *Commentarius in epistulas paulinas.* Text in *Theodori Episcopi Mopsuesteni in Epistulas B. Pauli Commentarii: The Latin Versions with the Greek Fragments.* 2 vols. Ed. H. B. Swete. Cambridge: Cambridge University Press, 1880. Text and tr. *Theodore of Mopsuestia: Commentary on the Pauline Epistles.* Writings from the Greco-Roman World 26. Ed. and tr. Rowan Greer. Atlanta: SBL Press, 2010.

Theodoret of Cyrus. *Eranistes.* Text in *Eranistes: Theodoret of Cyrrhus.* Ed. Gérard Ettlinger. Oxford: Clarendon Press, 1975.

Thomas Aquinas. *Summa Theologiae.* Text and tr. in *St. Thomas of Aquinas: Summa Theologiae.* 60 vols. Ed. Thomas Gilby (gen. ed.). Cambridge: Cambridge University Press, 1976.

Tours, Second Council of (567 CE). Text in *Concilia Galliae a. 511–596.* CCL 148a. Ed. C. de Clercq. Turnhout: Brepols, 1963. Pp. 175–99.

Traditio apostolica. Text in *La tradition apostolique.* SC 11bis. 2nd ed. Ed. B. Botte. Paris: Cerf, 1984.

Vincentius of Lerins. *Commonitorium.* Text in *Liber contra Arrianos; De laude sanctorum; Libellus emendationis; Epistulae; Commonitorium. Excerpta ex operibus s. Augustini; Altercatio legis inter Simonem Iudaeum et Theophilum christianum.* CCL 64. Ed. R. Demeulenaere et al. Turnhout: Brepols: 1985.

SECONDARY SOURCES

Abusch, Ra'anan. "Circumcision and Castration Under Roman Law in the Early Empire." In Mark, *Covenant of Circumcision* (q.v.). Pp. 75–86.

Adams, J. N. "'*Romanitas*' and the Latin Language." *Classical Quarterly* 53 (2003): 184–205.

Aland, Barbara. "Monophysitismus und Schriftauslegung: Der Kommentar zum Matthäus- und Lukasevangelium des Philoxenus von Mabbug." In *Unser ganzes Leben Christus unserm Gott überantworten: Studien zur ostkirchlichen Spiritualität.* Ed. Peter Hauptmann. Göttingen: Vandenhoeck & Ruprecht, 1982. Pp. 142–66.

Alexander, Loveday. "The Acts of the Apostles as an Apologetic Text." In Edwards, Goodman, and Price, *Apologetics in the Roman Empire* (q.v.). Pp. 15–44.

————. *The Preface to Luke's Gospel: Literary Conventions and Social Context in Luke 1.1–4 and Acts 1.1.* Society for New Testament Studies Monograph Series 78. Cambridge: Cambridge University Press, 1993.

Allen, Pauline. "Severus of Antioch and the Homily: The End of the Beginning?" In Allen and Jeffreys, *Sixth Century* (q.v.). Pp. 167–75.

————. "The Sixth-Century Greek Homily: A Reassessment." In Cunningham and Allen, *Preacher and Audience* (q.v.). Pp. 201–25.

————. *Sophronius of Jerusalem and Seventh-Century Heresy: The Synodical Letter and Other Documents.* Oxford Early Christian Texts. New York: Oxford University Press, 2009.

Allen, Pauline, and C. T. R. Hayward. *Severus of Antioch.* The Early Church Fathers. London: Routledge, 2004.

Allen, Pauline, and E. M. Jeffreys (eds.). *The Sixth Century—End or Beginning?* Byzantina Australiensia 10. Brisbane: Australian Association for Byzantine Studies, 1996.

Ando, Clifford. *Imperial Ideology and Provincial Loyalty in the Roman Empire.* Berkeley: University of California Press, 2000.

———. *The Matter of the Gods: Religion and the Roman Empire.* Transformation of the Classical Heritage 44. Berkeley: University of California Press, 2008.

Andresen, Carl. *Logos und Nomos: Die Polemik des Kelsos wider das Christentum.* Arbeiten zur Kirchengeschichte 30. Berlin: De Gruyter, 1955.

Aubineau, Michel. "Deux homélies de Cyrille d'Alexandrie *de hypapante* (*BHG* 1958w et 1963)?" *Analecta Bollandiana* 90 (1972): 100.

———. "Emprunts de Proclus de Constantinople à Cyrille d'Alexandrie dans son Homélie XXII, In illud 'et postquam consummati dies octo . . .' (Lc. 2,21)." In *After Chalcedon: Studies in Theology and Church History.* Orientalia Lovaniensia Analecta 18. Ed. C. Laga, J. Munitz, and L. van Rompay. Leuven: Peeters, 1985. Pp. 23–34.

———. "Les 'catenae in Lucam' de J. Reuss et Cyrille d'Alexandrie." *Byzantinische Zeitschrift* 80 (1987): 29–47.

Ayres, Lewis. "The Question of Orthodoxy." *Journal of Early Christian Studies* 14 (2006): 395–98.

Bagatti, Bellarmino. *L'église de la circoncision.* Studium Biblicum Franciscanum, collectio minor 2. Jerusalem: Imprimerie des pères franciscains, 1965.

Baker, Cynthia. "When Jews Were Women." *History of Religions* 45 (2005): 114–34.

Bakhtin, Mikhail. "Discourse in the Novel." In *The Dialogic Imagination: Four Essays.* Tr. Caryl Emerson and Michael Holquist. Austin: University of Texas Press, 1981. Pp. 259–422.

———. "From Notes Made in 1970–1971." In *Speech Genres and Other Late Essays.* University of Texas Slavic Series 8. Tr. Vern W. McGee. Ed. Caryl Emersen and Michael Holquist. Austin: University of Texas Press, 1986. Pp. 132–59.

Baldovin, John F. "The Empire Baptized." In Wainwright and Westerfield Tucker, *Oxford History of Christian Worship* (q.v.). Pp. 77–130.

———. *The Urban Character of Christian Worship: The Origins, Development, and Meaning of Stational Liturgy.* Orientalia Christiana Analecta 228. Rome: Pontificum Institutum Studiorum Orientalium, 1987.

Barclay, John M.G. *Jews in the Mediterranean Diaspora from Alexander to Trajan (323 BCE–117 CE).* Edinburgh: T & T Clark, 1996.

Bardy, Gustave. "La littérature patristique des 'quaestiones et responsiones' sur l'Écriture Sainte." *Revue Biblique* 41 (1932): 210–36, 341–60, 515–37; 42 (1933): 14–30, 211–29, 328–52.

Barkhuizen, J. H. "Amphilochius of Iconium: Homily 1 'On the Nativity.'" *Acta Patristica et Byzantina* 12 (2001): 1–23.

———. "Homily 3 of Amphilochius of Iconium: 'On the Four-day [Dead] Lazarus,' An Essay in Interpretation." *Acta Patristica et Byzantina* 5 (1994): 1–9.

———. "Imagery in the (Greek) Homilies of Amphilochius of Iconium." *Acta Patristica et Byzantina* 13 (2002): 1–33.

———. "Proclus of Constantinople: A Popular Preacher in Fifth-Century Constantinople." In Cunningham and Allen, *Preacher and Audience* (q.v.). Pp. 179–200.

Barnes, Timothy. "The Collapse of the Homoeans in the East." *Studia Patristica* 29 (1997): 6–13.

Barth, Fredrik. "Boundaries and Connections." In *Signifying Identities: Anthropological Perspectives on Boundaries and Contested Values*. Ed. Anthony Cohen. London: Routledge, 2001. Pp. 17–36.

———. *Ethnic Groups and Boundaries: The Social Organization of Cultural Difference*. Boston: Little, Brown, 1969.

Bauckham, Richard. "The Origin of the Ebionites." In Tomson and Lambers-Petry, *Image of the Judaeo-Christians* (q.v.). Pp. 162–81.

Bauer, Walter. *Orthodoxy and Heresy in Earliest Christianity*. Tr. Philadelphia Seminar on Christian Origins. Ed. Robert A. Kraft and Gerhard Krodel. Philadelphia: Fortress Press, 1971.

Baur, Ferdinand Christian. "Die Christuspartei in der korinthischen Gemeinde, der Gegensatz des petrinischen und paulinischen Christentums in der ältesten Kirche, der Apostel Petrus in Rom." *Tübinger Zeitschrift für Theologie* 5.4 (1831): 61–206.

Beard, Mary, John North, and Simon Price. *Religions of Rome*. Volume 1: *A History*. Cambridge: Cambridge University Press, 1998.

Beck, Edmund. "Philoxenos und Ephräm." *Oriens Christianus* 46 (1962): 61–76.

Becker, Adam H. *Fear of God and the Beginning of Wisdom: The School of Nisibis and Christian Scholastic Culture in Late Antique Mesopotamia*. Divinations. Philadelphia: University of Pennsylvania Press, 2006.

Becker, Adam H., and Annette Yoshiko Reed. "Introduction: Traditional Models and New Directions." In Becker and Reed, *Ways That Never Parted* (q.v.). Pp. 1–33.

———. (eds.). *The Ways That Never Parted: Jews and Christians in Late Antiquity and the Middle Ages*. Texts and Studies in Ancient Judaism 95. Tübingen: Mohr Siebeck, 2003. Repr. Minneapolis: Fortress Press, 2007.

BeDuhn, Jason D. "Augustine Accused: Megalius, Manichaeism, and the Inception of the *Confessions*." *Journal of Early Christian Studies* 17 (2009): 85–124.

Bell, Catherine. *Ritual Theory, Ritual Practice*. New York: Oxford University Press, 1992.

Bell, Michael Mayerfeld. "Culture as Dialogue." In *Bakhtin and the Human Sciences: No Last Words*. Theory, Culture & Society. Ed. Michael Mayerfeld Bell and Michael Gardiner. London: Sage, 1998. Pp. 49–62.

Bennett, Chris. "The Early Augustan Calendars in Rome and Egypt." *Zeitschrift für Papyrologie und Epigraphik* 142 (2003): 221–40.

Bergjan, Silke-Petra. "Celsus the Epicurean? The Interpretation of an Argument in Origen, *Contra Celsum*." *Harvard Theological Review* 94 (2001): 181–206.

Bhabha, Homi K. *The Location of Culture*. 2nd ed. London: Routledge, 2004.

Bible & Cultural Collective. *The Postmodern Bible*. New Haven, Conn.: Yale University Press, 1995.

Bickerman, Elias J. "Origines gentium." *Classical Philology* 47.2 (1952): 65–81.

Biddick, Kathleen. *The Typological Imaginary: Circumcision, Technology, History.* Philadelphia: University of Pennsylvania Press, 2003.

Billings, Bradley S. " 'At the Age of Twelve': The Boy Jesus in the Temple (Luke 2:41–52), the Emperor Augustus, and the Social Setting of the Third Gospel." *Journal of Theological Studies* n.s. 60 (2009): 70–89.

Bonney, Gillian. "The Exegesis of the Gospel of Luke in the *Expositio evangelii secundum Lucam* of Ambrose and in the *In Lucae evangelium expositio* of Bede as Observed in the Figure of Elisabeth." *Zeitschrift für Antikes Christentum* 5 (2001): 50–64.

Borgen, Peder, and Roald Skarsten. "Quaestiones et solutiones: Some Observations on the Form of Philo's Exegesis." *Studia Philonica* 4 (1976–77): 1–16.

Bovon, François. *Luke 1: A Commentary on the Gospel of Luke 1:1–9:50.* Tr. Christine M. Thomas. Ed. Helmut Koester. Hermeneia. Minneapolis: Fortress Press, 2002.

———. *Luke the Theologian: Fifty-five Years of Research (1950–2005).* 2nd ed. Waco, Tex.: Baylor University Press, 2006.

Boyarin, Daniel. *Border Lines: The Partition of Judaeo-Christianity.* Divinations. Philadelphia: University of Pennsylvania Press, 2004.

———. *Carnal Israel: Reading Sex in Talmudic Culture.* Berkeley: University of California Press, 1993.

———. "Homotopia: The *Fem*inized Jewish Man and the Lives of Women in Late Antiquity." *differences* 7 (1995): 41–81.

———. *Intertextuality and the Reading of Midrash.* Bloomington: Indiana University Press, 1990.

———. "Justin Martyr Invents Judaism." *Church History* 70 (2001): 427–61.

———. *A Radical Jew: Paul and the Politics of Identity.* Berkeley: University of California Press, 1994.

———. "Rethinking Jewish Christianity: An Argument for Dismantling a Dubious Category (to Which Is Appended a Correction of My *Border Lines*)." *Jewish Quarterly Review* 99 (2009): 7–36.

———. *Socrates and the Fat Rabbis.* Chicago: University of Chicago Press, 2009.

Boyarin, Daniel, and Virginia Burrus. "Hybridity as Subversion of Orthodoxy? Jews and Christians in Late Antiquity." *Social Compass* 52 (2005): 431–41.

Bradshaw, Paul F. *The Search for the Origins of Christian Worship: Sources and Methods for the Study of Early Liturgy.* 2nd ed. New York: Oxford University Press, 2002.

Brakke, David. *Demons and the Making of the Monk: Spiritual Combat in Early Christianity.* Cambridge, Mass.: Harvard University Press, 2006.

———. "The Early Church in North America: Late Antiquity, Theory, and the History of Christianity." *Church History* 71 (2002): 473–91.

———. *Evagrius of Pontus: Talking Back: A Monastic Handbook for Combatting Demons.* Cistercian Studies 229. Collegeville, Minn.: Liturgical Press, 2009.

———. "Jewish Flesh and Christian Spirit in Athanasius of Alexandria." *Journal of Early Christian Studies* 9 (2001): 453–81.

———. "Making Public the Monastic Life: Reading the Self in Evagrius' *Talking Back*." In *Religion and the Self in Antiquity*. Ed. David Brakke, Michael Satlow, and Steven Weitzman. Bloomington: Indiana University Press, 2005. Pp. 222–33.

Brent, Allen. *Hippolytus and the Roman Church in the Third Century: Communities in Tension Before the Emergence of the Monarch Bishop*. Leiden: Brill, 1995.

Broadhead, Edwin K. *Jewish Ways of Following Jesus: Redrawing the Religious Map of Antiquity*. Wissenschaftliche Untersuchungen zum neuen Testament 2:266. Tübingen: Mohr Siebeck, 2010.

Brock, Sebastian. *The Bible in the Syriac Tradition*. Gorgias Handbooks. Piscataway, N.J.: Gorgias Press, 2006.

———. "St. Ephrem in the Eyes of Later Syriac Liturgical Tradition." *Hugoye* [http://syrcom.cua.edu/syrcom/Hugoye] 2.1 (1999).

Brown, Francis. *The New Brown-Driver-Briggs-Gesenius Hebrew and English Lexicon*. Repr. Peabody, Mass.: Hendrickson, 1979.

Brown, Peter. *The Body and Society: Men, Women, and Sexual Renunciation in Early Christianity*. New York: Columbia University Press, 1988.

———. "In Gibbon's Shade." In *Society and the Holy in Late Antiquity*. Berkeley: University of California Press, 1982. Pp. 49–62.

Brown, Raymond E. *The Birth of the Messiah: A Commentary on the Infancy Narratives in the Gospels of Matthew and Luke*. 2nd ed. New York: Doubleday, 1993.

Bruce, F. F. *The Epistle to the Colossians, to Philemon, and to the Ephesians*. The New International Commentary on the New Testament. Grand Rapids, Mich.: Wm. B. Eerdmans, 1999.

Bryk, Felix. *Circumcision in Man and Woman: Its History, Psychology, and Ethnology*. Tr. David Berger. New York: American Ethnological Press, 1934.

Buell, Denise Kimber. "Rethinking the Relevance of Race for Early Christian Self-Definition." *Harvard Theological Review* 94 (2001): 449–76.

———. *Why This New Race? Ethnic Reasoning in Early Christianity*. New York: Columbia University Press, 2005.

Burrus, Virginia. *"Begotten, Not Made": Conceiving Manhood in Late Antiquity*. Figurae: Reading Medieval Culture. Stanford: Stanford University Press, 2000.

———. "The Gospel of Luke and the Acts of the Apostles." In *A Postoclonial Commentary on the New Testament Writings*. Ed. Fernando F. Segovia and R. S. Sugirtharajah. London: T & T Clark, 2007. Pp. 133–55.

———. "Hailing Zenobia: Anti-Judaism, Trinitarianism, and John Henry Newman." *Culture and Religion* 3 (2002): 163–77.

———. "Macrina's Tattoo." *Journal of Medieval and Modern Studies* 33 (2003): 403–18. Also in Martin and Miller, *Cultural Turn in Late Ancient Studies* (q.v.). Pp. 103–16.

———. *The Making of a Heretic: Gender, Authority, and the Priscillianist Controversy*. Transformation of the Classical Heritage 24. Berkeley: University of California Press, 1995.

———. "Mimicking Virgins: Colonial Ambivalence and the Ancient Romance." *Arethusa* 38 (2005): 49–88.

———. "Radical Orthodoxy and the Heresiological Habit: Engaging Graham Ward's Christology." In *Interpreting the Postmodern: Responses to "Radical Orthodoxy."* Ed. Rosemary Radford Ruether and Marion Grau. London: T & T Clark, 2006. Pp. 36–53.

———. *Saving Shame: Martyrs, Saints, and Other Abject Subjects.* Divinations. Philadelphia: University of Pennsylvania Press, 2007.

———. "Sexing Jesus in Late Antiquity." Paper presented at "Taking Off the Holy Shroud: 2000 Years of Gender in the Body of Jesus." New York University, March 25–27, 2001.

———. *The Sex Lives of Saints: An Erotics of Ancient Hagiography.* Divinations. Philadelphia: University of Pennsylvania Press, 2004.

Butler, Judith. *Gender Trouble: Feminism and the Subversion of Identity.* New York: Routledge, 1990.

———. *Giving an Account of Oneself.* New York: Fordham University Press, 2005.

Bynum, Caroline Walker. *Fragmentation and Redemption: Essays on Gender and the Human Body in Medieval Religion.* New York: Zone Books, 1991.

———. *The Resurrection of the Body in Western Christianity, 200–1336.* New York: Columbia University Press, 1995.

Cabrol, F. "Circoncision (Fête de la)." *Dictionnaire d'archéologie chrétienne et de liturgie* 3.2 (1914): 1718–28.

Cain, Andrew. "In Ambrosiaster's Shadow: A Critical Re-Evaluation of the Last Surviving Letter Exchange Between Pope Damasus and Jerome." *Revue des Études Augustiniennes* 51 (2005): 257–77.

Cameron, Averil. *Christianity and the Rhetoric of Empire: The Development of Christian Discourse.* Sather Classical Lectures 55. Berkeley: University of California Press, 1991.

———. "How to Read Heresiology." *Journal of Medieval and Early Modern Studies* 33 (2003): 471–92. Also in Martin and Miller, *Cultural Turn in Late Ancient Studies* (q.v.). Pp. 193–212.

———. "Jewish and Heretics—A Category Error?" In Reed and Becker, *Ways That Never Parted* (q.v.). Pp. 345–60.

Caner, Daniel. *Wandering, Begging Monks: Spiritual Authority and the Promotion of Monasticism in Late Antiquity.* Transformation of the Classical Heritage 33. Berkeley: University of California Press, 2002.

Caputo, John. *The Prayers and Tears of Jacques Derrida: Religion Without Religion.* Indiana Series in the Philosophy of Religion. Bloomington: Indiana University Press, 1997.

Caridad, Eva Castro. "The Hispanic Texts *In Diem Circumcisionis Domini.*" In *Hispania Vetus: Musical Liturgical Manuscripts from Visigothic Origins to the Franco-Roman Transition (9th–12th Centuries).* Ed. Susana Zapke. Bilbao: Fundación BBVA, 2007. Pp. 127–39.

Carleton Paget, James. "Barnabas 9:4: A Peculiar Verse on Circumcision." *Vigiliae Christianae* 45 (1991): 242–54.

———. *The Epistle of Barnabas: Outlook and Background.* Wissenschaftliche Untersuchungen zum Neuen Testament 2:64. Tübingen: Mohr Siebeck, 1994.

———. "Jewish Christianity." In *Cambridge History of Judaism*. Vol. 3: *The Early Roman Period*. Ed. W. D. Davies and William Horbury. Cambridge: Cambridge University Press, 1999. Pp. 731–75.

———. "The Terms *Jewish Christian* and *Jewish Christianity* in the History of Research." In Skarsaune and Hvalvik, *Jewish Believers in Jesus* (q.v.). Pp. 22–52.

Castelli, Elizabeth. *Martyrdom and Memory: Early Christian Culture Making*. Gender, Theory, and Religion. New York: Columbia University Press, 2004.

Caughie, Pamela L. *Passing and Pedagogy: The Dynamics of Responsibility*. Urbana: University of Illinois Press, 1999.

Chesnut, Roberta C. *Three Monophysite Christologies: Severus of Antioch, Philoxenus of Mabbug, and Jacob of Sarug*. Oxford Theological Monographs. London: Oxford University Press, 1976.

Chidester, David. *Savage Systems: Colonialism and Comparative Religion in Southern Africa*. Charlottesville: University of Virginia Press, 1996.

Chin, Catherine. *Grammar and Christianity in the Late Roman World*. Divinations. Philadelphia: University of Pennsylvania Press, 2008.

Clark, Elizabeth A. "Antifamilial Tendencies in Ancient Christianity." *Journal of the History of Sexuality* 5 (1995): 356–80.

———. "The Celibate Bridegroom and His Virginal Brides: Metaphor and the Marriage of Jesus in Early Christian Ascetic Exegesis." *Church History* 77 (2008): 1–25.

———. "From Patristics to Early Christian Studies." In Harvey and Hunter, *Oxford Handbook of Early Christian Studies* (q.v.). Pp. 7–41.

———. *History, Theory, Text: Historians and the Linguistic Turn*. Cambridge, Mass.: Harvard University Press, 2004.

———. *The Origenist Controversy: The Cultural Construction of an Early Christian Debate*. Princeton, N.J.: Princeton University Press, 1992.

———. "The Place of Jerome's *Commentary on Ephesians* in the Origenist Controversy: Apokatastasis and Ascetic Ideals." *Vigiliae Christianae* 41 (1987): 154–71.

———. *Reading Renunciation: Asceticism and Scripture in Early Christianity*. Princeton, N.J.: Princeton University Press, 1999.

Clark, Gillian. " 'In the Foreskin of Your Flesh': The Pure Male Body in Late Antiquity." In *Roman Bodies: Antiquity to the Eighteenth Century*. Ed. Andrew Hopkins and Maria Wyke. London: British School at Rome, 2005. Pp. 43–53.

Clarke, G. W. "Cyprian's *Epistle* 64 and the Kissing of Feet in Baptism." *Harvard Theological Review* 66 (1973): 147–52.

Cohen, Shaye J. D. *The Beginnings of Jewishness: Boundaries, Varieties, Uncertainties*. Hellenistic Culture and Society 31. Berkeley: University of California Press, 1999.

———. "Judaism Without Circumcision and 'Judaism' Without 'Circumcision' in Ignatius." *Harvard Theological Review* 95 (2002): 395–415.

———. "Menstruants and the Sacred in Judaism and Christianity." In *Women's History in Ancient History*. Ed. Sarah B. Pomeroy. Chapel Hill: University of North Carolina Press, 1991. Pp. 287–90.

———. " 'Those Who Say They Are Jews and Are Not': How Do You Know a Jew in Antiquity When You See One?" In *Diasporas in Antiquity*. Ed. Shaye J. D. Cohen and Ernest Frerichs. Atlanta: Scholars Press, 1993. Pp. 1–45.

———. *Why Aren't Jewish Women Circumcised? Gender and Covenant in Judaism*. Berkeley: University of California Press, 2005.

Cohick, Lynn. *The Peri Pascha Attributed to Melito of Sardis: Setting, Purpose, and Sources*. Brown Judaic Studies 327. Providence, R.I.: Brown Judaic Studies, 2000.

Cohn-Sherbok, Dan. "Modern Hebrew Christianity and Messianic Judaism." In Tomson and Lambers-Petry, *Image of the Judaeo-Christians* (q.v.). Pp. 287–98.

Coleman, Kathleen M. *M. Valerii Martialis Liber Spectaculorum*. Oxford: Oxford University Press, 2006.

Collins, John J. "A Symbol of Otherness: Circumcision and Salvation in the First Century." In *Seers, Sibyls, and Sages in Hellenistic-Roman Judaism*. Leiden: Brill, 1997.

Constas, Nicholas. *Proclus of Constantinople and the Cult of the Virgin Mary in Late Antiquity*. Supplements to *Vigiliae Christianae* 66. Leiden: Brill, 2003.

Conzelmann, Hans. *The Theology of Saint Luke*. Tr. Geoffrey Buswell. New York: Harper & Row, 1961.

Cordier, Pierre. "Les romains et la circoncision." *Revue des Études Juives* 160 (2001): 337–55.

Cox, Patricia. *Biography in Late Antiquity: A Quest for the Holy Man*. Transformation of the Classical Heritage 5. Berkeley: University of California Press, 1983.

Crouzel, Henri. "Le Christ Sauveur selon Origène." *Studia Missionalia* 30 (1981): 63–88.

Cumont, Franz. "La polémique de l'Ambrosiaster contre les païens." *Revue d'Histoire et de Littérature Religieuses* 8 (1903): 417–40.

Cunningham, Mary. "Andrew of Crete: A High-Style Preacher of the Eighth Century." In Cunningham and Allen, *Preacher and Audience* (q.v.). Pp. 267–94.

———. "The Sixth Century: A Turning Point for Byzantine Homiletics?" In Allen and Jeffreys, *Sixth Century* (q.v.). Pp. 176–86.

Cunningham, Mary B., and Pauline Allen (eds.). *Preacher and Audience: Studies in Early Christian and Byzantine Homiletics*. A New History of the Sermon 1. Leiden: Brill, 1998.

Curran, John R. *Pagan City and Christian Capital: Rome in the Fourth Century*. Oxford Classical Monographs. New York: Oxford University Press, 2000.

Daniélou, Jean. *The Theology of Jewish-Christianity*. Tr. John A. Baker. London: Darton, Longman & Todd, 1964

Darrouzès, J. "Manuscrits originaires de Chypre à la Bibliothèque Nationale de Paris." *Revue des Études Byzantines* 8 (1950): 162–96.

Davis, William D., and Dale Allison. *Matthew 1–7*. International Critical Commentary. London: T & T Clark, 1988.

Dawsey, James. "The Origin of Luke's Positive Perception of the Temple." *Perspectives in Religious Studies* 18 (1991): 5–22.

Dawson, David. *Allegorical Readers and Cultural Revision in Ancient Alexandria*. Berkeley: University of California Press, 1992.

Dawson, John David. *Christian Figural Reading and the Fashioning of Identity.* Berkeley: University of California Press, 2002.

Delehaye, Hippolyte. "Les ménologes grecs." *Analecta Bollandiana* 16 (1897): 311–29.

———. *Synaxaires byzantines, ménologes, typica.* London: Variorum, 1977.

Deliyannis, Deborah Mauskopf. *Ravenna in Late Antiquity.* Cambridge: Cambridge University Press, 2010.

Dench, Emma. *Romulus' Asylum: Roman Identities from the Age of Alexander to the Age of Hadrian.* Oxford: Oxford University Press, 2005.

Denysenko, Nicholas. "The *Hypapante* Feast in Fourth to Eighth Century Jerusalem." *Studia Liturgica* 37 (2007): 73–97.

Derrida, Jacques. *Archive Fever: A Freudian Impression.* Tr. Eric Prenowitz. Chicago: University of Chicago Press, 1996.

Dix, Gregory. *The Shape of the Liturgy.* 2nd ed. San Francisco: Harper & Row, 1982.

Dorival, Gilles. "Exégèse juive et exégèse chrétienne." In Geerlings and Schulze, *Kommentar* (q.v.). Pp. 131–50.

Douglas, Mary. *Natural Symbols: Explorations in Cosmology.* New York: Vintage Books, 1973.

Droge, Arthur. *Homer or Moses? Early Christian Interpretations of the History of Culture.* Hermeneutische Untersuchungen zur Theologie 26. Tübingen: Mohr Siebeck, 1989.

Duffy, John. "New Fragments of Sophronius of Jerusalem and Aristo of Pella?" Paper delivered at the Oxford International Conference on Patristic Studies, August 6–11, 2007.

Dunlop, Beth Elise. "Earliest Greek Patristic Orations on the Nativity: A Study Including Translations." Ph.D. diss., Boston College, 2004.

Dunn, Geoffrey D. "Mary's Virginity *in partu* and Tertullian's Anti-Docetism in *De carne Christi* Reconsidered." *Journal of Theological Studies* n.s. 58 (2007): 467–84.

———. "*Pro temporum condicione*: Jews and Christians as God's People in Tertullian's *adversus Iudaeos*." In *Prayer and Spirituality in the Early Church.* Vol. 2. Ed. Pauline Allen et al. Brisbane: Centre for Early Christian Studies, Australian Catholic University, 1999. Pp. 315–41.

———. "Rhetoric and Tertullian's *de virginibus velandis*." *Vigiliae Christianae* 59 (2005): 1–30.

———. "Tertullian and Rebekah: A Re-Reading of an 'Anti-Jewish' Argument in Early Christian Literature." *Vigiliae Christianae* 52 (1998): 119–45.

———. *Tertullian's "Adversus Iudaeos": A Rhetorical Analysis.* Patristic Monograph Series. Washington, D.C.: Catholic University of America Press, 2008.

———. "The Universal Spread of Christianity as a Rhetorical Argument in Tertullian's *adversus Iudaeos*." *Journal of Early Christian Studies* 8 (2000): 1–19.

Dunn, James D. G. *The Epistles to the Colossians and to Philemon.* The New International Greek Testament Commentary. Grand Rapids, Mich.: Wm. B. Eerdmans, 1996.

———. *Paul and the Mosaic Law.* Grand Rapids, Mich.: Wm. B. Eerdmans, 2001.

Duval, Yves-Marie. *L'affaire Jovinien: D'une crise de la société romaine à une crise de la pensée chrétienne à la fin du 4e et au début du 5e siècle.* Studia Ephemeridis Augustinianum 83. Rome: Institutum Patristicum Augustinianum, 2003.

Eagleton, Terry. *The Idea of Culture.* Blackwell Manifestos. Malden: Blackwell, 2000.

———. *Literary Theory: An Introduction.* 2nd ed. Minneapolis: University of Minnesota Press, 1996.

———. "Wittgenstein's Friends." *New Left Review* 135 (September–October 1982): 64–90.

Edmondson, Jonathan, and Alison Keith. *Roman Dress and the Fabric of Roman Culture.* Toronto: University of Toronto Press, 2008.

Edwards, Catharine. *Death in Ancient Rome.* New Haven: Yale University Press, 2007.

———. "Incorporating the Alien: The Art of Conquest." In Edwards and Woolf, *Rome the Cosmopolis* (q.v.). Pp. 44–70.

———. *Writing Rome: Textual Approaches to the City.* Cambridge: Cambridge University Press, 1996.

Edwards, Catharine, and Greg Woolf. "Cosmopolis: Rome as World City." In Edwards and Woolf, *Rome the Cosmopolis* (q.v.). Pp. 1–20.

———. *Rome the Cosmopolis.* Cambridge: Cambridge University Press, 2003.

Edwards, James R. "The *Gospel of the Ebionites* and the Gospel of Luke." *New Testament Studies* 48 (2002): 568–86.

Edwards, Mark J. *Origen Against Plato.* Ashgate Studies in Philosophy & Late Antiquity. Burlington, Vt.: Ashgate, 2002.

Edwards, Mark, Martin Goodman, and Simon Price (eds.). *Apologetics in the Roman Empire: Pagans, Jews, and Christians.* Oxford: Oxford University Press, 1999

Ehrhard, Albert. *Überlieferung und Bestand der hagiographischen und homiletischen Literatur der griechischen Kirche von den Anfängen bis zum Ende des 16. Jahrhunderts.* 3 vols. Texte und Untersuchungen 50–52. Leipzig: J. C. Hinrichs, 1937–52.

Ehrman, Bart D. "Heracleon, Origen, and the Text of the Fourth Gospel." *Vigiliae Christianae* 47 (1993): 105–18.

———. *Jesus: Apocalyptic Prophet of the New Millennium.* New York: Oxford University Press, 1999.

———. *Lost Christianities: The Battle for Scripture and the Faiths We Never Knew.* New York: Oxford University Press, 2003.

———. *The Orthodox Corruption of Scripture: The Effects of Early Christological Controversies on the Text of the New Testament.* New York: Oxford University Press, 1993.

Eilberg-Schwartz, Howard. *The Savage in Judaism: An Anthropology of Israelite Religion and Ancient Judaism.* Bloomington: Indiana University Press, 1990.

Eisenbaum, Pamela. *Paul Was Not a Christian: The Original Message of a Misunderstood Apostle.* San Francisco: HarperOne, 2009.

Elliott, Dyan. *Fallen Bodies: Pollution, Sexuality, and Demonology in the Middle Ages.* The Middle Ages Series. Philadelphia: University of Pennsylvania Press, 1999.

Elliott, James K. *The Apocryphal New Testament.* Oxford: Clarendon Press, 1993.

Elm, Susanna. " 'Pierced by Bronze Needles': Anti-Montanist Charges of Ritual Stigmatization in Their Fourth-Century Context." *Journal of Early Christian Studies* 4 (1996): 409–39.

———. *"Virgins of God": The Making of Asceticism in Late Antiquity.* Oxford Classical Monographs. Oxford: Oxford University Press, 1994.

Esbroeck, Michel van. "Col. 2, 11 «dans la circoncision du Christ»." In *Gnosticisme et monde hellénistique: Actes du colloque de Louvain-la-Neuve (11–14 mars 1980).* Ed. Julien Ries. Publications de l'Institut Orientalists de Louvain. Louvain-la-Neuve: Université Catholique de Louvain Institut Orientaliste, 1982. Pp. 299–35.

Eshel, Hanan. "The Bar Kochba Revolt, 132–35." In Katz, *Cambridge History of Judaism* (q.v.). Pp. 105–27.

Evans, Craig. "Assessing Progress in the Third Quest of the Historical Jesus." *Journal for the Study of the Historical Jesus* 4 (2006): 35–54.

Evans, Fred. "Bakhtin, Communication, and the Politics of Multiculturalism." *Constellations* 5 (1998): 403–23.

Falassi, Alessandro. *Time out of Time: Essays on the Festival.* Albuquerque: University of New Mexico Press, 1987.

Farag, Lois M. *St. Cyril of Alexandria, a New Testament Exegete: His Commentary on the Gospel of John.* Gorgias Dissertations 29. Piscataway, N.J.: Gorgias Press, 2007.

Farley, David. *An Irreverent Curiosity: In Search of the Church's Strangest Relic in Italy's Oddest Town.* New York: Gotham, 2009.

Farney, Gary. *Ethnic Identity and Aristocratic Competition in Republican Rome.* Cambridge: Cambridge University Press, 2007.

Farrell, Joseph. *Latin Language and Latin Culture: From Ancient to Modern Times.* Cambridge: Cambridge University Press, 2001.

Feeney, Denis. *Caesar's Calendar: Ancient Times and the Beginnings of History.* Sather Classical Lectures 65. Berkeley: University of California Press, 2007.

Ferguson, Everett. "Baptism According to Origen." *Evangelical Quarterly* 78 (2006): 117–35.

———. *Baptism in the Early Church: History, Theology, and Liturgy in the First Five Centuries.* Grand Rapids, Mich.: Wm. B. Eerdmans, 2009.

———. "Preaching at Epiphany: Gregory of Nyssa and John Chrysostom on Baptism and the Church." *Church History* 66 (1997): 1–17.

———. "Spiritual Circumcision in Early Christianity." *Scottish Journal of Theology* 41 (1988): 485–97.

Finley, Gregory C. "The Ebionites and 'Jewish Christianity': Examining Heresy and the Attitudes of Church Fathers." Ph.D. diss., Catholic University of America, 2009.

Finn, Thomas. *From Death to Rebirth: Ritual and Conversion in Antiquity.* New York: Paulist Press, 1997.

Fitzmyer, Joseph A. *The Gospel According to Luke I–IX: Introduction, Translation, Notes.* Anchor Bible 28. Garden City, N.Y.: Doubleday, 1982.

Fonrobert, Charlotte. *Menstrual Purity: Rabbinic and Christian Reconstructions of Biblical*

Gender. Contraversions: Jews and Other Differences. Stanford, Calif.: Stanford University Press, 2000.

Förster, Hans. *Die Anfänge von Weihnachten und Epiphanias: Eine Anfrage an die Entstehungshypothesen.* Studien und Texte zu Antike und Christentum 46. Tübingen: Mohr Siebeck, 2007.

Foster, Paul. "Polymorphic Christology: Its Origins and Development in Earliest Christianity." *Journal of Theological Studies* n.s. 58 (2007): 66–99.

Foucault, Michel. "The Discourse on Language." In *The Archaeology of Knowledge and the Discourse on Language.* Tr. Rupert Sawyer. New York: Pantheon Books, 1972. Pp. 215–38.

———. "Of Other Spaces." Tr. Jay Miskowiec. *Diacritics* 16 (1986): 22–27.

———. "The Order of Discourse." In *Untying the Text: A Post-Structuralist Reading.* Ed. Robert Young. Tr. Ian McLeod. London: Routledge, 1981. Pp. 48–78.

Frank, Georgia. "The Image in Tandem: Painting Metaphors and Moral Discourse in Late Antique Christianity." In *The Subjective Eye: Essays in Culture, Religion, and Gender in Honor of Margaret R. Miles.* Ed. Richard Valantasis, Deborah J. Hanynes, James D. Smith III. Princeton Theological Monograph Series 59. Eugene, Ore.: Pickwick, 2006. Pp. 33–47.

Frankfurter, David. "Beyond 'Jewish Christianity': Continuing Religious Sub-Cultures of the Second and Third Centuries and Their Documents." In Becker and Reed, *Ways That Never Parted* (q.v.). Pp. 131–43.

Frede, Michael. "Celsus' Attack on the Christians." In *Philosophia Togata II: Plato and Aristotle at Rome.* Ed. Jonathan Barnes and Miriam Griffen. Oxford: Clarendon Press, 1997. Pp. 218–40.

———. "Origen's Treatise Against Celsus." In Edwards, Goodman, and Price, *Apologetics in the Roman Empire* (q.v.). Pp. 131–55.

Fredriksen, Paula. *Augustine and the Jews: A Christian Defense of Jews and Judaism.* New York: Doubleday, 2008.

———. "*Excaecati Occulta Iustitia Dei*: Augustine on Jews and Judaism." *Journal of Early Christian Studies* 3 (1995): 299–324.

———. *Jesus of Nazareth, King of the Jews: A Jewish Life and the Emergence of Christianity.* New York: Alfred Knopf, 1999.

———. "Judaism, the Circumcision of Gentiles, and Apocalyptic Hope: Another Look at Galatians 1 and 2." *Journal of Theological Studies* n.s. 42 (1991): 532–64.

Frilingos, Christopher. "No Child Left Behind: Knowledge and Violence in the *Infancy Gospel of Thomas*." *Journal of Early Christian Studies* 17 (2009): 27–54.

———. *Spectacles of Empire: Monsters, Martyrs, and the Book of Revelation.* Divinations. Philadelphia: University of Pennsylvania Press, 2004.

Furst, Alfons. "Hieronymus über die heilsame Täuschung." *Zeitschrift für Antikes Christentum* 2 (1998): 97–112.

Futrell, Alison. *Blood in the Arena: The Spectacle of Roman Power.* Austin: University of Texas Press, 1997.

Gaddis, Michael. *There Is No Crime for Those Who Have Christ: Religious Violence in the Christian Roman Empire.* Transformation of the Classical Heritage 39. Berkeley: University of California Press, 2005.

Gager, John. *Reinventing Paul.* Oxford: Oxford University Press, 2000.

Galbiati, E. "La circoncisione di Gesù (*Luca* 2, 21)." *Bibbia e Oriente* 8 (1966): 37–45.

Gamble, Harry Y. *Books and Readers in the Early Church: A History of Early Christian Texts.* New Haven, Conn.: Yale University Press, 1995.

———. "Marcion and the 'Canon.'" In *The Cambridge History of Christianity.* Vol. 1: *Origins to Constantine.* Ed. Margaret M. Mitchell and Frances M. Young. Cambridge: Cambridge University Press, 2006. Pp. 195–213.

Garber, Marjorie. *Vested Interests: Cross-Dressing and Cultural Anxiety.* New York: Routledge, 1992.

Garroway, Joshua. "The Law-Observant Lord: John Chrysostom's Engagement with the Jewishness of Christ." *Journal of Early Christian Studies* 18 (2010): 591–615.

Geerard, Maurice (ed.). *Clavis Patrum Graecorum.* 6 vols. Turnhout: Brepols, 1974–2003.

Geerlings, Wilhelm. "Die lateinisch-patristischen Kommentare." In Geerlings and Schulze, *Kommentar in Antike und Mittelalter* (q.v.). Pp. 1–14.

Geerlings, Wilhelm, and Christian Schulze (eds.). *Der Kommentar in Antike und Mittelalter: Beiträge zu einer Erforschung.* Clavis Commentariorum Antiquitatis et Medii Aevi. Leiden: Brill, 2002.

Geller, Jay. *On Freud's Jewish Body: Mitigating Circumcisions.* New York: Fordham University Press, 2007.

Getcha, Job. "The Unity of the Mystery of Salvation According to the Festal Homilies of Hesychius of Jerusalem." *Studia Patristica* 37 (2001): 472–81.

Gilbert, Gary. "The List of Nations in Acts 2: Roman Propaganda and the Lukan Response." *Journal of Biblical Literature* 121 (2002): 497–529.

Gilman, Sander. "Decircumcision: The First Aesthetic Surgery." *Modern Judaism* 17 (1997): 201–10.

———. *The Jew's Body.* New York: Routledge, 1991.

Ginsberg, Elaine K. "Introduction: The Politics of Passing." In Ginsberg, *Passing* (q.v.). Pp. 1–18.

——— (ed.). *Passing and the Fiction of Identity.* Durham, N.C.: Duke University Press, 1996.

Glancy, Jennifer. *Corporal Knowledge: Early Christian Bodies.* New York: Oxford University Press, 2010.

———. "The Law of the Opened Body: Tertullian on the Nativity." *Henoch* 30 (2008): 45–66.

Gleason, Maud. *Making Men: Sophists and Self-Presentation in Ancient Rome.* Princeton, N.J.: Princeton University Press, 1995.

Goldhill, Simon (ed.). *Being Greek Under Rome: Cultural Identity, the Second Sophistic, and the Development of Empire.* Cambridge: Cambridge University Press, 2001.

Goldman, Norma. "Reconstructing Roman Clothing." In Sebesta and Bonfante, *World of Roman Costume* (q.v.). Pp. 213–37.

Goodman, Martin. "Nerva, the *fiscus iudaicus*, and Jewish Identity." *Journal of Roman Studies* 79 (1989): 40–44.

Goranson, Stephen. "The Joseph of Tiberias Episode in Epiphanius: Studies in Jewish and Christian Relations." Ph.D. diss., Duke University, 1990.

———. "Joseph of Tiberias Revisited: Orthodoxies and Heresies in Fourth-Century Galilee." In *Galilee Through the Centuries: A Confluence of Cultures*. Duke Judaic Studies 1. Ed. Eric M. Meyers. Winona Lake, Ind.: Eisenbrauns, 1999. Pp. 335–43.

Grafton, Anthony, and Megan Williams. *Christianity and the Transformation of the Book: Origen, Eusebius, and the Library of Caesarea*. Cambridge, Mass.: Belknap Press of Harvard University Press, 2006.

Grant, Robert. "Review of *Logos und Nomos*." *Journal of Religion* 36 (1956): 270–72.

Graumann, Thomas. *Christus Interpres: Die Einheit von Auslegung und Verkündigung in der Lukasklärung des Ambrosius von Mailand*. Patristische Texte und Studien 41. Berlin: De Gruyter, 1994.

Gregory, Andrew. *The Reception of Luke and Acts in the Period Before Irenaeus: Looking for Luke in the Second Century*. Wissenschaftliche Untersuchungen zum Neuen Testament 2:169. Tübingen: Mohr Siebeck, 2003.

Griffin, John Howard. *Black Like Me*. Boston: Houghton Mifflin, 1961.

Griffin, M. "Claudius in Tacitus." *Classical Quarterly* 40 (1990): 482–501.

———. "The Lyons Tablet and Tacitean Hindsight." *Classical Quarterly* 32 (1982): 404–18.

Griffith, Sidney H. "A Spiritual Father for the Whole World: The Universal Appeal of St. Ephraem the Syrian." *Hugoye* [http://syrcom.cua.edu/syrcom/Hugoye] 1.2 (1998).

Griffiths, Paul. *Religious Reading: The Place of Reading in the Practice of Religion*. New York: Oxford University Press, 1999.

Grillmeier, Aloys. *Christ in Christian Tradition*. Vol. 2: *From the Council of Chalcedon (451) to Gregory the Great (590–604)*. Part 2: *The Church of Constantinople in the Sixth Century*. Tr. Pauline Allen and John Cawte. Louisville, Ky.: Westminster John Knox Press, 1995.

Grosz, Elizabeth. "The Body of Signification." In *Abjection, Melancholia, and Love: The Work of Julia Kristeva*. Ed. John Fletcher and Andrew Benjamin. London: Routledge, 1990. Pp. 80–103.

Gruen, Erich. *Diaspora: Jews Amidst Greeks and Romans*. Cambridge, Mass.: Harvard University Press, 2002.

Guarino, Thomas. "Vincent of Lerins and the Hermeneutical Question: Historical and Theological Reflections." *Gregorianum* 75 (1994): 491–523.

Haberman, Bonna Devora. "Foreskin Sacrifice: Zipporah's Ritual and the Bloody Bridegroom." In Mark, *Covenant of Circumcision* (q.v.). Pp. 18–29.

Halkin, François. "Les manuscrits grecs de la Bibliothèque Laurentienne à Florence: Inventaire hagiographique." *Analecta Bollandiana* 96 (1978): 5–50.

Hall, Edith. *Inventing the Barbarian: Greek Self-Definition Through Tragedy*. Oxford Classical Monographs. Oxford: Clarendon Press, 1989.

Hall, Jonathan M. *Ethnic Identity in Greek Antiquity.* Cambridge: Cambridge University Press, 1997.

———. *Hellenicity: Between Ethnicity and Culture.* Chicago: University of Chicago Press, 2002.

Hall, Robert. "Epispasm and the Dating of Ancient Jewish Writings." *Journal for the Study of the Pseudepigrapha* 2 (1988): 71–86.

Halleux, André de. "Le commentaire de Philoxène sur *Matthieu* et *Luc*: Deux éditions récentes." *Le Muséon* 93 (1980): 5–35.

———. *Philoxène de Mabbog: Sa vie, ses écrits, sa théologie.* Louvain: Imprimerie Orientaliste, 1963.

Hamm, Dennis. "The Tamid Service in Luke-Acts: The Cultic Background Behind Luke's Theology of Worship (Luke 1:5–25; 18:9–14; 24:50–53; Acts 3:1; 10:3, 30)." *Catholic Biblical Quarterly* 25 (2003): 215–31.

Hanson, R. P. C. *Allegory and Event: A Study of the Sources and Significance of Origen's Interpretation of Scripture.* 2nd ed. Richmond, Va.: Westminster John Knox Press, 2002.

Harmless, William. *Desert Christians: An Introduction to the Literature of Early Monasticism.* Oxford: Oxford University Press, 2004.

Harnack, Adolf von. *Die Altercatio Simonis Iudaei et Theophili Christiani nebst Untersuchungen über die antijüdische Polemik in der alten Kirche.* Texte und Untersuchungen 1.3. Leipzig: J. C. Hinrichs, 1883.

Harpham, Geoffrey Galt. *On the Grotesque: Strategies of Contradiction in Art and Literature.* Princeton, N.J.: Princeton University Press, 1982.

Harrell, Charles L. "Saint Basil the Great as Icon: A Study in Late Antique and Byzantine Historiography, Hagiography, and Iconography." Ph.D. diss., Duke University, 1995.

Harrison, J. R. "Paul and the Imperial Gospel at Thessaloniki." *Journal for the Study of the New Testament* 25 (2002): 71–96.

Harvey, Graham. *The True Israel: Uses of the Names Jew, Hebrew, and Israel in Ancient Jewish and Early Christian Literature.* Arbeiten zur Geschichte des antiken Judentums und des Urchristentums 35. Leiden: Brill, 1996.

Harvey, Susan Ashbrook, and David G. Hunter (eds.). *The Oxford Handbook of Early Christian Studies.* Oxford: Oxford University Press, 2008.

Hasluck, Margaret M. "The Basil-Cake of the Greek New Year." *Folklore* 38 (1927): 143–77.

Hays, Christopher. "Marcion vs. Luke: A Response to the *Plädoyer* of Matthias Klinghardt." *Zeitschrift für die Neutestamentliche Wissenschaft* 99 (2008): 213–32.

Head, Thomas. "Guibert of Nogent, *On Saints and Their Relics*." In *Medieval Hagiography: An Anthology.* Ed. Thomas Head. London: Routledge, 2001. Pp. 399–428.

Heemstra, Marius. *The Fiscus Judaicus and the Parting of the Ways.* Wissenschaftliche Untersuchungen zum neuen Testament 2:277. Tübingen: Mohr Siebeck, 2010.

Hefele, Karl Joseph von, and H. Leclerq. *Histoire des conciles d'après les documents originaux.* 11 vols. Paris: Letouzey et Ané, 1907–52.

Hen, Yitzhak. *Culture and Religion in Merovingian Gaul, A.D. 481–751.* Cultures, Beliefs, and Traditions: Medieval and Early Modern Peoples 1. Leiden: Brill, 1995.

Henderson, John B. *The Construction of Orthodoxy and Heresy: Neo-Confucian, Islamic, Jewish, and Early Christian Patterns.* Albany: State University of New York Press, 1998.

Henry, Patrick. "Why Is Contemporary Scholarship So Enamored of Ancient Heresies?" *Studia Patristica* 17.1 (1982): 123–26.

Heschel, Susannah. "Jesus as a Theological Transvestite." In *Judaism Since Gender.* Ed. Miriam Peskowitz and Laura Levitt. London: Routledge, 1997. Pp. 188–212.

Heslin, Peter. "Augustus, Domitian, and the So-called Horologium Augusti." *Journal of Roman Studies* 97 (2007): 1–20.

Hill, Charles E. "Cerinthus, Gnostic or Chiliast? A New Solution to an Old Problem." *Journal of Early Christian Studies* 8 (2000): 135–72.

Hodge, Caroline Johnson. *If Sons, Then Heirs: A Study of Kinship and Ethnicity in the Letters of Paul.* Oxford: Oxford University Press, 2007.

Hoffman, Lawrence A. *Covenant of Blood: Circumcision and Gender in Rabbinic Judaism.* Chicago Studies in the History of Judaism. Chicago: University of Chicago Press, 1996.

Holl, Karl. *Amphilochius von Ikonium in seinem Verhältnis zu den grossen Kappadoziern.* Tübingen: J. C. B. Mohr, 1904.

Hollerich, Michael J. *Eusebius of Caesarea's "Commentary on Isaiah": Christian Exegesis in the Age of the Constantine.* Oxford Early Christian Studies. Oxford: Clarendon Press, 1999.

Holman, Susan. *The Hungry Are Dying: Beggars and Bishops in Roman Cappadocia.* Oxford Studies in Historical Theology. Oxford: Oxford University Press, 2001.

Hombergen, Daniël. "Barsanuphius and John of Gaza and the Origenist Controversy." In *Christian Gaza in Late Antiquity.* Ed. Brouria Bitton-Ashkelony and Aryeh Kofsky. Jerusalem Studies in Religion and Culture. Leiden: Brill, 2004. Pp. 173–81.

———. *The Second Origenist Controversy: A New Perspective on Cyril of Scythopolis' Monastic Biographies as Historical Sources for Sixth-Century Origenism.* Studia Anselmiana 132. Rome: Studio S. Anselmo, 2001.

Horbury, William. *Jews and Christians in Contact and Controversy.* Edinburgh: T & T Clark, 1998.

Horn, Cornelia. *Asceticism and Christological Controversy in Fifth-Century Palestine: The Career of Peter the Iberian.* Oxford Early Christian Studies. Oxford: Oxford University Press, 2006.

Horn, Friedrich Wilhelm. "Der Verzicht auf die Beschneidung im frühen Christentum." *New Testament Studies* 42 (1996): 479–505.

Horner, Timothy J. "Jewish Aspects of the *Protoevangelium of James.*" *Journal of Early Christian Studies* 12 (2004): 313–35.

———. *Listening to Trypho: Justin Martyr's Dialogue Reconsidered.* Contributions to Biblical Exegesis and Theology 28. Leuven: Peeters, 2001.

Horowitz, Elliott S. *Reckless Rites: Purim and the Legacy of Jewish Violence.* Jews, Christians, and Muslims from the Ancient to the Modern World. Princeton, N.J.: Princeton University Press, 2006.

Horsley, Richard. *Paul and Empire: Religion and Power in Roman Imperial Society.* Harrisburg, Pa.: Trinity Press International, 1997.

Horst, Pieter W. van der. "Philo and the Rabbis on Genesis: Similar Questions, Different Answers." In Volgers and Zamagni, *Erotapokriseis* (q.v.). Pp. 55–70.

Hoyland, Robert G. *Seeing Islam as Others Saw It: A Survey and Evaluation of Christian, Jewish, and Zoroastrian Writings on Early Islam.* Princeton, N.J.: Darwin Press, 1997.

Humphries, Mark. *Communities of the Blessed: Social Environment and Religious Change in Northern Italy, AD 200–400.* Oxford Early Christian Studies. Oxford: Oxford University Press, 1999.

Hunt, J. P. T. "Colossians 2:11–12, the Circumcision/Baptism Analogy, and Infant Circumcision." *Tyndale Bulletin* 41 (1990): 227–43.

Hunter, David G. "Fourth-Century Latin Writers." In *The Cambridge History of Early Christian Literature.* Ed. Frances Young, Lewis Ayres, and Augustine Casiday. Cambridge: Cambridge University Press, 2004. Pp. 302–17.

———. *Marriage, Celibacy, and Heresy in Ancient Christianity: The Jovinianist Controversy.* Oxford Early Christian Studies. Oxford: Oxford University Press, 2007.

———. "Rereading the Jovinianist Controversy: Asceticism and Clerical Authority in Late Ancient Christianity." *Journal of Medieval and Early Modern Studies* 33 (2003): 453–70. Also in Martin and Miller, *Cultural Turn in Late Ancient Studies* (q.v.). Pp. 119–35.

———. "Resistance to the Virginal Ideal in Late-Fourth-Century Rome: The Case of Jovinian." *Theological Studies* 48 (1987): 45–64.

———. "2008 NAPS Presidential Address: The Significance of Ambrosiaster." *Journal of Early Christian Studies* 17 (2009): 1–26.

Hutcheon, Cyprian Robert. "'God Is with Us': The Temple in Luke-Acts." *St. Vladimir's Theological Quarterly* 44 (2000): 3–33.

Hvalvik, Reidar. "Barnabas 9.7–9 and the Author's Supposed Use of *Gematria.*" *New Testament Studies* 33 (1987): 276–82.

———. *The Struggle for Scripture and Covenant: The Purpose of the "Epistle of Barnabas" and Jewish-Christian Competition in the Second Century.* Wissenschaftliche Untersuchungen zur Neuen Testament 2:82. Tübingen: Mohr Siebeck, 1996.

International Marian Research Institute. "Marian Feasts Past and Present." University of Dayton, http://campus.udayton.edu/mary/resources/dogmas.html.

Irvine, Martin. *The Making of Textual Culture: "Grammatica" and Literary Theory, 350–1100.* Cambridge: Cambridge University Press, 1994.

Isaac, Benjamin H. *The Invention of Racism in Classical Antiquity.* Princeton, N.J.: Princeton University Press, 2004.

———. "Orientals and Jews in the *Historia Augusta*: Fourth-Century Prejudice and Stereotypes." In *The Near East Under Roman Rule: Selected Papers.* Mnemosyne Supplementum 177. Leiden: Brill, 1998. Pp. 268–83.

Jacobs, Andrew S. "Blood Will Out: Jesus' Circumcision and Early Christian Readings of Exodus 4:24–26." *Henoch* 30 (2008): 310–32.

————. "The Disorder of Books: Priscillian's Canonical Defense of Apocrypha." *Harvard Theological Review* 93 (2000): 135–59.

————. "A Jew's Jew: Paul and the Early Christian Problem of Jewish Origins." *Journal of Religion* 86 (2006): 258–86.

————. "'Let Him Guard *Pietas*': Early Christian Exegesis and the Ascetic Family." *Journal of Early Christian Studies* 11 (2003): 265–81.

————. "The Lion and the Lamb: Reconsidering Jewish-Christian Relations in Antiquity." In Becker and Reed, *Ways That Never Parted* (q.v.). Pp. 95–118.

————. *Remains of the Jews: The Holy Land and Christian Empire in Late Antiquity.* Divinations. Stanford, Calif.: Stanford University Press, 2004.

————. "'Solomon's Salacious Song': Foucault's Author Function and the Early Christian Interpretation of the *Canticum Canticorum*." *Medieval Encounters* 4 (1998): 1–23.

————. "'What Has Rome to Do with Bethlehem?' Cultural Capital(s) and Religious Imperialism in Late Ancient Christianity." *Classical Receptions Journal* 3 (2011): 29–45.

Jensen, Robin. *Understanding Early Christian Art.* London: Routledge, 2000.

Jervell, Jacob. "The Circumcised Messiah." Tr. Roy A. Harrisville. In *The Unknown Paul: Essays on Luke-Acts and Early Christian History.* Minneapolis: Augsburg, 1984. Pp. 138–45. Originally published as "Den omskårne Messias." *Svensk Exegetisk Årsbok* 37–38 (1972–73): 145–55.

————. "The Divided People of God: The Restoration of Israel and Salvation for the Gentiles." In Jervell, *Luke and the People of God* (q.v.). Pp. 41–74.

————. "The Law in Luke Acts." In Jervell, *Luke and the People of God* (q.v.). Pp. 133–51.

————. *Luke and the People of God: A New Look at Luke-Acts.* Minneapolis: Augsburg, 1972.

Johnson, Aaron P. *Ethnicity and Argument in Eusebius' "Praeparatio Evangelica."* Oxford Early Christian Studies. Oxford: Oxford University Press, 2006.

————. "Identity, Descent, and Polemic: Ethnic Argumentation in Eusebius' *Praeparatio Evangelica*." *Journal of Early Christian Studies* 12 (2004): 25–56.

Johnson, Luke Timothy. *The Gospel of Luke.* Sacra Pagina 3. Ed. Daniel J. Harrington, S. J. Collegeville, Minn.: Liturgical Press, 1991.

————. "Luke-Acts, Book of." In *Anchor Bible Dictionary.* Ed. David Noel Freedman. New York: Doubleday, 1992. Vol. 4, pp. 403–20.

Johnson, Maxwell. "The Apostolic Tradition." In Wainwright and Westerfield Tucker, *Oxford History of Christian Worship* (q.v.). Pp. 32–76.

Katz, Steven T. (ed.). *The Cambridge History of Judaism.* Vol. 4: *The Late Roman-Rabbinic Period.* Cambridge: Cambridge University Press, 2006.

Kawash, Samira. "*The Autobiography of an Ex-Coloured Man*: (Passing for) Black Passing for White." In Ginsberg, *Passing* (q.v.). Pp. 59–74.

Keating, Daniel A. *The Appropriation of Divine Life in Cyril of Alexandria.* Oxford Theological Monographs. Oxford: Oxford University Press, 2004.

Keiser, Jeffrey. "The Circumcision of Jesus (Luke 2:21) and the Formation of Luke's Infancy Narrative." Paper delivered at the Society of Biblical Literature Annual Meeting, November 17–20, 2007.

Kim, Young Richard. "The Imagined Worlds of Epiphanius of Cyprus." Ph.D. diss., University of Michigan, 2006.

King, Daniel. "New Evidence on the Philoxenian Versions of the New Testament and the Nicene Creed." *Huyoge* 13.1 (2010): 9–30.

King, Karen L. *The Secret Revelation of John*. Cambridge, Mass.: Harvard University Press, 2006.

———. *What Is Gnosticism?* Cambridge, Mass.: Harvard University Press, 2005.

———. "Which Early Christianity?" In Harvey and Hunter, *Oxford Handbook of Early Christian Studies* (q.v.). Pp. 66–84.

Klijn, A. F. J. *Jewish-Christian Gospel Tradition*. Supplements to *Vigiliae Christianae* 17. Leiden: Brill, 1992.

Klijn, A. F. J., and G. J. Reinink. *Patristic Evidence for Jewish Christian Sects*. Supplements to *Novum Testamentum* 36. Leiden: Brill, 1973.

Klinghardt, Matthias. "The Marcionite Gospel and the Synoptic Problem: A New Suggestion." *Novum Testamentum* 50 (2008): 1–27.

———. "Markion vs. Lukas: Plädoyer für die Wiederaufnahme eines alten Falles." *New Testament Studies* 52 (2006): 484–513.

Klostermann, Erich. *Das Lukasevangelium*. Handbuch zum neuen Testament 5. Tübingen: Mohr Siebeck, 1929.

Knox, John. *Marcion and the New Testament: An Essay on the Early History of the Canon*. Chicago: University of Chicago Press, 1942.

———. "On the Vocabulary of Marcion's Gospel." *Journal of Biblical Literature* 58 (1939): 193–201.

———. "Philemon and the Authenticity of Colossians." *Journal of Religion* 18 (1938): 144–60.

Koch, Dietrich-Alex. "The God-Fearers Between Fact and Fiction." *Studia Theologica* 60 (2006): 62–90.

Koch, Glenn Alan. "A Critical Investigation of Epiphanius' Knowledge of the Ebionites: A Translation and Critical Discussion of *Panarion* 30." Ph.D. diss., University of Pennsylvania, 1976.

Koltun-Fromm, Naomi. "Re-Imagining Tatian: The Damaging Effects of Polemical Rhetoric." *Journal of Early Christian Studies* 16 (2008): 1–30.

Kotzé, Annemarré. "The 'Anti-Manichaean' Passage in *Confessions* 3 and Its 'Manichaean Audience.' " *Vigiliae Christianae* 62 (2008): 187–200.

Kraus, Christina Shuttleworth. "Introduction: Reading Commentaries/Commentaries as Reading." In *The Classical Commentary: Histories, Practices, Theory*. Ed. Christina Shuttleworth Kraus and Roy K. Gibson. *Mnemosyne* Supplement 323. Leiden: Brill, 2002. Pp. 1–27.

Kristeva, Julia. *Powers of Horror: An Essay on Abjection*. Tr. Leon S. Roudiez. New York: Columbia University Press, 1982.

Krueger, Derek. *Writing and Holiness: The Practice of Authorship in the Early Christian East*. Divinations. Philadelphia: University of Pennsylvania Press, 2004.

Kuefler, Mathew. *The Manly Eunuch: Masculinity, Gender Ambiguity, and Christian Ideology in Late Antiquity*. The Chicago Series on Sexuality, History, and Society. Chicago: University of Chicago Press, 2001.

Kuhn, Karl A. "The Point of the Step-Parallelism in Luke 1–2." *New Testament Studies* 47 (2001): 38–49.

Kunin, Seth D. "The Bridegroom of Blood: A Structuralist Analysis." *Journal for the Study of the Old Testament* 70 (1996): 3–16.

Labbie, Erin Felicia. *Lacan's Medievalism*. Minneapolis: University of Minnesota Press, 2006.

Lacan, Jacques. "The Mirror Stage as Formative of the Function of the I as Revealed in Pyschoanalytic Experience." In *Écrits: A Selection*. Tr. Alan Sheridan. New York: Norton, 1977. Pp. 1–7.

Lahey, Lawrence. "Evidence for Jewish Believers in Christian-Jewish Dialogues Through the Sixth Century (Excluding Justin)." In Skarsaune and Hvalvik, *Jewish Believers in Jesus* (q.v.). Pp. 581–639.

Lane, Christopher. Introduction. In *The Pyschoanalysis of Race*. Ed. Christopher Lane. New York: Columbia University Press, 1998. Pp. 1–37.

Lange, Christian. *The Portrayal of Christ in the Syriac Commentary on the Diatessaron*. CSCO 616, Subsidia 118. Leuven: Peeters, 2005.

Lapeyre, G. G. *Saint Fulgence de Ruspe: Un évêque catholique africaine sous la domination vandale*. Paris: Lethielleux, 1929.

Lardet, Pierre. *L'apologie de Jérôme contre Rufin: Un commentaire*. Supplements to *Vigiliae Christianae* 15. Leiden: Brill, 1993.

Layton, Richard. *Didymus the Blind and His Circle in Late-Antique Alexandria: Virtue and Narrative in Biblical Scholarship*. Urbana: University of Illinois Press, 2004.

———. "Plagiarism and Lay Patronage of Ascetic Scholarship: Jerome, Ambrose, and Rufinus." *Journal of Early Christian Studies* 10 (2002): 489–522.

Le Boulluec, Alain. *La notion de l'hérésie dans la littérature grecque, IIe–IIIe siècles*. Paris: Études Augustiniennes, 1985.

Leonhard, Clemens. "Die Beschneidung Christi in der syrischen *Schatzhöhle*: Beobachtungen zu Datierung und Überlieferung des Werks." In *Syriaca II*. Ed. Martin Tamcke. Münster: Lit, 2004. Pp. 11–28.

———. *The Jewish Pesach and the Origins of the Christian Easter: Open Questions in Current Research*. Berlin: De Gruyter, 2006.

Lepelley, Claude. "L'aristocratie lettrée païenne: Une menace aux yeux d'Augustin (à propos du sermon Dolbeau 26–Mayence 62)." In Madec, *Augustin prédicateur* (q.v.). Pp. 327–42.

Leyerle, Blake. "Blood Is Seed." *Journal of Religion* 81 (2001): 26–48.

———. "Chrysostom on the Gaze." *Journal of Early Christian Studies* 1 (1993): 159–74.

L'Huillier, Peter. *The Church of the Ancient Councils*. Crestwood, N.Y.: St. Vladimir's Seminary Press, 1995.

Liebescheutz, J. H. W. G. *Decline and Fall of the Roman City*. Oxford: Oxford University Press, 2001.

Lietzmann, Hans. *Apollinaris von Laodicea und seine Schule: Texte und Untersuchungen.* Tübingen: Mohr Siebeck, 1904.

Lieu, Judith. *Christian Identity in the Jewish and Graeco-Roman World.* Oxford: Oxford University Press, 2004.

———. "Circumcision, Women, and Salvation." *New Testament Studies* 40 (1994): 358–70.

———. *Image and Reality: The Jews in the World of the Christians in the Second Century.* London: T & T Clark, 1996.

———. "'Impregnable Ramparts and Walls of Iron': Boundary and Identity in Early 'Judaism' and 'Christianity.'" *New Testament Studies* 48 (2002): 297–313.

———. "The Parting of the Ways: Theological Construct or Historical Reality?" *Journal of the Study of the New Testament* 56 (1994): 101–19.

Lieu, Samuel. *Manichaeism in the Later Roman Empire and Medieval China.* 2nd ed. Wissenschaftliche Untersuchungen zum Neuen Testament 63. Tübingen: Mohr Siebeck, 1992.

Linder, Amnon. *The Jews in the Legal Sources of the Early Middle Ages.* Detroit: Wayne State University Press, 1997.

Livesey, Nina E. *Circumcision as a Malleable Symbol.* Wissenschaftliche Untersuchungen zum neuen Testament 2:295. Tübingen: Mohr Siebeck, 2010.

———. "Theological Identity Making: Justin's Use of Circumcision to Create Jews and Christians." *Journal of Early Christian Studies* 18 (2010): 51–79.

Long, D. Stephen. "Radical Orthodoxy." In *The Cambridge Companion to Postmodern Theology.* Ed. Kevin J. Vanhoozer. Cambridge: Cambridge University Press, 2003. Pp. 126–46.

Loomba, Ania. *Colonialism/Postcolonialism.* The New Critical Idiom. London: Routledge, 1998.

Lunn-Rockliffe, Sophie. *Ambrosiaster's Political Theology.* Oxford Early Christian Studies. Oxford: Oxford University Press, 2007.

Lyman, Rebecca. "The Politics of Passing: Justin Martyr's Conversion as a Problem of 'Hellenization.'" In *Conversion in Late Antiquity and the Early Middle Ages: Seeing and Believing.* Ed. Kenneth Mills and Anthony Grafton. Studies in Contemporary History. Rochester, N.Y.: University of Rochester Press, 2003. Pp. 36–60.

———. "2002 NAPS Presidential Address: Hellenism and Heresy." *Journal of Early Christian Studies* 11 (2003): 209–22.

MacDonald, Margaret Y. *Colossians and Ephesians.* Sacra Pagina 17. Collegeville, Minn.: Liturgical Press, 2000.

Madec, Goluven (ed.). *Augustin prédicateur (395–411), Actes du Colloque International de Chantilly, 5–7 septembre 1996.* Paris: Institut d'Études Augustiniennes, 1998.

Maier, Harry O. "'Manichee!' Leo the Great and the Orthodox Panopticon." *Journal of Early Christian Studies* 4 (1996): 441–60.

———. "A Sly Civility: Colossians and Empire." *Journal for the Study of the New Testament* 23 (2005): 323–49.

Maraval, Pierre. "Retour sur quelques dates concernant Basile de Césarée et Grégoire de Nysse." *Revue d'Histoire Écclesiastique* 99 (2004): 153–57.

Marguerat, Daniel. *The First Christian Historian: Writing the "Acts of the Apostles."* Tr. Ken McKinney. Society for New Testament Studies Monograph Series 121. Cambridge: Cambridge University Press, 2002.

Mark, Elizabeth Wyner (ed.). *The Covenant of Circumcision: New Perspectives on an Ancient Jewish Rite.* Brandeis Series on Jewish Women. Hanover, N.H.: Brandeis University Press, 2003.

Markus, Robert A. *The End of Ancient Christianity.* Cambridge: Cambridge University Press, 1990.

———. "The Problem of Self-Definition: From Sect to Church." In *Jewish and Christian Self-Definition.* Vol. 1: *The Shaping of Christianity in the Second and Third Centuries.* Ed. E. P. Sanders. London: S. C. M. Press, 1980. Pp. 1–15.

Martin, Dale B. *The Corinthian Body.* New Haven, Conn.: Yale University Press, 1995.

———. "Paul and the Judaism/Hellenism Dichotomy: Toward a Social History of the Question." In *Paul Beyond the Judaism/Hellenism Divide.* Ed. Troels Enberg-Pedersen. Louisville, Ky.: Westminster John Knox Press, 2001. Pp. 29–61.

———. *Sex and the Single Savior: Gender and Sexuality in Biblical Interpretation.* Louisville, Ky.: Westminster John Knox Press, 2006.

Martin, Dale, and Patricia Cox Miller (eds.). *The Cultural Turn in Late Ancient Studies: Gender, Asceticism, and Historiography.* Durham, N.C.: Duke University Press, 2005.

Martin, Ralph P. *Ephesians, Colossians, and Philemon.* Interpretation. Atlanta: John Knox Press, 1991.

Martin, Thomas F. "*Vox Pauli*: Augustine and the Claims to Speak for Paul, an Exploration of Rhetoric at the Service of Exegesis." *Journal of Early Christian Studies* 8 (2000): 237–72.

Mattelaer, Johan J., Robert A. Schipper, and Sakti Das. "The Circumcision of Jesus Christ." *Journal of Urology* 178 (2007): 31–34.

Matthews, Shelly. *Perfect Martyr: The Stoning of Stephen and the Construction of Christian Identity.* New York: Oxford University Press, 2010.

Maxwell, Jaclyn. *Christianization and Communication in Late Antiquity: John Chrysostom and His Congregation in Antioch.* Cambridge: Cambridge University Press, 2006.

May, Gerhard, and Katharina Greschat. *Marcion und seine kirchengeschichtliche Wirkung.* Texte und Untersuchungen 150. Berlin: De Gruyter, 2002.

McCabe, Matt Jackson. *Jewish Christianity Reconsidered: Rethinking Ancient Groups and Texts.* Minneapolis: Fortress, 2007.

McClintock, Anne. *Imperial Leather: Race, Gender, and Sexuality in the Colonial Contest.* New York: Routledge, 1995.

McDaniel, Justin T. *Gathering Leaves and Lifting Words: Histories of Buddhist Monastic Education in Laos and Thailand.* Critical Dialogues in Southeast Asian Studies. Seattle: University of Washington Press, 2008.

McDermott, Thomas. *Catherine of Siena: Spiritual Development in Her Life and Teaching.* Mahwah, N.J.: Paulist Press, 2008.

McGinn, Bernard. *Antichrist: Two Thousand Years of the Human Fascination with Evil.* San Francisco: HarperSanFrancisco, 1994.

McGowan, Andrew. *Ascetic Eucharists: Food and Drink in Early Christian Ritual Meals.* Oxford Early Christian Studies. Oxford: Oxford University Press, 1999.

McVey, Kathleen. *Ephrem the Syrian: Hymns.* Classics of Western Spirituality. New York: Paulist Press, 1989.

Michelson, David. "Practice Leads to Theory: Orthodoxy and the Spiritual Struggle in the World of Philoxenos of Mabbug (470–523)." Ph.D. diss., Princeton University, 2007.

Miles, Margaret M. *Art as Plunder: The Ancient Origins of Debate about Cultural Property.* New York: Cambridge University Press, 2008.

Miller, Patricia Cox. "'Differential Networks': Relics and Other Fragments in Late Antiquity." *Journal of Early Christian Studies* 6 (1998): 113–28.

———. "Is There a Harlot in This Text? Hagiography and the Grotesque." *Journal of Medieval and Early Modern Studies* 33 (2003): 419–35. Also in Martin and Miller, *Cultural Turn in Late Ancient Studies* (q.v.). Pp. 87–102.

———. "Jerome's Centaur: A Hyper-Icon of the Desert." *Journal of Early Christian Studies* 6 (1998): 209–33.

Mimouni, Simon. *La circoncision dans le monde judéen aux époques grecque et romaine: Histoire d'un conflit interne au judaïsme.* Paris: Peeters, 2007.

———. *Le judéo-christianisme ancien: Essais historiques.* Patrimoines. Paris: Cerf, 1998.

Mitchell, Margaret. *The Heavenly Trumpet: John Chrysostom and the Art of Pauline Interpretation.* Louisville, Ky.: Westminster John Knox Press, 2002.

Mitchell, W. J. T. *Picture Theory: Essays on Verbal and Visual Representation.* Chicago: University of Chicago Press, 1994.

Moore-Gilbert, Bart. *Postcolonial Theory: Contexts, Practices, Politics.* London: Verso, 1997.

Morin, G. *Miscellanea agostiniana.* Vol. 1: *Sancti Augustini sermones post mauritios reperti.* Rome: Tipografia poliglottia vaticana, 1930.

Mosshammer, Alden. "Gregory of Nyssa as Homilist." *Studia Patristica* 37 (2001): 212–39.

Moutsoulas, Élie D. "La lettre d'Athanase d'Alexandrie à Epictète." In *Politique et théologie chez Athanase d'Alexandrie.* Ed. Charles Kannengeisser. Théologie Historique 27. Paris: Beauchesne, 1974. Pp. 313–33.

———. "Le problème de la date de la mort de Basile de Césarée." *Studia Patristica* 33 (1997): 196–200.

Müller, Hildegund. "Zur Struktur des patristischen Kommentars: Drei Beispeile aus Augustins *Enarrationes in psalmos.*" In Geerlings and Schulze, *Kommentar* (q.v.). Pp. 15–31.

Muraviev, Alexei. "The Syriac Julian Romance as a Source of the Life of St. Basil the Great." *Studia Patristica* 38 (2001): 240–49.

Nasrallah, Laura. "The Acts of the Apostles, Greek Cities, and Hadrian's Panhellenion." *Journal of Biblical Literature* 127 (2008): 533–66.

———. *Christian Responses to Roman Art and Architecture: The Second-Century Church amid the Spaces of Empire.* Cambridge: Cambridge University Press, 2010.

———. "Mapping the World: Justin, Tatian, and the Second Sophistic." *Harvard Theological Review* 98 (2005): 283–314.

Niehoff, Maren R. "Circumcision as a Marker of Identity: Philo, Origen, and the Rabbis on Gen 17:1–14." *Jewish Studies Quarterly* 10 (2003): 89–123.

Nikulin, Dmitri. "Mikhail Bakhtin: A Theory of Dialogue." *Constellations* 5 (1998): 381–402.

Oberhelman, S. M. "Jerome's Earliest Attack on Ambrose: *On Ephesians*, Prologue (ML 26:469D-70A)." *Transactions of the American Philological Association* 121 (1991): 377–401.

Olster, David M. *Roman Defeat, Christian Response, and the Literary Construction of the Jew.* University of Pennsylvania Press Middle Ages Series. Philadelphia: University of Pennsylvania Press, 1994.

Oort, Johannes van. "*Secundini Manichaei Epistula*: Roman Manichaean 'Biblical' Argument in the Age of Augustine." In van Oort, Wermelinger, and Wurst, *Augustine and Manichaeism* (q.v.). Pp. 161–73.

Oort, Johannes van, Otto Wermelinger, and Gregor Wurst (eds.). *Augustine and Manichaeism in the Latin West.* Nag Hammadi and Manichaean Studies 49. Leiden: Brill, 2001.

Osborn, Eric. *Tertullian, First Theologian of the West.* Cambridge: Cambridge University Press, 1997.

Osiek, Carolyn and Margaret Y. MacDonald (eds). *A Woman's Place: House Churches in Earliest Christianity.* Minneapolis: Fortress Press, 2006.

Otten, Willamien. "Christ's Birth of a Virgin Who Became a Wife: Flesh and Speech in Tertullian's *De Carne Christi*." *Vigiliae Christianae* 51 (1997): 247–60.

Pagels, Elaine. *Adam, Eve, and the Serpent.* New York: Random House, 1988.

———. *The Gnostic Gospels.* New York: Random House, 1979.

———. *The Gnostic Paul: Gnostic Exegesis of the Pauline Letters.* Philadelphia: Fortress Press, 1975.

Papadoyannakis, Yannis. "Instruction by Question and Answer: The Case of Late Antique and Byzantine *Erotapokriseis*." In *Greek Literature in Late Antiquity: Dynamism, Didacticism, Classicism.* Ed. Scott Fitzgerald Johnson. Aldershot: Ashgate, 2006. Pp. 91–105.

Papsdorf, Joshua. "Ambrosiaster's Theological Anthropology: Nature, Law, and Grace in the Commentaries on the Pauline Epistles and the *Quaestiones veteris et novi testamenti cxxvii*." Ph.D. diss., Fordham University, 2008.

Parker, John. *The Aesthetics of Antichrist: From Christian Drama to Christopher Marlowe.* Ithaca, N.Y.: Cornell University Press, 2007.

Penn, Michael P. *Kissing Christians: Ritual and Community in the Late Ancient Church.* Divinations. Philadelphia: University of Pennsylvania Press, 2005.

———. "Moving Beyond the Palimpsest: Erasure in Syriac Manuscripts." *Journal of Early Christian Studies* 18 (2010): 261–303.

———. "Performing Family: Ritual Kissing and the Construction of Early Christian Kinship." *Journal of Early Christian Studies* 10 (2002): 151–74.

Perkins, Judith. "An Ancient 'Passing' Novel: Heliodorus' *Aithiopika*." *Arethusa* 32 (1999): 197–214.

————. *Roman Imperial Identities in the Early Christian Era.* Routledge Monographs in Classical Studies. London: Routledge, 2009.

Petersen, William. *Tatian's Dissertation: Its Creation, Dissemination, Significance, and History.* Supplements to *Vigiliae Christianae* 25. Leiden: Brill, 1994.

Peterson, Dale E. "Response and Call: The African American Dialogue with Bakhtin and What It Signifies." In *Bakhtin in Contexts: Across the Disciplines.* Ed. Amy Mandelker. Rethinking Theory. Evanston: Northern Illinois University Press, 1995. Pp. 89–98.

Pietz, William. "The Problem of the Fetish, I." *Res* 9 (1985): 5–17

————. "The Problem of the Fetish, II: The Origin of the Fetish." *Res* 13 (1987): 23–45

————. "The Problem of the Fetish, IIIa: Bosman's Guinea and the Enlightenment Theory of Fetishism." *Res* 16 (1988): 105–23.

Pilhofer, Peter. *Presbyteron Kreitton: Der Altersbeweis der jüdischen und christlichen Apologeten und seine Vorgeschichte.* Wissenschaftliche Untersuchungen zum Neuen Testament 2:39. Tübingen: J. C. B. Mohr, 1990.

Piper, Adrian. "Passing for White, Passing for Black." *Transition* 58 (1992): 4–32. Republished most recently in *Out of Order, Out of Sight.* Vol. 1: *Selected Writings in Meta-Art 1968–1992.* Cambridge, Mass.: MIT Press, 1996. Pp. 275–307.

Pittman, Robert. "The Marian Homilies of Hesychius of Jerusalem." Ph.D. diss., Catholic University of America, 1974.

Pourkier, Aline. *L'hérésiologie chez Épiphane de Salamine.* Paris: Beauchesne, 1992.

Pradels, Wendy, Rudolf Brändle, and Martin Heimgartner. "The Sequence and Dating of the Series of John Chrysostom's Eight Discourses *Adversus Iudaeos.*" *Zeitschrift für Antikes Christentum* 6 (2002): 90–116.

Pratt, Mary Louise. *Imperial Eyes: Travel Writing and Transculturation.* London: Routledge, 1992.

Prestige, G. L. "Apollinaris; or, Divine Irruption." In *Fathers and Heretics: Six Studies in Dogmatic Faith with Prologue and Epilogue.* Bampton Lectures for 1940. London: SPCK, 1940.

————. *St. Basil the Great and Apollinaris of Laodicea.* Ed. from his papers by Henry Chadwick. London: SPCK, 1956.

Pritz, Ray A. *Nazarene Jewish Christianity: From the End of the New Testament Until Its Disappearance in the Fourth Century.* Studia Post-Biblica 37. Leiden: Brill, 1988.

Propp, William H. "That Bloody Bridegroom (Exodus IV 24–6)." *Vetus Testamentum* 4 (1993): 495–523.

Rade, Martin. *Damasus: Bischof von Rom, ein Beitrag.* Tübingen: J. C. B. Mohr, 1882.

Rajak, Tessa. "Talking at Trypho: Christian Apologetic as Anti-Judaism in Justin's *Dialogue with Trypho the Jew.*" In *The Jewish Dialogue with Greece and Rome: Studies in Cultural and Social Interaction.* Arbeiten zur Geschichte des antiken Judentums und des Urchristentums 48. Leiden: Brill, 2001. Pp. 512–33.

Ramsey, Boniface. *Ambrose.* The Early Church Fathers. London: Routledge, 1997.

————. "Two Traditions of Lying and Deception in the Ancient Church." *Thomist* 49 (1985): 504–33.

Rapp, Claudia. *Holy Bishops in Late Antiquity: The Nature of Christian Leadership in an Age of Transition.* Transformation of the Classical Heritage 37. Berkeley: University of California Press, 2005.

Raven, Charles. *Apollinarianism: An Essay on the Christology of the Early Church.* Cambridge: Cambridge University Press, 1923.

Reed, Annette Yoshiko. "'Jewish Christianity' After the 'Parting of the Ways': Approaches to Historiography and Self-Definition in the Pseudo-Clementines." In Becker and Reed, *Ways That Never Parted* (q.v.). Pp. 189–231.

———. "The Trickery of the Fallen Angels and the Demonic Mimesis of the Divine: Aetiology, Demonology, and Polemics in the Writings of Justin Martyr." *Journal of Early Christian Studies* 12 (2004): 141–71.

Reggiani, C. Kraus. "I rapporti tra l'impero romano e il mondo ebraico al tempo di Caligula secondo la 'Legatio ad Gaium' di Filone Alessandrino." *Aufstieg und Neidergang der römischen Welt* II.21.1. Berlin: De Gruyter, 1982. Pp. 554–86.

Remensnyder, Amy. *Remembering Kings Past: Monastic Foundation Legends in Medieval Southern France.* Ithaca, N.Y.: Cornell University Press, 1995.

Rhoads, Bonita, and Julia Reinhard Lupton. "Circumcising the Antichrist: An Ethno-Historical Fantasy." *Jouvert: A Journal of Postcolonial Studies* [http://english.chass.ncsu.edu/jouvert] 3.1–2 (1999).

Ri, Andreas Su-Min. *Commentaire de la "Caverne des Trésors": Étude sur l'histoire du texte et de ses sources.* CSCO 581. Louvain: Peeters, 2000.

Ridings, Daniel. *The Attic Moses: The Dependency Theme in Some Early Christian Writers.* Studia Graeca et Latina Gothoburgensia. Göteborg: Acta Universitatis Gothoburgensis, 1995.

Ries, Julien. "La bible chez saint Augustin et chez les manichéens." *Revue des Études Augustiniennes* 7 (1961): 231–43; 9 (1963): 201–15; 10 (1964): 309–29.

Righetti, Mario. *Manuale di storia liturgica.* Vol. 2: *L'anno liturgico il brevario.* Milan: Ancora, 1959–66.

Roberts, Michael. *The Jeweled Style: Poetry and Poetics in Late Antiquity.* Ithaca, N.Y.: Cornell University Press, 1989.

Robinson, Amy. "It Takes One to Know One: Passing and Communities of Common Interest." *Critical Inquiry* 20 (1994): 715–36.

Robinson, James M., and Helmut Koester. *Trajectories Through Early Christianity.* Philadelphia: Fortress Press, 1971.

Rohy, Valerie. "Displacing Desire: Passing, Nostalgia, and *Giovanni's Room.*" In Ginsberg, *Passing* (q.v.). Pp. 218–33.

Rokéah, David. *Justin Martyr and the Jews.* Jewish and Christian Perspectives Series 5. Leiden: Brill, 2002.

Roll, Susan K. *Toward the Origins of Christmas.* Liturgia condenda 5. Kampen: Kok Pharos, 1995.

Rompay, Lucas van. "*Mallpânâ dilan Suryâyâ*: Ephrem in the Works of Philoxenus of Mabbog: Respect and Distance." *Hugoye* [http://syrcom.cua.edu/syrcom/Hugoye] 7.1 (2004).

Rose, Els (ed.). *Missale Gothicum.* CCL 159D. Turnhout: Brepols, 2005.

Rosenblum, Jordan D. "'Why Do You Refuse to Eat Pork?' Jews, Food, and Identity in Roman Palestine." *Jewish Quarterly Review* 100 (2010): 95–110.

Roth, Dieter. "Marcion's Gospel and Luke: The History of Research in Current Debate." *Journal of Biblical Literature* 127 (2008): 513–27.

Rottenberg, Catherine. "*Passing*: Race, Identification, and Desire." *Criticism* 45 (2003): 435–52.

Rousseau, O. "La rencontre de saint Ephrem et de saint Basile." *L'Orient Syrien* 2 (1957): 261–84; 3 (1958): 73–90.

Rousseau, Philip. *Basil of Caesarea.* Transformation of the Classical Heritage 20. Berkeley: University of California Press, 1994.

———. "Homily and Exegesis: Reflection on Their Intersection." Plenary lecture delivered at the Annual Meeting of the North American Patristics Society. May 27, 2010.

Rouwhorst, Gerard. "The Reception of the Jewish Sabbath in Early Christianity." In *Christian Feast and Festival: The Dynamics of Western Liturgy and Culture.* Liturgia condenda 12. Ed. P. Post, Gerard Rouwhorst, L. van Tongern, and A. Scheer. Leuven: Peeters, 2001. Pp. 233–66.

Rubin, Miri. *Gentile Tales: The Narrative Assault on Late Medieval Jews.* New Haven, Conn.: Yale University Press, 1999.

Rubin, Nissan. "*Brit Milah*: A Study of Change in Custom." In Mark, *Covenant of Circumcision* (q.v.). Pp. 87–97.

Ruether, Rosemary Radford. *Sexism and God-Talk: Toward a Feminist Theology.* Boston: Beacon Press, 1983.

Rusch, William. "Some Comments on Origen's *Homilies on the Gospel According to Luke*." In *Origeniana Octava: Origen and the Alexandrian Tradition* (= *Origene e la tradizione alessandrina*). Ed. L. Perrone with P. Bernardino and D. Marchini. Bibliotheca Ephemeridum Theologicarum Lovaniensum 164. Leuven: Peeters Press, 2003. Pp. 727–32.

Russell, Norman. *Cyril of Alexandria.* The Early Church Fathers. London: Routledge, 2000.

Russell, Paul. "The Image of the Infant Jesus in Ephrem the Syrian." *Hugoye* [http://syrcom. cua.edu/syrcom/Hugoye] 5.1 (2002).

Rust, Marion. "The Subaltern as Imperialist: Speaking of Olaudah Equiano." In Ginsberg, *Passing* (q.v.). Pp. 21–36.

Salzman, Michele Renée. *On Roman Time: The Codex-Calendar of 354 and the Rhythms of Urban Life in Late Antiquity.* Transformation of the Classical Heritage 17. Berkeley: University of California Press, 1990.

Sanders, E. P. *Jesus and Judaism.* Philadelphia: Fortress, 1985.

———. "Literary Dependence in Colossians." *Journal of Biblical Literature* 85 (1966): 28–45.

Sanders, Jack T. *The Jews in Luke-Acts.* Philadelphia: Fortress Press, 1987.

Sanders, James A. "The Canonical Process." In Katz, *Cambridge History of Judaism* (q.v.). Pp. 230–43.

Sandweiss, Martha A. *Passing Strange: A Gilded Age Tale of Love and Deception Across the Color Line*. New York: Penguin, 2009.

Sandwell, Isabella. *Religious Identity in Late Antiquity: Greeks, Jews, and Christians in Antioch*. Cambridge: Cambridge University Press, 2007.

Satlow, Michael. "Fictional Women: A Study in Stereotypes." In *The Talmud Yerushalmi and Graeco-Roman Culture III*. Ed. Peter Schäfer and Catherine Hezser. Texts and Studies in Ancient Judaism 93. Tübingen: Mohr Siebeck, 2002. Pp. 225–43.

Sauget, J.-M. "Nouvelles homélies du Commentaire sur l'Évangile de s. Luc de Cyrille d'Alexandrie dans leur traduction syriaque." In *Symposium Syriacum I*. Orientalia Christiana Analecta 197. Rome: Pontificium Institutum Orientalium Studiorum, 1974. Pp. 439–56.

Savon, Hervé. "Le prêtre Eutrope et la 'vraie circoncision.'" *Revue de l'Histoire des Religions* 199 (1982): 273–302, 381–404.

Schäfer, J. *Basilius des Grossen Beziehungen zum Abendlande*. Münster: Aschendorffschen, 1909.

Schäfer, Peter. *Jesus in the Talmud*. Princeton, N.J.: Princeton University Press, 2007.

Scheid, John. "Les réjouissances des calendes de janvier d'après le *sermon* Dolbeau 26: Nouvelle lumières sur une fête mal connue." In Madec, *Augustin prédicateur* (q.v.). Pp. 353–65.

Schott, Jeremy M. *Christianity, Empire, and the Making of Religion in Late Antiquity*. Divinations. Philadelphia: University of Pennsylvania Press, 2008.

———. "Founding Platonopolis: The Platonic πολιτεία in Eusebius, Porphyry, and Iamblichus." *Journal of Early Christian Studies* 11 (2003): 501–31.

———. "Heresiology as Universal History in Epiphanius's *Panarion*." *Zeitschrift für Antikes Christentum* 10 (2006): 546–63.

Schwartz, Daniel. "On Barnabas and Bar-Kokhba." In *Studies in the Jewish Background of Christianity*. Wissenschaftliche Untersuchungen zur Neuen Testament 60. Tübingen: Mohr Siebeck, 1992. Pp. 147–54.

Scott, Joan Wallach. "Gender as a Useful Category of Historical Analysis." In *Gender and the Politics of History*. Rev. ed. Gender and Culture. New York: Columbia University Press, 1999.

Sebesta, Judith Lynn, and Larissa Bonfante (eds.). *The World of Roman Costume*. Madison: University of Wisconsin Press, 1994.

Setzer, Claudia. *Jewish Responses to Early Christians: History and Polemics, 30–150 CE*. Minneapolis: Fortress Press, 1994.

Shell, Marc. *Art and Money*. Chicago: University of Chicago Press, 1995.

———. "The Holy Foreskin; or, Money, Relics, and Judeo-Christianity." In *Jews and Other Differences: The New Jewish Cultural Studies*. Ed. Jonathan Boyarin and Daniel Boyarin. Minneapolis: University of Minnesota Press, 1997. Pp. 345–59.

Shepardson, Christine C. *Anti-Judaism and Orthodoxy: Ephrem's Hymns in Fourth-Century Syria*. Patristic Monograph Series 20. Washington, D.C.: Catholic University of America Press, 2008.

———. "Controlling Contested Places: John Chrysostom's *Adversus Iudaeos* Homilies and the Spatial Politics of Religious Controversy." *Journal of Early Christian Studies* 15 (2007): 483–516.

Shoemaker, Stephen J. *Ancient Traditions of the Virgin Mary's Dormition and Assumption.* Oxford Early Christian Studies. Oxford: Oxford University Press, 2002.

———. "Epiphanius of Salamis, the Kollyridians, and the Early Dormition Narratives: The Cult of the Virgin in the Fourth Century." *Journal of Early Christian Studies* 16 (2008): 371–401.

———. "'Let Us Go and Burn Her Body': The Image of the Jews in the Early Dormition Traditions." *Church History* 68 (1999): 775–823.

Sickenberger, Joseph. *Titus von Bostra: Studien zu dessen Lukashomilien.* Texte und Untersuchungen 21.1. Leipzig: J. C. Hinrichs, 1901.

Siker, Jeffrey S. *Disinheriting the Jews: Abraham in Early Christian Controversy.* Louisville, Ky.: Westminster John Knox Press, 1991.

Silverman, Eric Kline. *From Abraham to America: A History of Jewish Circumcision.* Lanham, Md.: Rowman & Littlefield, 2006.

Simon, Marcel. *Verus Israel: A Study of the Relations Between Christians and Jews in the Roman Empire (135–425).* Tr. H. McKeating. Oxford: Oxford University Press for the Littman Library, 1986.

Sinkewicz, Robert E. *Manuscript Listings for the Authors of the Patristic and Byzantine Periods.* Greek Index Project Series 4. Toronto: PIMS, 1992.

Sizgorich, Thomas. *Violence and Belief in Late Antiquity: Militant Devotion in Christianity and Islam.* Divinations. Philadelphia: University of Pennsylvania Press, 2009.

Skarsaune, Oskar. "The Ebionites." In Skarsaune and Hvalvik, *Jewish Believers in Jesus* (q.v.). Pp. 419–62.

———. *In the Shadow of the Temple: Jewish Influences on Early Christianity.* Downer's Grove, Ill.: InterVarsity Press, 2002.

Skarsaune, Oskar, and Reidar Hvalvik (eds.). *Jewish Believers in Jesus: The Early Centuries.* Peabody, Mass.: Hendrickson, 2007.

Smallwood, E. Mary. *The Jews Under Roman Rule: From Pompey to Diocletian.* Studies in Judaism in Late Antiquity 20. Leiden: Brill, 1976.

———. *Philonis Alexandrini Legatio ad Gaium.* Leiden: Brill, 1970.

Smith, Jonathan Z. "Good News Is No News: Aretalogy and Gospel." In *Map Is Not Territory: Studies in the History of Religions.* Studies in Judaism in Late Antiquity 23. Leiden: Brill, 1978. Pp. 190–207.

———. *Relating Religion: Essays in the Study of Religion.* Chicago: University of Chicago Press, 2004.

———. *To Take Place: Toward Theory in Ritual.* Chicago Studies in the History of Judaism. Chicago: University of Chicago Press, 1987.

———. "What a Difference a Difference Makes." In *"To See Ourselves as Others See Us": Christians, Jews and "Others" in Late Antiquity.* Ed. Jacob Neusner and Ernest S. Frerichs. Chico, Calif.: Scholars Press, 1985. Pp. 3–48. Repr. in Smith, *Relating Religion* (q.v.). Pp. 251–302.

Souter, Alexander. *A Study of Ambrosiaster.* Texts and Studies 7.4. Cambridge: Cambridge University Press, 1905.

Speller, Lydia. "Ambrosiaster and the Jews." *Studia Patristica* 17.1 (1982): 72–78.

Staab, K. (ed.) *Pauluskommentar aus der griechischen Kirche aus Katenenhandshriften gesammelt.* Münster: Aschendorff, 1933.

Stauffer, Annemarie. "Clothing." In *Late Antiquity: A Guide to the Postclassical World.* Ed. Glen Bowersock, Peter Brown, and Oleg Grabar. Cambridge, Mass.: Harvard University Press, 1999. Pp. 381–82.

Stein, Robert H. "What Is Redaktionsgeschichte?" *Journal of Biblical Literature* 88 (1969): 45–56.

Steinberg, Leo. *The Sexuality of Christ in Renaissance Art and Modern Oblivion.* New York: Pantheon, 1983.

Sterk, Andrea. "On Basil, Moses, and the Model Bishop: The Cappadocian Legacy of Leadership." *Church History* 67 (1998): 227–53.

Stern, Julia. "Spanish Masquerade and the Drama of Racial Identity in *Uncle Tom's Cabin.*" In Ginsberg, *Passing* (q.v.). Pp. 103–30.

Stern, Menahem. *Greek and Latin Authors on Jews and Judaism.* 3 vols. Jerusalem: Israel Academy of Sciences and Humanities, 1974–84.

———. "The Jews in Greek and Latin Literature." In *The Jewish People in the First Century: Historical Geography, Political History, Social, Cultural, and Religious Life and Institutions.* Ed. Shemuel Safrai, Menahem Stern, and David Flusser. Compendia rerum Iudaicarum ad Novem Testamentum 1.2. Minneapolis: Fortress Press, 1976.

Stern, Sacha. *Calendar and Community: A History of the Jewish Calendar, 2nd Century* B.C.E. *–10th Century* C.E. Oxford: Oxford University Press, 2001.

Stevenson, Jane. *The "Laterculus Malalianus" and the School of Archbishop Theodore.* Cambridge Studies in Anglo-Saxon England 14. Cambridge: Cambridge University Press, 1995.

Stewart, Columba. "Imageless Prayer and the Theological Vision of Evagrius Ponticus." *Journal of Early Christian Studies* 9 (2001): 173–204.

Stewart-Sykes, Alistair. *The Lamb's High Feast: Melito, Peri Pascha, and the Quartodeciman Paschal Liturgy at Sardis.* Supplements to *Vigiliae Christianae* 42. Boston: Brill, 1998.

———. "Melito's Anti-Judaism." *Journal of Early Christian Studies* 5 (1997): 271–83.

Still, T. D. "Eschatology in Colossians: How Realized Is It?" *New Testament Studies* 50 (2004): 125–38.

Stock, Brian. *Augustine the Reader: Meditation, Self-Knowledge, and the Ethics of Interpretation.* Cambridge, Mass.: Harvard University Press, 1996.

Stökl Ben Ezra, Daniel. "An Ancient List of Christian Festivals in *Toledot Yeshu*: Polemics as Indication for Interaction." *Harvard Theological Review* 102 (2009): 481–96.

———. "Canonization—A Non-Linear Process? Observing the Process of Canonization through the Christian (and Jewish) Papyri from Egypt." *Zeitschrift für Antikes Christentum* 12 (2008): 193–214.

———. "'Christians' Observing 'Jewish' Festivals of Autumn." In Tomson and Lambers-Petry, *Image of the Judaeo-Christians* (q.v.). Pp. 53–73.

———. *The Impact of Yom Kippur on Early Christianity: The Day of Atonement from Second Temple Judaism to the Fifth Century*. Wissenschaftliche Untersuchungen zum Neuen Testament 163. Tübingen: Mohr Siebeck, 2003.

Streete, Gail P. C. "Redaction Criticism." In *To Each Its Own Meaning: An Introduction to Biblical Criticisms and Their Applications*. 2nd ed. Ed. Stephen Haynes and Steven McKenzie. Louisville, Ky.: Westminster John Knox Press, 1999. Pp. 105–24.

Stroumsa, G. Guy. "Christ's Laughter: Docetic Origins Reconsidered." *Journal of Early Christian Studies* 12 (2004): 267–88.

Sumney, Jerry L. *Colossians: A Commentary.* Louisville, Ky.: Westminster John Knox Press, 2008.

Syed, Yasmin. "Romans and Others." In *A Companion to Latin Literature*. Ed. S. J. Harrison. Oxford: Blackwell, 2005. Pp. 360–71.

Taboray, Joseph. "Jewish Festivals in Late Antiquity." In Katz, *Cambridge History of Judaism* (q.v.). Pp. 556–72.

Taft, Robert. "Historicism Revisited." *Studia Liturgica* 14 (1982): 97–109.

Talley, Thomas. *The Origins of the Liturgical Year*. Collegeville, Minn.: Liturgical Press, 1991.

Tardieu, Michel. "Une définition du Manichéisme comme *secta christianorum*." In *Ritualisme et vie intérieure: Religion et culture*. Ed. A. Caquot and P. Canivet. Le Point Théologique 52. Paris: Beauschesne, 1989. Pp. 167–77.

Taylor, David G. K. "St. Ephraim's Influence on the Greeks." *Hugoye* [http://syrcom.cua.edu/syrcom/Hugoye] 1.2 (1998).

Taylor, Joan E. *Christians and the Holy Places: The Myth of Jewish-Christian Origins*. Oxford: Clarendon Press, 1993.

———. "The Phenomenon of Early Jewish-Christianity: Reality or Scholarly Construct?" *Vigiliae Christianae* 44 (1990): 313–34.

Teske, Ronald J., S.J. "Augustine of Hippo and the Quaestiones et Responsiones Literature." In Volgers and Zamagni, *Erotapokriseis* (q.v.). Pp. 127–44.

Thompson, Thomas A. "Mary in Western Liturgical Tradition." *Liturgical Ministry* 6 (Winter 1997): 1–10.

Tilg, Stefan. *Chariton of Aphrodisias and the Invention of the Greek Love Novel*. New York: Oxford University Press, 2010.

Tomson, Peter. "The Wars Against Rome, the Rise of Rabbinic Judaism and of Apostolic Gentile Christianity, and the Judaeo-Christians: Elements for a Synthesis." In Tomson and Lambers-Petry, *Image of the Judaeo-Christians* (q.v.). Pp. 1–31.

Tomson, Peter, and Doris Lambers-Petry (eds.). *The Image of the Judaeo-Christians in Ancient Jewish and Christian Literature*. Wissenschaftliche Untersuchungen zum neuen Testament 158. Tübingen: Mohr Siebeck, 2003.

Trakatellis, Demetrios. "Justin Martyr's Trypho." *Harvard Theological Review* 79 (1986): 289–97.

Trigg, Joseph W. *Origen: The Bible and Philosophy in the Third-Century Church*. Atlanta: John Knox Press, 1983.

Turner, H. E. W. *The Pattern of Christian Truth: A Study in the Relations Between Orthodoxy and Heresy in the Early Church*. London: Mowbray, 1954.

Tyson, Joseph. *Images of Judaism in Luke-Acts*. Columbia: University of South Carolina Press, 1992.

——. *Luke, Judaism, and the Scholars: Critical Approaches to Luke-Acts*. Columbia: University of South Carolina Press, 1999.

——. *Marcion and Luke-Acts: A Defining Struggle*. Columbia: University of South Carolina Press, 2006.

Usener, Hermann. *Das Weihnachtsfest*. Bonn: M. Cohen & Sohn, 1889.

Vainio, Raija. "On the Concept of *Barbarolexis* in the Roman Grammarians." *Arctos* 28 (1994): 129–40.

Vannier, Marie-Anne. "L'apport du *Sermon Dolbeau 26*." *Studia Patristica* 38 (2001): 331–27.

Verheyden, Joseph. "Epiphanius on the Ebionites." In Tomson and Lambers-Petry, *Image of the Judaeo-Christians* (q.v.). Pp. 182–208.

Verme, Marcello del. *Didache and Judaism: Jewish Roots of an Ancient Christian-Jewish Work*. London: T & T Clark, 2004.

Vessey, Mark. "Peregrinus Against the Heretics: Classicism, Proviniciality, and the Place of the Alien Writer in Late Roman Gaul." In *Cristianesimo e specificità regionali nel Mediterraneo latino (sec. IV–VI)*. Studia Ephemeridis Augustinianum 46. Rome: Institutum Patristicum Augustinianum, 1994. Pp. 529–65.

Volgers, Annelie. "Ambrosiaster: Persuasive Powers in Progress." In Volgers and Zamagni, *Erotapokriseis* (q.v.). Pp. 99–125.

Volgers, Annelie, and Claudio Zamagni (eds.). *Erotapokriseis: Early Christian Question-and-Answer Literature in Context, Proceedings of the Utrecht Colloquium, 13–14 October 2003*. Contributions to Biblical Exegesis and Theology 37. Leuven: Peeters, 2004.

Wainwright, Geoffrey, and Karen B. Westerfield Tucker (eds.). *The Oxford History of Christian Worship*. Oxford: Oxford University Press, 2006.

Walaskay, Paul. *"And So We Came to Rome": The Political Perspective of Saint Luke*. Society for New Testament Studies Monograph Series 49. Cambridge: Cambridge University Press, 1983.

Wald, Gayle. " 'A Most Disagreeable Mirror': Reflections on White Identity in *Black Like Me*." In Ginsberg, *Passing* (q.v.). Pp. 151–77.

Wallace-Hadrill, D. S. "Eusebius of Caesarea's *Commentary on Luke*: Its Origin and Early History." *Harvard Theological Review* 67 (1974): 55–63.

Ward, Graham. *Christ and Culture*. Challenges in Contemporary Theology. Malden: Blackwell, 2005.

——. "The Displaced Body of Jesus Christ." In Ward, Milbank, and Pickstock, *Radical Orthodoxy: A New Theology* (q.v.). Pp. 163–81.

——. "Uncovering the Corona: A Theology of Circumcision." In *The Birth of Jesus:*

Biblical and Theological Reflections. Ed. George J. Brooke. Edinburgh: T & T Clark, 2000. Pp. 35–46.

Ward, Graham, John Milbank, and Catherine Pickstock (eds.). *Radical Orthodoxy: A New Theology.* London: Routledge, 1999.

Ward-Perkins, Bryan. *The Fall of Rome and the End of Civilization.* Oxford: Oxford University Press, 2005.

Warnke, Georgia. *After Identity: Rethinking Race, Sex, and Gender.* Cambridge: Cambridge University Press, 2007.

Whitmarsh, Tim. *Greek Literature and the Roman Empire: The Politics of Imitation.* Oxford: Oxford University Press, 2001.

———. *The Second Sophistic.* Oxford: Oxford University Press, 2005.

Whittaker, C. R. *Frontiers of the Roman Empire: A Social and Economic Study.* Baltimore: Johns Hopkins University Press, 1994.

———. *Rome and Its Frontiers: The Dynamics of Change.* London: Routledge, 2004.

Wilken, Robert. *The Christians as the Romans Saw Them.* New Haven, Conn.: Yale University Press, 1984.

———. "Cyril of Alexandria as Interpreter of the Old Testament." In *The Theology of St. Cyril of Alexandria: A Critical Appreciation.* Ed. Thomas G. Weinandy and Daniel A. Keating. London: T & T Clark, 2003. Pp. 1–21.

———. *John Chrysostom and the Jews: Rhetoric and Reality in the Late 4th Century.* Transformation of the Classical Heritage 4. Berkeley: University of California Press, 1983.

———. *Judaism and the Early Christian Mind: A Study of Cyril of Alexandria's Exegesis and Theology.* New Haven, Conn.: Yale University Press, 1971.

Wilson, R. McL. "Jewish Christianity and Gnosticism." *Recherche de Sciences Réligieuses* 50 (1972): 261–72.

Wilson, Stephen G. *The Gentiles and the Gentile Mission in Luke-Acts.* Society for New Testament Monograph Series 23. Cambridge: Cambridge University Press, 1973.

———. *Related Strangers: Jews and Christians, 70–170 C.E.* Minneapolis: Fortress Press, 1995.

Winkelmann, F. *Euseb von Kaisareia: Der Vater der Kirchengeschichte.* Berlin: Anstalt Union, 1991.

Winter, Paul. "The Proto-Source of Luke 1." *Novum Testamentum* 1 (1956): 184–99.

Witherington, Ben, III. *The Letters to Philemon, the Colossians, and the Ephesians: A Socio-Rhetorical Commentary on the Captivity Epistles.* Grand Rapids, Mich.: Wm. B. Eerdmans, 2007.

Wolfson, Elliot. "Circumcision and the Divine Name: A Study in the Transmission of Esoteric Doctrine." *Jewish Quarterly Review* 78 (1987): 77–112.

———. "Circumcision, Vision of God, and Textual Interpretation: From Midrashic Trope to Mystical Symbol." *History of Religions* 27 (1987): 189–215.

Woolf, Greg. "Becoming Roman, Staying Greek: Culture, Identity, and the Civilizing Process in the Roman East." *Proceedings of the Cambridge Philological Society* 40 (1994): 116–43.

———. *Becoming Roman: The Origins of Provincial Civilization in Gaul.* Cambridge: Cambridge University Press, 1998.

Wortley, John. "The Pseudo-Amphilochian *Vita Basilii*: An Apocryphal *Life* of Saint Basil the Great." *Florilegium* 2 (1980): 217–39.

Wright, N. T. *Colossians and Philemon*. The Tyndale New Testament Commentaries. Grand Rapids, Mich.: Wm. B. Eerdmans, 1986.

Wurst, Gregor. "Bemerkungen zu Struktur und *genus litterarium* der *Capitula* des Faustus von Mileve." In van Oort, Wermelinger, and Wurst, *Augustine and Manichaeism* (q.v.). Pp. 307–24.

———. "Manichäismus um 375 in Nordafrika und Italien." In *Augustin Handbuch*. Ed. Volker Henning Drecoll. Tübingen: Mohr Siebeck, 2007. Pp. 85–92.

Young, Frances M. *Biblical Exegesis and the Formation of Christian Culture*. Cambridge: Cambridge University Press, 1997.

Young, Robert J. C. *Colonial Desire: Hybridity in Theory, Culture, and Race*. London: Routledge, 1995.

———. *Postcolonialism: An Historical Introduction*. Oxford: Blackwell, 2001.

Yuval, Israel. *Two Nations in Your Womb: Perceptions of Jews and Christians in Late Antiquity and the Middle Ages*. Tr. Barbara Harshav and Jonathan Chipman. Berkeley: University of California Press, 2006.

Zamagni, Claudio. "Une introduction méthodologique à la littérature patristique des questions et réponses: Le cas d'Eusèbe de Césarée." In Volgers and Zamagni, *Erotapokriseis* (q.v.). Pp. 7–24.

Zettersteén, K. von. "Ein Homilie des Amphilochius von Ikonium über Basilius von Caesarea." In *Festschrift Eduard Sachau*. Ed. Gustav Weil. Berlin: Georg Reimer, 1915. Pp. 223–47.

———. "Ein Homilie des Amphilochius von Ikonium über Basilius von Caesarea." *Oriens Christianus* 31 (1934): 67–98.

Zimmerman, Ulrich. *Kinderbeschneidung und Kindertaufe: Exegetische, dogmengeschichtliche und biblisch-theologische Betrachtungen zu einem alten Begründungszusammenhang*. Beiträge zum Verstehen der Bibel 15. Hamburg: Lit Verlag, 2006.

Index

Acknowledgments

This project has spanned every institution of higher education with which I have been affiliated, as a student or faculty member. My interest in Christ's circumcision was sparked by a senior seminar in religious studies on "Circumcision: Male and Female, Jewish and Gentile" offered in the spring of 1994 by Shaye J. D. Cohen at Brown University; my final paper was on Jesus' circumcision in Jacobus de Voragine and Thomas Aquinas (for which I think I received a B+). I entered graduate school at Duke University in the fall of 1995 with Jesus' circumcision as a notional topic for study, before ultimately turning elsewhere for my doctoral dissertation. After the publication of my first book, I returned to Christ's circumcision (with generous research support) at the University of California, Riverside, where I taught from 2001 to 2008, and now at my present institution, Scripps College in Claremont, California. I can only hope that the final product, the fruits of my (somewhat more) mature scholarship, will do justice to all those who have contributed to it along the way.

I presented various bits and pieces of this work over the years at the following conferences, at which other presenters and audience members provided vigorous and invaluable comment: the Society of Biblical Literature, the North American Patristics Society, and the International Conference on Patristic Studies at the University of Oxford. I must also thank the following institutions for inviting me to present my work in progress in multiple, lively venues: McMaster University; the Claremont Graduate University, both the Institute for Antiquity and Christianity and the Institute for Signifying Scriptures; Brown University; Duke University; Boston University, both at a conference on sacrifice and in a joint presentation with the inimitable Paula Fredriksen; Indiana University; the University of California, Riverside; and Scripps College.

I offer tremendous thanks to the following scholars who provided assistance over the years, from reading pieces of the manuscript to helping decode ancient texts and contexts to alerting me to previously unknown sources on Christ's circumcision: Timothy Barnes, Jason BeDuhn, Daniel Boyarin, Ra'anan Boustan, Denise Buell, Virginia Burrus, Catherine Chin, Elizabeth Clark, Eugene Clay, Shaye Cohen, John Duffy, Bart D. Ehrman, Susanna Elm (who helped me come up with a title), James Ernest, Georgia Frank, Christopher Frilingos, Jay Geller, Susan Holman, David Hunter, Dayna Kalleres, Jeffrey Keiser, Lawrence Lahey, Shelly Matthews, Simon Mimouni, Laura Nasrallah, Claudia Rapp, Walter Ray, Annette Yoshiko Reed, Philip Rousseau, Jeanne-Nicole Saint-Laurent, Christine Shepardson, Stephen Shoemaker, Maureen Tilley, Lucas van Rompay, Susan Weingarten, and Terry Wilfong. The generosity of colleagues enlivens the solitary nature of our work.

I must also thank my research assistants over the years who helped in the day-to-day work, including final manuscript preparation: Kelly Meister at the University of California, Riverside, and Bonita Wilson and Beatrice Schuster-Smith at Scripps College. The staffs of Tomás Rivera Library at the University of California, Riverside, and Honnold-Mudd Library of the Claremont Colleges helped me acquire the most obscure of titles, in the most obscure of languages.

My special thanks go to the editors of the Divinations series, who have encouraged this project over the years: Daniel Boyarin, Virginia Burrus, and Derek Krueger. I especially appreciate the attention and care given by the editorial staff at the University of Pennsylvania Press: Jerome Singerman, senior editor; Caroline Winschel, assistant editor; Noreen O'Connor, project editor; and Robert Milks, freelance copyeditor.

Portions of this book previously appeared as follows: Early versions of pieces of multiple chapters: "The Kindest Cut: Christ's Circumcision and the Signs of Early Christian Identity," *Jewish Studies Quarterly* 16 (2009): 97–117. Chapter 2: Copyright © 2007 The Johns Hopkins University Press. This article, "Dialogical Differences: (De-)Judaizing Jesus' Circumcision," was first published in *Journal of Early Christian Studies* 15, no. 3 (Fall 2007): 291–335. Reprinted with permission by The Johns Hopkins University Press. Conclusion: "Passing: Jesus' Circumcision and Strategic Self-Sacrifice," in *Ancient Mediterranean Sacrifice*, ed. Jennifer Wright Knust and Zsuzsanna Várhelyi (Oxford: Oxford University Press, 2011), which appears here by permission of Oxford University Press, Inc.

This book, like my first, is dedicated to my family, which now includes at its head my spouse, Catherine Allgor, without whom the completion of this book would have been impossible. *Placet, magistra.*